Tilde *skills*

Design and Produce Text Documents

Plus Challenges and Assessment Tasks

Microsoft Word 2010

2nd Edition

Tilde *skills* Design and Produce Text Documents plus Challenges and Assessment Tasks
Microsoft Word 2010
2nd edition, 3rd printing

Authors
Tilde Publishing and Distribution

ISBN-13: 978-0-7346-0791-1

Published in Australia by:

Tilde Publishing and Distribution
PO Box 72
Prahran VIC 3181, Australia
Tel: 1300 880 935
www.tilde.com.au

Ts-Design&ProdTxt-Wrd2010-BSB07-2e3p

Table of Contents

Preface

Introduction

This publication can be used as a tutorial for self-paced learning or for instructor-led teaching. Its purpose is to enable students to become competent in the design and development of predominately text-based documents, using the advanced features of *Microsoft Word 2010*. If kept conveniently near your computer workstation it can also be used as your primary reference, reminding you of the most efficient ways to approach word processing tasks.

This course is written using *Microsoft Word 2010* running on *Windows 7*.

Business Services Training Package

The contents of this publication can contribute to achieving the following unit of competency in the Business Services Training Package:

BSBITU303A Design and produce text documents.

Learning outcomes – Business Services Training Package Unit BSBITU303A Design and produce text documents

1. **Prepare to produce word processed documents**
   - 1.1. Use safe work practices to ensure ergonomic, work organisation, energy and resource conservation requirements are addressed
   - 1.2. Identify document purpose, audience and presentation requirements, and clarify with relevant personnel as required
   - 1.3. Identify organisational and task requirements for text-based business documents to ensure consistency of style and image
2. **Design word processed documents**
   - 2.1. Design document structure and layout to suit purpose, audience and information requirements of the task
   - 2.2. Design document to enhance readability and appearance, and to meet organisational and task requirements for style and layout
   - 2.3. Use style sheets and automatic functions to ensure consistency of design and layout
3. **Add tables and other data**
   - 3.1. Insert a standard table into a document, changing cells to meet information requirements
   - 3.2. Insert and delete columns and rows as necessary
   - 3.3. Insert images and other data to meet required specifications

4. **Produce text documents**
   - 4.1. Use advanced software functions to enable efficient production of documents
   - 4.2. Enter or import, and edit text and other data to meet required specifications
   - 4.3. Preview, adjust and print documents in accordance with organisational and task requirements
   - 4.4. Name and store text documents, in accordance with organisational requirements and exit the application without information loss/damage
   - 4.5. Prepare text documents within designated time lines and organisational requirements for speed and accuracy
   - 4.6. Use manuals, user documentation and online help to overcome problems with document design and production

How this publication is organised

This publication contains **15** topics. Each topic contains: concept overviews; detailed **How to** explanations; and abundant **Hands-on** exercises.

Consolidation tasks are used at intervals to bring skills together, and the course finishes with a number of **Workplace scenarios, Challenge tasks** and **Assessment tasks** which firmly place knowledge in a workplace setting and can act as assessment tools.

Information contained in the **Appendices** can be brought into the course at any time.

Tilde conventions

The following conventions are used throughout Tilde publications.

Convention explained	Example
Each topic begins with an overview of relevant theory (a narrative). In narratives, important terms are shown in **bold**.	'Using **styles** you can ensure a consistent and professional ...'
Narratives are often followed by examples or useful additional information (an aside).	***For example*** *...* ***As an aside*** *...*
A set of **How to** steps follows a narrative. These steps detail the procedure required to perform a task. These can be read by a student, presented by a trainer, or referred to when using the manual as a reference.	**How to: Apply a quick style** 1. ... 2. ... 3. ...
A command button is shown beside the relevant **How to** step, and often as a reminder in **Hands-on exercises**.	
In **How to** steps, names of command buttons are highlighted in **bold**. Steps also include the name of the ribbon where the button is located, and the group.	'Display the Home ribbon, point to any option in the **Quick Styles Gallery** (Styles group).'

Keyboard shortcuts can often save you time and effort. These are illustrated with the required keys from the keyboard.	New document Ctrl N
An exercise to be undertaken by a student is called a **Hands-on exercise**. Each exercise step is described in detail and is used to practise and reinforce the skill being learned.	
In exercises, file names are shown in *italics*. Key actions are also highlighted in bold.	'**Open** the document *Health centre*.'
Additional useful **Hints & tips** are used to help students apply their skills more successfully, overcome problems and extend their knowledge.	
Terms & concepts review questions are used to review key terms and concepts covered in a topic.	
To review or consolidate student skills a **Consolidation task** is used. This task can be undertaken individually by students, or as a team review in the classroom.	
To help students apply their new skills in realistic scenarios a work-based task called a **Workplace scenario** is used.	

How to use this publication in a self-paced manner

Read through the **How to** step(s), and then work through the following **Hands-on** exercise.

Accompanying exercise files are required to work through the exercises. These can be downloaded from the Tilde website <www.tilde.com.au>, or obtained from the publisher. It is recommended that they are pre-loaded into a suitable folder on a hard/network drive, or used directly from a (USB) flash drive.

Downloaded with the accompanying files is a document used for reference within the course. Please print out the following file prior to course commencement: *OH&S guide*.

How to use this publication in an instructor-led classroom

Present to students the material in the **How to** steps; then, have them work through the **Hands-on** exercises.

Accompanying exercise files are required to work through the exercises. These can be downloaded from the Tilde website <www.tilde.com.au>. It is recommended that they be pre-loaded into a suitable folder on a hard/network drive, or used directly from a (USB) flash drive. Exercise files can be freely copied onto student PCs, instructor PCs, or network drives when used for education purposes with a Tilde™ publication.

Spelling

The Macquarie dictionary is used except for the names of features from the application, e.g. Center Align, where the original (American) spelling is used.

Instructor email list

To be notified regularly of new educational developments from Tilde Publishing, go to the Tilde Publishing website <www.tilde.com.au> and add yourself to our instructor email list.

Tilde *skills* series

This publication is just one in Tilde *skills* series that addresses the educational needs of adults in the workplace. It is suitable for anyone wishing to learn using Tilde's enjoyable methodology.

Before you start

To ensure you get the best results from this course please check the following for your students (standards settings from a fresh installation of Microsoft Word 2010):

- □ Print Layout view & 100% zoom.
- □ Maximised screen.
- □ Quick Access Toolbar in default location and reset if buttons added.
- □ Maximised ribbon.
- □ Nothing added/removed from Status bar.
- □ No add-ins.
- □ Default font/size of Calibri 11 pts, multiple of 1.15 line spacing and 10 pt spacing after paragraph. These are the defaults of a fresh installation (not necessarily an upgrade). However, these settings have minimal effect on exercises.
- □ Margins 2.54 cm – all.
- □ Any saved Quick Part items removed.
- □ All reviewing marks and colours as per defaults.
- □ Page size – please change default to A4.

Please note:

- □ The ribbon expands or contracts to fit the window in which it is displayed. Resizing a window may result in buttons becoming smaller or text on buttons being removed. Different screen resolutions can also have the same effect. To see Microsoft's recommendations for screen resolution search Windows 7 Help on 'Getting the best display'.

Topic 1 – Word processing and the Word environment

Word processors today seem to be almost everywhere. In businesses, in government, in home offices, as well as in schools, colleges and universities. They are used by all sorts of people – regardless of age, job, language, background, or geography – from all walks of life. It seems there is almost no limit to the growing popularity of word processors.

Word processing software comes under many names, from numerous different companies. While different word processing programs have different features, all have one strong similarity – they all help us to process text, i.e. to create letters, memos, reports, etc. In the past, typewriters were used to create such documents, and before that documents were produced longhand. In fact, for many people, word processors are the modern equivalent of a pencil and paper.

Today, word processors are extremely sophisticated and can help you perform tasks far beyond those a typewriter could ever achieve, including spelling, grammar and context checking, plus extensive design and layout tools.

Microsoft Word is one of the world's most popular word processing programs. Word makes it easy for you to create professional-looking documents that present your written work to others more effectively. Word can save you valuable time, and is enjoyable to use.

The Word environment

Before you can use Microsoft Word to its best advantage you first need to be familiar with the Word environment. Let's begin by starting Word.

How to: Start Word

1. Click on the **Start** button. The **Start menu** is presented.
   Click on Microsoft Word 2010

   Or, if Word is not in your list of recently used programs …

   From the **Start menu** type: *word* word
   Microsoft Word will be presented in your list of **Programs**.

   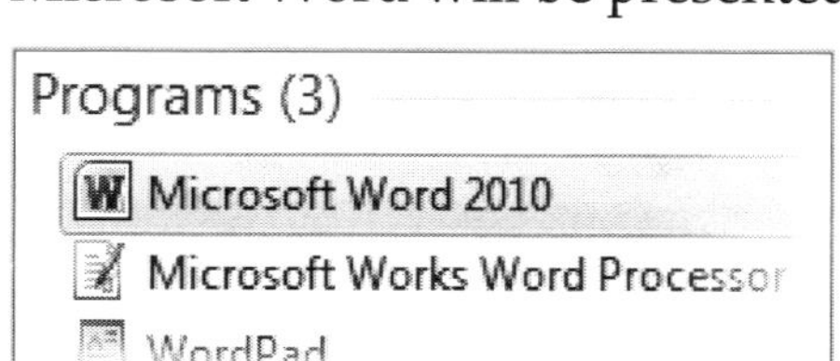

2. Press Enter to start the selected program.
   Word opens and presents a new blank document ready for you to commence your tasks.

> ***As an aside*** *… If you are using Windows XP, and if Word is not in your list of recently used programs, click on the* ***Start*** *button, point to* ***All programs****, point to* ***Microsoft Office****, then click on* ***Microsoft Word 2010****.*

As an aside ... *Each organisation has its own procedures for when you start work on a computer (log-on). Typically you are prompted for a* ***User name*** *and* ***Password****, particularly if you are connecting to a network. These security requirements are necessary to keep the organisation's data safe, ensuring only authorised staff access company computers.*

Understanding the Word screen

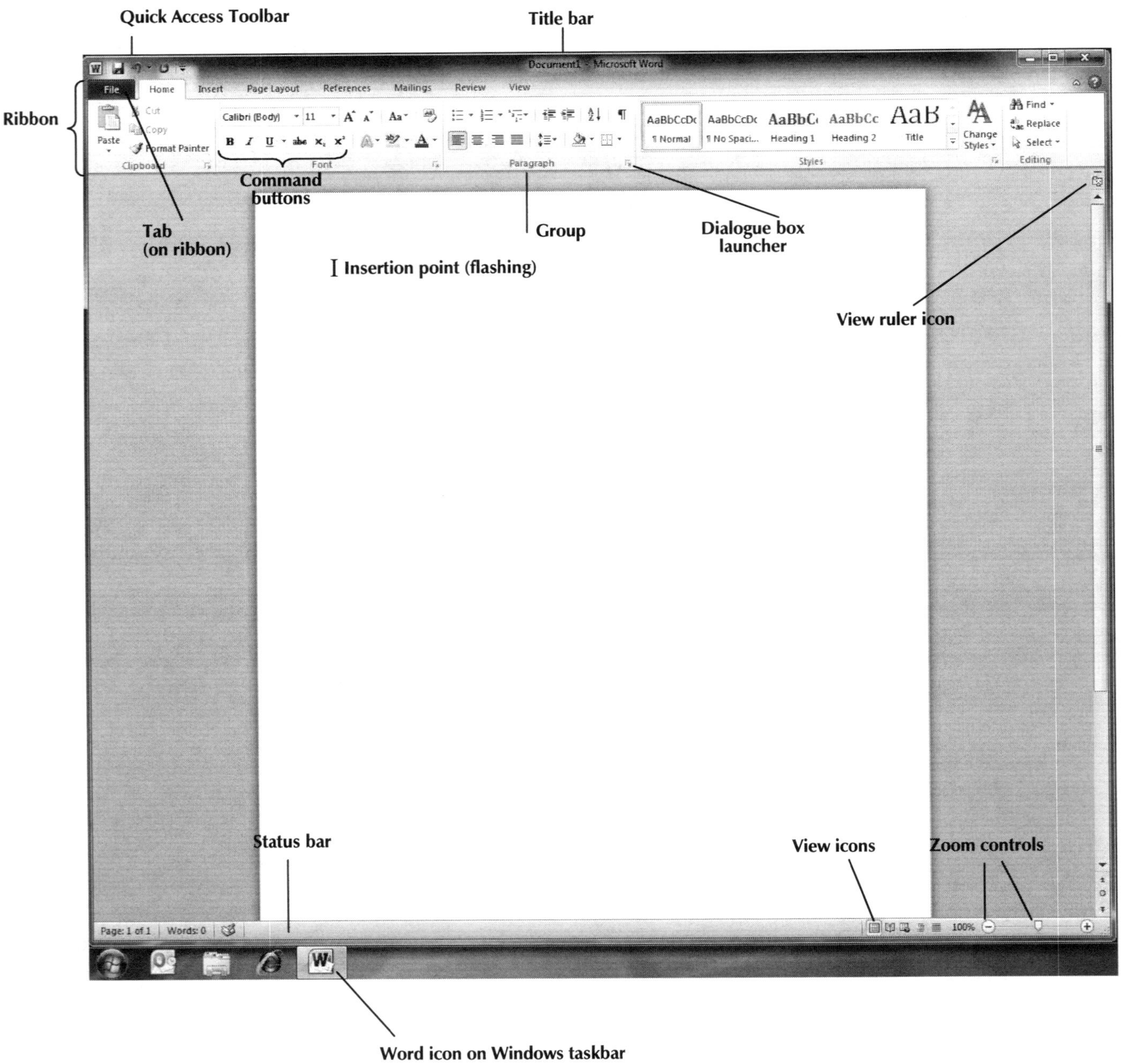

Quick Access Toolbar	A toolbar which contains a set of commands which can be added to and used as your personal collection. The basic commands are Save, Undo and Redo. This toolbar is always on display.
Title bar	Indicates the name of your current document (e.g. Document1), and the name of your program (Microsoft Word).
Ribbon	Ribbons house your **command buttons**. Each ribbon represents a type of activity. For example, the Home ribbon has all your formatting options, and the Page Layout ribbon your document layout options. Certain ribbons only appear when needed (contextual ribbons). If you point to a command button on a ribbon, without clicking on it, a ScreenTip displays a description of the button.
Tab	Each ribbon has a tab displaying its name. Click on a tab to display a ribbon.
Group (of commands)	The commands on each ribbon are organised into groups, e.g. the Home ribbon, Paragraph group.
Dialog box launcher	Some groups have a Dialog box launcher which opens a dialogue box of further commands (downward-facing arrow in bottom-right of group).
Insertion point	Flashing in the document area is the insertion point (flashing vertical line). This is where new typing and editing takes place. If you glide your mouse pointer around the document area you notice that the pointer changes shape. This is to help you select and position text.
View ruler icon	Click to turn the ruler display on/off.
Status bar	Indicates the status of your document, e.g. physical page number/total number of pages and word count. It also displays any messages that you receive, e.g. when saving a document. You can right-click on the Status bar to see a list of items that can be added to the bar.
View icons	Indicates your current view and allows you to move between views. Each view has particular benefits at different stages of document creation and editing. The default (starting) view is Print Layout view.
Zoom controls	Use to enlarge or reduce the magnification level of your document.
Windows taskbar	At the bottom of the screen the Windows taskbar displays icons for a selection of files and programs.

Topic 2 – Basics review

The following chapter is a review of basic skills in Word. There are no exercises included in the chapter. If you need to practice these skills, you will find hands-on exercises in *Tilde Publishing and Distribution's - Produce Simple Word Processed Documents*.

Creating a new blank document

Although Word presents you with a new document when launched, additional tasks require new documents. You can create a new document at any time, even when an existing document is displayed.

How to: Create a new blank document

1. Click on the **File** tab to display **Backstage** view.
2. Click on **New** (left panel).
   The Available Templates are presented.

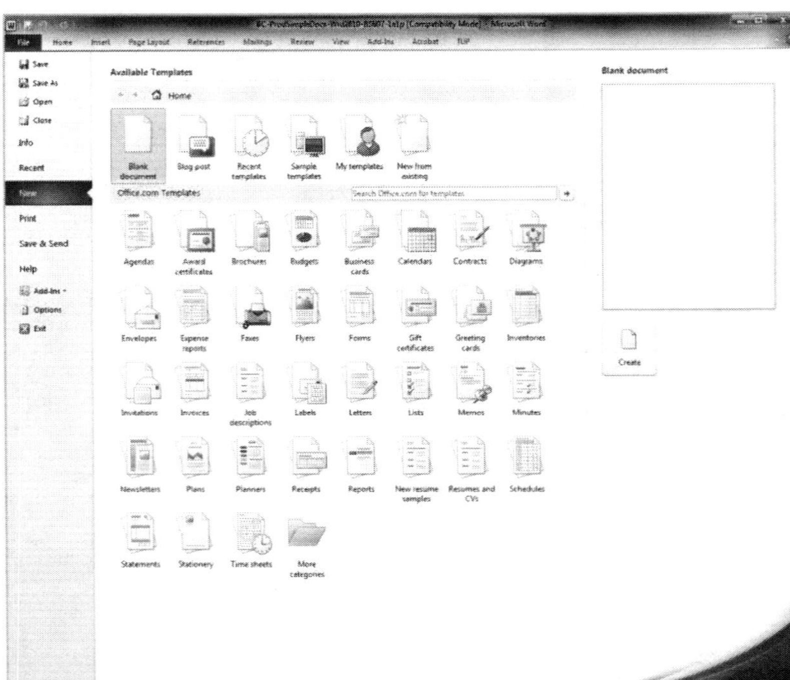

3. Ensure that the **Blank document** template is selected (top left of screen).
4. Click on **Create** (right panel) ~ *or* ~
   Double-click on **Blank document**.
5. A new blank document is created.

New document Ctrl N

Working with multiple documents

You can work on several documents at the same time. This is particularly useful if you are working on a number of tasks together, e.g. a letter to accompany a report. It is easy to move between your open documents.

How to: Switch between open documents

Single document open

1. Point to the Word icon on the Windows taskbar.
2. You are presented with a small (thumbnail) preview of each open document. Note document names at the top of each preview.
3. Point to a thumbnail for a full-screen view.
4. Click to select.

Multiple documents open

Saving your documents

How to: Save a new document

1. Click on the **Save** button (Quick Access Toolbar)
   ~or~
   Display **Backstage** view, then click on **Save**.

   The Save As dialogue box is presented.
   The default storage location is displayed at the top of the dialogue box.

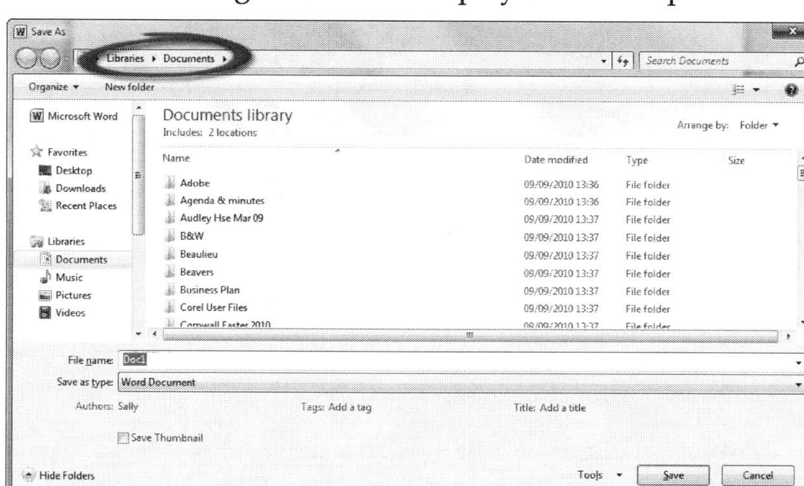

2. Type a **File name**.
   Your typing replaces the highlighted text which is only a suggestion.
3. To select an alternative storage location, click on a folder or other location in the panel on the left of the dialogue box (**Navigation pane**).
4. Click on **Save**.
   A Save message appears briefly in the Status bar.
   The document name then appears in the Title bar at the top of the screen.

Save document Ctrl S

*As an aside … You can also use the **Address Bar** list in Windows 7 to locate folders in a folder structure. In Windows XP use the **Save in** list.*

Address Bar

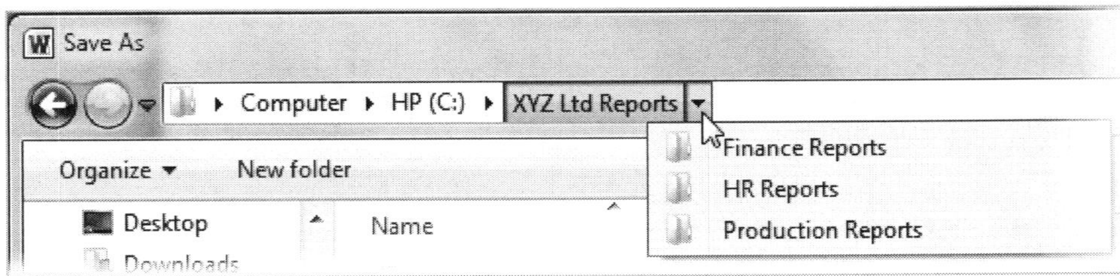

*As an aside … Word 2010 documents have a file extension of .docx (XML file format). File extensions can be viewed in the Save As dialogue box if this view option has been selected in the **Windows** environment.*

Saving your documents regularly

How to: Save regularly

1. Click on the **Save** button (Quick Access Toolbar).
   The previously saved version of the document is overwritten by the displayed version.

Save document — Ctrl S

Saving a document with a new name (creating a copy)

You can return to the Save As dialogue box to re-save a document with a new name or to re-save a document to a new location (or both). Selecting a new name or location creates a copy of the displayed document.

How to: Return to the Save As dialogue box

1. Display **Backstage** view, then click on **Save As**.
   The Save As dialogue box is presented.
2. Complete the dialogue box with a new name and/or location.

Save As — F12

As an aside … You can also use the 'Save As' procedure to create a backup copy of a document to another drive in case of computer failure or error. Saving to a CD or an external flash drive is ideal as it is also portable so can be kept offsite. If you are using a network, typically your data is being backed up for you. Talk to your network administrator or PC support staff.

*As an aside … You can also use the 'Save As' procedure to save a copy of a file in an earlier file format, so you can share files with users on Word 2003 or earlier. In the Save As dialogue box select **Word 97-2003 Document** from the **Save as type** list.*

Saving to PDF

Word 2010 provides the ability to save a document to a PDF (Portable Document Format).

***As an aside** ... PDF is a popular format for sharing documents particularly on the internet.*
To read a PDF you need a reader program, the most popular being Acrobat which is available free from the Adobe website.

How to: Save to a PDF

1. Display the required document, then click on **Save**. The Save As dialogue box is presented.
2. Select a storage location and type a file name if necessary, then click on **PDF** from the drop down box beside **Save as type**.
   The PDF is presented.

Closing your documents

How to: Close a document

1. Display **Backstage** view, then click on **Close**. 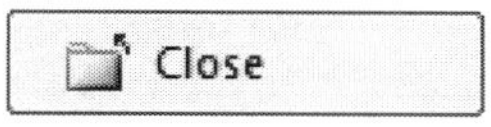

2. If you have *already* saved your work the document closes immediately. If you have *not* saved your work you are prompted to save.

3. Click on **Save** to save your changes. Click on **Don't Save** to close the document without saving your changes.

Close document 

To try to remember the 'W' key, think about closing a Window.

***As an aside** ... You can also click on the **Close** button in the top-right corner of your screen.*

If this is your only open document this button also closes Word.

Opening existing documents

How to: Open a document

1. Display **Backstage** view, then click on **Open**.
   The Open dialogue box is presented.
   The selected storage location is displayed at the top of the dialogue box.

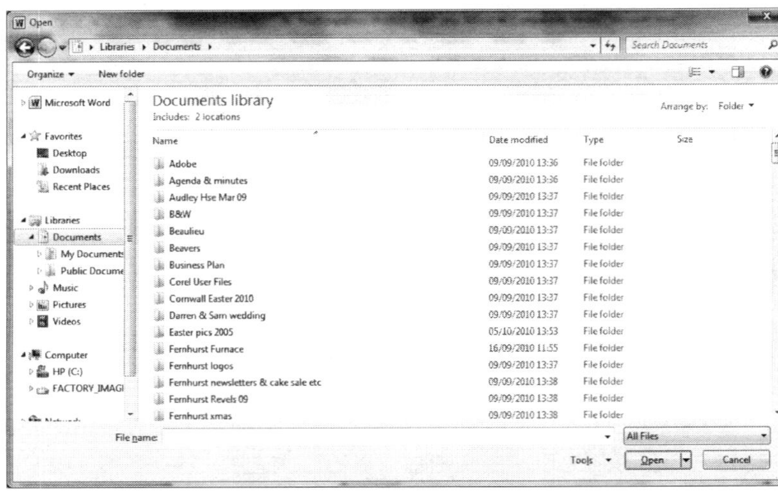

2. To select an alternative storage location, click on a folder or other location in the panel on the left of the dialogue box (**Navigation pane**).
3. To select your document, double-click on the file name *~or~*
   Click on the file name, then click on **Open**.

Open document Ctrl O

---

*As an aside … To list a number of recently-used documents or locations, display **Backstage** view then click on **Recent**, or right-click on the Word icon on the taskbar for a more limited list.*

*As an aside … If you open a document directly from an email message, the document will open in **Protected View** and cannot be edited. The Protected View message displays on the ribbon. If the document is from a trustworthy source and you want to make changes, click on the **Enable Editing** button which is located on the Protected View message.*

Migrating documents to Word 2010

If you open a document from an earlier version of Word it will display **Compatibility Mode** in the Title bar (after the document's name). You can continue working in compatibility mode or convert the document to Word 2010 to gain access to all the new 2010 features.

How to: Convert a document to Word 2010

1. Display **Backstage** view, click on **Info**, then click on **Convert**.
2. The following message is presented:

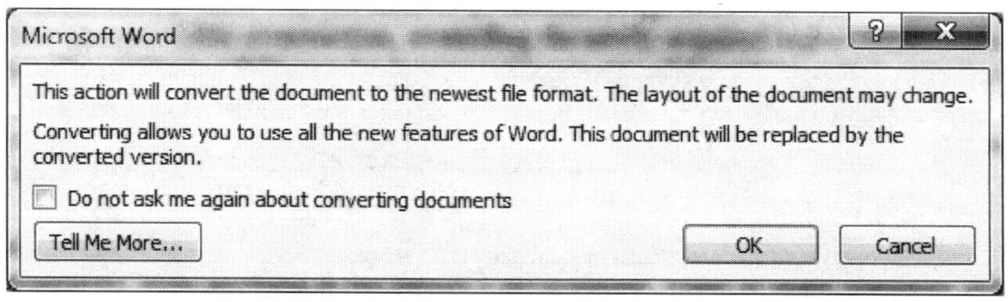

3. Click on **OK**.
   The compatibility notice is removed from the Title bar.

As an aside *... Word 2007 and Word 2010 share the same file format, but earlier versions use a different file format.*

As an aside *... If you are working between Word 2010 and previous versions continue to work in Compatibility mode to avoid inserting features from Word 2010 that are not supported in earlier versions. To* ***save*** *a document in Word 2010 format (instead of converting the original), use Save As to create a copy. In the Save As dialogue box select* ***Word Document*** *from* ***Save as type****.*

Navigating using a Browse Object

You can navigate your document by selecting a **browse object**.

For example *... You can browse by page, graphic or table – and move directly to these items.*

When you first start Word *browse by page* is automatically selected.

How to: Select a browse object

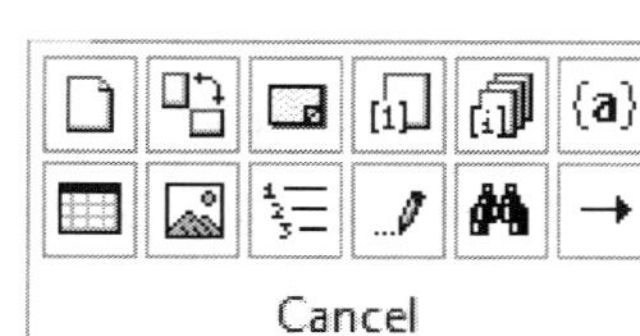

1. Click on the **Select Browse Object** button (located at the base of the vertical scroll bar).
   A list of browse objects is presented.
2. Click on the required browse object. (Point to each object and its purpose is displayed at the bottom of the list.)
3. Use the **navigation arrows** to move through your document using the selected browse object.

As an aside ... *If you rest your mouse pointer on the navigation arrows, a* ***ScreenTip*** *indicates the browse object currently selected.*

Navigating using Go To

The **Go To** feature is a particularly efficient way to move directly to a page.

How to: Go to a specific page

1. Display the Home ribbon, click on the **Find** down-arrow, then click on the **Go To...** button (Editing group).

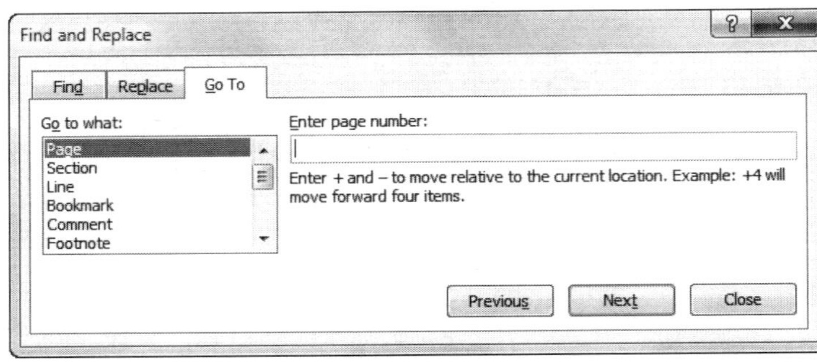

2. Click on **Page** in the **Go to what** list (if not already selected).
3. Click on **Enter page number** and type the required page number.
4. Click on **Go To**, click on **Close**.

Go To 

As an aside … If you click on the ***Find*** *button instead of the* ***Find down-arrow*** *a Navigation pane opens to the left of the window. You explore this later, for now click on the* ***Close*** *button in the top right of the pane.*

As an aside … Click on the page number on the Status bar to also quickly access the ***Go To*** *feature.*

Selecting your text

There are a number of ways to efficiently select text. These techniques are worth mastering as they save you a lot of time when editing.

One of the most efficient ways of selecting larger amounts of text involves using an area called the **selection bar**. The selection bar is an invisible area that runs down the left side of your text. The mouse pointer changes to a right-pointing arrow when you move it into the selection bar area. When text is selected, a coloured block highlights the text.

Serif typefaces

Serif, or "roman", typefaces are named for the features at the ends of their strokes. Times Roman and Garamond are common examples of serif typefaces. Serif fonts are probably the most used class in printed materials, including most books, newspapers and magazines.

"Roman" and "oblique" are also terms used to differentiate between upright and italic variations of a typeface.

Sans serif typefaces

Sans serif designs appeared relatively recently in the history of type design. The two-line English so-called "Egyptian" font, released in 1816 by the William Caslon foundry in England apparently produced the first specimen. Sans serif fonts are commonly but not exclusively used for display typography such as signage, headings, and other situations demanding visual clarity rather than high readability. The text on web pages offers an exception: it appears mostly in sans serif font because serifs often detract from readability at the low resolution of displays.

> ***As an aside*** *... When text is selected you may see a semi-transparent mini toolbar alongside the selection.*

How to: Select text

Select characters	Drag over the characters.
Select a word	Double-click on the word.
Select a line	Point to the line from the selection bar then click.
Select a sentence	Hold down the Ctrl key then click in the middle of the sentence. (Before you start, ensure you have no other text selected.)
Select a paragraph	Point to the paragraph from the selection bar then double-click *~or~* triple-click in the paragraph.
Select multiple, non-adjacent text	Hold down the Ctrl key to make a second, third, fourth, etc., selection. Use for example to select a paragraph from the top, middle and bottom of a page.
Select the entire document	Move the mouse pointer to the selection bar and triple-click *~or~* display the Home ribbon, click on the **Select** button, then click on **Select All** (Editing group) *~or~* press Ctrl A
Select text with similar formatting	Click in a sample of the text. Display the Home ribbon, click on the **Select** button, then click on **Select Text with Similar Formatting** (Editing group).

How to: Deselect a selection

1. To cancel a selection of text, click anywhere on the document (even inside the selected area).

Zooming for a better view

Zoom allows you to focus on certain areas of your text by enlarging or reducing the magnification level.

How to: Zoom

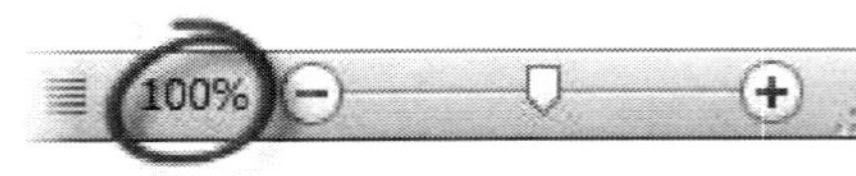

1. Click on the **Zoom level** button (Status bar). The Zoom dialogue box is presented.
2. Click on the desired zoom level, or type the required **Percentage of zoom**.
3. Click on **OK**. The selected zoom is now displayed on the **Zoom level** button.

~ *or* ~

1. Click on the plus (**Zoom In**) or minus (**Zoom Out**) buttons on the **Zoom slider**, slide to the percentage zoom you require, or click along the Zoom slider. Again the selected zoom is displayed on the **Zoom level** button.

> ***As an aside*** *… The mid-point of the Zoom slider is 100%. If you slide along the Zoom slider the indicator is quite easily attracted back to the mid-point.*

Editing text (inserting and deleting)

Text is edited at the insertion point. When you type new text it is placed at the insertion point location, in front of existing text. Text can be deleted before or after the insertion point. A selected block of text can also be deleted.

How to: Insert text

1. Click to position the insertion point where the new text is to start ~*or*~ Use your keyboard navigation actions to position the insertion point.

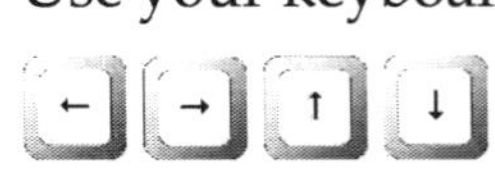

2. Type the new text.

How to: Delete text

Text in front of the insertion point	Press Delete
Text behind the insertion point	Press Back Space
A selection	Select text, then press Delete ~*or*~ Type directly over selected text. Typing replaces a selection. You need to take care with this feature. Do not leave a selection active when no longer needed in case you accidentally type over the selected text.

Checking your spelling and grammar

Word marks spelling and grammar errors as you type with a red, blue or green wavy underline depending on the type of error.

- Red wavy underline – spelling error.
- Blue wavy underline – contextual spelling error, i.e. a word spelled correctly but being used in the wrong context.
- Green wavy underline – grammar error.

You can ignore the wavy underlines until your typing is complete, then check the document throughout. Alternatively, you can correct the errors as they appear.

As an aside … *The wavy underlines do not print.*

How to: Check your spelling and grammar throughout

1. Press Ctrl Home to return to the top of the document.

2. Display the Review ribbon, then click on the **Spelling & Grammar** button (Proofing group). When a spelling or grammar error is encountered a dialogue box is displayed. Note the message at the top of the dialogue box (in this case: **Not in Dictionary**).

3. Correct the spelling or grammar error directly in the textbox *~or~* Click on one of the following options.

Main spelling options

Ignore Once or **Ignore All**	Leaves the selected word - or all occurrences of that word – unchanged, e.g. it could be someone's name.
Add to Dictionary	Adds the selected word (e.g. a name) to the custom dictionary. This dictionary is shared by all installed Office programs.
Change or **Change All**	Changes the selected word - or all occurrences of the selected word - to the suggestion highlighted.
Delete and **Delete All**	These buttons appear only when a repeated word is encountered. Click to remove repetition(s).
AutoCorrect	Adds an error and its correction to the AutoCorrect list.
Options	Allows you to change how Word corrects your text, e.g. ignore words in uppercase, ignore words that contain numbers, and ignore Internet and file addresses.
Undo	Allows you to Undo (reverse) previous responses.
Resume	If you click outside the dialogue box, you can edit the document directly. Click back on this button to continue your spell check.

Main grammar options

Ignore Once	Leaves this occurrence of the grammar error unchanged.
Ignore Rule	Leaves all occurrences of the grammar error unchanged.
Next Sentence	This ignores all grammar errors marked in the selected sentence and moves to the next sentence.
Change	This changes the grammar error marked, replacing it with the selected item from the list of **Suggestions**.
Explain	Provides more information about the grammar error.
☑ Check grammar	This switches off the Grammar Check feature. Uncheck the box if you do not want to check grammar and spelling together.
Options	Allows you to set options for your grammar check.
Undo	Allows you to Undo (reverse) previous responses.
Resume	If you click outside the dialogue box, you can edit the document directly. Click back on this button to continue your grammar check.

***As an aside** … The document is checked from the insertion point forwards or if a selection is active, the selection is checked first.*

Spell check F7

***As an aside** … You should always do a final read proofread of your document as the Spelling & Grammar checker cannot pick up all errors. This is best from a printed copy. Printing is discussed shortly.*

Correcting spelling and grammar as you type

You can use the following method to correct errors as they appear instead of using the Spelling & Grammar button later.

How to: Correct errors as you type

1. Right-click on the red, blue or green wavy underline.
2. Click on the required spelling or grammar option from the list presented.

As an aside ... *The Spelling & Grammar status icon on the Status bar indicates whether or not there are errors in your document. (A cross indicates errors, a tick indicates no errors.) If there are errors, click on the icon to move directly to the next error.*

Hints & tips

The Review ribbon also offers a Thesaurus. Click on a word then click on the ***Thesaurus*** *button (Proofing group). A task pane opens on the right with suggested alternatives. To insert, point to a word in the list, click on the down-arrow next to the word, then click on* ***Insert****. Click on the* ***Close*** *button to close the pane.*

You can add a ***Language*** *indicator to the Status bar to show which dictionary is being used to review a document. Right-click on the Status bar, then click on* ***Language****. Click back in the document to close the list.*

What if the language selected says English (United States) and I want to change this option?

Click on the **Language** indicator on the Status bar to see the Language dialogue box. Click on the language required, then click on **Set As Default**. Click on **OK.**

Inserting a date field

Many documents, particularly letters, require a date. Word can add the date automatically for you in a variety of formats. The date can be automatically updated each time the document is opened or printed to reflect the current date.

How to: Insert the date

1. Display the Insert ribbon, then click on the **Date & Time** button (Text group). The Date and Time dialogue box is presented.

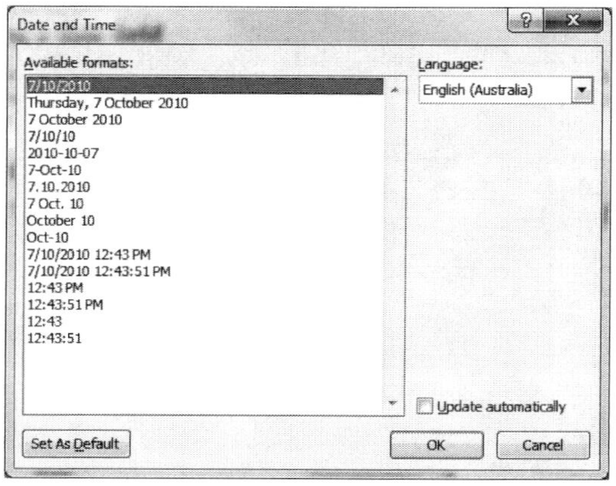

2. Under the list of **Available formats**, click on the required date format.
3. Click on **Update automatically** if you want the date to be updated each time the document is opened or printed.
4. Click on **OK**.

Cutting and copying text

A major part of your editing activities can involve re-arranging text, e.g. moving paragraphs into a different order, or copying text to another location. The **Cut** and **Paste** or **Copy** and **Paste** commands are efficient ways of achieving these tasks.

Cutting text

When you **cut** text, it is removed from the document and placed in a temporary storage area known as the **Clipboard**. Storing text on the clipboard enables you to **Paste** the text elsewhere in the current document, in another document, or in another program.

How to: Cut (move) text

1. Select the text to be moved.

2. Display the Home ribbon, then click on the **Cut** button (Clipboard group).

3. Position the insertion point where you want to insert the text.
4. Click on the **Paste** button (Clipboard group).

Cut Ctrl X Paste Ctrl V

To try to remember the Cut key 'X', think about a pair of scissors—as shown on the Cut button—blades crossing.

Copying text

Copying text means that you place duplicate text on the Clipboard without removing existing text from the document. Copying text enables you to repeat existing text elsewhere in the current document, in another document, or in another program.

How to: Copy text

1. Select the text to be copied.

2. Display the Home ribbon, then click on the **Copy** button (Clipboard group).

3. Position the insertion point where you want to insert the text.
4. Click on the **Paste** button (Clipboard group).

Copy Ctrl C Paste Ctrl V

To try to remember the Paste key 'V', think about pasting a wall with a 'V' (down and up) arm action.

As an aside ... *The same text can be pasted again and again until you copy or cut new information to the Clipboard.*

As an aside *... You can preview what you are about to paste. Copy/cut text as you would normally, then position the insertion point where you want to paste. Click on the* ***Paste*** *drop-down (Clipboard group), then point to each of the* ***Paste Options*** *to preview the possibilities. (The options generally relate to whether you use the formatting of the original text or the formatting of the area you are pasting into – and this might be particularly important when pasting between documents.)*

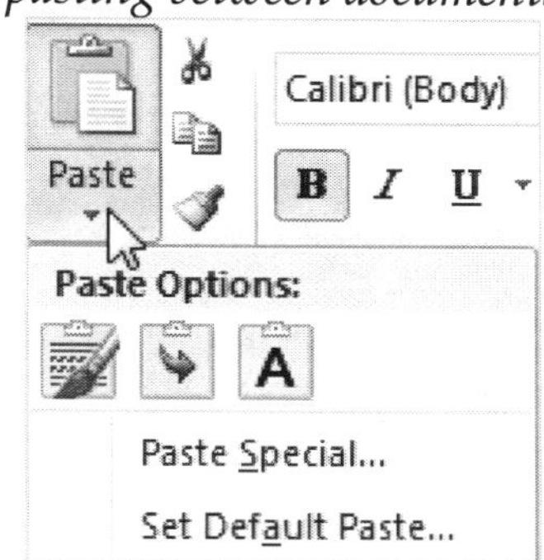

Similarly, the ***Paste Options*** *button is displayed when text is pasted. Click on the down-arrow to reveal the same paste options.*

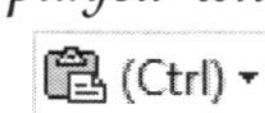

Reversing an action (Undo)

You can reverse or **undo** the majority of actions you perform - particularly useful if you make a mistake when copying and moving text!

How to: Undo an action

1. Click on the **Undo** button (Quick Access Toolbar).
2. Repeat to **Undo** previous steps in sequence.
3. If you undo too many steps, click on the **Redo** button (Quick Access Toolbar).
   The **Redo** button is only available directly after using **Undo**.

Undo Ctrl Z Redo Ctrl Y

As an aside ... *The down-arrow to the right of the* ***Undo*** *button allows you to select multiple actions. The actions are highlighted as you move down the list. Note that you can only undo actions in sequence, and not selectively.*

Moving text using drag and drop

Another useful technique for re-arranging text is called **drag and drop**. Use this method to move small amounts of text over short distances, e.g. a few words or a paragraph.

As an aside ... *Using drag and drop bypasses the Office Clipboard.*

How to: Move text by drag and drop

1. Select the text to be moved.
2. Point into the highlighted text block and drag.
   (An arrow and a dotted vertical line indicate where the text will be positioned when you release the mouse.)

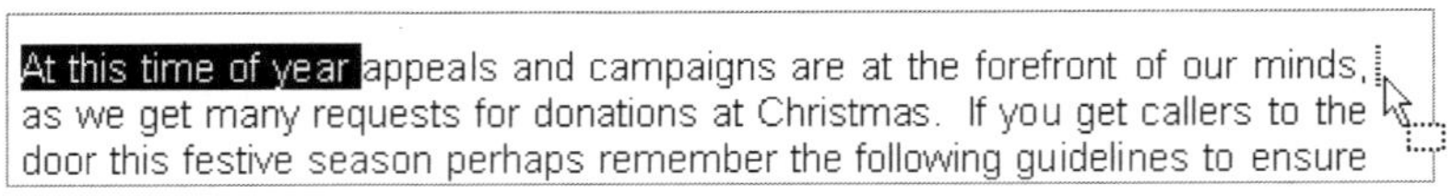

3. Release when the dotted vertical line is positioned where you want the text to appear.

As an aside ... *You can also copy text with a drag and drop by holding down* Ctrl *as you drag. An arrow with a plus sign and a dotted vertical line indicate where the text will be positioned when you release the mouse.*

Previewing your work

To avoid wasting paper and to gain an overall view of how your printed document will look, use **Print Preview** prior to printing.

How to: View in Print Preview

1. Display **Backstage** view, then click on **Print**.
   Print Preview is presented on the right of the window.

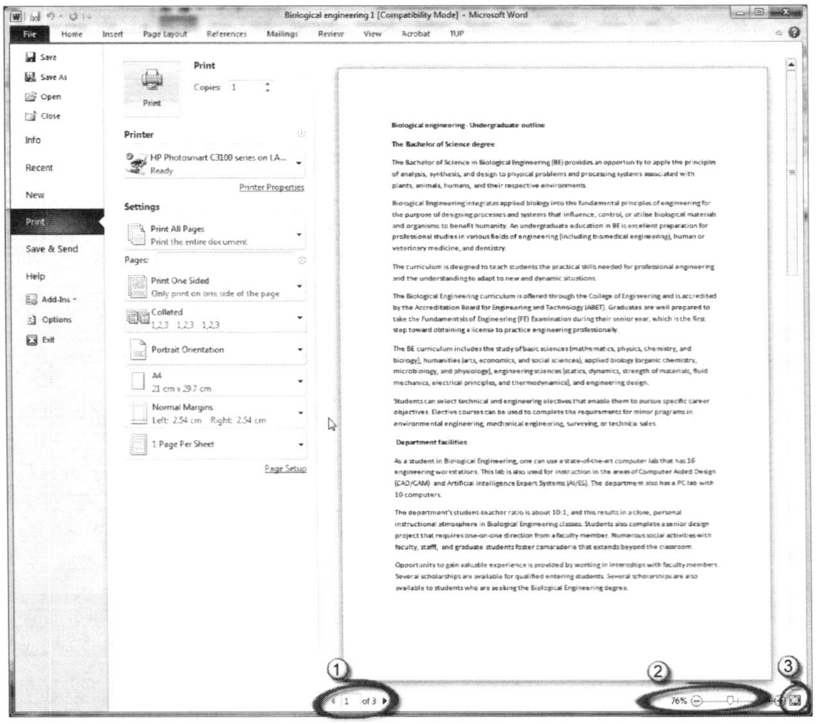

2. Note the buttons to move to **Previous Page** or **Next Page** (**1**).
   You can also type the required page number in the text box and press [Enter].
3. Note the **Zoom Out** or **Zoom In** buttons (**2**).
4. Note the **Zoom to Page** button in the lower-right corner of the window (**3**), to display a whole page after zooming.

Print Place [Ctrl] [P]

Printing your work

When you are ready to print, you can quickly print the entire active document, or select from a range of print options from the **Print Place**, e.g. print only selected pages, direct to a different printer.

How to: Print using the current settings

1. Display **Backstage** view, then click on **Print**.
   If you are ready to print simply click on the **Print** button, or press [Enter]
   You return to where you were originally working. A print message appears briefly on the Status bar.

How to: Select your print options

1. Display **Backstage** view, then click on **Print**.
2. A number of options are presented including:

Main printing options

Print: Copies	Select the number of print copies.
Printer: Name	Click on the down-arrow to select the required printer.
Settings: Print what	Choose the pages to print – **All Pages**, **Selection** (need to select first), **Current Page** (where insertion point is located), **Custom Range**. To print a range of pages, select Custom Range, then enter the page numbers in the **Pages** box, e.g. 3, 5, 8-10.
Sides	Some printers offer the option of automatically printing on both sides of a sheet of paper (automatic duplexing). Depending on your printer, if you choose **Print on Both Sides**, your printer will either print duplex automatically, or prompt you to turn the paper. Otherwise you may see an additional option **Manually Print on Both Sides** (and you will need to manually reinsert the paper).
Collated	When printing multiple copies, **Collated** prints each copy in order, **Uncollated** prints all the copies of page 1 together, then all the copies of page 2, etc.
Orientation	The choices are Landscape or Portrait.
Page size	Choose a paper size. In Australia it is usually A4.

Margins	The width around the outside of the paper that will not be printed on.
Pages per sheet	Some printers have the capability to print more than one page on a piece of paper.

3. Click on **Print**.

Changing document orientation

Your text may be better presented in a different orientation.

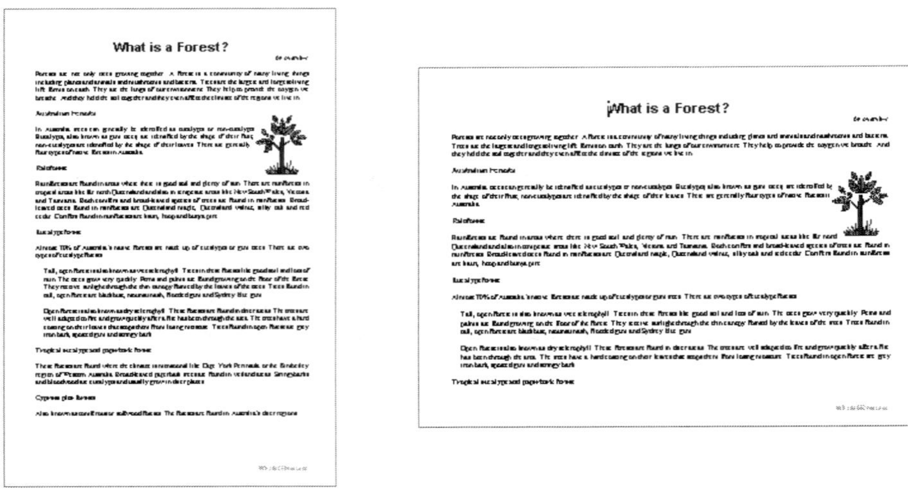

A document in portrait orientation, then in landscape orientation.

How to: Change document orientation

1. Display the Page Layout ribbon, click on the **Orientation** button (Page Setup group), then select the required option.

Changing vertical alignment

Your text may be better presented aligned to the centre of the page, e.g. for flyers or invitations.

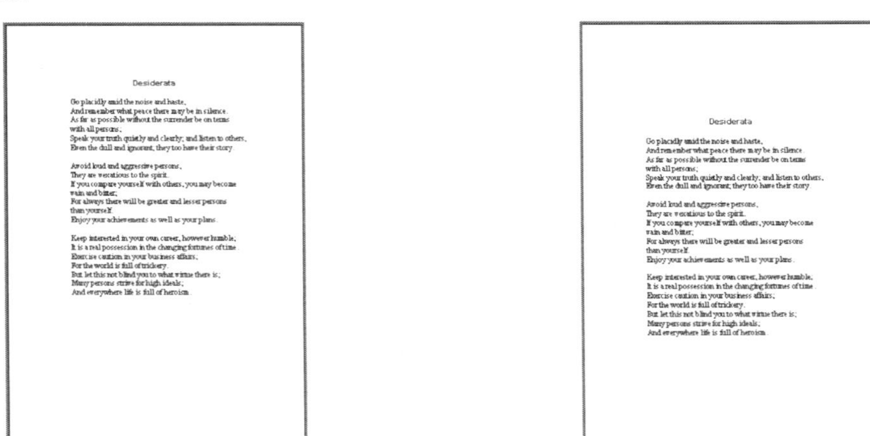

A document where the text starts at the top margins, then where the text is centred vertically on the page

How to: Change vertical alignment to centre

1. Display the Page Layout ribbon, locate the **Page Setup** group, then click on the dialogue box launcher. The Page Setup dialogue box is presented.
2. Click on the **Layout** tab.

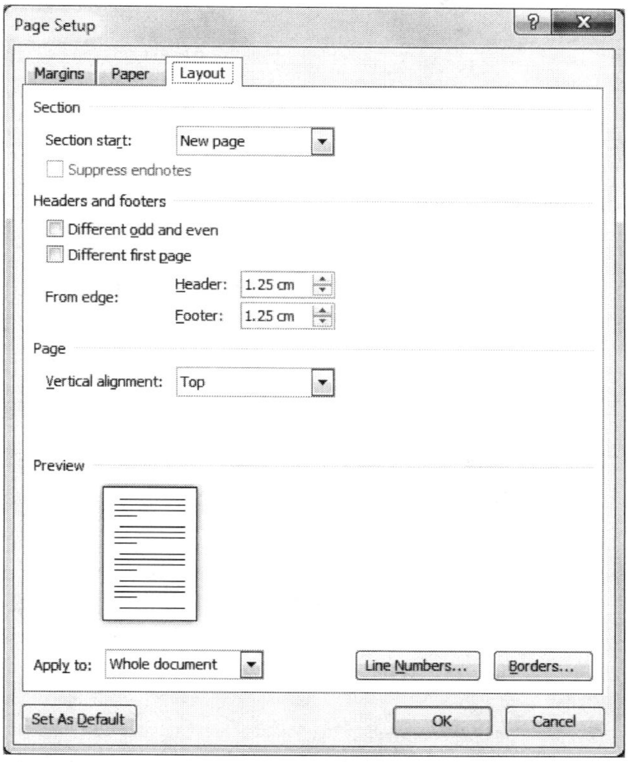

3. Click on the **Page**: **Vertical alignment** down-arrow, then click on **Center**.
4. Under **Apply to** select **Whole Document** or **This point forward** or **Selected text**.
5. Click on **OK**.

Topic 3 – Enhancing your document

Formatting can enhance the appearance and readability of your work. Formatting can be divided into two main groups:

- character formatting
- paragraph formatting.

Both can be applied either to existing text or to new text as you type.

Formatting using the mini toolbar

Formatting commands are primarily located on the **Home** ribbon, but you may have noticed a useful **Mini Toolbar** floating alongside your work. The Mini Toolbar also houses formatting commands, and appears when you select text.

Mini Toolbar

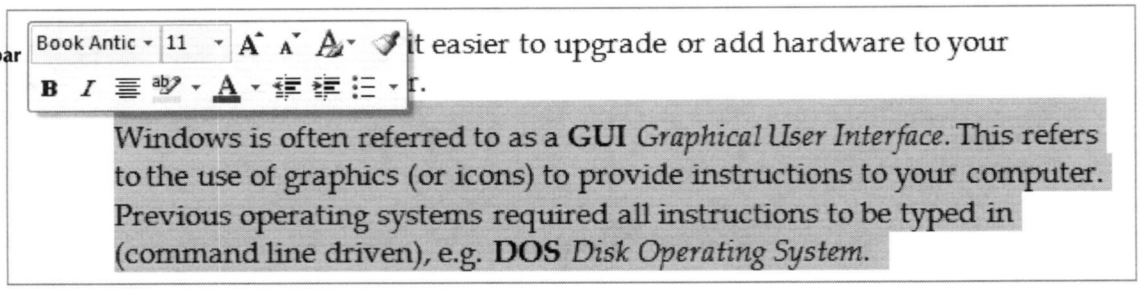

The toolbar is semi-transparent until you point to it. It disappears when you point away from it.

In the following sections although the command buttons are documented from the Home ribbon, use of the Mini Toolbar is equally efficient and can save you changing ribbons. You can also right-click on text to provide more formatting options, but again we concentrate on the **Home** ribbon and keyboard shortcuts.

> ***As an aside** …The Mini Toolbar can be switched off. Display **Backstage** view, click on **Options**, under **General** deselect **Show Mini Toolbar on selection**. Click on **OK**.*

Applying character formats

Basic character formats include: **bold**, *italics*, underline, font, and font size. Character formats can be applied to a single character, to an entire document, or to anything in between. You can apply new formatting to existing text, or turn on the formatting options you require and then start typing.

How to: Apply bold, italic or underline

1. Select the required text *~or ~*
   Position the insertion point where the new text and formatting is to begin.
2. Display the Home ribbon, then click on the **Bold**, **Italic** or **Underline** buttons (Font group). You can apply more than one format to the selection/new text. Click on the **Underline** down-arrow for different underlining options. The last underline option selected is remembered by this button until you next start Word.

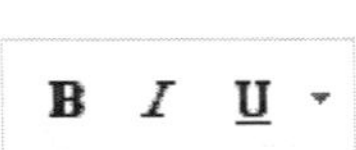

How to: Remove bold, italic or underline

1. Select the required text *~or~*
   Position the insertion point where the change is required from. The buttons representing the formats already applied are 'lit up', i.e. selected.
2. Click on the **Bold**, **Italic**, or **Underline** buttons to remove the required formatting.

Bold, Italic, Underline Ctrl B Ctrl I Ctrl U

How to: Apply a different font

1. Select the required text *~or~*
   Position the insertion point where the new text and font is to begin.
2. Display the Home ribbon, then click on the **Font** down-arrow (Font group). The fonts that you have used most recently appear towards the top of the drop-down font list, the rest are then listed alphabetically.

Calibri (Body)

3. Point to a font in the list for a live preview in your document (i.e. the font you are pointing to is shown in your document).

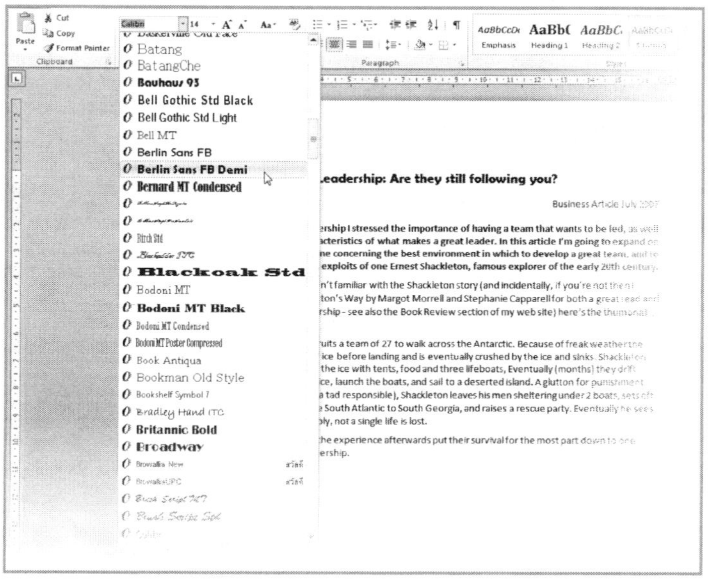

4. Click on the font of your choice.

Font dialogue box Ctrl Shift F

How to: Apply a different font size

1. Select the required text *~or ~*
   Position the insertion point where the new text and font size is to begin.
2. Display the Home ribbon, then click on the **Font Size** down-arrow (Font group). A drop-down list is presented.
3. Point to a font size in the list for a live preview in your document.
4. Click on the font size of your choice.
   Font size is measured in points (pts). There are 72 points in 1 inch.
   Most text in the body of a document falls in the range of 8-14 points.

***As an aside** … In a fresh installation of Word 2010 the default font is **Calibri** and the default font size in **11 points** (pts).*

Font Size Ctrl Shift P

Hands-on exercise 1

In this exercise you practise basic formatting. (Use the command buttons or try some keyboard shortcuts.)

- **Open** the document *Sunshine Days annual report.*
- Format the document as follows (use shortcut keys where possible):
  - Select all and change the font to: Calibri
  - To the heading *Sunshine Days Annual Report*
    (i) Apply **Bold**
    (ii) Increase the **Font** size to 20 pt
  - To the heading *Managing Director's Review*
    (i) Apply **Bold**
    (ii) Increase the **Font** size to 18 pt
  - To the following headings: *Transformation over the last three years, Sunshine Days values, Sunshine Days in a strong position, The future is energy, Opportunities for Sunshine Days Energy*
    (i) Apply **Bold**
    (ii) Increase the **Font** size to 16 pt
- Format the document from page 2 as follows:
  - To the following headings: *Leadership, Respect, Focus, Performance, Persistence*
    (i) Apply **Bold**
    (ii) Increase the **Font** size to 14 pt
- Return to page 1.

- Select the first paragraph *"Sunshine Days key objective..."*, then apply **Italics**.
- Select the first paragraph under the heading *Transformation over the last three years*, then apply **Italics**. (*A major part of the transformation process..)*
- Repeat the first paragraph in italics under the headings: *Sunshine Days in a strong position* and *Opportunities for Sunshine Days Energy*.
- **Save** your changes.
- Leave your document open for the next exercise.

Applying special effects for characters

Simple font effects were discussed earlier, however additional formatting options are available to maximise the presentation of your text.

> **For example ...** *Wave underline*, ***shadow***, *engraving*, *SMALL CAPS*, *superscript* ($3m^2$), *and subscript* (H_20).

How to: Apply more font options

1. Select the text to be formatted *~or~*
   Position the insertion point where the formatted text is to begin.
2. Display the Home ribbon, then click on the required button (Font group).

Grow Font and **Shrink Font**
Use to increase/reduce font size.

Strikethrough
Use to indicate text to be removed.

Subscript and **Superscript**
Use for H_2O or MC^2 .

Change Case
Use to change capitalisation. Click on the down-arrow to select a different capitalisation.

Text Effects
Apply a visual effect to selected text.

Text Highlight Color
Use to highlight text as you would with a pen. Click on the down-arrow to select a different colour/no colour.

Font Color
Use to change the colour of your text. Click on the down-arrow to select a colour.

Clear Formatting
Use to remove character and paragraph formatting. This strips formatting back to the original defaults in a document – so using **Undo** might sometimes be more appropriate.

As an aside ... Don't forget the basic design principles: simplicity, consistency and contrast. Use decorative features sparingly. Colour might be useful on a poster or flyer but in a business letter?

Applying character spacing

Character spacing can adjust the amount of space between characters.

For example *... Normal text, e x p a n d e d t e x t, condensedtext.*

Expanded text can be used to make headings more attractive and to increase the readability of text typed in a small point size. Condensed text can be used to ensure that text fits into a small area.

How to: Expand or condense text

1. Select the text to be formatted *~or~*
   Position the insertion point where the formatted text is to begin.
2. Display the Home ribbon, locate the **Font** group, then click on the dialogue box launcher. The Font dialogue box is presented.
3. Click on the **Advanced** tab.

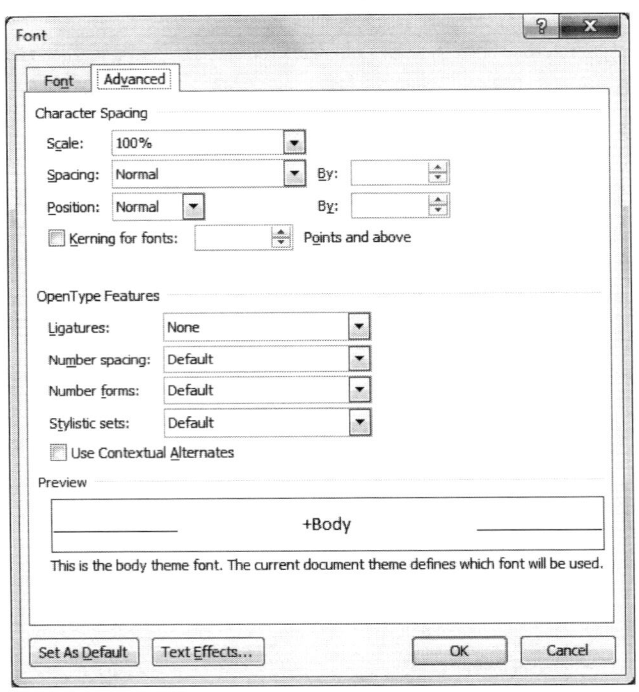

4. Click on the **Spacing** down-arrow.
5. Click on **Expanded** or **Condensed**.
6. Default spacing of 1 point appears in **By**. Click on the up- or down-arrow to select a larger or smaller spacing size.
7. Click on **OK**.

Copying formats (Format Painter)

If you have manually applied lots of formatting to text you can easily copy or 'paint' these formats to other areas.

How to: Copy formats using the Format Painter

1. Click on text that has the formatting to be copied.
2. Display the Home ribbon, then click on the **Format Painter** button (Clipboard group). A brush becomes attached to your mouse pointer.
3. Click on or drag over the text to be formatted.

As an aside ... *Double-clicking on the Format Painter button allows you to paint formats onto multiple text areas. Click back on the Format Painter button to switch this feature off.*

Hands-on exercise 2

In this exercise you work with spacing, font colours and the format painter.

- Using the document *Sunshine Days annual report*, select the document heading.
- Click on the **Change Case** button (Font group), then select UPPERCASE.
- Locate the **Font** group, then click on the dialogue box launcher. The Font dialogue box is presented.
- Click on the **Advanced** tab.
- Click on the **Spacing** down-arrow.
- Click on **Expanded**.
- Set a spacing of **1.5 pt**.
- Click on **OK**.
- Return the heading to sentence case.
- Display the Font dialogue box (Font tab) and click on Small caps.
- Reduce the spacing to 1 pt.
- Apply a dark green font colour to the main heading.
- Apply one shad lighter font colour to the heading: *Managing Director's Review*
- Using the Format painter, copy the format from the heading: *Managing Director's Review* to all the other headings with 16 pt. (You will save time, double click on the Format Painter button to make multiple changes then press ESC or click on the button again to turn it off.)
- **Save** your changes.

Applying paragraph formats

Paragraph formatting controls the alignment, spacing and appearance of entire paragraphs.

> ***For example*** *... Aligning a heading to the centre of a document, increasing the spacing between lines in a draft, adding bullet points to highlight a list.*

Alignment is a good place to start. Word includes simple tools to enable you to align your paragraphs to the: left, centre, right or to justify the text (align text to both the left and right creating a 'block' appearance). Paragraphs are aligned to the margins of your document, i.e. the borders on all four sides of a page which surround your document's text, and create an area of white space.

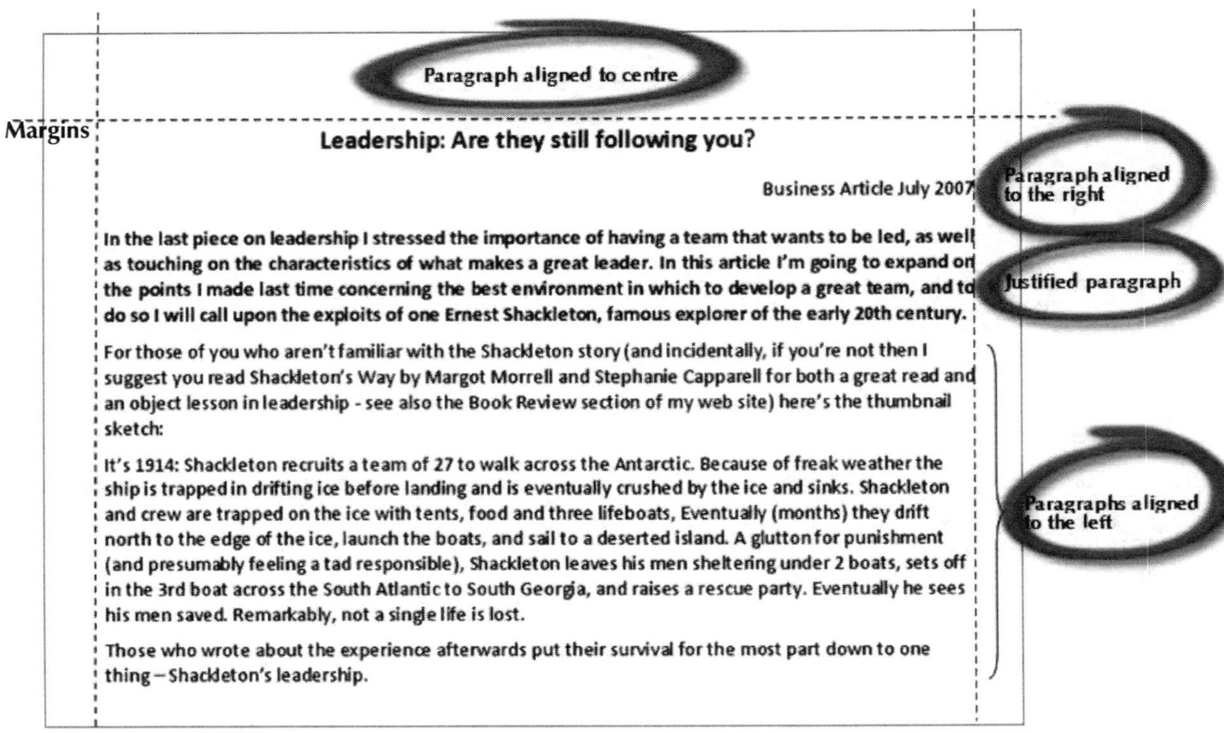

Leadership: Are they still following you?

Business Article July 2007

In the last piece on leadership I stressed the importance of having a team that wants to be led, as well as touching on the characteristics of what makes a great leader. In this article I'm going to expand on the points I made last time concerning the best environment in which to develop a great team, and to do so I will call upon the exploits of one Ernest Shackleton, famous explorer of the early 20th century.

For those of you who aren't familiar with the Shackleton story (and incidentally, if you're not then I suggest you read Shackleton's Way by Margot Morrell and Stephanie Capparell for both a great read and an object lesson in leadership - see also the Book Review section of my web site) here's the thumbnail sketch:

It's 1914: Shackleton recruits a team of 27 to walk across the Antarctic. Because of freak weather the ship is trapped in drifting ice before landing and is eventually crushed by the ice and sinks. Shackleton and crew are trapped on the ice with tents, food and three lifeboats, Eventually (months) they drift north to the edge of the ice, launch the boats, and sail to a deserted island. A glutton for punishment (and presumably feeling a tad responsible), Shackleton leaves his men sheltering under 2 boats, sets off in the 3rd boat across the South Atlantic to South Georgia, and raises a rescue party. Eventually he sees his men saved. Remarkably, not a single life is lost.

Those who wrote about the experience afterwards put their survival for the most part down to one thing – Shackleton's leadership.

A paragraph is created when you press Enter after typing some text. It is particularly useful to *view* paragraph marks ¶ to understand where paragraphs occur. Paragraph marks do not print, but simply indicate where a paragraph ends. When you choose to view paragraph marks you can also see other non-printing characters, e.g. dots between words to represent spaces.

How to: Display non-printing characters

¶

1. Display the Home ribbon, then click on the **Show/Hide** button (Paragraph group).
2. Click on the button again to hide these non-printing characters.

How to: Change the alignment of paragraph(s)

1. Click in the paragraph you want to re-align *~or~*
   Select the paragraphs you want to re-align *~or~*
   Click to position the insertion point where the new text and alignment is to begin (usually a new paragraph).

2. Display the Home ribbon, then click on the required alignment button - **Align Text Left, Center, Align Text Right, Justify** (Paragraph group).

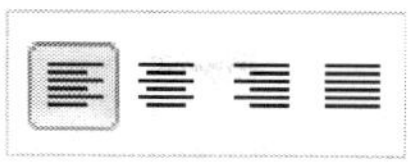

Left, Centre, Right, Justify

Changing line spacing

Line spacing determines the amount of vertical space **between** lines of text in a paragraph. Many documents simply use single-line spacing (1.0). Draft copies of documents often use double-line spacing (2.0) as it leaves space for editing or comments to be added.

> ***As an aside*** *… The default line spacing on a fresh installation of Word 2010 is a multiple of 1.15.*

How to: Adjust line spacing

1. Click in the required paragraph *~or~*
   Select the required paragraphs *~or~*
   Click to position the insertion point where the new text and line spacing is to begin (usually a new paragraph).
2. Display the Home ribbon, then click on the **Line Spacing** down-arrow (Paragraph group).

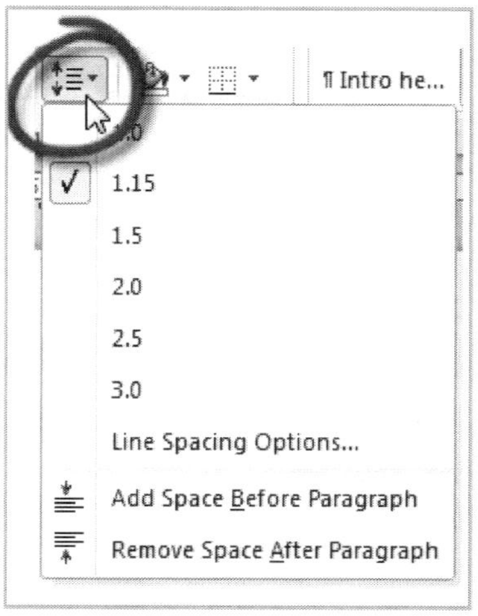

3. Select your line spacing, e.g. 1.0 (single) or 2.0 (double).
4. To set more precise spacing measurements, click on **Line Spacing Options** (see above). The Paragraph dialogue box is presented.

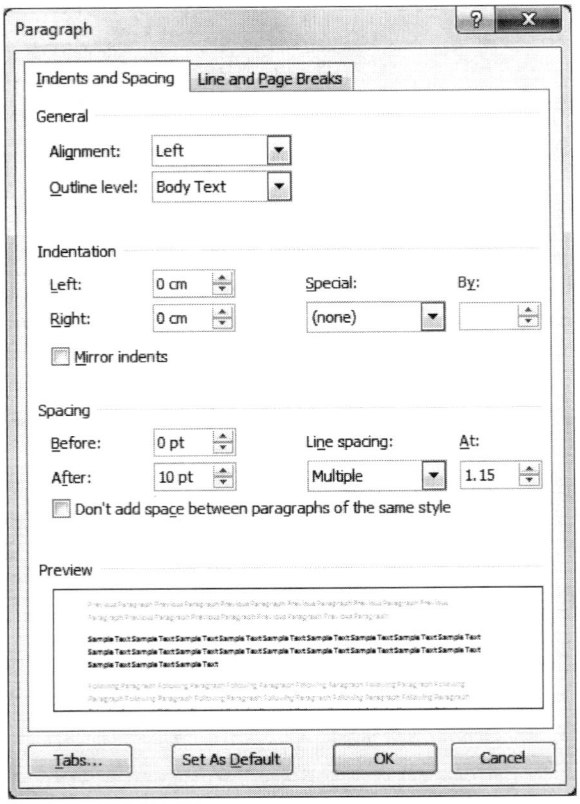

5. Select the required **Line spacing/At** options.

Line spacing options

Single	Line height adjusts to the height of the largest font in the line plus a small amount of extra space.
1.5	One and a half times single spacing.
2	Twice single spacing.
At least	The line height you have set is used but will increase if necessary for tall characters, graphics, etc.
Exactly	The line height is fixed and does not adjust. Be aware that this may cut off the tops of tall characters if you have not left enough space.
Multiple	Sets line spacing that is increased or decreased from single line spacing by a percentage you specify, e.g. 1.15 increases space by 15%.

6. Click on **OK**.

Single, Double, 1.5 line spacing: Ctrl 1 | Ctrl 2 | Ctrl 5

Changing paragraph spacing

Paragraph spacing determines the amount of vertical space **above or below** a paragraph. It allows you to control the spacing *between paragraphs* more exactly than by simply pressing Enter.

How to: Change paragraph spacing

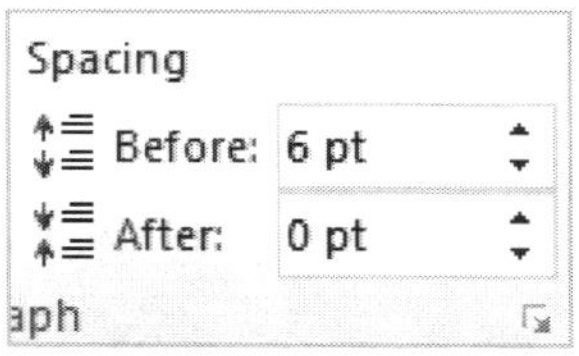

1. Click in the required paragraph *~or~* Select the required paragraphs.
2. Display the Page Layout ribbon, then adjust the **Spacing: Before** or **Spacing: After** measurements (Paragraph group).
   To adjust the measurements, click on the measurement to select, type new measurement digits, then press Enter, or simply use the up/down arrows to adjust. Note the adjustment in the document.

   ~or~

1. Display the Home ribbon, click on the **Line spacing** button (Paragraph group). At the bottom of the list are options to add/remove paragraph spacing. Particularly useful for removing.

As an aside *... In a fresh installation of Word 2010 the default spacing for paragraphs is 10 pts after. You can change this default.*

Hands-on exercise 3

In this exercise you practise aligning your text.

- Using the document *Sunshine Days annual report*, press Ctrl Home to go to the top of the document.
- Select the first heading and apply a **Centre** alignment: *Sunshine Days Annual Report.*
- Select the second heading and apply a **Right** alignment: *Managing Director's Review.*
- Apply this alignment to all 16 pt headings (format painter).
- Click into all the paragraphs and apply a **Justified** alignment.
- Click on the **Show/Hide** button to display non-printing characters.
- Delete the paragraph mark between the paragraphs through the whole document (see following example).

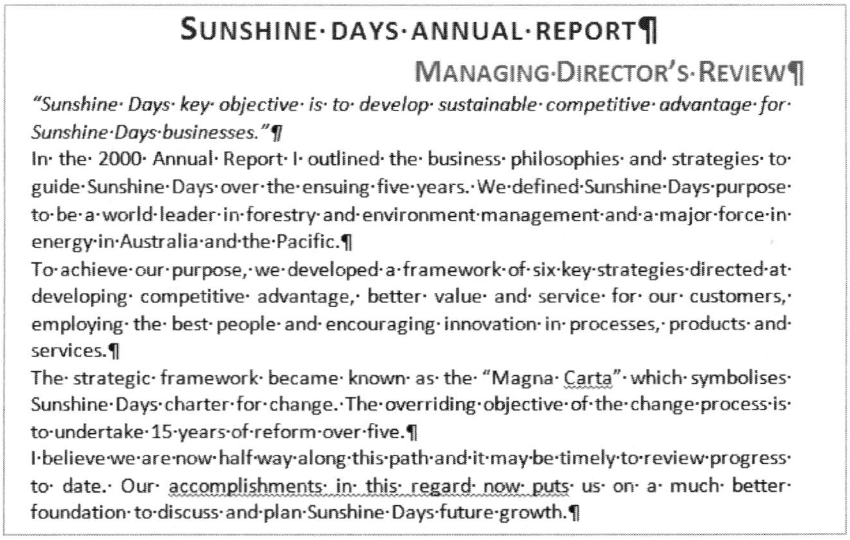

SUNSHINE DAYS ANNUAL REPORT¶

MANAGING DIRECTOR'S REVIEW¶

"Sunshine Days key objective is to develop sustainable competitive advantage for Sunshine Days businesses."¶

In the 2000 Annual Report I outlined the business philosophies and strategies to guide Sunshine Days over the ensuing five years. We defined Sunshine Days purpose to be a world leader in forestry and environment management and a major force in energy in Australia and the Pacific.¶

To achieve our purpose, we developed a framework of six key strategies directed at developing competitive advantage, better value and service for our customers, employing the best people and encouraging innovation in processes, products and services.¶

The strategic framework became known as the "Magna Carta" which symbolises Sunshine Days charter for change. The overriding objective of the change process is to undertake 15 years of reform over five.¶

I believe we are now half way along this path and it may be timely to review progress to date. Our accomplishments in this regard now puts us on a much better foundation to discuss and plan Sunshine Days future growth.¶

- Select the text between the headings *Managing Director's Review* and *Transformation over the last three years.*

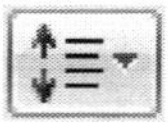

- Click on the **Line and Paragraph Spacing** button.
- Select **Line Spacing Options**.
- Set a spacing after as: 12 pt.
- Update this throughout your document.
- Select the first heading: *Sunshine Days Annual Report*.
- Set a line spacing of 6 pt after.
- Select the second heading: *Managing Director's Review.*
- Set a line spacing of 6 pt after. Copy this spacing to all the other right aligned headings.
- Click on the **Show/Hide** button again to hide non-printing characters.
- **Save** your changes.

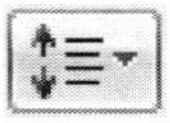

- Select the list of qualities. Using the **Line Spacing** button remove the space after paragraph (Home ribbon, Paragraph group).
- **Save** your document as *Leadership extract.*
- **Close** all open documents.

Indenting text

Indenting changes a paragraph(s) distance from the document margins. Margins are the borders on all four sides of a page which surround your document's text, and create an area of white space. At times you may like to adjust the amount of indentation to make a document easier to read and understand. This can be particularly useful with sub-headings and lists in a document. The command buttons change indentation from the left margin only.

> ***For example*** *... The heading 'Things to Remember' and subsequent points are all indented from the left.*

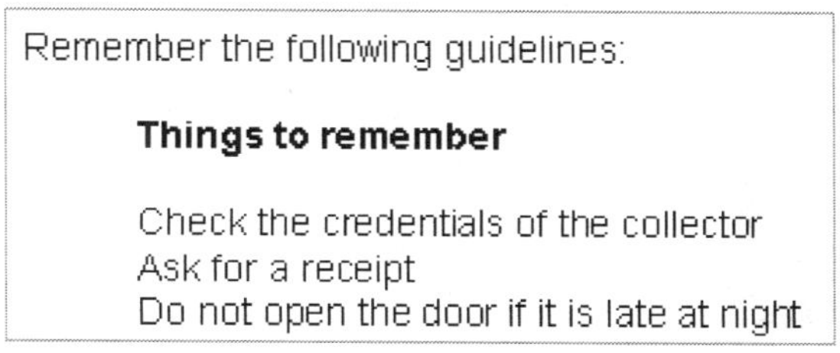

How to: Change the left indent of paragraph(s)

1. Click in the paragraph you want to indent *~or~*
   Select the paragraphs you want to indent *~or~*
   Click to position the insertion point where the new indented text is to begin (usually a new paragraph).

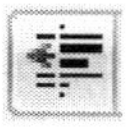

2. Display the Home ribbon, then click on the **Increase Indent** button (Paragraph group) *~or~*
   Display the Home ribbon, then click on the **Decrease Indent** button (Paragraph group).

Indenting text from both margins (blocked paragraphs)

The **Increase** and **Decrease Indent** buttons only allow you to indent from the left margin. Blocked paragraphs are indented from both the left and right margins.

How to: Adjust a left or right indent

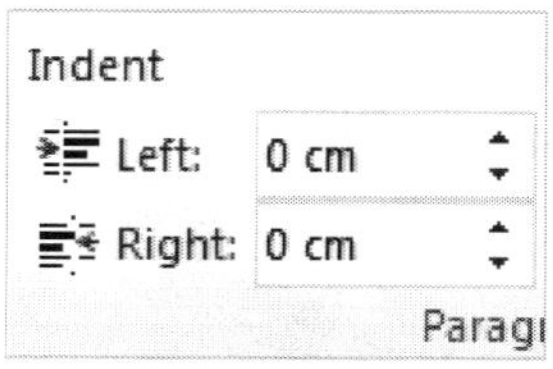

1. Click in the paragraph you want to re-align *~or~*
   Select the paragraphs you want to re-align *~or~*
   Position the insertion point where the new text and alignment is to begin (usually a new paragraph).
2. Display the Page Layout ribbon, then adjust the **Indent: Left** and **Indent: Right** measurements (Paragraph group). To adjust the measurements, click on the measurement to select, type new measurement digits, then press Enter, or simply use the up/down arrows to adjust. Note the adjustment in the document.

Hands-on exercise 4

In this exercise you create a blocked paragraph.

- Using the document *Sunshine Days annual report*, select the first paragraph.
- Display the Page Layout ribbon, then apply **Left** and **Right indent** measurements of **0.5 cm** (Paragraph group).
- Repeat this to all paragraphs that have italics (first paragraph under *Transformation over the last three years, Sunshine Days in a strong position, Opportunities for Sunshine Days Energy).*
- **Save** your changes.

Working with special indents

As discussed earlier, basic indents can be increased and decreased using the Home and Page Layout ribbons. The Paragraph dialogue box can also be used for additional forms of indentation, e.g.

- a **first line indent** (indents first line of a paragraph only),

> Working as an organizational change consultant for companies all over the world, I have learned that there are some basic "rules" or organisational behaviours that are too simple not to know. An example is quoted below:

- a **hanging indent** (indents all lines except the first line of a paragraph, e.g. in a bibliography).

> **Contemporary Issues and Challenges in HRM**
>
> **References**
>
> Apgar, M I 1998, 'The alternative workplace: Changing where and how people work', *Harvard Business Review*, May–June, 121–136.
>
> Bailey, D E & Kurland, N B 2002, 'A review of telework research: Findings, new directions, and lessons for the study of modern work', *Journal of Organizational Behavior*, 23: 383-400.
>
> Bell, B S & Kozlowski, S W J 2002, 'A typology of virtual teams: Implications for effective leadership', *Group and Organization Management*, 27: 14-49.

How to: Set a first line or hanging indent

1. Position the insertion point in the required paragraph *~or~* Select the required paragraphs.
2. Display the Home or Page Layout ribbon, locate the **Paragraph** group, then click on the dialogue box launcher. The Paragraph dialogue box is presented.
3. Ensure the **Indents and Spacing** tab is selected.
4. Click on the **Special** down-arrow, and click on the required option. (Note the default is **None**.)
5. Click on the **By** up/down-arrow to select your measurement.
6. Click on **OK**.

Applying bullets and numbering

Bullets and numbering are often used to clarify the items in a list or steps in a procedure. Multilevel numbering may be required for more complex lists or legal documents.

How to: Apply basic bullets or numbering

1. Select the required text ~ *or* ~
   Position the insertion point where the new text and formatting is to begin.
2. Display the Home ribbon, then click on the **Bullets** or **Numbering** buttons (Paragraph group). Click on the down-arrow beside each button to select alternative button symbols or numbering options.
3. If you are typing new text and formatting, press Enter twice to complete the list.

How to: Remove basic bullets and numbering

1. Select the formatted text, then click back on the **Bullets** or **Numbering** buttons (Paragraph group).

As an aside ... *If you need to alter the number at which a list starts, right-click on the required paragraph to **Restart at 1**, **Continue Numbering** or **Set Numbering Value** (useful for legal numbering).*

How to: Apply a multilevel list

1. Select the required text ~ *or* ~
   Position the insertion point where the new text and formatting is to begin.
2. Display the Home ribbon, then click on the **Multilevel List** button (Paragraph group). A gallery of options is presented.
3. Click on the required list.
4. Press Tab to move to a lower level item in the list. Press Shift Tab to move to a higher level item in the list.
5. If you are typing new text press Enter twice to complete the list.

How to: Remove a multilevel list

1. Select the formatted text, then click back on the **Multilevel List** button (Paragraph group). A gallery of options is presented.
2. Click on **None**.

As an aside ... *You can quickly add an additional numbered or bulleted item into an existing list by positioning the insertion point where you require the new item and pressing* Enter.

Hands-on exercise 5

In this exercise you practise applying numbering.

- Using the document *Sunshine Days annual report,* display page 2.
- Select the line: *Creates and contributes to...*

- Click on the **Numbering** drop-down button (Home ribbon, Paragraph group).

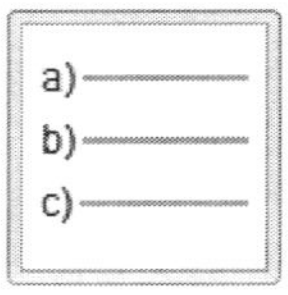

- Select the a) option.
- Select the next list: *Employees, Customers, Communities, the Environment.*
- Apply the same numbering option.
- Repeat with the next 3 paragraphs: *Makes critical choices, Makes timely..., Gets on with the job, sets challenging..., and Strives to be...*
- *NOTE*: if your second numbered list begins with the letter b), right click on the letter and click on **Restart at a.**
- Add a line spacing to all numbered list of 1.15
- **Save** your changes.

Applying paragraph borders and paragraph shading

Borders and shading can be used to make a document more attractive and eye-catching. Borders and shading can be applied to one or more paragraphs, and extend to the left and right indent positions.

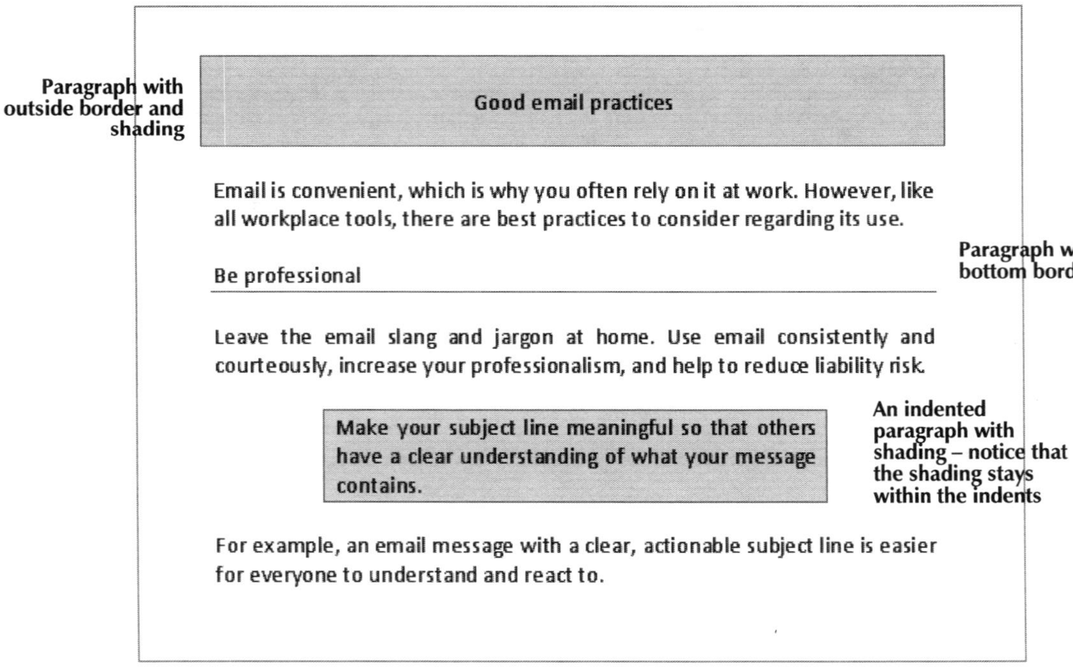

How to: Apply paragraph borders

1. Position the insertion point in the required paragraph *~or~* Select the required paragraphs.
2. Display the Home ribbon, click on the **Borders** down-arrow (Paragraph group). A list of options is presented.
3. Click on the **Outside Borders** option to apply to all sides of the paragraph, or select particular borders.

How to: Remove paragraph borders

1. Position the insertion point in the required paragraph *~or~* Select the required paragraphs.
2. Display the Home ribbon, then click on the **No Border** option (Paragraph group).

How to: Apply paragraph shading

1. Position the insertion point in the required paragraph *~or~* Select the required paragraphs.
2. Display the Home ribbon, click on the **Shading** down-arrow (Paragraph group). A gallery of colours is presented organised by themes. Point to a colour selection for a live preview in your document.
3. Click on a colour of your choice.

How to: Remove paragraph shading

1. Position the insertion point in the required paragraph *~or~* Select the required paragraphs.
2. Display the Home ribbon, click on the **Shading** down-arrow, then click on **No Color** (Paragraph group).

Hands-on exercise 6

In this exercise you practise applying paragraph borders and shading.

- Using the document *Sunshine Days annual report,* display page 1.
- Select the first heading.
  Click on the **Borders** down-arrow (Home ribbon, Paragraph group), then click on **Outside Borders**.
- Keeping the heading selected, click on the **Borders** down-arrow, then de-select the **Left Border**.
- Keeping the heading selected, click on the **Borders** down-arrow, then de-select the **Right Border**.
- Keeping the heading selected, display the Page Layout ribbon.
  Set a **Left** and **Right Indent** of **1 cm**. (Notice that your borders only extend to the indents.)

Next, you apply some shading.

- With the heading still selected, click on the **Shading** down-arrow (Home ribbon, Paragraph group).
- Click on the lightest green. Note the live preview in the document.
- **Save** your changes.

Applying page borders, page colour and watermarks

Pages can be made more attractive with **borders** and **colour**, e.g. for flyers or invitations. **Watermarks** appear behind text and are useful to indicate that a document is a draft, should not be copied or is confidential.

How to: Apply a page border

1. Display the Page Layout ribbon, click on the **Page Borders** button (Page Background group). The Borders and Shading dialogue box is presented.

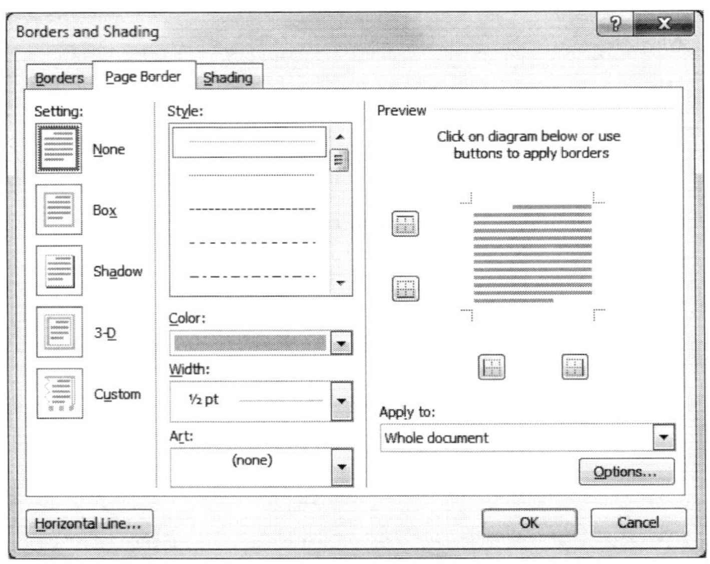

2. To design your page border, click on a combination of **Setting**, **Style**, **Color**, **Width** or use **Art**.
3. Click on **OK**.

> ***As an aside*** *... To remove a border select a Setting of* **None** *from the dialogue box options.*

How to: Apply a page colour

1. Ensure you are working in Print Layout view.

2. Display the Page Layout ribbon, click on the **Page Color** button. (Page Background group). A gallery of colours is presented organised by themes. Point to a colour selection for a live preview in your document.
3. Click on a colour of your choice.

How to: Apply a watermark

1. Ensure you are working in Print Layout view.
2. Display the Page Layout ribbon, click on the **Watermark** button (Page Background group). A gallery of watermarks is presented.
3. Click on the required option.

***As an aside** … To remove a watermark select **Remove Watermark** from the gallery.*

Hands-on exercise 7

In this exercise you practise applying a watermark.

- Using the document *Sunshine Days annual report*, display page 1.

- Click on the **Watermark** button (Page Layout ribbon, Page Background group). A gallery of watermarks is presented.
- Scroll down and click on either DRAFT option.
- Review your pages in **Print Preview**.
- **Print** a copy of your document and review.
- **Save** your changes.
- **Close** your document.

Terms & concepts review

- Why would you use expanded text?

- What are the shortcut keys for the following functions?

	Shortcut key combination
Underline	
Right alignment	
1.5 line spacing	
Font dialogue box	

- Where do you find the following buttons and what do they do?

	Ribbon? Group?	What does this button do?

Consolidation task 1

You have been asked to prepare the following document for a hand-out at a presentation. Using the following hints, update the given 2 page file: *Trees of the Australian Forest.*

- Spacing throughout: Line 1.15 / Paragraph 12pt after unless otherwise stated. (You will need to remove current paragraph markings.)
- Some text needs to be added.
- Font: Calibri.

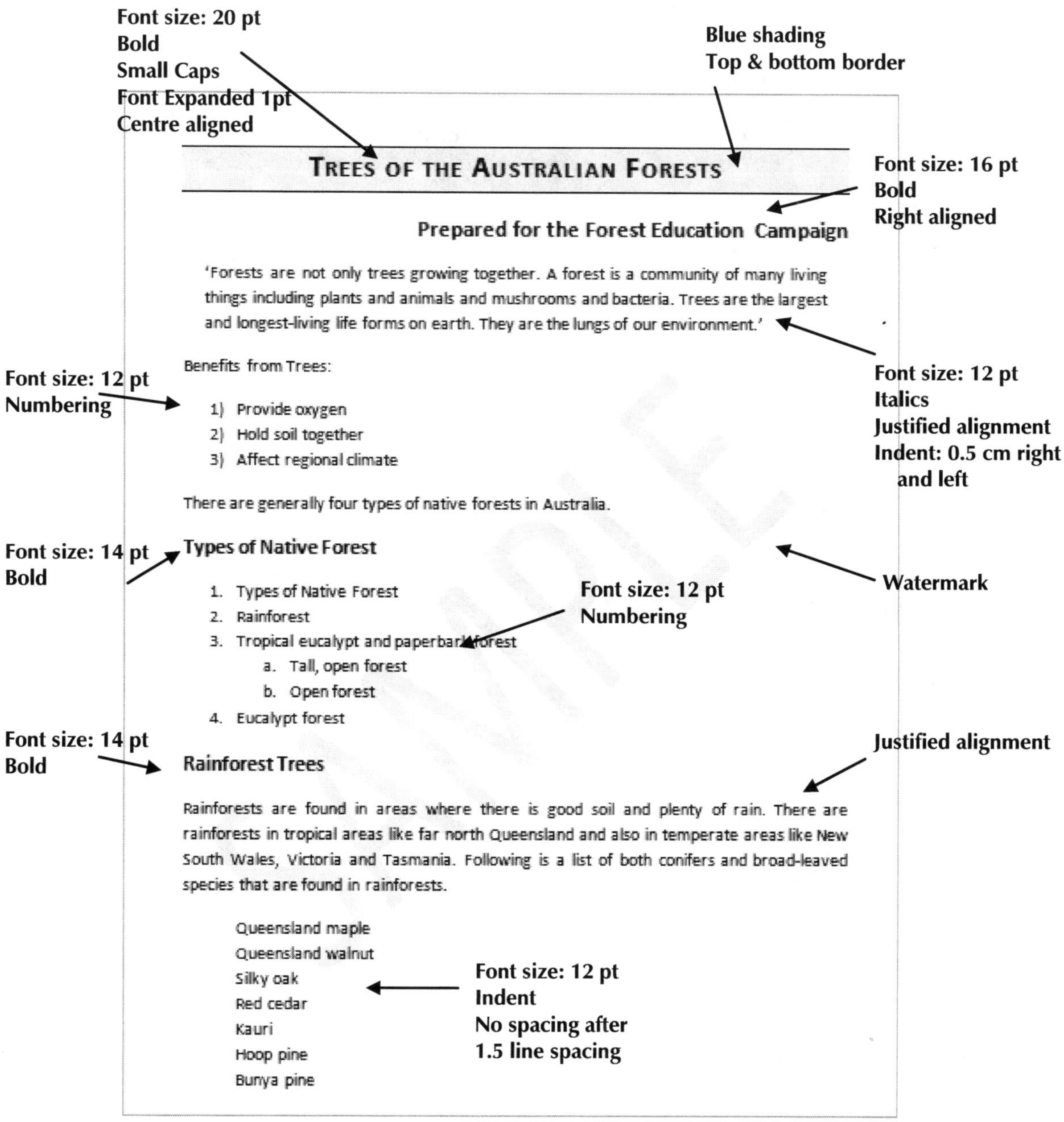
TREES OF THE AUSTRALIAN FORESTS

Prepared for the Forest Education Campaign

'Forests are not only trees growing together. A forest is a community of many living things including plants and animals and mushrooms and bacteria. Trees are the largest and longest-living life forms on earth. They are the lungs of our environment.'

Benefits from Trees:

1) Provide oxygen
2) Hold soil together
3) Affect regional climate

There are generally four types of native forests in Australia.

Types of Native Forest

1. Types of Native Forest
2. Rainforest
3. Tropical eucalypt and paperbark forest
    a. Tall, open forest
    b. Open forest
4. Eucalypt forest

Rainforest Trees

Rainforests are found in areas where there is good soil and plenty of rain. There are rainforests in tropical areas like far north Queensland and also in temperate areas like New South Wales, Victoria and Tasmania. Following is a list of both conifers and broad-leaved species that are found in rainforests.

Queensland maple
Queensland walnut
Silky oak
Red cedar
Kauri
Hoop pine
Bunya pine

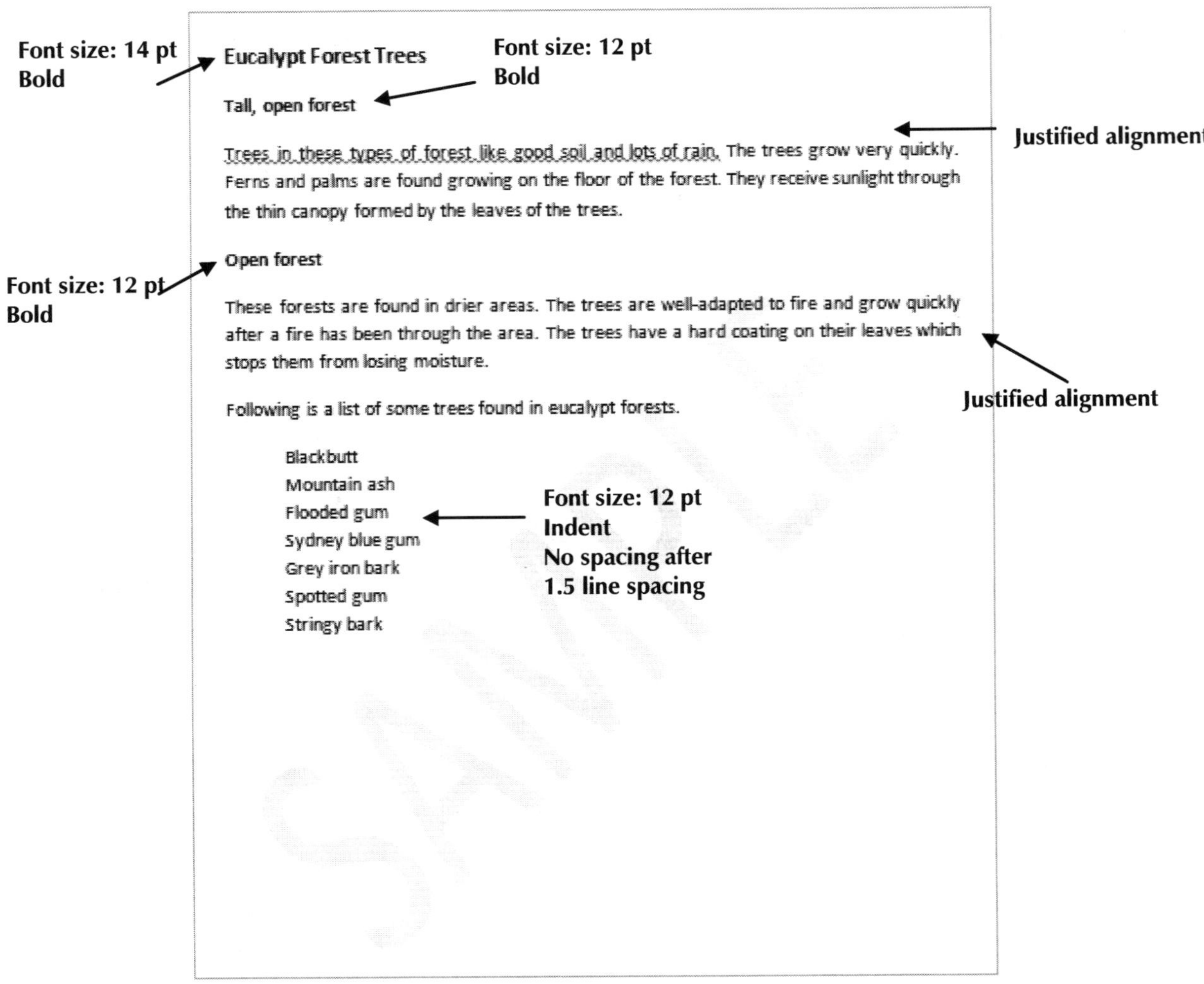

- **Print** your document.
- **Save** and **Close** your document.

After this Consolidation task, do you feel confident... tick the appropriate box:

	Editing a document
	Aligning text (centre, right & justified)
	Changing font size
	Indenting text
	Formatting small caps
	Formatting text (bold & italics)
	Numbering / multi-level
	Shading text
	Adding borders
	Adding watermark

Topic 4 – Consistent layout with templates

Templates are used as patterns - or blueprints - for all documents of a certain type.

> ***For example ...*** *Letters, memos, faxes and reports can all be based on different templates that specify their layout.*

Using templates you can ensure that your document layout is consistent and you can create a template for each document type to present a standard corporate image.

All documents that you create in Word are based on a template. When you create a new blank document, the document presented is based on the **Normal** template. This means that when you start typing, Word uses the margins, tab settings, paper size, orientation and styles defined in the associated Normal template.

In this topic you first review how to use a template; then you create a template; then you incorporate a custom style into that template. Creating your own styles in a custom template ensures that documents created from your templates not only have a common layout, but also have consistently formatted text.

Using a template

How to: Create a new document using a template

1. Click on the **File** tab to display **Backstage** view.
2. Click on **New** (left panel).
   The Available Templates are presented.
3. Click on **Sample templates**, select a template, ensure **Document** is selected, then click on **Create**. A new document is produced from the selected template.

Hands-on exercise 8

In this exercise you create a document with the assistance of the Equity Letter template.

- Click on the **File** tab to display **Backstage** view.
- Click on **New** (left panel).
  The Available Templates are presented.
- Click on **Sample templates**, click on the *Equity Letter* template from the selection presented in the centre of the pane.
- Click on **Create**.
  A new document is produced from the selected template.
- **Save** your document as *Letter example*.
- Leave your document open.

Viewing the applied template

To view the template associated with a document you need to customise a button onto the Quick Access toolbar.

How to: Customise the Quick Access Toolbar

1. Click on the **Customize Quick Access Toolbar** button, then click on **More Commands** from the list presented.
   The Word Options dialogue box is presented.

2. Under **Choose commands from** select **All Commands**, then scroll down and find **Templates** (they are in alphabetical order).
3. Click on **Add**, click on **OK**.

How to: Remove buttons from the Quick Access Toolbar

1. Right-click on a command button added to the Quick Access Toolbar, then click on **Remove from Quick Access Toolbar**.

Hands-on exercise 9

In this exercise you practise adding the Templates button to the Quick Access Toolbar.

- Click on the **Customize Quick Access Toolbar** button, then click on **More Commands** from the list presented.
- The Word Options dialogue box is presented.
- Under **Choose commands from** select **All Commands**, then scroll down and find **Templates** (they are in alphabetical order).
- Note the selected default **For all documents (default)**.
- Click on **Add**, click on **OK**.
- Now, with your *Letter example* document displayed, click on the new **Templates** button on your Quick Access toolbar.
  The Templates and Add-ins dialogue box is presented.

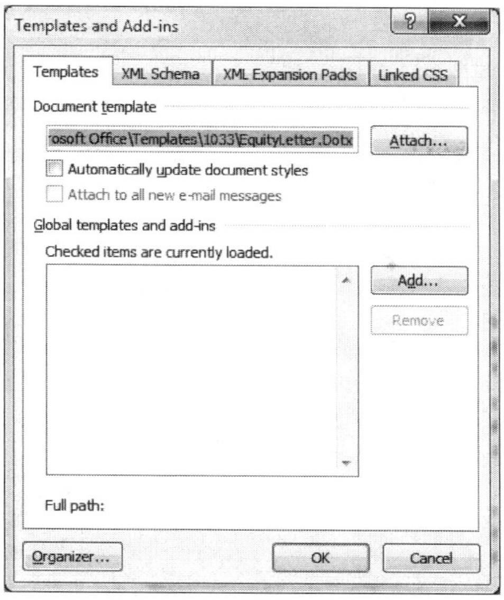

- Note the filename of the template *EquityLetter.Dotx*. (Note then that the file extension of a general template is *.dotx*.
- Click on **OK**.
- **Close** your document.

Creating a custom template

Word supplies a variety of templates to help you get started. However, advanced users of Word will want to create their own.

How to: Create a new template

1. Click on the **File** tab to display **Backstage** view.
2. Click on **New** (left panel).
   The Available Templates are presented.
3. To create a template based on the Normal template, click on **My Templates**. The New dialogue box is presented.

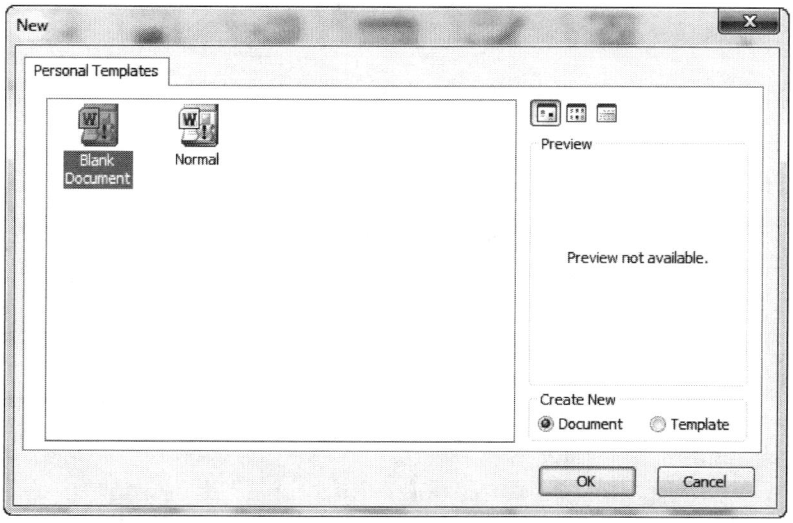

4. Click on **Normal**.
   (You may have **NormalOld** if your installation is an upgrade.)

5. Click on the **Template** option, then click on **OK**.
   A new template is displayed.
   Note in the Title Bar the title: Template *no.* (e.g. Template1).

How to: Save your template

1. Click on the **Save** button (Quick Access Toolbar).
   The Save As dialogue box is presented.
2. Type a **File name**.
3. Ensure **Save as type** is set to **Word Template**.
4. Scroll to the top of **Navigation pane** and click on **Microsoft Word**.

5. The Templates folder is displayed.

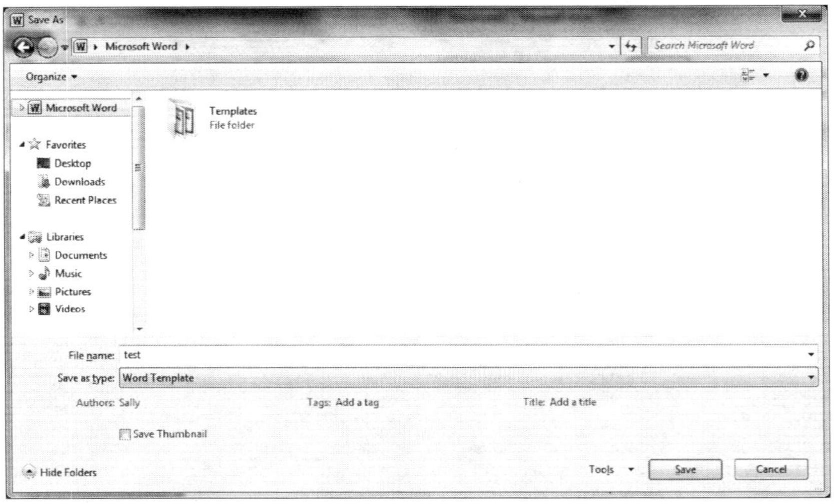

6. Double-click on the **Templates** folder (to select).
7. Note the path displayed in the **Address Bar**.
   This is where your templates are stored. For example,

8. Click on **Save**.

> ***As an aside*** *... In a standard installation of Office 2010 on Windows 7, the Templates folder is in the AppData\Roaming\Microsoft\Templates folder within your user folder. If you cannot find your Templates folder, display* ***Backstage*** *view, then click on* ***Options****. The Word Options task pane is presented. Click on* ***Advanced****. Scroll down to the bottom, click on* ***File Locations****. Double-click on* ***User templates*** *to see your full path.*

Hands-on exercise 10

In this exercise you practise creating your own template.

- Click on the **File** tab to display **Backstage** view.
- Click on **New** (left panel).
  The Available Templates are presented.
- To create a template based on the Normal template, click on **My Templates**. The New dialogue box is presented.
- Click on **Normal**.
- Click on the **Template** option, then click on **OK**.
  A new template is displayed.
  Note in the Title Bar the title: Template *no.* (e.g. Template1).
- Select the basic style of **No Spacing** (from the Quick Style Gallery).
- Type the following organisation name and contact details at the top of the template, and format them appropriately for a letterhead.

Greenwood National Forest

25 Woody Way

BARKINGTON NSW 2988

02 9889 5555

- Press Enter three times to leave some space.
- Insert the date (Insert ribbon, Date & Time).
- Press Enter six or seven times to leave some space.
- Type a standard letter closure and sign-off for a letter.
  For example:

Yours sincerely

<Your Name>

Director of Forest Marketing

- Change the margins in your template as follows (Page Layout ribbon, Margins).

Top	4 cm
Bottom	3 cm
Left	5 cm
Right	5 cm

- Click on **OK**.

- Click on the **Save** button.
  The Save As dialogue box is presented.
- Type the **File name**: *Standard letter*
- Ensure **Save as type** is set to **Word Template**.
- Scroll to the top of **Navigation Pane** and click on **Microsoft Word**.
- Double-click on the **Templates** folder displayed.
  Ensure your templates folder is selected.
- Click on **Save**.
- **Close** the template.

Next, you create a new document based on your *Standard letter* template.

- Display **Backstage** view.
- Click on **New** (left panel).
- To create a document based on your *Standard letter* template, click on **My Templates**. The New dialogue box is presented.
- Click on the *Standard letter* template from the selection presented.
  Leave the option set to Document.
- Click on **OK**.
  A new document is produced from the selected template.
  Note that the Title Bar says: Document *no*.
- **Close** your document.

Finally, you review the associated template for this document.

- With your *Standard letter* document displayed, click on the new **Templates** button on your Quick Access toolbar.
  The Templates and Add-ins dialogue box is presented.
- Note the filename of the template *Standard letter.dotx*.
- Click on **OK**.
- **Close** your *document*.

Editing a template

To open a template for editing you follow the usual procedure for opening a document. The main difference is selecting your templates folder as your file location.

How to: Open a template for editing

1. Click on the **Open** button.
2. Scroll to the top of **Navigation Pane** and click on **Microsoft Word**.
3. Double-click on the **Templates** folder displayed.
   Ensure your templates folder is selected.
4. Double-click on your template to open it.
   Check for the correct name in the Title bar

As an aside ... *If your template is not displayed check file type is set to All Files.*

Hands-on exercise 11

In this exercise you first locate and open your template for editing.

- Display the **Open** dialogue box.
- Scroll to the top of **Navigation Pane** and click on **Microsoft Word**.
- Double-click on the **Templates** folder displayed.
  Ensure your templates folder is selected.
- Double-click on the *Standard letter* template to open it.
- Note the template name in the Title bar.

First, you make a change to the margins of your template.

- Change the document margins as follows:

Left	2 cm
Right	2 cm

- Click on **OK**.
- **Save** your changes to the template.
- **Close** your template.

Next, you produce a new document using your updated template.

- Display **Backstage** view.
- Click on **New** (left panel).
- Under **Available Templates**, click on **My Templates**.
- Click on the *Standard letter* template from the selection presented.
  Leave the option set to Document.
- Click on **OK**.
  A new document is presented with the changes to the margins, and it includes the new styles.

- Type the following into your letter.

Mr Bill Walker
117 Currawong Parade
BIRDYVILLE NSW 2899

Dr Mr Walker

We are pleased to confirm your reservation to visit the Greenwood National Forest next month. Please be sure to bring the following items with you:

Binoculars
Hat
Insect repellent
Sturdy walking shoes
Plenty of water

- Apply **Bullets** to the listed items.
- Spell and grammar check your document.
- **Save** your document as *Walker letter*.
- **Close** your document.

Creating Quick Part items

Other Word features can be used to ensure consistency. These include **Quick Parts**.

Standard paragraphs of text can be saved into the **Quick Parts** gallery. These paragraphs can then be quickly inserted into any document. Word refers to these as building blocks.

How to: Add to the Quick Parts gallery

1. Select the text to be stored.

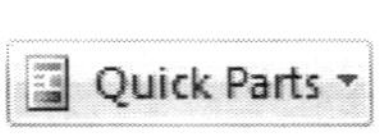

2. Display the Insert ribbon, click on the **Quick Parts** button, then click on the **Save Selection to Quick Parts Gallery** option (Text group). The Create New Building Block dialogue box is presented.

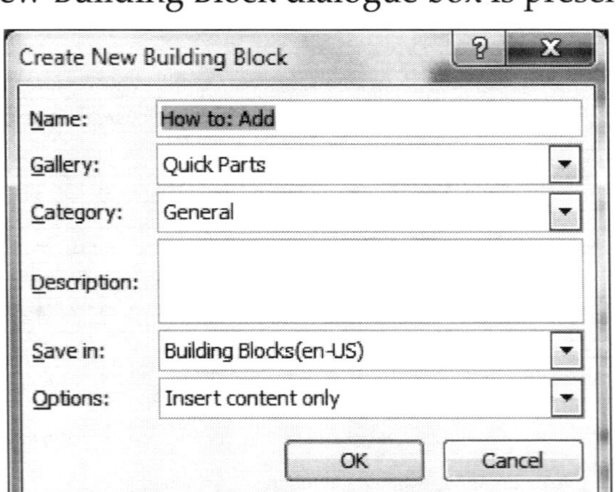

3. Complete the following information:

Name	Be unique and descriptive.
Gallery	There are many. If you store under the default **Quick Parts** gallery the item can quickly be selected later from the Quick Parts list.
Category	**General** is the only one to begin with. More can be created later to manage extensive lists.
Description	Be clear to help locate later on.
Save In	Select **Building Blocks** so item is available to all documents you create or the item can be stored in specific templates to restrict availability to only specific types of documents.
Options	Select **Insert content only** to insert item wherever required (most flexible), **Insert content in its own paragraph**, to make item into its own paragraph (paragraph markers before and after), or **Insert content in its own page**, with page breaks before and after, e.g. for a cover page.

4. Click on **OK**.

***As an aside** … If you want to retain the paragraph formatting of selected text, ensure that you include the paragraph marker in the selection.*

How to: Insert a Quick Part item

1. Position insertion point where item required.

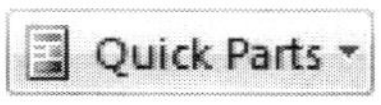

2. Display the Insert ribbon, click on the **Quick Parts** button (Text group).
3. Note your item under **General** in the Quick Parts list.
4. Click on the item required.

How to: Delete a Quick Part item

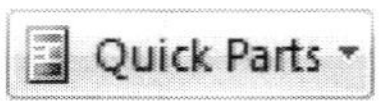

1. Display the Insert ribbon, click on the **Quick Parts** button, then click on the **Building Blocks Organizer** option (Text group).
   The Building Blocks Organizer dialogue box is presented
2. Scroll down the list to locate your item. The Gallery is Quick Parts. (Word has provided most of these items.)
3. Click on your item, then click on **Delete**.

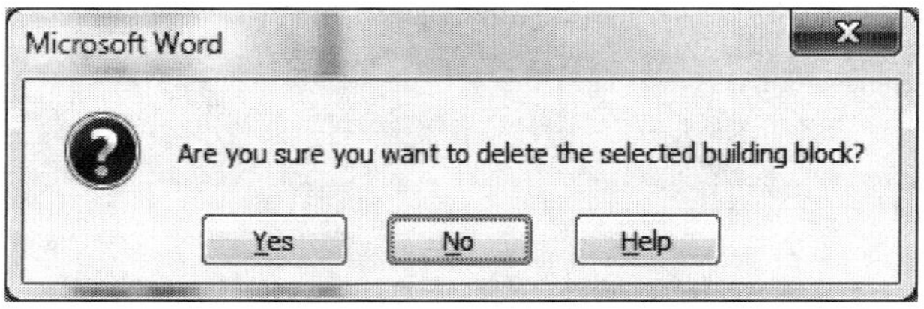

4. Click on **Yes**.
5. Click on **Close**.

Hands-on exercise 12

In this exercise you practise creating and using Quick Parts.

First, you create your Quick Part item.

- Create a **new** blank document. Select the style **No Spacing**.
- Type the following text:

> The Landlord warrants that he is the sole owner of the leasehold and or freehold interest of the Premises and that all consents necessary to enable him to enter into this agreement have been obtained.

- Select the text then display the Insert ribbon, click on the **Quick Parts** button, then click on the **Save Selection to Quick Parts Gallery** option (Text group). The Create New Building Block dialogue box is presented.
- Complete the following:

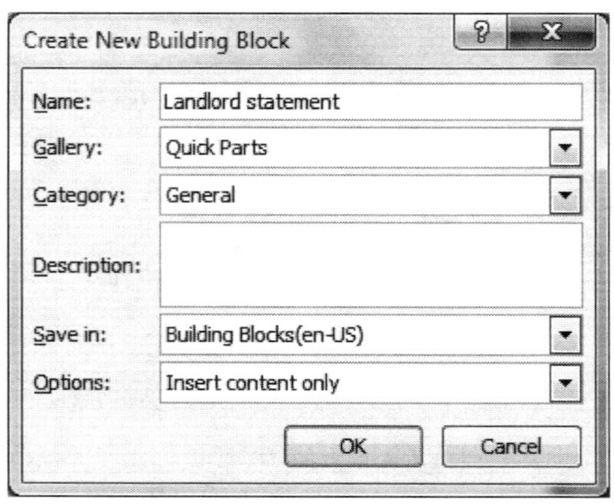

Note: By choosing Building Blocks the Quick Part item will be available to all documents.

- Click on **OK**.

Next, you insert your Quick Part item.

- **Close** your document without saving.
- Display a **new** blank document.

- Click on the **Quick Parts** button (Insert ribbon, Text group).
- Note your item under **General** in the Quick Parts list.
- Click on your item. It is inserted into your document.
- Close your document without saving.

Storing a Quick Part item into a custom template

By default, Quick Part items are stored in the Normal template (when you select Building Blocks under **Save in**). By storing a Quick Part item here it is available to all documents. If you have a Quick Part item that is only useful for a particular type of document, you should create a suitable template and add the Quick Part item to it. The Quick Part item is then only available to documents based on that template, and not to every document.

How to: Save a Quick Part item to a custom template

1. Select the text to be stored.

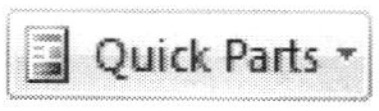

2. Display the Insert ribbon, click on the **Quick Parts** button, then click on the **Save Selection to Quick Parts Gallery** option (Text group). The Create New Building Block dialogue box is presented.
3. Complete the following as previously but under **Building Blocks** select the name of your template.
4. Click on **OK**.

Hands-on exercise 13

In this exercise you practise adding a Quick Part item to a previously created template.
To complete this exercise you will need to have created the *Standard letter* template.

- **Open** the template *Standard letter*.
- Go to the end of the template.
- Select the standard letter closure you created in this template.
  You will create a Quick Part item from this selection.

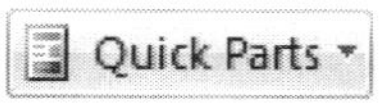

- Display the Insert ribbon, click on the **Quick Parts** button, then click on the **Save Selection to Quick Parts Gallery** option (Text group). The Create New Building Block dialogue box is presented.
- Complete the following as previously but under **Building Blocks** select the name of your template. Leave the suggested name of Yours sincerely.
- Click on **OK**.
  You return to the template.
- Delete the letter closure details, leaving just three lines after the date.
- **Save** your changes to the template.
- **Close** the template.
- Create a new document based on the *Standard letter* template.
- Insert your new Quick part item at the bottom of the letter.
- Create another Quick Part item for Yours faithfully and store with the *Standard letter* template.
- **Close** all open documents without saving.

- Create a **new** blank document (which is based on the Normal template). Note that your Quick Part items are not available in this template.
- **Close** your document without saving.

> ***As an aside*** ... *You can only select the Standard letter template as a Building Block if you have the template open, or a document based on the template.*

Hints & tips

After adding items to the Quick Parts list (Normal template) you are prompted as follows when you exit Word: Click on ***Save****.*

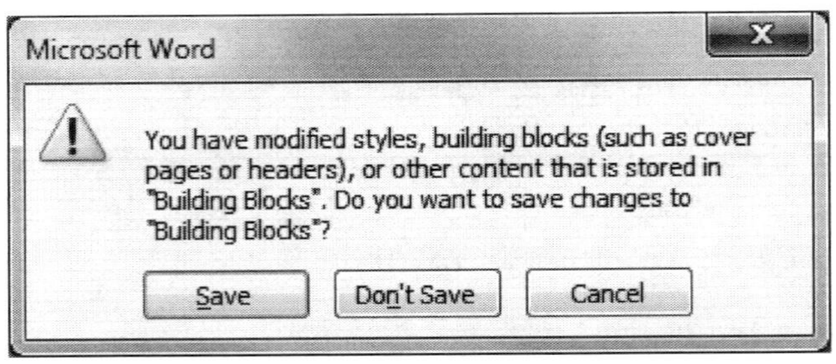

To save you recreating styles in different templates or documents you can use the ***Organizer*** *feature to copy them. Access via the Templates and Add-ins dialogue box (see page 44).*

Hands-on exercise 14 (Optional)

In this exercise you exit Word and do not save the Quick Part items stored in the Normal template. This is simply to clean up your PC. Your custom template with Quick Part items remains.

- **Exit** Word and when prompted to save Building Blocks, click on **No**.
- **Start** Word.

Terms & concepts review

- Simply put, what is a **template**?

- How do you add the **Templates** button to the Quick Access toolbar?

- Why store a **Quick Part item** to a custom template?

Topic 5 – Consistent formatting with styles

Using **styles** you can ensure a consistent and professional appearance for your documents. A style is created by bringing together a number of formatting characteristics and giving that set of formatting characteristics a name.

> ***For example ...*** *Instead of applying bold, a font, and a font size to each heading in a document (three actions), you can save these formatting characteristics into a single style. Then, you simply use one action to apply the style.*

If you update any of the formatting characteristics in a style, all instances of the style are updated.

Microsoft Word supplies numerous built-in **'quick'** styles for elements in a document. These are organised in **style sets**. You can create your own styles if you have particular corporate or personal requirements.

Styles fall into five categories: **paragraph**, **character**, **linked** (elements of paragraph and character), **table** and **list**. Paragraph styles control the appearance of an entire paragraph, whereas character styles control only selected text (usually selected words within a paragraph). Table styles control the appearance of a table, such as borders, shading and fonts. List styles control the appearance of alignment, numbering, bullet characters and fonts displayed in lists.

Applying a quick style

Text in a new document uses (by default) the **Normal** style. Use the Quick Styles Gallery to apply a different built-in style. Styles can be applied in a number of ways.

How to: Apply a quick style using the Quick Styles Gallery

1. Click in a paragraph, or select the required text.
2. Display the Home ribbon, point to any option in the **Quick Styles Gallery** (Styles group). The style is previewed in your paragraph(s). Click on the **More** button to display the full gallery of styles.
3. Click on the required style to apply.

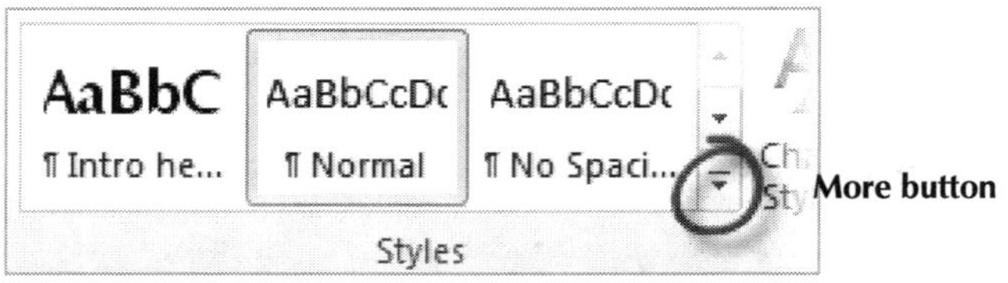

> ***As an aside*** *... Note the* ***Normal*** *style for Word 2010 is Calibri 11 pt, 1.15 line spacing, and 10 pts spacing after paragraph. The second option* ***No Spacing*** *is the same but with single line spacing and no spacing after paragraph.*

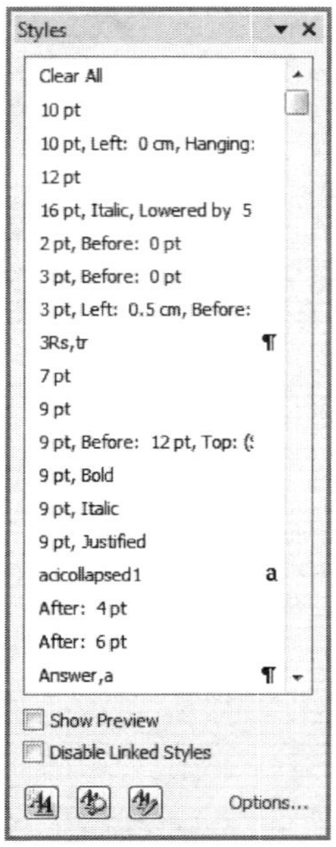

How to: Apply a quick style using the Styles task pane

1. Click in a paragraph, or select the required text.
2. Display the Home ribbon, locate the Styles group, then click on the dialogue box launcher ~*or*~
   Click on the **Styles** button in the Apply Styles box.
   The Styles task pane is presented.
3. Click on the required style.

> ***As an aside ...*** *This task pane is useful as it identifies the type of style, e.g. paragraph style* ¶, *character style* a, *or a style that has properties of both (linked style* ¶a*). Also if you point to each style you get full details of what the style comprises.*

How to: Remove quick styles

1. Select the required text.
2. Display the Home ribbon, in the **Quick Styles Gallery** click on the **More** button, then click on **Clear All**.

Hands-on exercise 15

In this exercise you practice applying quick styles.

- **Open** the document *Book reviews*
- Ensure the insertion point is located in the heading paragraph: Leadership Book Reviews
- Display the Home ribbon, point to the option **Heading 1** in the **Quick Styles Gallery** (Styles group). The style is previewed in your paragraph(s).
- Click on the **More** button in the **Quick Styles Gallery** to display the full gallery of styles. Click on **Heading 1** to apply the style.

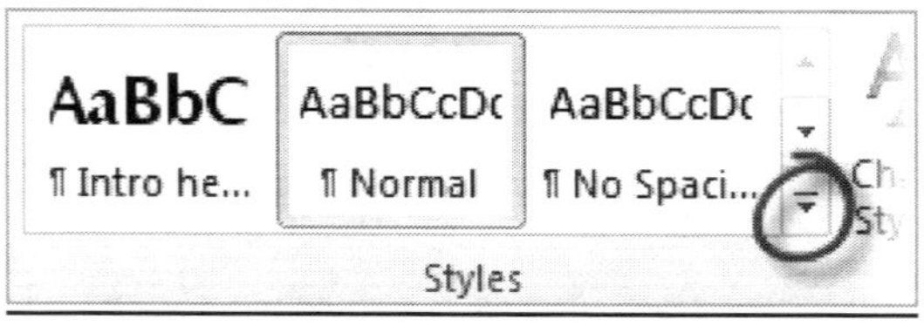

- Click in the paragraph: Maverick! Ricardo Semler
- Click on the option **Heading 2** in the **Quick Styles Gallery**.

Next, you try an alternative method to apply styles. (Ultimately which method you choose is your preference.)

- Scroll to page 2 and click in the heading paragraph at the top of the page.
- Click on the styles dialogue box launcher.
  The Styles task pane is presented.
- Click on **Heading 2**.

- Scroll to page 3 and click in the heading paragraph at the top of the page.
- Click on the **Heading 2** style in the task pane.
- **Close** the task pane.
- Return to the top of the document.
- Select the word **Maverick!** in the first body paragraph on page 1.
- Click on the **More** button in the **Quick Styles Gallery**, then point to the style **Emphasis**, then point to the style **Intense Emphasis**. Click on the style **Book Title**. (All of these styles are character styles.)
- Select the following text in the second line of this paragraph: 'success story behind the world's most unusual workplace'. Apply the style **Quote**.
- Apply the style **Book Title** to the book title **Shackleton's Way** in the first body paragraph on page 2.
- Apply the style **Heading 3** to the text: **Our star rating** at the bottom of every page. (Note that once you have applied a style once you can use the F4 repeat key to reapply the same style to the next selected text, i.e. repeat your last action.)
- **Save** your changes.

***As an aside** ... Only the Heading styles 1 and 2 are initially listed in the gallery and task pane. However, when you use the Heading 2 style, Heading 3 is added. When you use the Heading 3 style, Heading 4 is added and so on.*

Changing a quick style set

You can quickly change the entire appearance of a document you using a different **style set**.

How to: Change a quick style set

1. Display the required document.
2. Display the Home ribbon, click on the **Change Styles** button (Styles group), then point to **Style Set**.
3. Point to an alternative set, e.g. Formal. Wait for the live preview to display your potential new document look.
4. Click on the required set.

How to: Reset a style set

1. Display the required document.
2. Display the Home ribbon, click on the **Change Styles** button (Styles group), then point to **Style Set**.
3. Click on the option **Reset to Quick Styles from Template** or **Reset Document Quick Styles**.

> ***As an aside** … You'll learn more on templates later. At this stage you have set your styles purely within the document.*

Hands-on exercise 16

In this exercise you practise changing and resetting your style set.

- Using the document *Book reviews*, return to the top of the document.
- Click on the **Change Styles** button (Styles group), then point to **Style Set**.
- Point to an alternative set, e.g. Formal. Wait for the live preview to display your potential new document look.
- Click on **Distinctive**. You document is displayed using the new style set.
- **Save** your changes.

Updating a quick style

When required, any style can be updated. Updating a style is the quickest way to change formatting throughout a document. When a style is updated, all text with the selected style is immediately changed to the new look.

> ***For example …** You have just completed formatting a 40 page document when you decide to change the appearance of all major headings.*

For simple changes update the style by example.

How to: Update a quick style by example

1. Apply your formatting changes to any text formatted with the existing style.
2. Select the text.
3. Display the **Styles** task pane.
4. Point to the style in the task pane. A down-arrow appears beside the style. Click on the down-arrow.

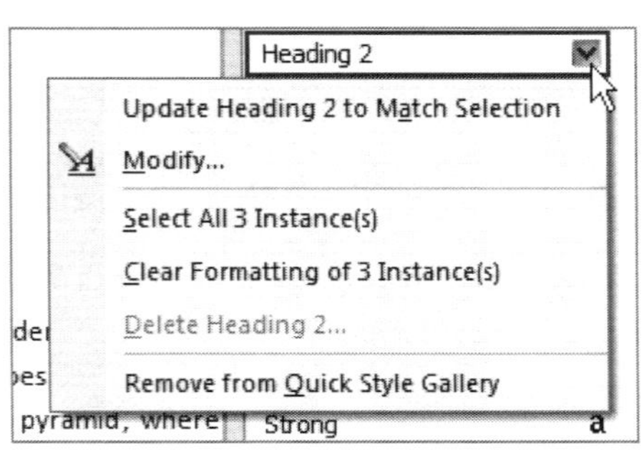

5. Click on **Update 'style name' to Match Selection**.
6. All occurrences of the style in the document are updated to reflect the changes

Hands-on exercise 17

In this exercise you practice updating styles.

- Using the document *Book reviews*, return to the top of the document.
- Select the heading: Maverick! Ricardo Semler
  (This paragraph is already formatted with a Heading 2 style.)

First, you apply your formatting changes.

- Keeping the text selected, apply **Bold** and a font colour of **Aqua**.

Next, you update the Heading 2 style using your text as the example.

- Keeping the text selected, display the Styles task pane.
- Point to the Heading 2 style in the task pane. A down-arrow appears beside the style. Click on the down-arrow.
- Click on **Update Heading 2 to Match Selection**.
- Scroll down and view your other headings formatted with the Heading 2 style – at the top of each page. Each has been updated.

Next, you repeat with different formatting.

- Select any heading formatted with the Heading 3 style (bottom of each page).
- Increase the font size to **14**, apply **Bold** and a font colour of **Red**.
- Keeping the text selected, point to the Heading 3 style in the task pane. A down-arrow appears beside the style. Click on the down-arrow.
- Click on **Update Heading 3 to Match Selection**.
- View your other headings formatted with the Heading 3 style – at the bottom of each page. Each has been updated.
- **Close** the task pane.
- **Save** your changes.

Normal style	Ctrl Shift N
Heading 1	Alt Ctrl 1
Heading 2	Alt Ctrl 2
Heading 3	Alt Ctrl 3

Using the Navigation Pane

You can use the **Navigation Pane** to browse through a document. This gives you a big-picture look at a document, and provides clickable links to browse. There are **three tabs** within the navigation pane allowing you to browse by headings, pages and results (from a search).

As an aside *... Headings need to be defined using heading styles.*

How to: Show the Navigation Pane

1. Display the View ribbon, then select the **Navigation Pane** option (Show group). A Navigation Pane opens to the left of the window.
2. Click on the first tab (Headings). Any headings in the document formatted with heading styles are listed. Click on a heading to move to it.
3. Click on the second tab (Pages) to see page thumbnails.
4. Close on the **Close** button to close the pane.

Hands-on exercise 18

In this exercise you practice using the navigation pane.

- Using the document *Book reviews*, return to the top of the document.
- Experiment with the Navigation Pane.
- **Close** your document without saving.

As an aside *... You can also drag and drop headings in the Navigation Pane and click on the triangles to collapse expand a heading level.*

Consolidation task 2

In this task you further practise applying and modifying styles.

- Open the document *Leadership characteristics.*

  Ensure your insertion point is located in the document heading.
- Apply the **Heading 1** style.
- Using the Styles task pane, apply the **Heading 2** style to the following headings:

  Knowledge

  Decision making

  Ruthlessness

  Planning

  Self-discipline

  Leading by example

  Seeking counsel

  Communication

Next, you update the appearance of Heading 2 text, then update the style.

- Return to the top of the document.
- Select the heading: Knowledge
  (This has the style Heading 2 applied.)
- Change the font colour to **Red**, and add a space after paragraph measurement of **6 pts** (Page Layout ribbon).
- Keeping the text selected, point to the **Heading 2** style in the Styles task pane. A down-arrow appears beside the style.
  Click on the down-arrow.
- Click on **Update Heading 2 to Match Selection**.
- View your other headings formatted with the Heading 2 style. Each has been updated.
- Update the style again to return the font colour to black.
- **Close** the task pane.
- View the **Navigation Pane**.
- Click on the first tab (Headings). Note the headings listed to which you have applied heading styles.
- Click on a heading to move to it.
- Click on the second tab (Pages). Note the page view.
- Save your changes.
- Close your document.

After this Consolidation task, do you feel confident... tick the appropriate box:

	Applying styles
	Updating styles

Creating a simple paragraph style

If the built-in quick styles are not suitable for your corporate or personal needs, then you can create your own styles. If you require a simple paragraph style, there is a quick method using the Apply Styles box.

How to: Create a style using the Apply Styles box

1. Select the entire paragraph that contains the formatting you want to use for your style.
2. Display the **Apply Styles** box.
3. Type a new style name.
4. Press Enter
   Your new style is created in the document, and it is added to the **Quick Styles Gallery**.

Hands-on exercise 19

In this exercise you practise creating new styles. First, you clear the existing quick styles.

- Using the document *Book reviews*, scroll to the bottom of page 1
- Select the paragraph: Our star rating.
- Return the paragraph to the **Normal** style.
- Keeping the paragraph selected, increase the font size to **12**, **Bold**, and apply a **Bottom Border**.
- Keeping the paragraph selected, display the **Apply Styles** box.
- Type the new style name: *Star ratings*
- Press Enter
  Your new style is created in the document, and it is added to the **Quick Styles Gallery**.
- Apply your new style to the other star rating paragraphs.
- **Close** your Apply Styles box.
- **Save** your changes
- **Close** your document.

Consolidation task 3

In this task you further practise creating and updating paragraph styles. (You need to complete the previous Consolidation task before commencing this task.)

- Open the document *Leadership characteristics*.
- Select the second paragraph in the document, 'Previously, … .

First, you apply some formatting changes before creating a paragraph style.

- Apply **Italics** and a font colour of **Blue**.
- Keeping the paragraph selected, display the **Apply Styles** box.
- Type the new style name: *Opening*
- Press Enter
- Apply this style to the following paragraph.

Next, you update this style. You begin by changing the current formatting.

- Select either paragraph formatted with the Opening style.
- Update the style to return the font colour to black.
- Close the Apply Styles box.
- Close the task pane.
- Save your changes.
- Close your document.

After this Consolidation task, do you feel confident... tick the appropriate box:

	Apply formatting changes
	Update styles

Creating an advanced style

For more advanced features, including creating character styles, you use an alternative approach.

How to: Create an advanced style

1. Display the **Styles** task pane.
2. Click on the **New Style** button (at the bottom of the pane).
   The **Create a New Style from Formatting** dialogue box is presented.

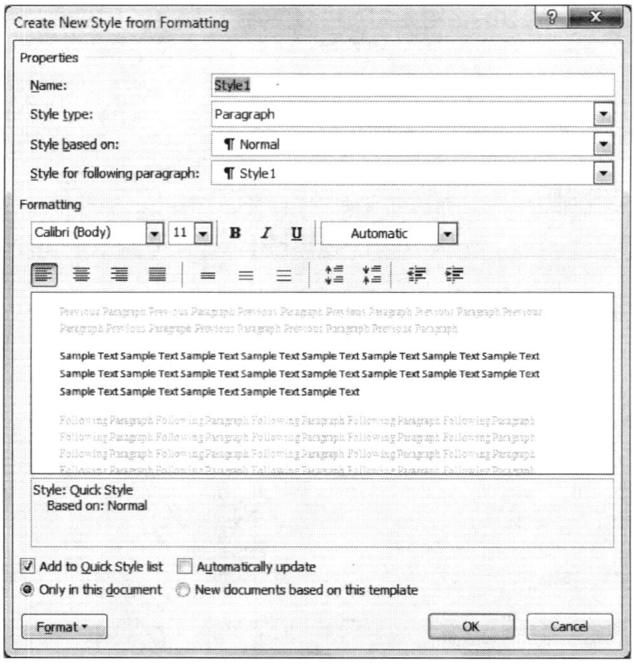

3. Type a **Name** for your style.
4. Select a **Style type**.
5. If your style can use another style for its basic formatting characteristics, click on the **Style based on** down-arrow and select that style. For example, if you select Normal your style starts with the characteristics of the Normal style, plus any changes made in this dialogue box.
6. If a particular style always follows this style, e.g. the *Caption* style always follows the *Picture* style, click on the **Style for following paragraph** down-arrow and select the name of a style here. (You type something with the *Pictures* style, the *Captions* style is automatically applied after you press Enter.)
7. Note in the **Formatting** section that the characteristics of any selected text are displayed (or where the insertion point is located). You can add further changes here. More options are listed under the **Format** button. (For a paragraph style you can change nearly everything, for a character style your options are more limited.)
8. Note the option to add to the **Quick Styles list** is selected.
9. Note new styles by default are **Only in this document**.

10. Click on **OK**.
    The text has the style applied, and the style is displayed in the Quick Styles Gallery

Hands-on exercise 20

In this exercise you create a paragraph and a character style.

- **Open** the document *Leadership article.*
- Apply the style **Heading 1** to the first (heading) paragraph.

First, you create a paragraph style.

- Click in the second paragraph.
- Display the **Styles** task pane.
- Click on the **New Style** button (at the bottom of the task pane).
  The **Create a New Style from Formatting** dialogue box is presented.
- Type the **Name**: *Introduction*
- Press Tab
- Ensure the **Style type** is **Paragraph**.
- Leave the **Style based on** as **Normal** style.
- The **Style for following paragraph** can be left as Introduction also.
- Note in the **Formatting** section that the characteristics of the second paragraph are displayed. Change the font to **Cambria**, apply **Bold**, and a font colour of **Blue**.

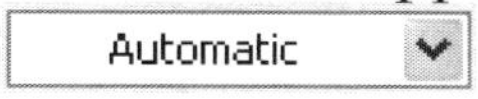

- Note the option to add to the **Quick Styles list** is selected.
- Note new styles by default are **Only in this document**.
- Click on **OK**.
  The paragraph has the style applied, and the style is displayed in the Quick Styles Gallery.
- Apply the **Introduction** style to the following two paragraphs.

Next, you create a character style.

- Select the words **Common Purpose** on page 2.
- Click on the **New Style** button (at the bottom of the Styles task pane).
  The **Create a New Style from Formatting** dialogue box is presented.
- Type the **Name**: *Highlight*
- Press Tab
- Select a **Style type** of **Character**.
- Change the font colour to **Blue**.

- Click on **OK**.
  The selected text has the character style applied, and the style is displayed in the Quick Styles Gallery.
- Apply the **Highlight** style to the rest of the bold terms in the list.
  (You can make use of the F4 *repeat key.)*

- **Save** your changes.

Modifying styles

Any style can be modified using the Modify Style dialogue box, but particularly required for the advanced styles.

How to: Modify styles using the Modify Style dialogue box

1. Display the **Styles** task pane.
2. Point to the style in the task pane. A down-arrow appears beside the style. Click on the down-arrow.

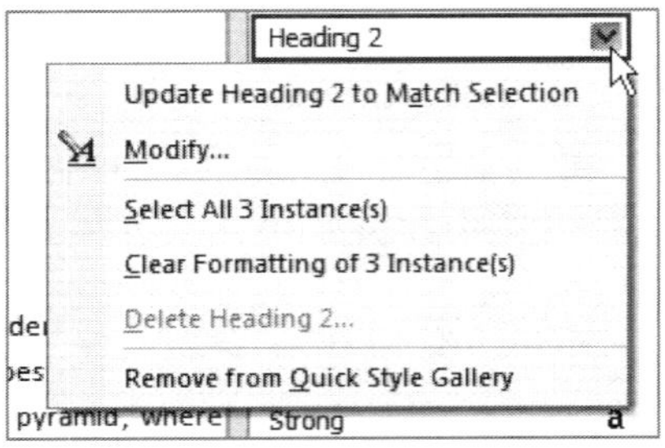

3. Click on **Modify**.
   The Modify Style dialogue box is presented.
4. Make your changes.
5. Click on **OK**.
   All occurrences of the style in the document are updated to reflect the changes

As an aside ... *Rather than modifying the Normal style, it is often better to create a new style.*

Hands-on exercise 21

In this exercise you practise modifying paragraph and character styles using the Modify Style dialogue box.

- Using the document *Leadership article*, return to the top of the document.

First, you make changes to the **Introduction** paragraph style.

- Click in the second paragraph of the document.
- Point to the style **Introduction** in the task pane. A down-arrow appears beside the style. Click on the down-arrow.
- Click on **Modify**. The Modify Style dialogue box is presented.
- Change the font colour to **Olive Green**.
- Click on **OK**.
  All occurrences of the style in the document are updated to reflect the changes.

Next, you make changes to the **Highlight** character style.

- Scroll to the end of the document a click in any of the terms formatted with the **Highlight** style.

- Point to the style **Highlight** in the task pane. A down-arrow appears beside the style. Click on the down-arrow.
- Click on **Modify**. The Modify Style dialogue box is presented.
- Change the font colour to **Olive Green**.
- Click on **OK**. All occurrences of the style in the document are updated to reflect the changes.
- **Save** your changes.
- **Close** your document.

Hands-on exercise 22

In this exercise you practise creating a follow-on style.

- **Open** the document *Proposal*.
  Note that **below** each heading using a **Heading 2** style that the following text uses the **Intro** style. This could be defined as a follow-on style and so automatically applied as you type.
- Click in the heading: Introduction.
  This heading is currently formatted with the **Heading 2** style.
- Point to the style **Heading 2** in the task pane. A down-arrow appears beside the style. Click on the down-arrow.
- Click on **Modify**. The Modify Style dialogue box is presented.
- Change the **Style for following paragraph** to **Intro**.
- Click on **OK**.
  When you next type a paragraph using the **Heading 2** style, the style **Intro** will be automatically applied to the following paragraph.
- **Close** the task pane.
- Go to the end of the document.
- Type the heading: *Preparatory Work*
- Leaving your insertion point in the heading, display the **Apply Styles** box.
- Type 'h'. Note in the style box that the style name has been completed for you. Press Enter to accept the style.
- Press Enter to type your next paragraph. Note in the style box that the style **Intro** has been automatically selected.
- Type the following paragraph using the **Intro** style:

> For the period of the internal modernisation and redecoration of the house, Enterprise will relocate the family to suitable family and business accommodation.

- Press Enter to type your next paragraph. Note in the style box that the style **Intro** is still selected.
- Type the following paragraph using the **Normal** style. (Click in the style box to select a style.)

> Enterprise shall be responsible for all site preparatory work, provision of general building trades and for ensuring that all rubbish is removed.

- Press Enter
- Type the following heading in the **Heading 2** style: *External Works*
- Press Enter to type the next paragraph. Note in the style box that the style **Intro** has been automatically selected.
- Type the following paragraph using the **Intro** style:

> External works will commence following the completion of the detailed design phase.

- Spell and grammar check your document.
- **Save** your changes.
- **Close** your document.

Consolidation task 4

In this task you create a letter using styles to make you more efficient.

- Open the document *New mortgage letter*.
- Select the first body paragraph after the subject heading, commencing 'Following the completion … '.
- Display the Style task pane.
- Create a new paragraph style called **Body** with a space after paragraph measurement of **12 pts** (use the Format button in the dialogue box and look under Paragraph).
- Apply this new style to the following paragraph commencing:
  As a new customer …
- Select the next paragraph commencing:
  interest is charged …
- Create a new paragraph style called **Bullets** with a bullet of your choice (use the Format button and look under Numbering), and a space after paragraph measurement of **6 pts**.
- Apply the Bullets style to the next two paragraphs.
- Close the task pane.
- Type the following text formatted with your new styles:

I would also remind you of the following regarding life cover premiums being used to cover your mortgage:

- premiums are not included in your payments
- it is your responsibility to pay premiums
- pay your insurance company not us
- maintain them every month.

As a company committed to service, we want to ensure that your mortgage runs smoothly at all times. If you have any queries about your mortgage, our Customer Service team is there to offer you help.

Yours sincerely

<Your name>

Operations Leader

- Remove the space after paragraph on the <Your name> paragraph.
- Spell and grammar check your document.
- Save your changes.
- Print and proofread, correcting any errors.
- Close your document.

After this Consolidation task, do you feel confident... tick the appropriate box:

	Creating styles
	Applying bullets

Hints & tips

If you see the following in your Style list, the document has originated from a previous Word version.

Heading 1 + Centered, Befo

Terms & concepts review

- What are **styles** and how can they save you time?

  ____

  ____

- What is the difference between **character** and **paragraph** styles?

  ____

  ____

- What style is used by **default** on text in a document?

  ____

  ____

- How do you display the **Apply Styles box**?

  ____

  ____

- How do you display the **Styles task pane**?

  ____

  ____

Consolidation task 5

In this task you create a report outline in a template, defining in the template the required styles.

- Display **Backstage** view.
- Click on **New.**
- Under **Available Templates** click on **My Templates**.
- Click on **Normal**.
- Click on the **Template** option, then click on **OK**.
  A new template is displayed.
- Type the following text into the template.

> South Coast – Annual Report Summary
>
> Financial Performance

- Apply Heading 1 style to the document heading.
  Apply Heading 2 style to the second heading.
- Display the Styles task pane.
- Return the font colour of the Heading 2 style to black and add a space after paragraph measurement of **6 pt,** then update the style.
- Position your insertion point below the Financial Performance heading.
- Create a new paragraph style called **Body** featuring a space after paragraph measurement of **12** pts, and **single line** spacing.
- **Close** the task pane.
- Ensure the paragraph marker below the Financial Performance heading is set to the Body style.
- Click on the **Save** button.
  The Save as dialogue box is presented.
- Type the **File name**: *Annual report*
- Ensure **Save as type** is set to **Word Template**.
- Scroll to the top of **Navigation Pane** and click on **Microsoft Word**.
- Double-click on the **Templates** folder displayed.
  Ensure your templates folder is selected.
- Click on **Save**.
- Close the template *Annual report.*
- Create a new document based on your *Annual report* template (**My Templates**). (Ensure the Title Bar says Document *no.* before you continue.)

- Type the following information into your *document* using the heading, paragraph and character styles (you may like to display the Apply Styles dialogue box):

South Coast - Annual Report Summary

Financial Performance

The company's financial performance improved significantly over the year, culminating in record-breaking final quarter profits.

Profitability

An increase in profit margin was reported in the manufacturing area. This requires investigation in the next financial year.

Next Financial Year

Investment will be made primarily in the information technology infrastructure of the organisation, to simplify operating procedures and order processing.

- Spell and grammar check your document.
- Save your document as *Report 1.*
- **Close** your document.

After this Consolidation task, do you feel confident... tick the appropriate box:

	Creating new template
	Updating styles
	Saving a template

Consolidation task 6

In this task you practise creating a new template for a weekly report

- Create a new **template** (based on Normal).

First, you change a number of layout settings in the template.

- Change all **margins** to 2 cm (Page Layout ribbon).
- Ensure the **Orientation** is set to **Portrait**.
- Click on **OK**.

Next, you add the headings required for your weekly report template.

- Type the following text into the template (use Insert/Date ...).

NORTH COAST PTY LTD

Acquisitions Department – Weekly Report

<Insert Day Month Year>

- Apply Heading 1 style to the document heading.
  Apply Heading 2 style to the second heading.

- Return the font colour of the Heading 2 style to black and add a space after paragraph measurement of **6 pt,** then update the style.

Next, you add an attractive border to the template.

- Select **Box** and a **Color** of **Blue** for your page border.
- Save your template as *Weekly report.*
- Close your template.

Finally, you create a new document based on your template.

- Create a new document based on your *Weekly report* template.
- Go to the end of the document, then add the following text:

> NORTH COAST PTY LTD
>
> Acquisitions Department – Weekly Report
>
> 15th November <year>
>
> Client visits
>
> Visits were made to two prospective clients. Quick is a progressive printing company that is turning over $30,000 per month. I am putting a proposal together for them.
>
> Snack Eats is a fast food company that has recently expanded into our district. I will follow-up in six months' time.
>
> New clients
>
> A new client has joined us called Global Travel. They have signed a three month trial contract.

- Ensure you apply the style Heading 2 to the two headings in your document.
- Spell and grammar check your document.
- Save your document as *Week 1.*
- Close your document.

After this Consolidation task, do you feel confident... tick the appropriate box:

	Creating a new template
	Changing margins
	Adding a page border

Consolidation task 7

In this task you practise editing a **template**.

- Open the *Weekly report* template.
- Create a character style called **Keywords** featuring **Bold** and the font colour **Blue**.
- Save and close.
- Create a new document from the template to ensure the character style is included.
- Close the document, without saving.

Hints & tips

Changes to a template only affect new documents. Old documents created from the template will not be automatically updated with changes.

Also note that the next time you open a document your template storage location may still be selected.

Topic 6 – Basic tables

Tables are a great way to organise columns of information. Tables can contain text, numbers and even graphics. Tables are easy to create, flexible, and offer a variety of attractive formatting features.

Surname	First Name	Department	Extension
Vickers	Joan	Finance	334
Wong	Jim	Admin	456
Smith	George	Management	457
Tadski	John	Administration	925
Orchard	June	Finance	769

Lists of text and numbers in a table

Tables are simply a series of cells (boxes) arranged in rows and columns.

Surname	First Name	Department	Extension
Vickers	Joan	Finance	334
Wong	Jim	Admin	456
Smith	George	Management	457
Tadski	John	Administration	925
Orchard	June	Finance	769

*Columns run vertically (see highlighted **column**)*

Surname	First Name	Department	Extension
Vickers	Joan	Finance	334
Wong	Jim	Admin	456
Smith	George	Management	457
Tadski	John	Administration	925
Orchard	June	Finance	769

*Rows run horizontally (see highlighted **row**)*

If you enter text that is wider than the cell, it wraps to a new line just as it would in a normal paragraph.

Serious, quiet, earn success by concentration and thoroughness. Practical, orderly, matter-of-fact, logical, realistic and dependable. See to it that everything is well organised.	Quiet, friendly, responsible and conscientious. Work devotedly to meet their obligations. Lend stability to any project or group. Thorough, painstaking, accurate.
Cool onlookers – quiet, reserved, observing and analysing life with detached curiosity and unexpected flashes of original humour.	Retiring, quietly friendly, sensitive, kind, modest about their abilities. Shun disagreements, do not force their opinions or values on others.

Parallel paragraphs in a table (borders can be removed)

The table **gridlines** mark the boundaries of cells. **Paragraph marks** and **end-of-cell/ row marks** control the formatting of data in a cell.

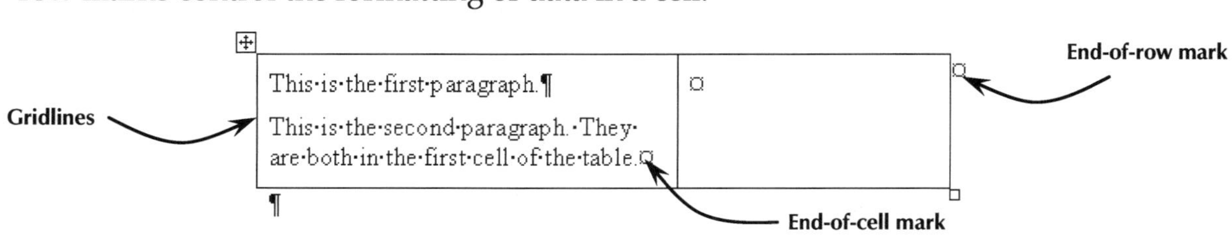

As an aside *... Cell and row marks do not print. Ensure you have your **Show/Hide** button on (Home ribbon) to display these non-printing characters.*

Creating a basic table and entering text

A table can be created in a number of ways to give you complete control.

How to: Insert a basic table

1. Position the insertion point where the table is required.
2. Display the Insert ribbon, then click on the **Table** button (Tables group). A drop-down box is presented.
3. Drag over the cells in the grid to indicate the number of rows and columns required. Note the proposed table in your document. Click to complete, and a table of the selected number of rows and columns is inserted. The borders are printable.
4. Note the **Table Tools** spanning the new Design and Layout ribbons.

~or~

1. Display the Insert ribbon, then click on the **Table** button (Tables group). A drop-down box is presented.
2. Click on **Insert Table**.
   The Insert Table dialogue box appears.

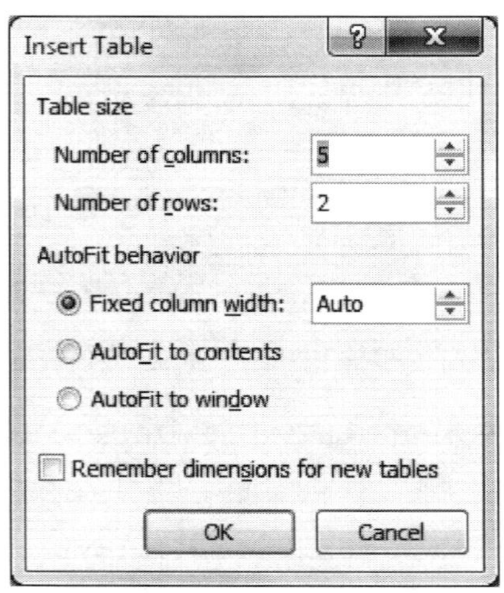

3. Specify the **Number of columns/rows.**
4. Click on **OK**.
   A table with printable borders is inserted into your document.
5. Note the **Table Tools** spanning the Design and Layout ribbons.

How to: Enter data

1. Type the required data.
2. Press Tab to move to the next cell.
   (If you press Enter you simply get a new paragraph within the same cell.)

How to: Add a new row as you enter data

1. Type your data in the last cell of the last row.
2. Press Tab to create a new row.

Hands-on exercise 23

In this exercise you practise inserting a basic table and adding text.

- Create a **new** blank document.
- Remove spacing after.
- Type the following text: *Sales reps by state*
- Remove
- Press Enter twice.

- Click on the **Insert Table** button.
  The drop-down box appears.
- Drag over the cells in the grid to indicate a table of four columns and three rows. Click to complete. A table with printable borders is inserted into your document.

  Note: If you insert a table of the incorrect size, simply **Undo** and try again.
- Note the **Table Tools** spanning the Design and Layout ribbons.
- Display the Layout ribbon, then return to the Design ribbon.
- Enter the following information, pressing Tab to move to the next cell.

Sales reps by state

	Jan-Feb	March-April	May-June
NSW	$23,432	$12,893	$12,987
TAS	$18,293	$15,922	$9,372

- After typing the final row, press Tab to add another row.
- Type the following additional information:

Sales reps by state

	Jan-Feb	March-April	May-June
NSW	$23,432	$12,893	$12,987
TAS	$18,293	$15,922	$9,372
NT	$19,873	$15,098	$10,382
QLD	$34,938	$22,231	$10,382
VIC	$38,223	$19,832	$15,291
SA	$32,987	$19,483	$14,873

- **Save** your document as *Sales reps by state.*

Moving and editing within a table

To work efficiently in a table let's learn some useful keyboard actions. Using the keyboard actions also repositions the insertion point ready for editing.

How to: Move within a table - mouse method

1. Point to the new location and click.

How to: Move within a table - keyboard methods

Next cell	Tab or →
Previous cell	Shift Tab or ←
Next row	↓
Previous row	↑

Selecting in a table

Editing data in a table is more efficient with the effective use of table selection activities.

How to: Select within a table - mouse methods

Table	Rest the mouse pointer on the table until the **table move handle** ⊞ appears in the top-left corner of the table, then click on the handle. (Ensure you are in **Print Layout** view.)	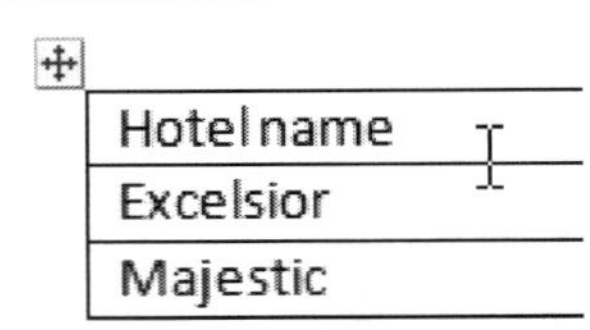
Row	Position the mouse pointer outside the table, beside a row. The mouse pointer becomes a white arrow. Click once to select the whole row.	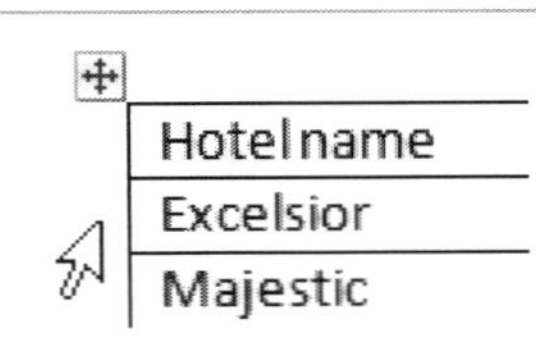
Column	Position the mouse pointer at the top of a column until a black down-arrow is displayed, then click to select the whole column.	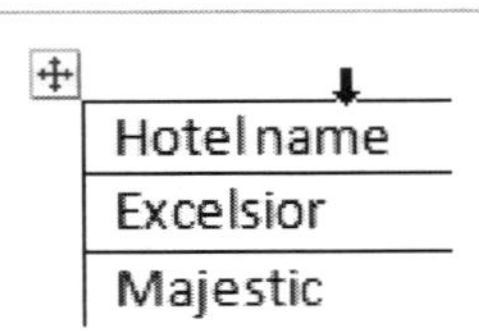
Cell	Position the mouse pointer in the cell to the left of the text. The mouse pointer becomes a black arrow. This space left of the text is the **cell selection bar**. Click in the cell selection bar.	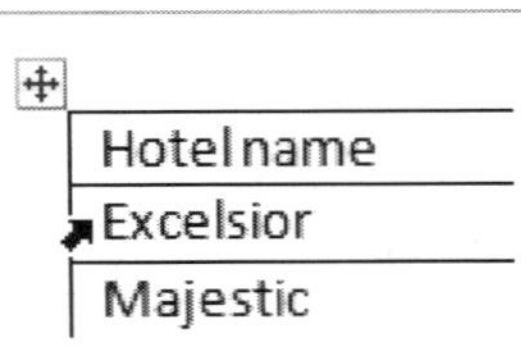

As an aside ... *To select multiple cells, rows or columns, select the required item, then drag to extend the selection.*

As an aside ... *To select multiple cells, rows or columns, select the required item then drag to extend the selection. To select non-adjacent cells, rows or columns, select the first required item, hold down* Ctrl *and continue to select all other required items.*

Modifying a table means changing its structure. For example, perhaps you need to add an extra column, delete a row, or widen a column or row.

Inserting rows and columns

One of the first modifications required is often inserting a row or column.

How to: Insert a row

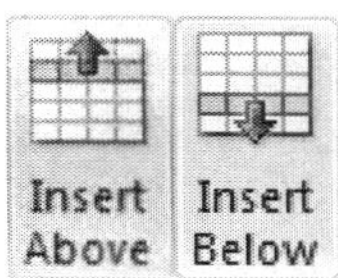

1. Select the required row (rows can be inserted above or below).
2. Display the Layout ribbon, then click on the **Insert Above** or **Insert Below** buttons (Rows & Columns group).
3. Click in the required cell and begin typing.

How to: Insert a column

1. Select the required column (columns can be inserted left or right).
2. Display the Layout ribbon, then click on the **Insert Left** or **Insert Right** buttons (Rows & Columns group).
3. Click in the required cell and begin typing.

> ***As an aside** ... The Table Tools do not appear unless your insertion point is in the table or you have a table component selected.*

Hands-on exercise 24

In this exercise you practise inserting rows and columns.

- Using the document *Sales reps by state*, change the document orientation to **Landscape** (Page Layout ribbon).

- Insert a new column to the right for the next group of sales **Europa** hotel as shown below (Layout ribbon):

-June	July-August
987	$22,493
72	$19,889
382	$15,382
382	$32,121
291	$22,983
873	$22,332

- **Save** your changes.

Deleting rows, columns, tables and table text

Another common activity when modifying a table includes removing rows and columns. You may even want to remove the entire table.

How to: Delete a row, column or table

1. Select the required row, column or click in the table.
2. Display the Layout ribbon, then click on the **Delete** button (Rows & Columns group).
3. Click on the required option.

> ***As an aside ...*** *To delete multiple columns or rows, select before you choose the required Delete option.*

How to: Delete text only

1. Select the column, row, or cell, and press Delete

Changing column widths

Column widths may need to be made wider or narrower to best present your data.

How to: Change a column width

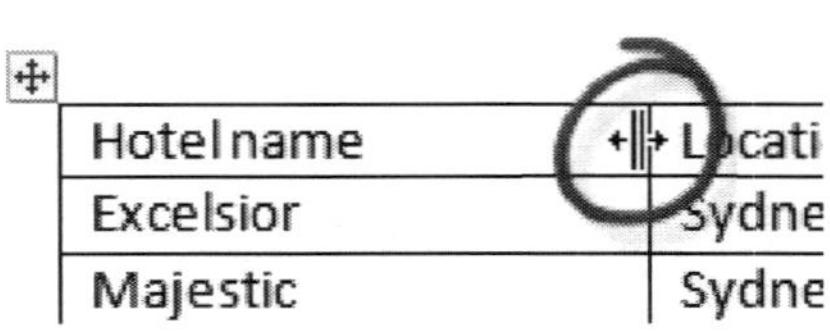

1. Position the mouse pointer on the right gridline of the column you want to adjust. The mouse pointer becomes a double-headed arrow.
2. Drag the gridline left or right to a new position.

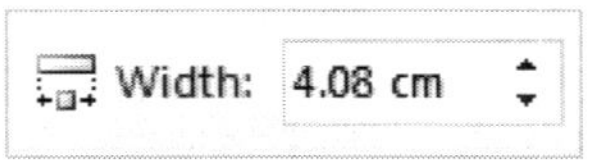

~or~

1. Click in the required column, or select the required columns.
2. Display the Layout ribbon, then adjust the measurements on the **Table Column Width** option (Cell Size group).

> ***As an aside ...*** *You can automatically adjust the width of a column to fit its contents by double-clicking on a gridline. The column is automatically resized. This feature is called* ***AutoFit****.*

> ***As an aside ...*** *Hold* Alt *as you drag a gridline to display measurements on the horizontal ruler.*

Changing row height

If you need to change the width of any rows, perhaps to create more white space, you can simply adjust the row height.

How to: Change a row height

1. Position the mouse pointer on the gridline of the row you want to adjust.
   The mouse pointer becomes a double-headed arrow.
2. Drag the gridline to a new position.

   ~or~

1. Click in the required row, or select the required rows.
2. Display the Layout ribbon, then adjust the measurements on the **Table Row Height** option (Cell Size group).

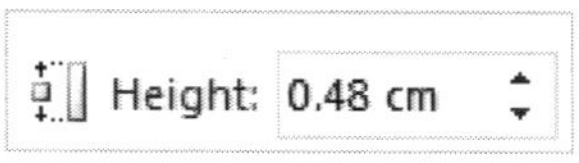

> ***As an aside*** *... Hold* Alt *as you drag a gridline to display measurements on the vertical ruler.*

Hands-on exercise 25

In this exercise you practise adjusting column widths.

First, you set approximate widths.

- Drag the column gridlines of the first three columns to reduce the column widths.

Next, you set precise column widths.

- Click in the first column of the table.
- Display the Layout ribbon, then adjust the measurements on the **Table Column Width** option (Cell Size group) to **3 cm.**
- With the table still selected, increase the height of the columns to 1cm.

Finally, you use AutoFit.

- Double-click on the gridline to the left of *Jan-Feb* to **AutoFit** each column.
- Undo this action so all the columns are 4 cm.
- **Save** your changes.

Moving and copying rows and columns

Generally, the steps for moving and copying rows and columns are the same as moving and copying ordinary text. One important difference, however, is the required *selection* of the destination *row or column.*

How to: Move or copy a row

1. Select the row to be moved or copied.

2. Click on the **Cut** or **Copy** buttons (Home ribbon, Clipboard group).

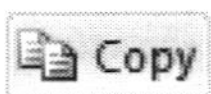

3. Select the destination row.
   (The new row is pasted *above* the selected row.)

4. Click on the top half of the **Paste** button (Home ribbon, Clipboard group).

How to: Move or copy a column

1. Select the column to be moved or copied.
2. Click on the **Cut** or **Copy** buttons (Home ribbon, Clipboard group).
3. Select the destination column.
   (The new column is inserted *to the left.*)
4. Click on the **Paste** button (Home ribbon, Clipboard group).

Hands-on exercise 26

In this exercise you practise moving rows and columns.

- Using the document *Sales reps by state,* select the row with the details of the NT sales rep.
- Move (**Cut**) this row to the top of the table - beneath the NSW sales rep. (Simply click on **Undo** and try again if you make a mistake.)
- Move the rows so the states are in alphabetical order.

Changing table and table text alignment

You can easily change the alignment of a table on a page, and you can also choose how text aligns in a cell(s).

How to: Align a table on the page

1. Click in the table to select.
2. Display the Layout ribbon, then click on the **Properties** button (Table group). The Table Properties dialogue box is presented.

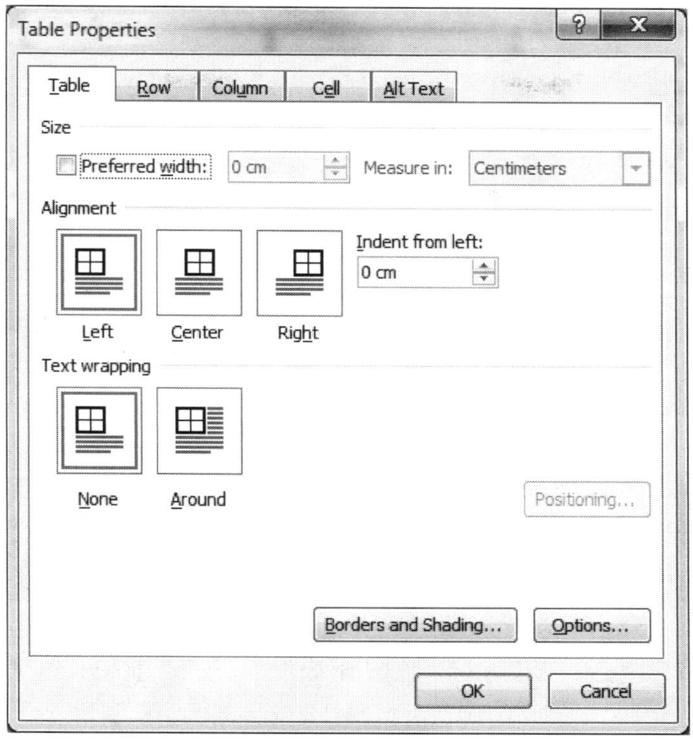

3. Click on the required **Alignment** option, i.e. **Left** (default), **Center**, or **Right**.
4. Click on **OK**.

How to: Align text in cells

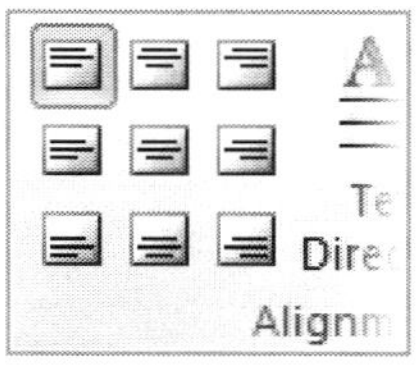

1. Select the required cell(s).
2. Display the Layout ribbon, then click on the required alignment button, e.g. **Align Center** (Alignment group).

Examples of alignment buttons

	**Align Top Center**	Aligns text to top and centre of a cell.
	**Align Center**	Aligns text to the middle and centre of a cell.
	**Align Bottom Center**	Aligns text to the bottom and centre of a cell.

Hands-on exercise 27

In this exercise you practise aligning your table and text in cells.

- Using the document *Sales rep by state,* select the table to select.
- Display the Layout ribbon, then click on the **Properties** button (Table group). The Table Properties dialogue box is presented.
- Click on the **Table** tab (if not still selected).
- Click on **Center**.
- Click on **OK**.

- While still selected, display the Layout ribbon, then click on **Align Center Left** (Alignment group).

- Select the table (if not still selected).

- Display the Layout ribbon, then click on **Align Center** (Alignment group).
- **Save** your changes.

Applying table styles, borders and shading

Formatting skills you have already acquired can be applied in a table, e.g. font, font size, bold, italics, alignment, etc. You can also apply pre-designed table styles and manually adjust borders and shading.

How to: Apply table styles

1. Click in the table.
2. Display the Design ribbon, point to any option in the **Tables Styles** group to see the design effect previewed on your table. Click on the **More** button to display the full gallery of styles.
3. Click on the required style to apply. The first option on the ribbon is plain.

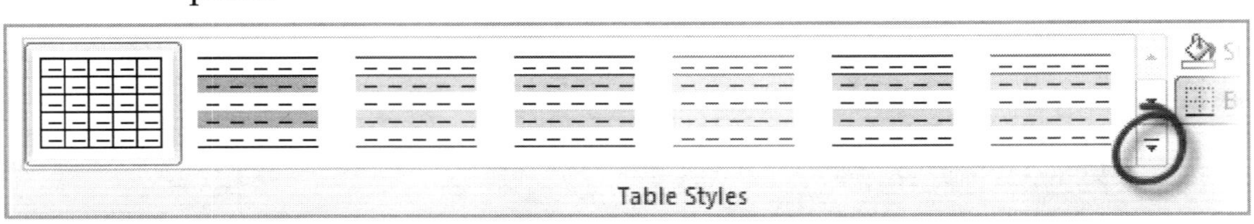

How to: Remove table style options

1. Click in the table.
2. Display the Design ribbon, click to remove a selected option in the **Table Style Options** group, e.g. to remove formatting on the first (header) row.

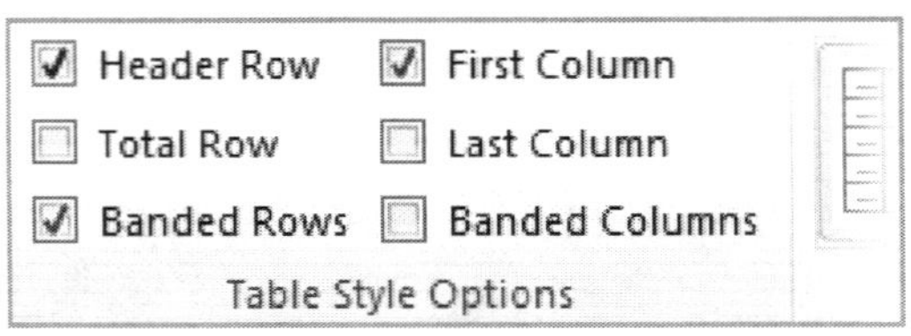

How to: Adjust table borders

1. Select the required cell, row or column.

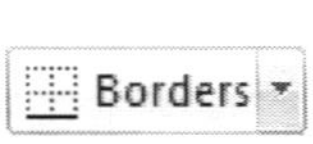

2. Display the Design ribbon, click on the **Borders** down-arrow (Table Styles group). A list of options is presented.
3. Click on the required border option.

> ***As an aside*** *...Note that the last border selected is stored behind the button (note the picture on the button) so if you click directly on the button instead of the down-arrow the currently selected option is applied immediately.*

How to: Adjust table shading

1. Select the required cell, row or column.

2. Display the Design ribbon, click on the **Shading** button (Table Styles group). A gallery of colours is presented organised by themes. Point to a colour selection to see the design effect previewed on your table.
3. Click on a colour of your choice.

> ***As an aside*** *... To remove shading from a table, select the cells, click on the* ***Shading*** *button, then click on* ***No Color.***

Hands-on exercise 28

In this exercise you practise applying formatting techniques to your table.

- Using the document *Sales reps by state*, display the Design ribbon, point to a few options in the **Tables Styles** group to see the design effect previewed on your table. If you apply an option click back on the first option on the ribbon to remove.

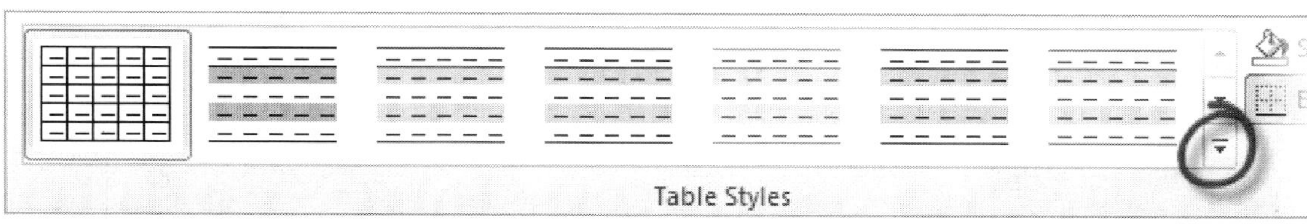

Next, you work simply with borders.

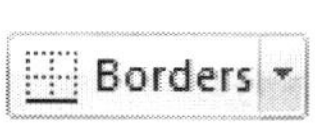

- Select the table, then display the Design ribbon. Click on the **Borders** down-arrow (Table Styles group), click on **No Borders**.
- While the table is still selected, click on **Outside Borders.**
- Select the top row only.
- Click on the **Borders** down-arrow (Table Styles group), click on **Bottom Border**.
- Keeping the top row selected apply **bold**.

Next, you work simply with shading.

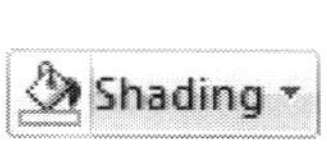

- Keeping the top row selected, on the Design ribbon click on the **Shading** button (Table Styles group). Apply a shade of your choice.
- Review your pages in **Print Preview**. Press Esc to exit.
- **Save** your changes.

Changing border styles, widths and colour

Basic borders can be made more attractive.

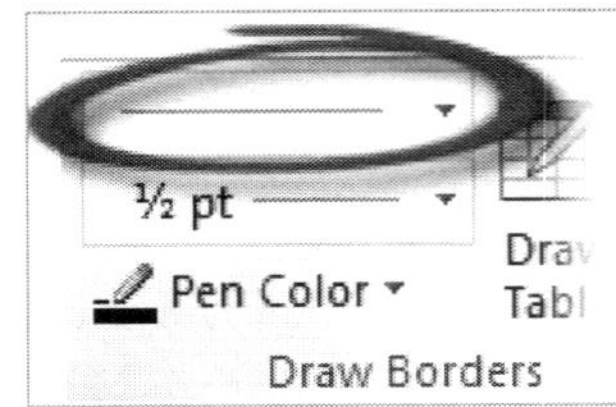

How to: Change a border style

1. Display the Design ribbon, click on the **Line Style** button, then click on one of the options presented (Draw Borders group).
2. Your mouse pointer becomes a pencil. Draw the new border over the existing border or gridline.
3. To switch off the pencil press Esc

As an aside *… Take care with the pencil as this feature also can create new cells.*

How to: Change a border width

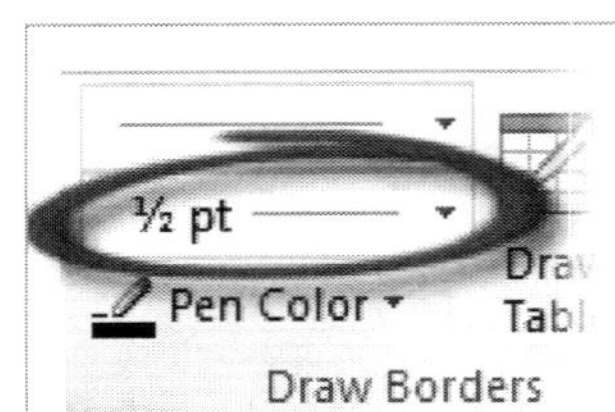

1. Display the Design ribbon, click on the **Line Weight** button, then click on one of the options presented (Draw Borders group).
2. Your mouse pointer becomes a pencil. Draw the new border over the existing border or gridline.
3. To switch off the pencil press Esc

How to: Change a border colour

1. Display the Design ribbon, click on the **Pen Color** button, then click on one of the options presented (Draw Borders group).
2. Your mouse pointer becomes a pencil. Draw the new border over the existing border or gridline.
3. To switch off the pencil press Esc

As an aside *… Select your border style, width and colour before you draw your new line.*

Hands-on exercise 29

In this exercise you practise more techniques with tables and borders.

- Using the document *Sales reps by state,* display the Table Tools/Design ribbon (if the top line is still selected, click away).
- Click on the **Line Style** button, then click on one of the options presented.
- ½ pt — Click on the **Line Weight** button, then click on one of the options presented.
- Pen Color — Click on the **Pen Color** button, then click on one of the options presented.
- Draw a new line over the existing border under the top row.
- Draw a new line over the gridline to the right of the state column.
- To switch off the pencil press Esc
- Click into the first cell and remove the bottom border.
- Review your pages in **Print Preview**. Press Esc to exit.
- **Save** your changes.
- **Close** your document.

Sales reps by state

	Jan-Feb	March-April	May-June	July-August
NSW	$23,432	$12,893	$12,987	$22,493
NT	$19,873	$15,098	$10,382	$15,382
QLD	$34,938	$22,231	$10,382	$32,121
SA	$32,987	$19,483	$14,873	$22,332
TAS	$18,293	$15,922	$9,372	$19,889
VIC	$38,223	$19,832	$15,291	$22,983

As an aside *... If you remove all table borders you may not be able to see your table unless you are viewing gridlines. Display the Layout ribbon, then click on* ***View Gridlines*** *(Table group).*

Hands-on exercise 30

In this exercise you review your basic table skills.

- In a **new** blank document, create the following table.

Destination	Metro	Suburbs
Sydney	$18	$12
Melbourne	$15	$20
Perth	$25	$35

- Apply the table style **Light List.**
- Add additional borders beside the columns.
- **Insert** the 'Brisbane' row shown below:

Destination	Metro	Suburbs
Sydney	$18	$12
Melbourne	$15	$20
Perth	$25	$35
Brisbane	$20	$23

- **Insert** the 'State' column shown below:

Destination	State	Metro	Suburbs
Sydney	NSW	$18	$12
Melbourne	VIC	$15	$20
Brisbane	QLD	$25	$23
Perth	WA	$20	$35

Finally, you practise moving a row.

- Move the Brisbane row above the Sydney row.
- Move the Suburbs column before the Metro column.
- Reduce the size of your columns.
- **Save** your document as *Courier rates.*
- **Close** your document.

Hints & tips

What if you have created a table at the very top of a document and you need to add a paragraph above it?

Position your insertion point at the beginning of the first cell of the table, then press Enter.

Consolidation task 8

In this task you create the following document with the skills you have learnt in the previous topics.

- Start with a new blank A4 document.
- Change the vertical alignment to centre.
- Spacing after is 10 pt.
- Font: Arial 11 pt
- Save your document as: *William Willow results*
- Following the hints below.
- Colour theme of your choice.

Dear Mrs Willow

In the past 5 weeks we have been assessing the children in 5T on the following subjects:

i) Maths
ii) English
iii) Creative Arts
iv) Sport

Please see below the marks that William has received.

Row height: 0.9 cm
Column widths are moved to fit

Bold
Dark shading
White bold font

Bold font
Light shading

Term 2	Maths	English	Creative Arts	Sport
Week 1	14/20	12/30	Satisfactory	Soccer – Achieved Grade
Week 3	16/20	16/30	Satisfactory	Athletics – Satisfactory
Week 5	19/20	19/30	Achieved Grade	Swimming – Grade 4

Dotted lines

If you have any questions, please contact me to discuss.

Yours sincerely

Janice Teatree

Lucida Handwriting 14 pt

Top and bottom border, 1 ½ pt Dark colour

After this Consolidation task, do you feel confident... tick the appropriate box:

	Changing vertical alignment
	Inserting a table
	Formatting a table

Topic 7 – Advanced tables

Working with the Draw table feature

If your tables are more advanced and contain irregularly-sized rows and columns, you can use the **Draw Table** feature to create and format your tables. This feature gives you more flexibility when building advanced tables.

For example ...

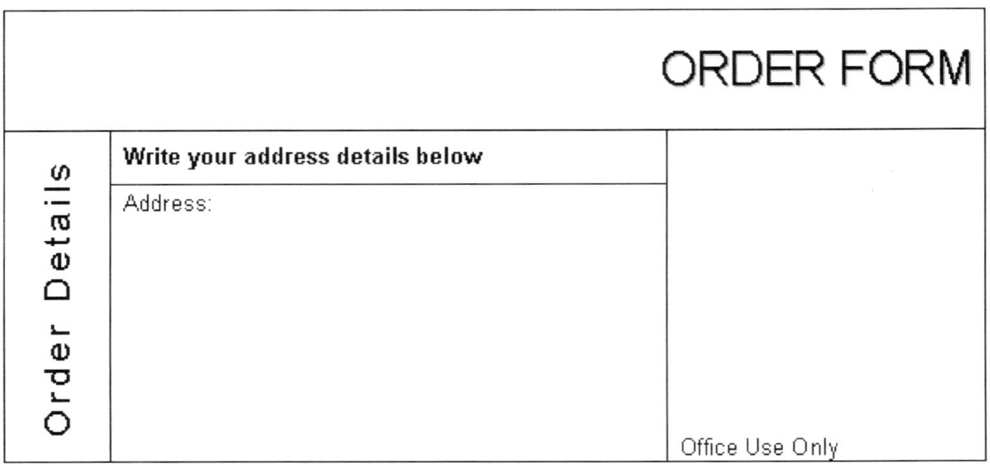

The Draw Table feature for advanced table layouts

How to: Draw your advanced table

1. Display the Insert ribbon, then click on the **Table** button (Tables group). A drop-down box is presented. Click on **Draw Table**. Your mouse pointer becomes a pencil, ready to start drawing.
2. Drag the pencil from top left to bottom right to create the boundaries of your table.

3. Drag the pencil to create row and column gridlines.

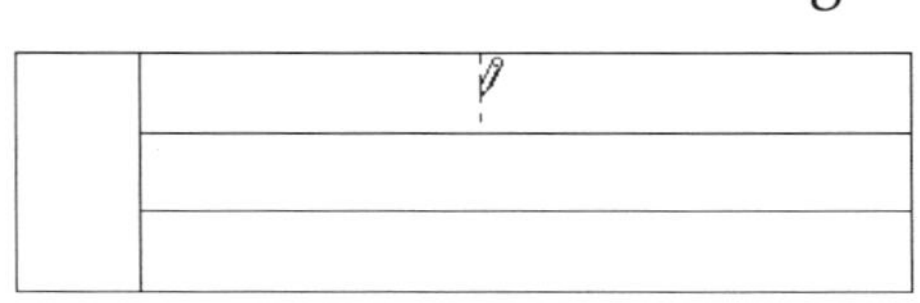

4. Click on the **Draw Table** button to switch off the pencil *~or~* Press Esc
5. Click back on the **Draw Table** button to return to drawing.

How to: Erase a line

1. Click on the **Eraser** button (Design ribbon, Draw Borders group). Your mouse pointer becomes an eraser.
2. Drag over the gridline to be removed.
3. Click back on the **Eraser** button to switch off the eraser *~or~* Press Esc
4. Click on the **Draw Table** button to return to drawing.

Hands-on exercise 31

In this exercise you practise creating a table using the Draw Table feature.

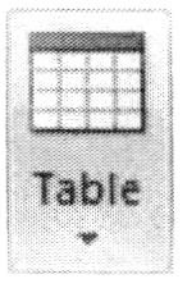

- Create a **new** blank document.
- Display the Insert ribbon, then click on the **Table** button (Tables group). A drop-down box is presented. Click on **Draw Table**. Your mouse pointer becomes a pencil, ready to start drawing.
- Drag the pencil downwards and to the right to create a box to cover about half of your page.
  Draw table lines to create the following outline. The lines only need to be in approximate positions.

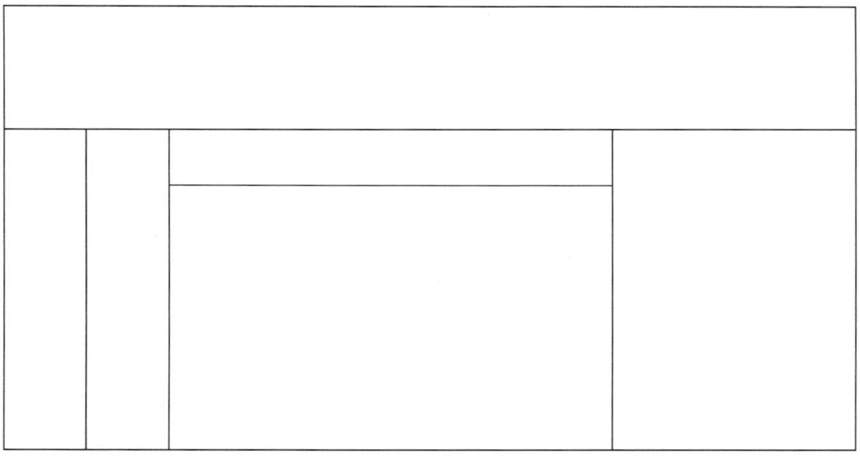

- Click on the **Draw Table** button to switch off the pencil.
- **Save** your document as *Order form*.
- Click in the first cell of your table.
  Align the text to the right.
- Type the text: *Order Form*
- Add the following additional text (all left aligned).

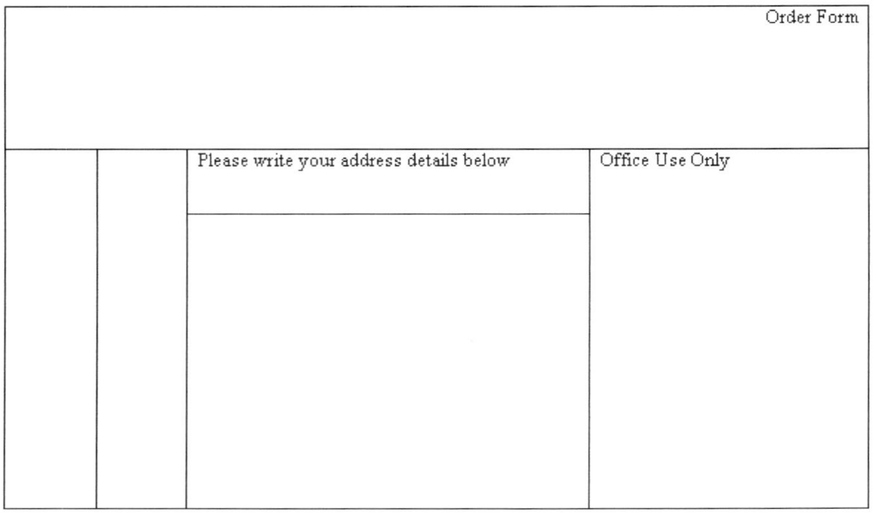

- Click on the **Eraser** button (Design ribbon, Draw Borders group). Your mouse pointer becomes an eraser.
- Drag over the second vertical line in the table.

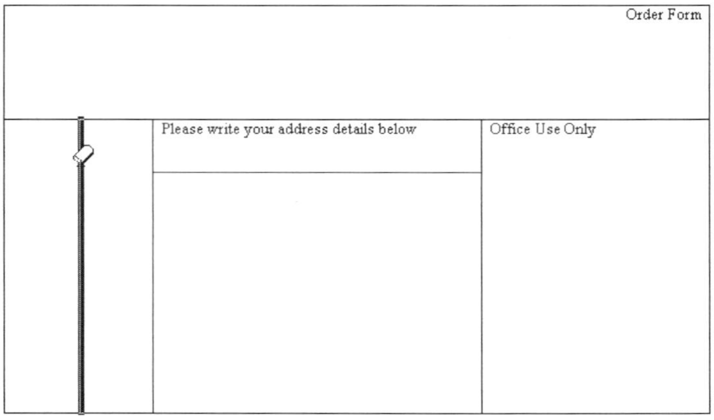

- Click back on the **Eraser** button to switch off the eraser.
- **Save** your changes.

Modifying uneven rows or columns

If you have drawn uneven rows or columns, you can quickly re-distribute them to even them out.

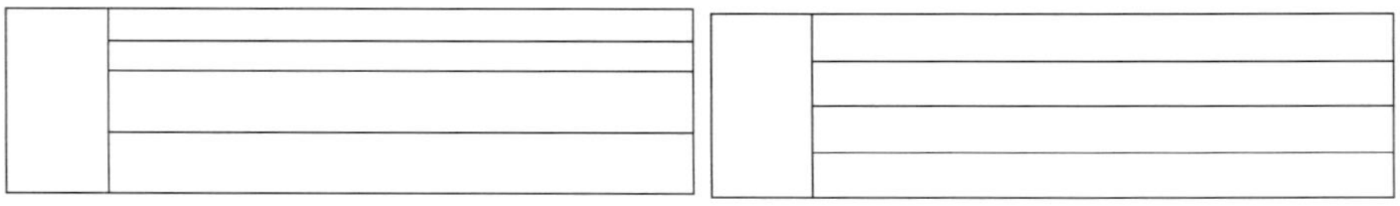

Rows drawn unevenly can be quickly re-distributed

How to: Distribute rows and columns

1. Select the required rows or columns.

2. Display the Layout ribbon, then click on the **Distribute Rows** or **Distribute Columns** button (Cell Size group).

Hands-on exercise 32

In this exercise you practise re-distributing uneven rows and columns. First, you add some more rows.

- Using the document *Order form*, click on the **Draw Table** button.
- Draw four horizontal lines beneath the text: Please write your address … . Don't worry about making the space between the lines even.

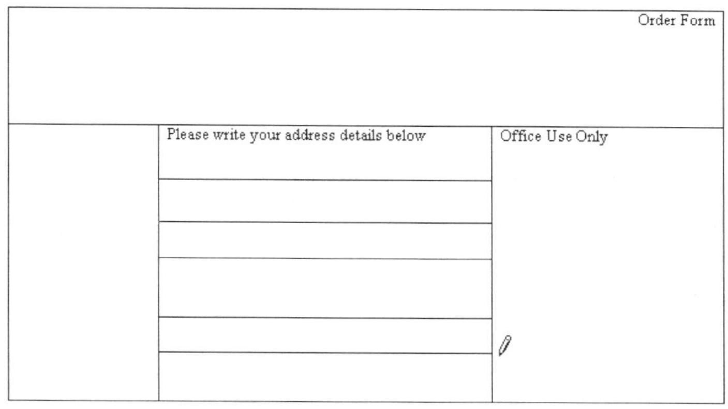

- Click on the **Draw Table** button to switch off the pencil.

Next, you ensure that the space between the rows is evenly distributed.

- Drag down over all rows in the middle section of the table to select them (include the first row 'Please write …').

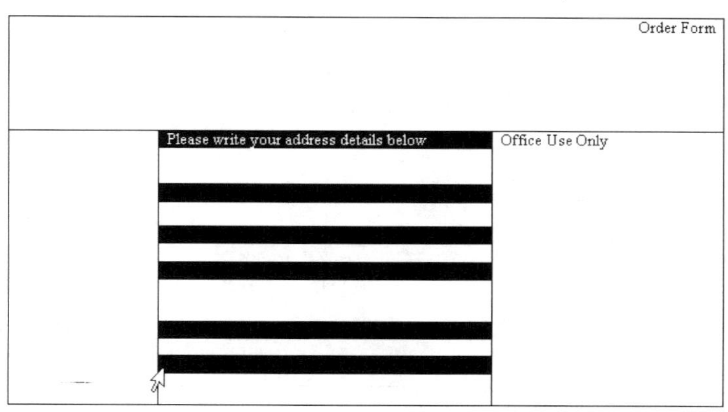

- Display the Layout ribbon, then click on the **Distribute Rows** button (Cell Size group).

Next, you ensure that the space between the columns is evenly distributed.

- Draw another vertical line down the Office Use Only column. Again, do not worry if the spacing is uneven.

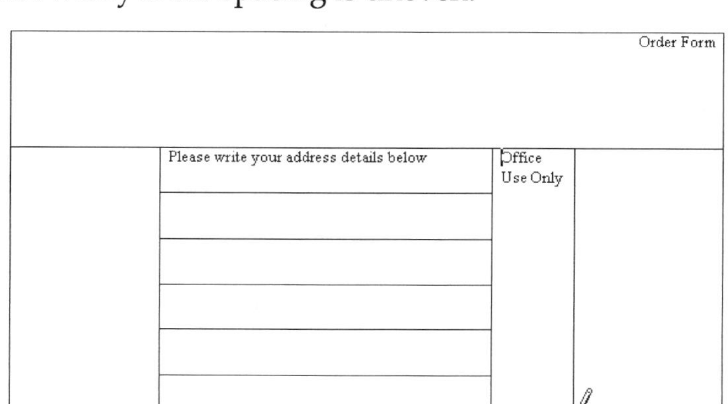

- Switch off the pencil.

- Drag over the columns in the Office Use Only section to select them.

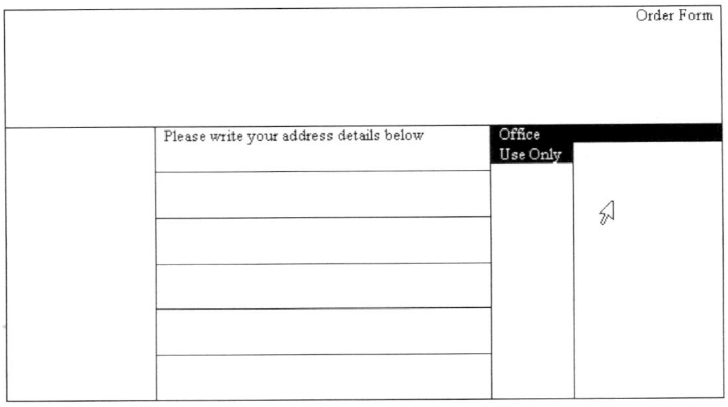

- Display the Layout ribbon, then click on the **Distribute Columns** button (Cell Size group).

Next, you reduce the size of a column.

- Position the mouse pointer on the right gridline of first the column. Drag the gridline to the left to reduce the size of the column.

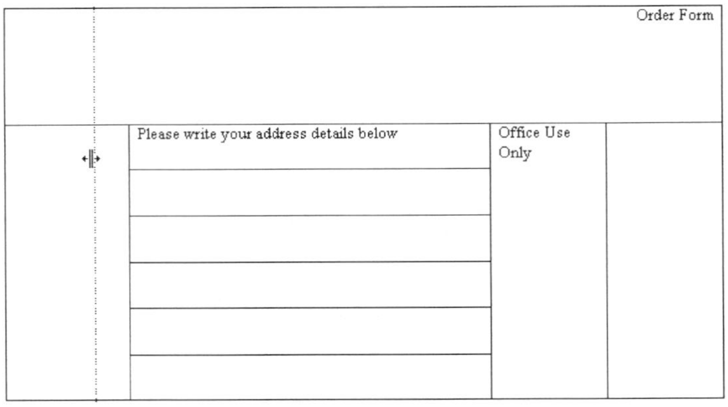

Finally, you reduce the width of a row.

- Position the mouse pointer on the horizontal gridline at the base of the top row. The mouse pointer becomes a double-headed arrow.
- Drag the gridline upwards by a small amount to slightly reduce the size of the top row
- **Save** your changes.

Aligning text and changing text direction

Your table can look more attractive if the text is evenly positioned both horizontally and vertically in a cell. An additional effect can be achieved by rotating the text.

Annual figures	June 2002 Results	June 2003 Results

Before

Annual figures	June 2002 Results	June 2003 Results

After

> ***For example ...*** *In the second table above, the 'Results' headings have been aligned to the centre of the cells (horizontally and vertically), with the 'Annual Figures' title rotated and centred.*

How to: Change text direction

1. Select the required cell(s).
2. Display the Layout ribbon, then click on the **Text Direction** button (Alignment group).
3. Click on the button again to continue rotating.

> ***As an aside ...*** *Once text has been rotated, you will notice that the text alignment buttons also rotate.*

Hands-on exercise 33

In this exercise you enhance the appearance of text in your table.

- Using the document *Order form*, select the heading text: Order Form
- Change the font size to **26 pt**.
- Keeping the text selected, expand the character spacing by **3 pt**.
  Font dialogue box, Advanced tab.)
- Select the text: Please write your address ...
- Change the font size to **12 pt**.
- Apply the same formatting to the text: Office Use Only
  (Consider using the **Format Painter** button or the F4 repeat key.)
- Click back on the text: Please write your address ...
  Display the Layout ribbon, then click on the **Align Center Left** button.
- Click on the heading text, Order Form, then click on the **Align Center Right** button.
- Click in the first column and type the text: *Customer Details*
- Select the text and change the font size to **16 pt**.
- Display the Layout ribbon, then click on the **Text Direction** button twice.
- Click on the **Align Center** button. (Note how the button has rotated.)

- Click on the text: Office Use Only
- Click on the **Align Bottom Left** button.

Order Form			
Customer Details	Please write your address details below	Office Use Only	

- Review your document in Print Preview.
- **Save** your changes.
- **Close** your document.

Aligning a table

In additional to aligning text within a table, you can also quickly align the whole table on the page, e.g. you can align a table to the centre of a page, horizontally and vertically.

How to: Align a table on the page

1. Click in the table to select.

2. Display the Layout ribbon, then click on the **Properties** button (Table group). The Table Properties dialogue box is presented.
3. Click on the required **Alignment** option, e.g. **Center** or **Right**.
4. Click on **OK**.

How to: Align a table vertically

1. Display the Page Layout ribbon and launch the Page Setup dialogue box.
2. Click on the **Layout** tab.
3. Click on the **Vertical alignment** down-arrow, then click on **Center**.
4. Click on **OK**.

Hands-on exercise 34

In this exercise you practise aligning a table to the centre of the page.

- Using the document *Order* form, click in the table to select.

- Display the Layout ribbon, then click on the **Properties** button (Table group). The Table Properties dialogue box is presented.
- Click on the **Center** alignment.
- Click on **OK**.
  The table aligns to the centre of the page horizontally.
- Launch the Page Setup dialogue box.
- Click on the **Layout** tab.
- Click on the **Vertical alignment** down-arrow, then click on **Center**.
- Click on **OK**.
  The table aligns to the centre of the page vertically.
- Review your document in Print Preview.
- **Save** your changes.

Merging and splitting cells

To create a heading in a table, you can **merge** cells together. Merging combines two or more cells from a row or column into one cell. If you discover you need to break a table to add a paragraph of text you can split the table.

For example ...

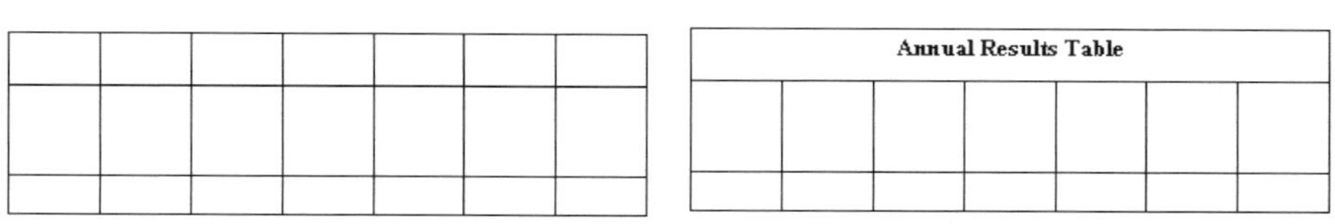

Cells in the first row are easily merged to become a single cell for a heading

As an alternative to drawing more lines you can quickly split cells.

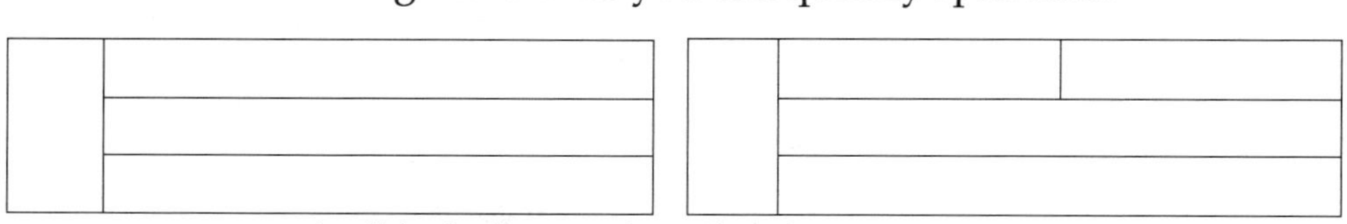

A cell in the first row is easily split into two cells

How to: Merge cells

1. Select the cells to be merged.

2. Display the Layout ribbon, then click on the **Merge Cells** button (Merge group).

How to: Split cells

1. Select the cell(s) to be split.

2. Display the Layout ribbon, then click on the **Split Cells** button (Merge group). The Split Cells dialogue box is presented.

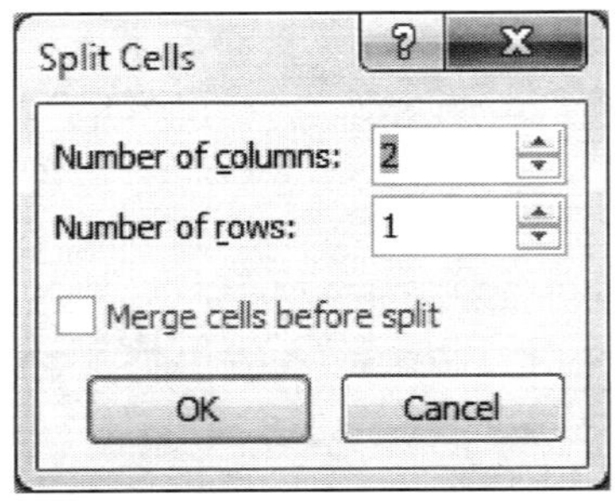

3. Click on the up/down-arrows to select the required **Number of columns**.
4. Click on the up/down-arrows to select the required **Number of rows**.
5. Click on **OK**.

Hands-on exercise 35

In this exercise you practise merging and splitting cells in an existing table.

- **Open** the document *Order form 2*. This is a slightly different version of the document you have created.
- Select the two cells at the top of the Office Use Only section.

- Display the Layout ribbon, then click on the **Merge Cells** button (Merge group).
- Align the text to the centre of the cell.
- Select the two blank cells at the bottom of this section.
- Click on the **Merge Cells** button.
- Type the following text: *Two approval stamps required*
- Align the text to the centre of the cell.
- Reduce the font size to **10 pts**.
- Type and align the following additional text.

Order Form

Customer Details

Please write your address details below

Name:

Address:

Post Code:

Office Use Only

Two approval stamps required

- Select the cell containing the text: Post Code

- Click on the **Split Cells** button. The Split Cells dialogue box is presented. Ensure the **Number of columns** is set to **2**.
  Click on **OK**.
- Align the Post Code text to the right of the cell.
- Apply appropriate shading to the top row of the table, and the Customer Details cell.
- **Save** your changes.
- **Close** your document.

Adding tabs within tables

When aligning data in an advanced column layout, tables are generally more flexible and easier to use than tabs. However, a tab may still be needed *within* a table to achieve a desired alignment.

For example ... *This table has a decimal tab in the second and third columns.*

Cash Management Trusts		
	Ave Rate Per Wk this week	**Size of Trust $m this week**
ASP CMT	4.15	66.44
AT Aust.	4.05	509.2
CommonPlus	4.0003	1476.9
General & Low	4.336	29.7

Decimal tabs used in table columns to align numeric data

How to: Set a tab stop in a table

1. Select the cell(s) or column(s) where the tab is required.

2. Click on the **Tab** button on the far left of the horizontal ruler until the required tab is displayed.

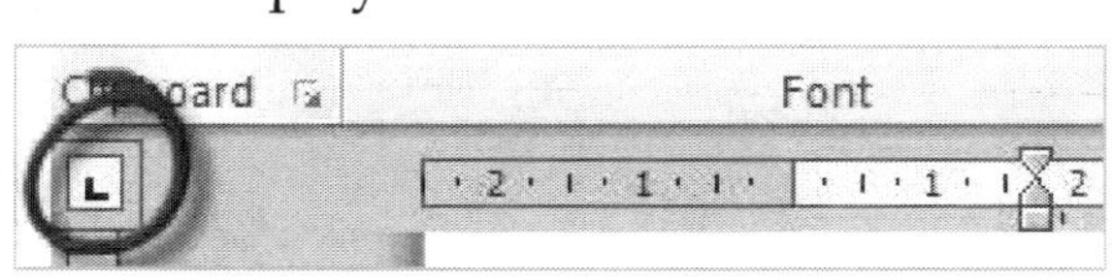

3. Click on the horizontal ruler at the required position above the selected cells.

As an aside ... *If you require the same tab position over multiple columns, select all the columns, then set the tab above the first column of the selection only.*

Hands-on exercise 36

In this exercise you practise adding decimal tabs to a table, and review some of your advanced table formatting skills.

- In a **new** blank document, create a table of three columns and two rows using the **Table** button. (As the table does not have irregularly sized rows and columns at this stage the **Draw Table** feature is not necessary.)
- Enter the following text and numeric data. At this stage do not worry about aligning the numeric data.

	Ave. Rate	Size of Trust $M
JPC	5.6	67.5
All Australian	5.79	100.2
General Plus	5.004	27.4
Safe & Low	5.39	209.25

- **Save** your document as *Mgnt rates.*

Next, you insert a decimal tab in the second column of the table in order to align the decimal numbers. To help you to set the tabs you split off the table heading.

- Select the second row.
- Split off the table header (Layout ribbon, **Split Table** button).
- Select the second column of numeric data (it is now easier to select purely the data you require).

> ***As an aside ...*** *You could of course have simply selected the required cells, but in a longer table this is more difficult.*

- Click on the **Tab** button on the horizontal ruler until the **Decimal** tab is displayed.
- Click in the centre of the horizontal ruler above the second column (about **8 cm**). Note that the decimals align automatically to the decimal tab.
- Repeat, setting a decimal tab above the third column at about **13.5 cm**.
- Delete the paragraph separating the heading row from the table.
- Centre and apply bold to the text in the top row.
- Add a new row at the top of the table.
- Merge the cells.
- Type the new heading: *Management Trusts*
- Format the text as **22 pts**.
- Increase the row height on this new header row.
- Align the text to the centre of the cell.
- Using the Draw Table feature, add a new 'column' to the start of the table as follows:

	Management Trusts		
		Ave Rate	Size of Trust $m
	JPC	5.6	67.5
	All Australian	5.79	100.2
	General Plus	5.004	27.4
	Safe & Low	5.39	209.25

- Type the following new text: *2011/2012*
- Change the text direction to align the text vertically.
- Reduce the font size if appropriate.
- Centre the text in the cell.
- Change the document layout to landscape.
- Centre the table on the page (horizontally).
- Review your document in Print Preview.
- **Save** your changes.
- **Close** your document.

Hands-on exercise 37

In the following exercise you use a table to create an attractive layout incorporating tabs and paragraphs of text displayed side by side (parallel columns).

- In a **new** blank document, create a table of three columns and four rows using the **Table** button.
- Insert text on the following page.
- Spell and grammar check your document.
- **Save** your document as *Investment funds.*

First, you change a column width - to some precise measurements.

- Select the first column of the table.
- Display the Layout ribbon, then adjust the measurements on the **Table Column Width** option (Cell Size group) as follows
  Set the width of column 1 to: **3.5 cm**, column 2 to **9.5 cm**, and column 3 to **2 cm**.
- Click on **OK**.

Next, you insert a decimal tab in the third column of the table in order to align the decimal numbers.

- Select the third column.
- Click on the **Tab** button on the horizontal ruler until the **Decimal** tab is displayed.
- Click in the centre of the horizontal ruler above the third column.

Fund Name	Overview	2001% Return
Share Fund High Risk	This fund is an actively managed portfolio of Australian shares and is considered to offer the most attractive returns. However, there is a higher short-term risk associated with this investment. Features of this fund are: diversification across company and industrial sectors; active management strategies to reduce volatility; and significant tax advantages	12.45
Property Fund Medium Risk	The aim of this fund is to provide growth whilst mantaining flexibility. This is not generally available with direct property investments. Features of this fund are: diversification across commercial and retail sectors; quality tenants; consistent income.	10.76
Capital Fund Low Risk	This fund delivers money market rates of return via our cash management trust and is most suited to investors looking for a short-term option. Features of this fund are: security; no entry fee; and a credit rating of AAA.	8.7

Next, you apply bullets and indents to selected text in the second column of the table.

- Select the three points under the first heading:
  Features of this fund are:
- Apply **Bullets**. (Change the bullet symbols if they are inappropriate.)
- Locate the two remaining lists of features in this text and apply the same bullet formatting. (Hint: This could be made into a style.)
- **Save** your changes.

Finally, you improve the appearance of your table by applying alignment, adding shading, and removing the borders. (Note that removal of borders is very common when tables are used to present parallel columns of text.)

- Select the entire table.
- Remove all borders.
- Select the first row of the table.
- Apply **Bold** and align the text to the centre.
- Select the first column of the table.
- Apply **Bold**. (You may need to press the **Bold** button twice because of the mixture of bold/no bold text.)
- Add a new row to the top of the table.
- Merge the cells in the new row.
- Type the text: *Investment Funds*
- Increase the width of the top row.
- Select the text in the top row and apply the font size of **16 pts**.
- Add any further formatting you think would improve the appearance of your table, e.g. shading.
- Review your document in Print Preview.
- **Save** your changes.
- **Close** your document.

Sorting information

When working with tables it is very useful to know the **Sort** feature. This can save you lots of time if text needs to be rearranged.

> ***For example ...*** *You have created a telephone list to which you are often adding new employees, and you need to maintain the list in alphabetical order.*

How to: Sort information

1. Click on a table, or select the paragraphs to be sorted.
2. Display the Layout ribbon, then click on the **Sort** button (Data group). The Sort dialogue box is presented. The options in the dialogue box change depending on the text selected.
3. Select the required options.
4. Click on **OK**.

Hands-on exercise 38

In this exercise you practise sorting data in a table and sorting paragraphs of information.

- **Open** the document *Telephone list*.

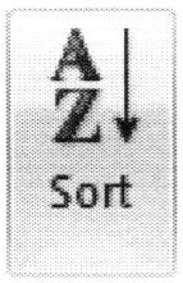

- Click in the table.
- Display the Layout ribbon, then click on the **Sort** button (Data group). The Sort dialogue box is presented.

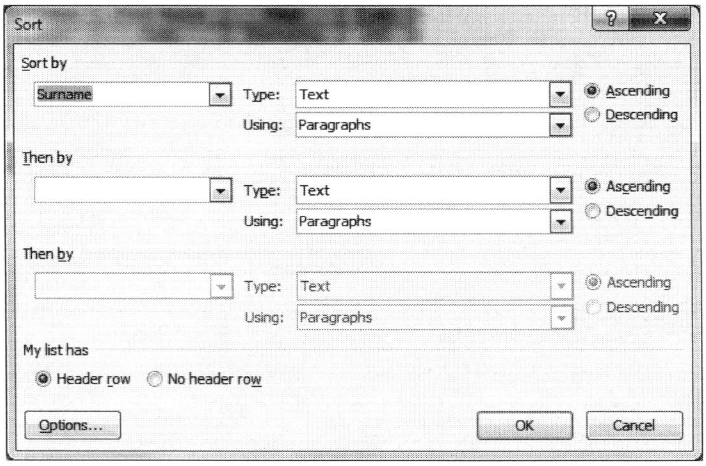

- The first column (**Surname**) is selected as the sort key (**Sort by**).
- Ensure **Ascending** is selected as the sort order.
- Ensure the option **Header row** is selected so that the first row in the table is not included in the sort.
- Click on **OK**.
  The data in the table is sorted in Surname order.
- Click on **Undo**.

Next, you sort the information in the table by Department.

- Click in the table.

- Display the Layout ribbon, then click on the **Sort** button.
  The Sort dialogue box is presented.
- The first column is selected as the sort key.
  Click on the **Sort by** down-arrow, then click on Dept.
- Ensure **Ascending** is selected as the sort order.
- Ensure the option **Header row** is selected.
- Click on **OK**.
  The data in the table is sorted in Department order.
- Click on **Undo**.

Next, you sort the information in the table by Surname within Department.

- Click on the table.
- Display the Layout ribbon, then click on the **Sort** button.
  The Sort dialogue box is presented.
- Select **Dept** as the first sort key (**Sort by**).
- Click in **Then by** and select **Surname** as the second sort key.
- Ensure **Ascending** is selected as the sort order.
- Ensure the option **Header row** is selected.
- Click on **OK**.
  The data in the table is sorted by Surname within Department.
- **Save** your changes.
- **Close** your document.

As an aside *... Note if you need to sort paragraphs of text (not in a table), use the* ***Sort*** *button on the Home ribbon.*

Hands-on exercise 39

In this exercise you further practise sorting.

- **Open** the document Hughs store.
- In the top row, align the text to the centre.
- Align the numeric data in the Unit Price column using a decimal tab.
- Sort the data by the Product Name, alphabetically, ascending.
- **Save** your changes.
- **Close** your document.

Consolidation task 9

In this task you create an attractive table to display holiday pricing information.

- In a new blank document create the following table:

	People per room	Low Season		High Season	
		7 days	Extra Night	7 days	Extra Night
Queenstown	2	$1200	$90	$1379	$110
	4-6	$1068	$60	$1280	$97
Mount Hutt	2-6	$980	$50	$1050	$80

- **Save** your document as Holiday pricing.
- Select the top row and insert a new row.
- Merge the cells in the new top row.
- Type the new heading: *Skiing Holiday Pricing 2011*
- Format this new heading attractively.
- Review your document in Print Preview.
- Save your changes.
- Close your document.

After this Consolidation task, do you feel confident... tick the appropriate box:

	Inserting a table
	Merging cells
	Inserting borders
	Inserting shading

Consolidation task 10

In this task you create an attractive table to publicise local events.

- In a new blank document create the following table:

Major Events	
January 25-27	Taree Aquatic Festival
March 9-17	Wauchope Lasiandra Festival
May 3-5	Coffs Harbour Show
August 16-18	Bellingen Jazz Festival
Sept. 18 - Oct. 2	Coffs Harbour Festival
October 5-7	Oyster Festival, Forster
October 6	Food and Wine Festival, Port Macquarie
Australia's Holiday Coast	

- Centre the table horizontally and vertically on the page.
- Apply new formatting of your choice to the table to maximise readability and appearance.
- Save your document as *Major events*.
- Close your document.

After this Consolidation task, do you feel confident... tick the appropriate box:

	Inserting a table
	Merging cells
	Inserting borders
	Inserting shading
	Changing text direction
	Changing text alignment

Topic 8 – Inserting pictures, text & charts

In this topic you learn how to insert, format and effectively display pictures in Word documents. You also look at importing text and creating charts.

Before you start working with pictures and layout, a few thoughts on document design and picture placement.

Document design

There are three basic rules of thumb for good document design and layout:

- keep the design simple
- keep the design consistent
- add contrast.

Simplicity

With a simple design the reader gets the message immediately. Limit the number of elements on a page, e.g. limit fonts, decorative elements and pictures.

Consistency

Consistency in design helps a reader to move through a document more easily and to understand quickly how information is organised. Be consistent with the size of headings, spacing between paragraphs, borders and effects.

Contrast

Contrast catches the reader's eye and helps draw it to what is important. White space helps to create contrast, i.e. the parts of your page that remain unprinted.

Filling a page with information can overwhelm your audience and distract them to the point that they fail to understand your message (or simply decide that it is easier to ignore). Therefore, give your layout room to breathe by using white space, e.g. space around headings, around pictures and making sure margins are not too small.

Picture placement

For an effective page layout with pictures you need to consider your picture placement.

Generally, a reader scans a page from the top-left corner down to the bottom-right corner. Clever picture placement can be used to lead the reader's eye across the page, enhancing readability and making information easier to digest.

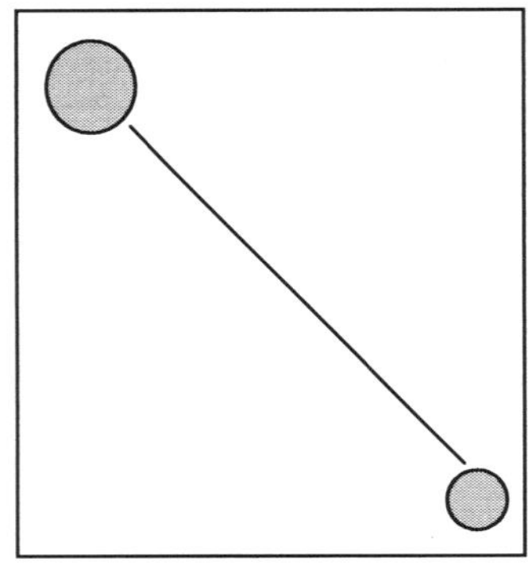

A picture or title is often placed in the top-left corner so that the reader's eye is drawn into the page. Company logos are frequently placed alongside a title for immediate identification, or in the bottom-right corner.

The bottom-right corner of a page is the last place that the eye rests as it scans the page. So, a logo that has been placed in the bottom-right corner is likely to form part of the final impression left with the reader.

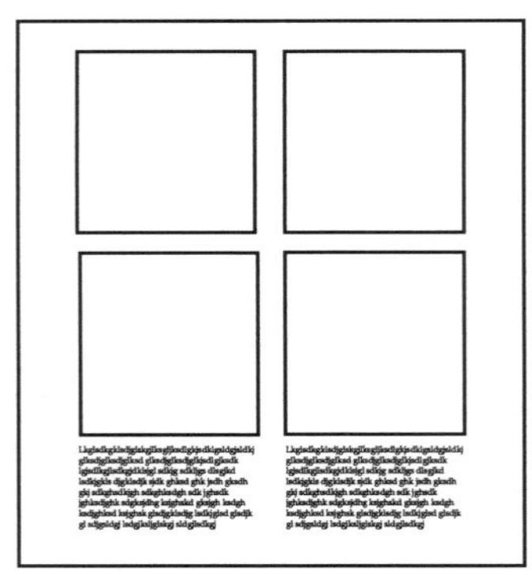

If you have a lot of pictures consider placing them together.

Use a large picture to be dramatic – or make your picture very small with lots of white space around it.

Adding Clip Art pictures

Word provides a great number of pictures in a **Clip Art** library that can be quickly and easily inserted into a document.

How to: Insert a Clip Art picture

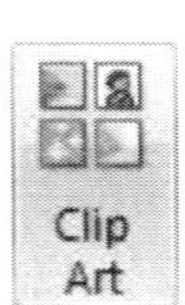

1. Click in your document where you want to insert a picture.
2. Display the Insert ribbon, then click on the **Clip Art** button (Illustrations group). The Clip Art task pane is presented on the right.
3. Type a word or phrase that best describes the picture you want in the **Search for** text box.
4. Use **Results should be** to limit file types, e.g. to remove Audio from search options.
5. Select **Include Office.com content** for searching online images.
6. Click on **Go**.
   A number of pictures are displayed.

7. Click on the required Clip Art picture. The picture is inserted into your document. Note the Picture Tools added on a new Format Ribbon. This is displayed while the picture is selected.

Manipulating your pictures

You can easily re-size a picture once it has been inserted.

How to: Re-size a picture

1. Sizing handles appear around a picture when it is selected. (Click on a picture if it is not selected.)

2. Point to a sizing handle. Your mouse pointer becomes a two-way arrow. To ensure you size your picture proportionately, point to one of the corner handles.
3. Drag the sizing handle to a new size.

How to: Move and align a picture (basic actions)

1. You can drag your picture to a new position in a document (dragging to another paragraph marker), and you can align using your **Align Text Left**, **Centre** or **Align Text Right** buttons.

Hints & tips

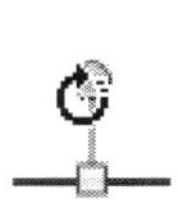

If you want to resize a picture around its centre point, press Ctrl *and drag on a corner handle. For exact measurements, you can also resize using the Size controls on the Format ribbon. The green rotate handle is used to rotate a picture. Drag to rotate to a different angle. To delete a picture ensure it is selected then press* Delete.

Cropping a picture

If you want to show only part of a picture you can trim off unwanted parts. You can also crop to a shape, e.g. a triangle or a bubble.

How to: Crop (trim) a picture

1. Double-click on a picture to select it (and display Format ribbon).
2. Click on the top-half of the **Crop** button (Size group).
3. Drag on one of the sizing handles that now surround the picture.

4. Click back on the **Crop** button to finish.

As an aside *… When you crop the 'removed' part of the picture is still there just hidden. You can restore by changing the cropping (e.g. dragging back out). Be careful if you then distribute the picture and you have cropped sensitive information as it can be restored. To remove completely you need to* ***Compress Pictures*** *(Adjust group). Use this to reduce file size and delete the cropped areas of pictures.* 

How to: Crop to a shape

1. Double-click on a picture to select it (and display Format ribbon).
2. Click on **Crop** button down-arrow (Size group).
3. Point to **Crop to Shape**, then click on a shape.

Wrapping text around a picture

You can change how text wraps around a picture. This also provides more flexibility when positioning a picture (more than simply using the **Align Text Left**, **Centre** or **Align Text Right** buttons).

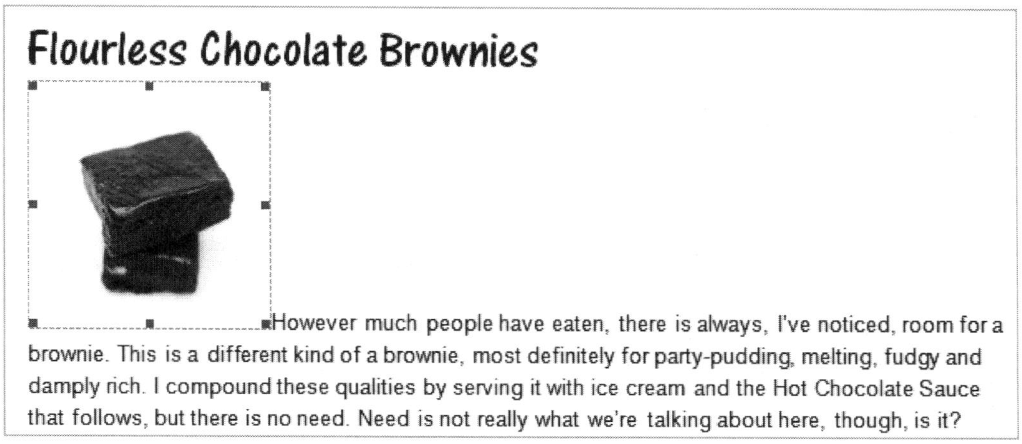

Picture as it is first inserted (in-line)

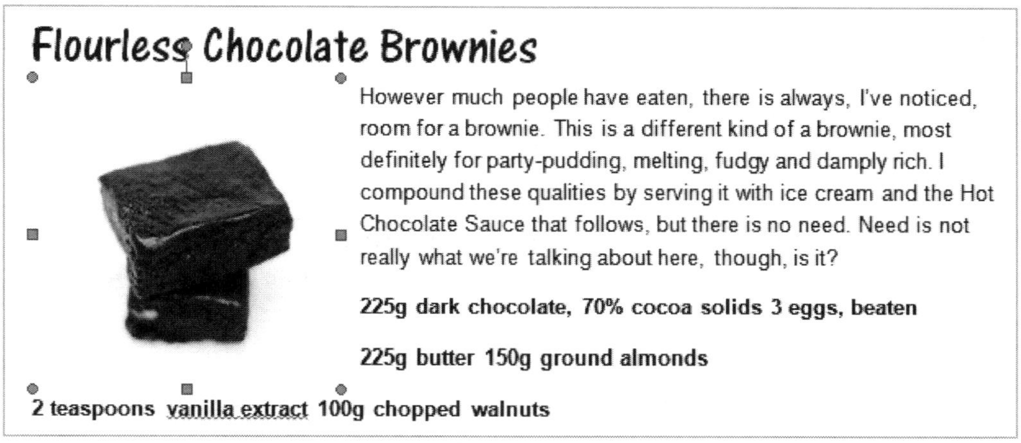

*Picture with **Square** wrapping applied*

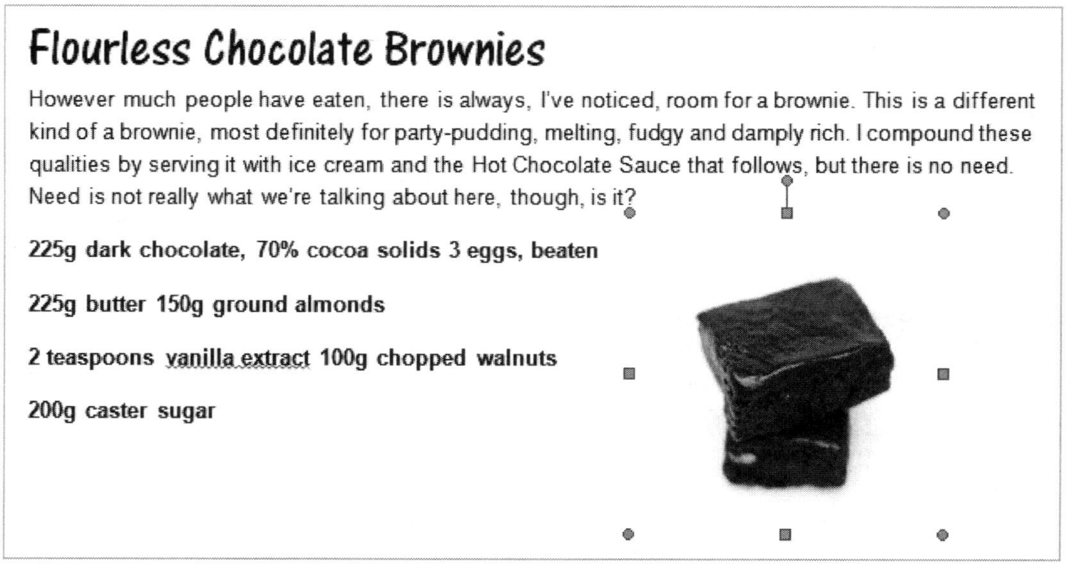

*Picture with **In Front of Text** wrapping applied, and dragged to the right*

How to: Wrap text around a picture

1. Double-click on the picture to select it (and display the Format ribbon).
2. Click on the **Wrap Text** button (Arrange group).
3. Click on the required text wrapping option.

In Line With Text	Wraps text in line with the bottom of the picture. The picture remains where it was placed and moves with the text.
Square	Wraps text around all sides of the square bounding box that surrounds a picture or object.
Tight	Wraps text tightly around the edges of the actual image (instead of wrapping to the square bounding box). You can change the dotted wrapping perimeter using the **Edit Wrap Points** button (see below).
Through	Wraps text around the image as best it can, similar to the Tight option.
Top and Bottom	Wraps text above and below the selected picture or object (only).
Behind Text	Removes text wrapping and places the selected picture or object behind the document text in its own layer.
In Front of Text	Removes text wrapping and places the selected picture or object on top of the document text in its own layer.
Through	Wraps text around the perimeter and inside any open portions of a picture or object.

4. The text wraps to the sides of the picture.

How to: Select a preset position and wrap

1. Double-click on the picture to select it (and display the Format ribbon).
2. Click on the **Position** button (Arrange group).
   A list of options is presented, each has Square wrapping applied.
3. Click on the required position.

Hands-on exercise 40

In this exercise you practise improving the visual presentation of a document by inserting and working with pictures.

- **Open** the document *Occupational health.*
- Display the Insert ribbon, then click on the **Clip Art** button (Illustrations group). The Clip Art task pane is presented.
- In the **Search for** text box, type: *people at work*
  Use **Results should be** to search **All media file types**.
- Click on **Go**.
  A number of pictures are displayed.

- Click on a Clip Art picture of your choice (choose one of the initial more complex pictures/photos).
  The picture is inserted into your document.
- The picture is displayed full-size. Scroll down the document if necessary to fully view the picture. Note the Picture Tools added on a new Format Ribbon.

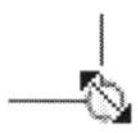

- Ensuring your picture is still selected, point to the sizing handle in the bottom right corner of the picture. Drag it diagonally towards the top left to reduce the size of the picture.
- **Save** your changes.

Next, you practice cropping.

- Keeping your picture selected, click on the top-half of the **Crop** button (Size group).
- Drag on one of the sizing handles that now surround the picture to remove a portion.
- Click back on the **Crop** button to finish.
- Keeping your picture selected, click on the **Crop** button down-arrow, point to **Crop to Shape**, then click on a heart shape.

Next, you practice wrapping text.

- Keeping your picture selected, click on the **Wrap Text button** (Arrange group).
- Click on **Square**.
  The text wraps around your picture.
- Drag your picture towards the centre of the document.
- Click on the **Wrap Text** button, then click on **Tight**.
- Click on the **Wrap Text** button, then click on **In Front of Text**.

- Keeping your picture selected, click on the **Position** button (Arrange group). A list of options is presented, each has Square wrapping applied.
- Click on the top left option (**With Text Wrapping**).
- Return your crop shape to a simple rectangle.
- **Close** the task pane.
- **Save** your changes.

Enhancing your picture style

A number of effects can be used to enhance your picture style, including:

- applying a picture style
- applying a picture border
- applying picture effects.

There are lots of styles and effects to experiment with.

How to: Apply a picture style

1. Double-click on the picture to select it (and display the Format ribbon).
2. Point to any option in the **Picture Styles** group to see the design effect previewed on your picture. Click on the **More** button to display the full gallery of styles.

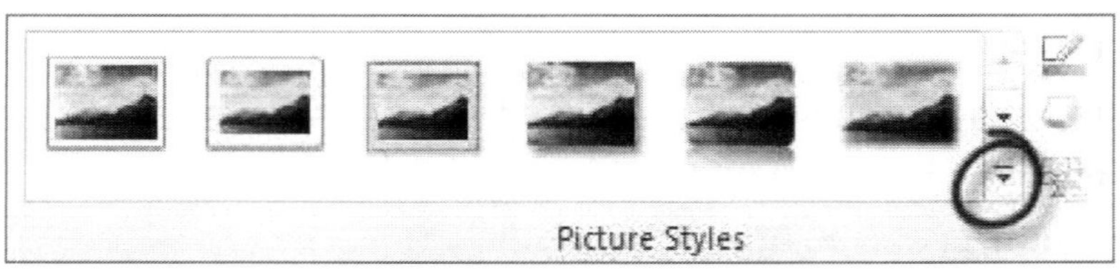

3. Click on the required style to apply.

How to: Apply a picture border

1. Double-click on the picture to select it (and display the Format ribbon).

2. Click on the **Picture Border** button (Picture Styles group).
   A number of border colours are presented.
3. Click on the required border colour (note the live preview).

As an aside *... Note you can also change the border Weight here.*

How to: Apply a picture effects

1. Double-click on the picture to select it (and display the Format ribbon).

2. Click on the **Picture Effects** button (Picture Styles group).
   A gallery of options is presented. Point to the required category, then sub-category.
3. Click on the required effect (note the live preview)

Hands-on exercise 41

In this exercise you practise further enhancing your picture.

- Using the document *Occupational health*, experiment with the above features.

Adjusting your picture

A number of effects can be used to adjust your picture, including:

- removing a picture background (which removes unwanted parts of a picture)
- adjusting sharpness, brightness and contrast
- re-colouring
- adding artistic effects.

Again, there are lots of adjustments to experiment with. When removing a background on a simple picture Word can easily remove all in one go, on others you will need to adjust.

How to: Remove a background (adjustments)

1. Double-click on the picture to select it (and display the Format ribbon).
2. Click on the **Remove Background** button (Adjust group).
   Note the new Background Removal Ribbon. Word colours purple those areas of the picture that it chooses as background and displays an outline around the area to keep.
3. Drag the handles to resize and reposition the rectangle around the part of the picture you want to keep.

4. Refine the areas to keep/remove further by using the **Mark Areas to Keep/Mark Areas to Remove** buttons (Refine group). Click on the required button, your insertion point becomes a pen. Click or click and drag on an area of the picture. Word marks with a + or – sign. Click the buttons again to switch off.

5. On the Background ribbon, click on **Keep Changes** (Close group).

> ***As an aside*** *... Click on* ***Discard All Changes*** *(Background Removal ribbon) if you do not like changes made, or use* ***Reset Picture*** *(Adjust group).*

How to: Correct sharpness, brightness and contrast

1. Double-click on the picture to select it (and display the Format ribbon).

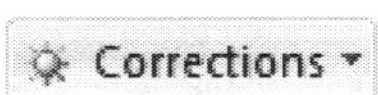

2. Click on the **Corrections** button (Adjust group).
3. Click on one of the correction options (note the live preview).
   Also note the separate categories Sharpen and Soften, and Brightness and Contrast.

How to: Recolor a picture

1. Double-click on the picture to select it (and display the Format ribbon).

2. Click on the **Color** button (Adjust group).
3. Click on one of the colour variations (note the live preview).

How to: Add an artistic effect

1. Double-click on the picture to select it (and display the Format ribbon).

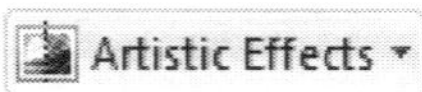

2. Click on the **Artistic Effects** button (Adjust group).
3. Click on one of the effects (note the live preview).

Hands-on exercise 42

In this exercise you practise enhancing your picture.

- Using the document *Occupational health,* delete the existing picture.
- Add another suitable Clip Art picture.
- Resize, crop and wrap text/position as required.
- Experiment with removing backgrounds.
- Experiment with sharpness, brightness and contrast.

- Experiment with re-colouring.
- Add an artistic effect.
- **Close** the task pane.
- **Save** your changes.

Inserting captions

Once inserted, pictures or diagrams can often benefit from a description or **caption**. Using the Word caption feature you can insert an automatically numbered caption, e.g. **Figure 1**. Caption numbers are updated if a picture is moved or deleted, and you can add text after the caption label, e.g. **Figure 1 Correct posture**.

How to: Insert a caption

1. Click on the object to be captioned.
2. Display the References ribbon, then click on the **Insert Caption** button (Captions group). The Caption dialogue box is presented.

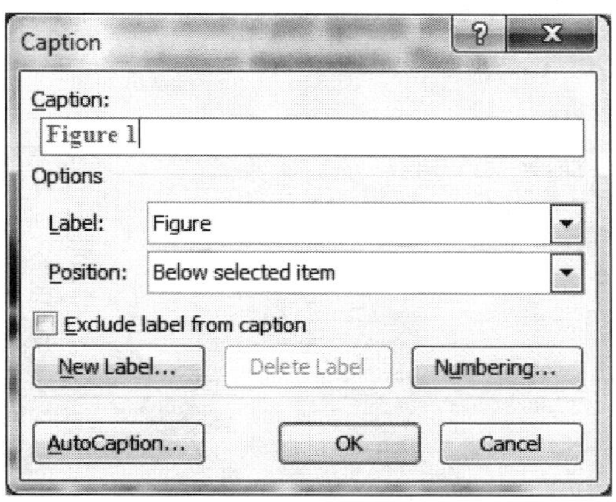

3. Click on the **Label** down-arrow to select the best label for your object, e.g. Figure, Table.
4. Click on the **Position**, e.g. **Below** or **Above selected item**.
5. Click to the right of the **Caption** (e.g. Figure 1) and type any additional text and punctuation. Note you cannot delete the default text.
6. Click on **OK**.

As an aside ... *To change the caption text use the* ***New Label*** *option. To change the number style use* ***Numbering****. Use* ***AutoCaption*** *to select objects to be automatically captioned on insertion.*

Hands-on exercise 43

In this exercise you practise inserting captions.

- Using the document *Occupational health*, select your picture then display the References ribbon.

- Click on the **Insert Caption** button (Captions group).
  The Caption dialogue box is presented.
- Click to the right of the **Caption** (Figure 1) and type: *Correct posture* (or something suitable to your picture).
- Click on **OK**.
  The caption is added beneath your picture.
- Click on the **Center** align button.
- Click beside the heading **Good habits**.
- Insert another suitable Clip Art picture into your document.
- Resize as necessary, add **Square** wrapping and drag alongside the text.
- Enhance the picture as required.
- Keeping the picture selected, add a caption. Note the automatic numbering.

- Periodically evaluate your environment for ways to reduce stress.
- Try to keep your desk uncluttered so your can find things easily and so that your thoughts don't get cluttered.
- Vary your tasks throughout the day.
- Take a break every hour. Do some relaxation or stretching exercises, or talk with someone. Give your mind and body a rest.
- Drink plenty of water.
- Massage your hands and forearms several times a day, with hand cream if desired. This will improve circulation and will enforce a break - and if you use hand cream you cannot then touch the keyboard for a few minutes! (This applies to men as well as women.)

Figure 2: Take a break

- **Close** the task pane.
- **Save** your changes.

As an aside *... The caption text is a style called Caption, so can easily be updated throughout a document.*

Inserting a picture file

You can insert pictures from other programs or locations on your computer, i.e. if they are not part of the Clip Art Gallery.

For example ... *You can insert a company logo, a scanned signature, pictures of staff or products, etc.*

How to: Insert a picture file

Picture

1. Click in your document where you want to insert a picture.
2. Display the Insert ribbon, then click on the **Picture** button (Illustrations group). The Insert Picture dialogue box is presented.

3. Locate and click on the required picture.
4. Click on **Insert**.
5. Click to select the picture before resizing, etc.

Hands-on exercise 44

In this exercise you insert a picture that is not part of the Clip Art Gallery.

Picture

Position

- Using the document *Occupational health*, press Ctrl End to go to the bottom of the document.
- Display the Insert ribbon, then click on the **Picture** button (Illustrations group). The Insert Picture dialogue box is presented.
- Locate the supplied graphic file: *Health logo*.
(This picture file is located with your exercise documents.)
Locate and click on the picture file, then click on **Insert**.
- **Position** the picture in the bottom right of the document.
- Review your document in Print Preview.
- **Save** your changes.

Inserting a text file

If you have text in another file that you want to insert into your current document, you can use the Text from File command.

How to: Insert a file

1. Click in your document where you want to insert the text.
2. Display the Insert ribbon, click on the **Object** down-arrow, then click on **Text from File** (Text group). The Insert File dialogue box is presented.

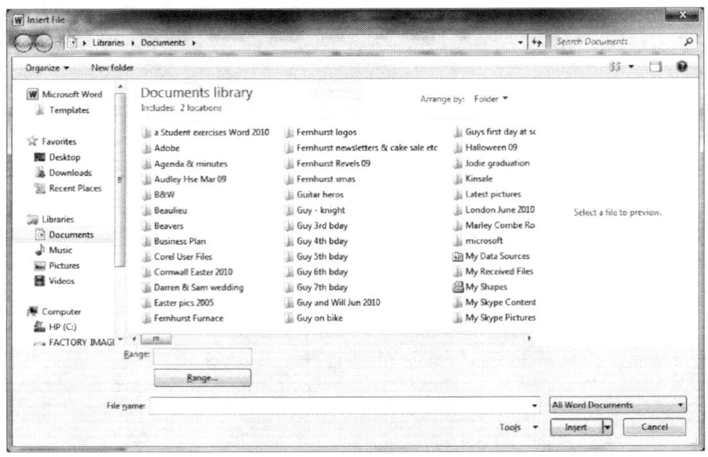

3. Locate and click on the required file.
4. Click on **Insert**.

Hands-on exercise 45

In this exercise you experiment with the Insert File feature.

- Using the document *Occupational health*, press Ctrl End to go to the end of the document (beneath text).
- Display the Insert ribbon, click on the **Object** down-arrow, then click on **Text from File** (Text group). The Insert File dialogue box is presented.
- Locate and insert the file *Office safety checklist*. (This file is located with your exercise documents.)
- The text is added to your document.
- Apply the **Heading 2** style to all headings in the imported text.
- Apply the **BulletedList** style to all text under the headings in the imported text.
- Update the **Caption** style enlarging the font text and ensuring the font colour is black.
- Re-**position** the logo to the bottom right of the final page.
- Review your document in Print Preview.
- **Save** your changes.
- **Close** your document.

Inserting a chart object

In Word you can insert a chart object to display data in graphical form. When you insert a chart Word opens Excel which then displays a workbook with sample data. You then replace the sample data in Excel with your own information, and Word creates a chart.

How to: Create a chart

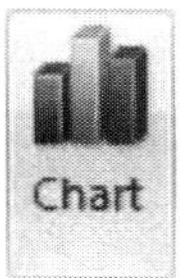

1. Click where you want to insert the chart.
2. Display the Insert ribbon, then click on the **Chart** button (Illustrations group). The Insert Chart dialogue box is presented.

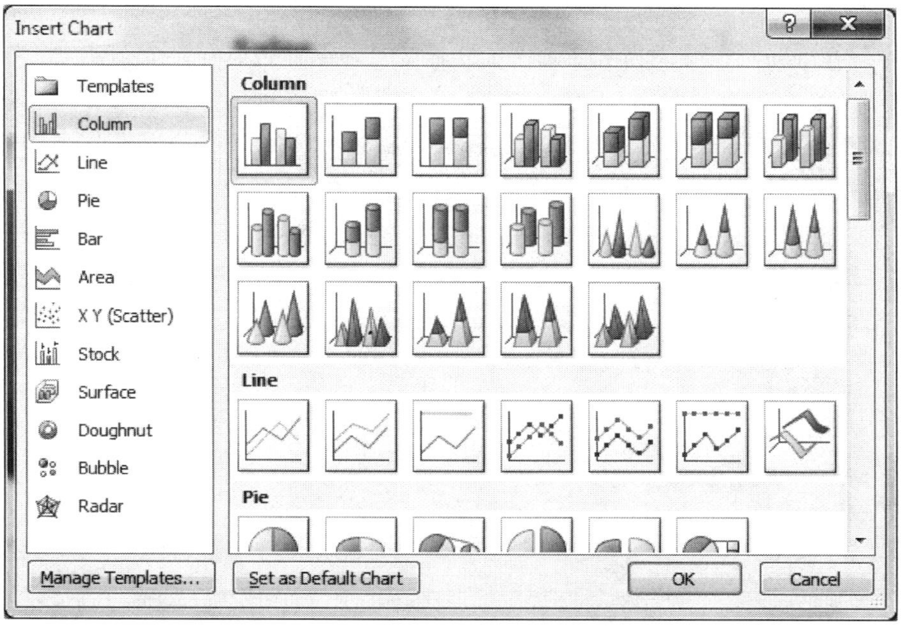

3. Click on one of the charting options in the left pane, e.g. Column, Line, then click on one of the chart styles from the right pane, e.g. Clustered Column.
4. Click on **OK**.
   Word opens Excel which displays a workbook with sample data. Your chart is in the Word document, and your data is in an Excel worksheet. Three new ribbons are displayed in Word with Chart Tools (Design, Layout and Format). The Design ribbon is active.
5. To replace the sample data in the Excel worksheet, click on a cell and type the new text or numbers required. The chart in Word automatically updates with the new data. If you need to create a larger data area in Excel, drag the sizing handle in the bottom right corner until the area is the required size.

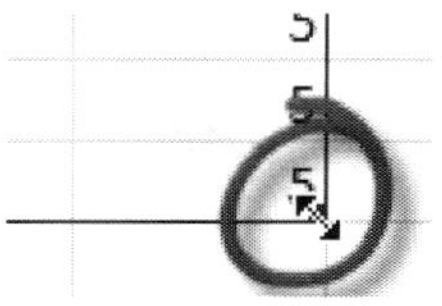

6. **Save** your document in the usual way and the (embedded) worksheet data is also saved. Closing the Word document also closes the Excel worksheet.

How to: Edit chart data

1. Click on the chart to activate the Chart Tools.
2. On the Design ribbon, click on the **Edit Data** button (Data group). Excel is re-displayed with your worksheet data.
3. Edit the data in the worksheet as previously.

How to: Change your chart type

1. Click on the chart to activate the Chart Tools.
2. Click on the **Change Chart Type** button (Design ribbon, Type group). The Change Chart Type dialogue box is presented.

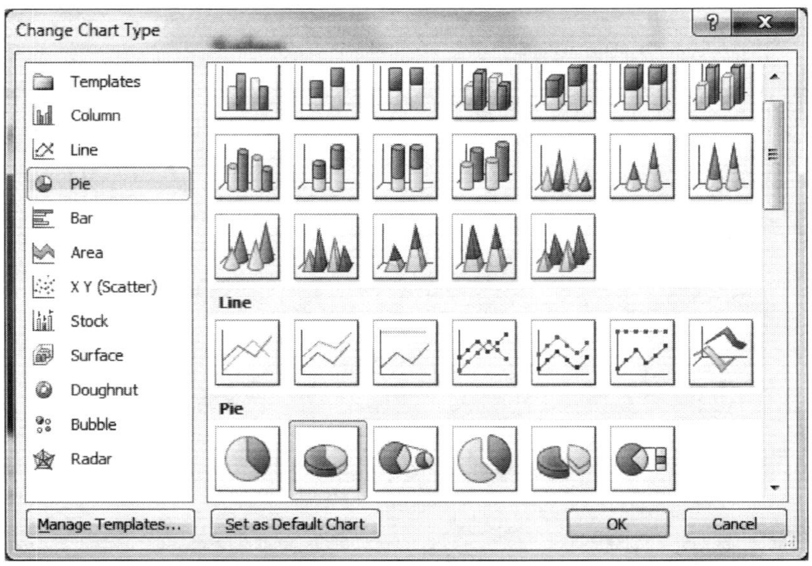

3. Click on the chart type required from the left pane, then click on a variation from the right pane.
4. Click on **OK**.
   The chart is updated.

Hands-on exercise 46

In this exercise you practise creating a chart to present numerical data.

- **Open** the document *Commissions*.
- Press Ctrl End to go to the end of the document.
- Display the Insert ribbon, then click on the **Chart** button (Illustrations group). The Insert Chart dialogue box is presented.
- Ensure the option **Column** is selected in the left pane, then ensure the first option **Clustered Column** is selected from the right pane.
- Click on **OK**.
  Word opens Excel which displays a workbook with sample data. Your chart is in the Word document.
  Three new ribbons are displayed in Word with Chart Tools (Design, Layout and Format). The Design ribbon is active.

- To replace the sample data in the worksheet, click in the required cell and type the new data. Press Tab to move to the next cell. Type the following data (note how the chart also develops):

	A	B	C	D
1	Rep	April	May	June
2	A. Davis	27,050	32,500	56,500
3	J. Bromley	35,750	72,600	28,960
4	S. Fredricks	76,900	88,100	59,500
5	N. Yu	108,000	75,820	84,650
6	F Georgiou	46,950	52,350	49,850

- Ensure the blue border surrounds your data. (If not, point to the bottom right corner of the blue border. Your mouse pointer becomes a two-way arrow. Drag to resize.)
- Your chart is complete.
- Return to Word and press Ctrl Home to go to the top of the document.

- Click on the chart to activate the Chart Tools.
- On the Design ribbon, click on the **Edit Data** button (Data group). Excel is re-displayed with your worksheet data.
- Change the data for **A. Davis** to **35,000** for each month. Note the effect on the chart.

- Ensuring the chart is selected, click on the **Change Chart Type** button (Design ribbon, Type group). The Change Chart Type dialogue box is presented.
- Select a **Bar** chart.
- Click on **OK**.
  The chart is updated.
- Review your document in Print Preview.
- To remove a chart border, display the Format ribbon, click on **Shape Outline** (Shape Styles group), then click on **No Outline**.
- **Save** your changes.
- **Close** your document. Your Excel worksheet also closes.

Hints & tips

If you are working in Compatibility mode you will not have full Chart functionality – only that available in previous versions. Your functionality will also be limited if you do not have Excel installed.

You can also copy and paste a chart into Excel, and copy and paste data into the sample worksheet.

Terms & concepts review

- What are the three basic rules of good document **design** and layout?

- Where would be a good place to position a **logo** on a page, and why?

- How can you remove completely **cropped** parts of a picture?

- Name a number of features you can use to **enhance** a picture?

- What are the following buttons used for?

- What effect has been used on the following photograph?

- Where do you find the command **Text from File** (to insert a text file)?

Consolidation task 11

In this task you experiment further with inserting text and graphics.

- Open the document Western Australia.
- Go to the end of the document and insert the file Western Australia 2.
- Apply the **Heading 2** style to any headings.
- Display the document footer.
- Insert the following graphic file: WA logo.
- Reduce the size of the logo so that it fits into the footer.
- Apply square wrapping and drag to the right.
- Close your footer.
- Review your document in Print Preview.
- Save your changes.
- Close your document.

After this Consolidation task, do you feel confident... tick the appropriate box:

	Editing a footer
	Applying heading styles
	Inserting a picture file
	Resizing pictures
	Applying text wrapping

Topic 9 – Document layout

Word offers a variety of document views. Each view has particular benefits at different stages of document creation and editing. Changing the view of a document does not affect its printed appearance.

The five main document views are Print layout, Full Screen Reading, Web Layout, Outline and Draft.

> ***As an aside** … In Word 2003 and earlier, Draft view was known as Normal view, and Full Screen Reading view was known as Reading Layout view.*

Changing document views

In this topic you look at the variety of views available, then begin looking at document layout tasks.

How to: Change your view

1. Click on the required **View icon** (far right of Status bar)
   ~or~
   Display the View ribbon and click on the required button (Document Views group).

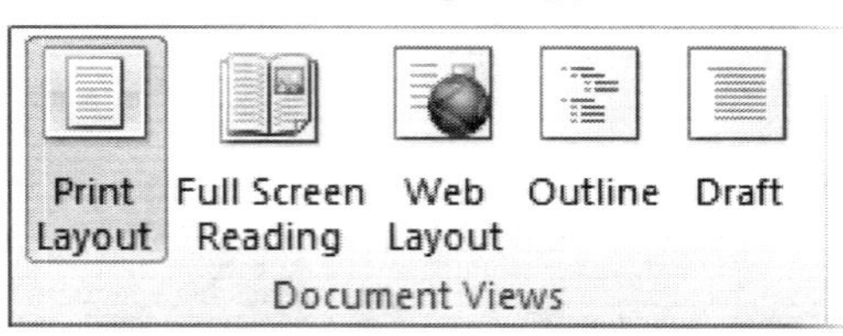

Document views

Print Layout	Shows a document as it will appear when printed, e.g. graphics in true position, headers and footers.
Full Screen Reading	This view presents your documents in 'book' format with two pages displayed at a time. Pages are rearranged to read well, so may not be what is printed. A number of useful tools for reviewing are also displayed. To exit click on the **Close** button.
Web Layout	This is a specialised view for creating web pages and other documents that you expect to be seen on screen rather than on paper. It wraps text to fit the window and places graphics on screen the same way they would appear in a browser.
Outline	This view is designed for working with long documents that use heading styles. It allows you to view selected headings and to quickly re-organise text. To exit click on the **Close Outline View** button.
Draft	This view is the fastest for entering plain text. However, you cannot see text in the margin areas (e.g. headers and/or footers), or some graphics in their true (printed) location (dependant on text wrapping option selected). Useful for very large documents where speed is an issue, and for working with section breaks

Hands-on exercise 47

In this exercise you practise using the variety of views available in Word.

- **Open** the document *Book reviews2*.
  The document opens in **Print Layout** view (see Status bar icon).

- View the document in **Draft** view.
  Note that you can no longer see the graphics.

- Return to **Print Layout** view.

- View the document in **Outline** view.
- Click on the **Close Outline View** button to exit the view.

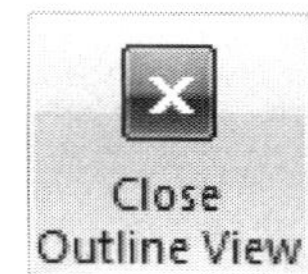

- View the document in **Full Screen Reading** view.

- Click on the **Close** button to exit the view (far right corner).
- **Close** your document.

Hints & tips

In Print Layout view you can hide the white space at the top and bottom of your page (header and footer area). Point to the space between two pages and the ***Hide White Space*** *icon is displayed (two arrows pointing inwards).*

Double-click and the white space disappears leaving a thick blank line to define pages. To return to full ***Print Layout*** *view, double-click on the thick black line.*

You can split your document window horizontally to give you two panes looking in on the same document. This is useful if you need to compare two different parts of a document side-by-side. Display the View ribbon, then click on the ***Split*** *button ((Window group). Click to position the split. Click on the* ***Remove Split*** *button to remove.*

Word can also assist you to compare two different documents side-by-side. Open both documents, display the View ribbon, then click on the ***View Side by Side*** *button (Windows group). To restore, click on the Windows group button to expand, then click back on* ***View Side By Side****. The* ***Synchronous Scrolling*** *option lets you scroll both documents together, and the* ***Reset Window Position*** *option allows you to restore a window if you have positioned side by side and then adjusted the window size.*

Adding page breaks, blank pages and cover pages

When you fill a page Word inserts an **automatic** page break and starts a new page. As you edit, Word is constantly recalculating and repositioning the automatic page breaks.

> **Serif typefaces**
>
> Serif, or "roman", typefaces are named for the features at the ends of their strokes. Times Roman and Garamond are common examples of serif typefaces. Serif fonts are probably the most used class in printed materials, including most books, newspapers and magazines.
>
> ....
>
> "Roman" and "oblique" are also terms used to differentiate between upright and italic variations of a typeface.

An automatic page break in Draft view

You can add your own page breaks. Page breaks that you add are called **manual** page breaks. You can delete manual page breaks but automatic page breaks are controlled by Word.

> ....Page Break..........¶
>
> **Serif·typefaces¶**
>
> Serif,·or·"roman",·typefaces·are·named·for·the·features·at·the·ends·of·their·strokes.·Times·Roman· and·Garamond·are·common·examples·of·serif·typefaces.·Serif·fonts·are·probably·the·most·used· class·in·printed·materials,·including·most·books,·newspapers·and·magazines.¶
> ¶
> "Roman"·and·"oblique"·are·also·terms·used·to·differentiate·between·upright·and·italic·variations·of· a·typeface.¶

A manual page break in Draft view (Show/Hide button on).
Note that with the insertion of a manual page break the automatic page break has disappeared as it is no longer needed.

In Draft view page breaks are shown as a line across the page as shown in the examples above. In Print Layout view a new page is displayed.

You can also insert an entire blank page into a document and a pre-designed cover page.

How to: Insert a manual page break

1. Click your insertion point where the break is required (usually at the beginning or end of a line of text).
2. Display the Insert ribbon, then click on the **Page Break** button (Pages group). [Page Break]
3. Information after the insertion point now starts a new page.

Page Break Ctrl Enter

How to: Insert a blank page

1. Click your insertion point where the blank page is required (usually at the end of a line of text).

2. Display the Insert ribbon, then click on the **Blank Page** button (Pages group). A blank page is inserted.

How to: Remove a manual page break/blank page

1. Switch on the **Show/Hide** button (Home ribbon).
2. Click the insertion point on the page break location (at the start of the line).

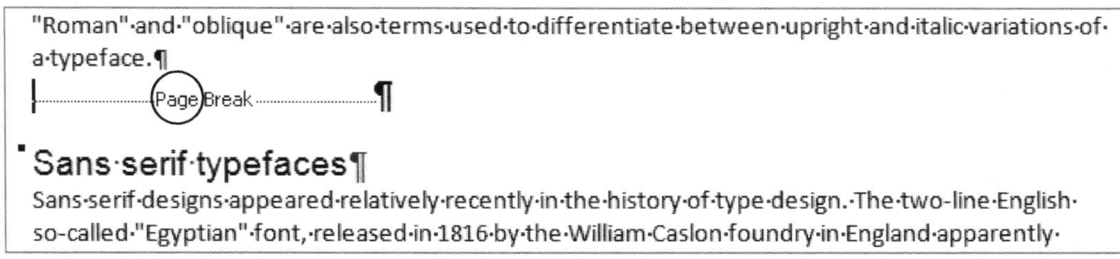

"Roman"·and·"oblique"·are·also·terms·used·to·differentiate·between·upright·and·italic·variations·of· a·typeface.¶

Page Break ¶

Sans·serif·typefaces¶

Sans-serif·designs·appeared·relatively·recently·in·the·history·of·type·design.·The·two-line·English· so-called·"Egyptian"·font,·released·in·1816·by·the·William·Caslon·foundry·in·England·apparently·

3. Press 

How to: Insert a cover page

1. Display the Insert ribbon, then click on the **Cover Page** button (Pages group).
2. Click on a pre-designed cover from the gallery of options presented.
3. Replace any sample text with your own text.

How to: Remove a cover page

1. Display the Insert ribbon, click on the **Cover Page** button (Pages group), then click on the **Remove Current Cover Page** option.

***As an aside** … If you insert another cover page it replaces any existing cover page.*

Hands-on exercise 48

In this exercise you practise inserting page breaks.

- **Open** the document *Biological engineering 2.*
- Scroll to the bottom of the document and click your insertion point at the front of the heading: For more information.

First, you insert a manual page break.

- Display the Insert ribbon, then click on the **Page Break** button (Pages group). The heading and following information now start a new page.
- Switch on the **Show/Hide** button (Home ribbon). Note the manual page break.
- View your document in **Draft** view.
- Note the automatic and manual page break.

- **Delete** the manual page break and any spare paragraph marker.
- Return to **Page Layout** view.
- Press Ctrl Home to return to the top of the document.
- Click your insertion point at the front of the heading: Department facilities.
- **Insert** a manual page break using the keyboard shortcut.
- **Delete** your page break.
- Again, click your insertion point at the front of the heading: *Department facilities*.

Next, you insert a blank page.

Blank Page

- Display the Insert ribbon, then click on the **Blank Page** button (Pages group). A blank page is inserted.
- View the manual page breaks in **Draft** view.
- **Delete** the page breaks and any spare paragraph markers.
- Return to **Print Layout** view.

Finally, you add a cover page.

- Press Ctrl Home to return to the top of the document.
- Display the Insert ribbon, then click on the **Cover Page** button (Pages group). Cover Page
- From the gallery of options presented, click on **Mod**.
- Scroll down and click on the marker: **Type the document subtitle**.
  Type: *The Bachelor of Science degree*
- Click on the marker: Pick the date.
  Click on the down-arrow. Click on the button **Today**.
  (If the date field is not suitable others can be inserted. You look at fields in more detail later.)
- Review your pages in **Print Preview**. Press Esc to exit.
- Switch off the **Show/Hide** button (Home ribbon).
- **Save** your changes.
- Leave your document open for the next exercise.

Changing document margins

Margins are the borders on all four sides of a page which surround your document's text. Your document's text is surrounded by the margins. Margins are not always empty. They can contain text, graphics, page numbers, etc.

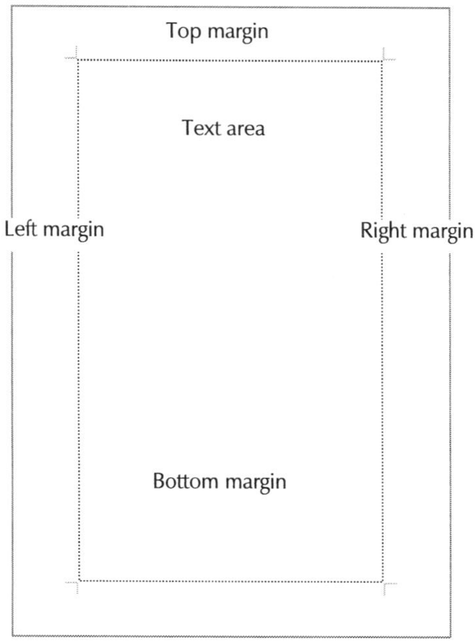

Margins on a page

How to: Change document margins (predefined options)

1. Display the Page Layout ribbon, then click on the **Margins** button (Page Setup group). Select a predefined option from the list presented. Margins are applied to the whole document.

How to: Change document margins (custom)

1. Display the Page Layout ribbon, click on the **Margins** button, then click on **Custom Margins** (Page Setup group). The Page Setup dialogue box is presented.

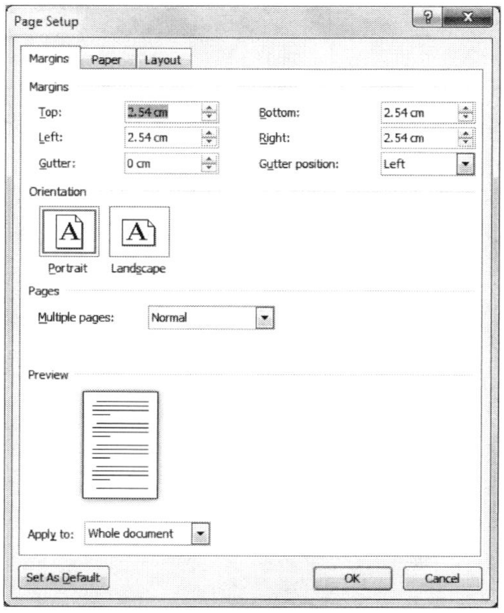

2. Ensure the Margins tab is selected, then adjust the margin settings (**Top**, **Bottom**, **Left**, **Right**) as required.
3. Under **Apply to** select **Whole Document** or **This point forward** or **Selected text**.
4. Click on **OK**.

> ***As an aside** … To change the margins for all new documents that you create, set your requirements in the dialogue box then click on **Set As Default**. Respond **Yes** to the question that follows.*

Hands-on exercise 49

In this exercise you practise changing document margins.

First, you select from the predefined options.

- Using the document *Biological engineering 2*, display the Page Layout ribbon, then click on the **Margins** button (Page Setup group).
- Click on the option **Narrow**. Note the effect to the margins throughout the document.
- Click on the option **Wide**. Note the effect to the margins.
- Click on the option **Normal**.

Next, you set custom margins.

- Display the Page Layout ribbon, click on the **Margins** button, then click on **Custom Margins** (Page Setup group).
  The Page Setup dialogue box is presented.
- Ensure the Margins tab is selected, then set the **Top** and **Bottom** margins to **3 cm**.
- Ensure under **Apply to** that the **Whole document** is selected.
- Click on **OK**.
- **Save** your changes.
- Leave your document open for the next exercise.

> ***As an aside** …Using the **This point forward** option for margins introduces a section break into your document which starts a new page with the new margin measurements, e.g. a continuation sheet for a letter. Use it instead of a page break when different margins are required.*

Changing page size

The standard Australian page size is A4 (210 x 297mm). Often a new installation of Word uses Letter size (American).

How to: Change standard page size

1. Display the Page Layout ribbon, then click on the **Size** button (Page Setup group). Select an option from the list presented.

> ***As an aside*** *... To change the page size default select* ***More Paper Sizes*** *from the list presented. Set your Paper size, then click on* ***Set As Default****. Respond* ***Yes*** *to the question that follows.*

Selecting a paper source

If your printer has a selection of paper sources, e.g. two paper trays, you can choose where various pages of your document are printed from.

> ***For example ...*** *You may select the first page of your letter to print from the top tray (which holds your letterhead paper), and the remaining pages from the second tray (which holds your continuation paper).*

How to: Choose a paper source

1. Display the Page Layout ribbon, click on the **Size** button, then click on **More Paper Sizes** (Page Setup group). The Page Setup dialogue box is presented. Ensure the Paper tab is active.

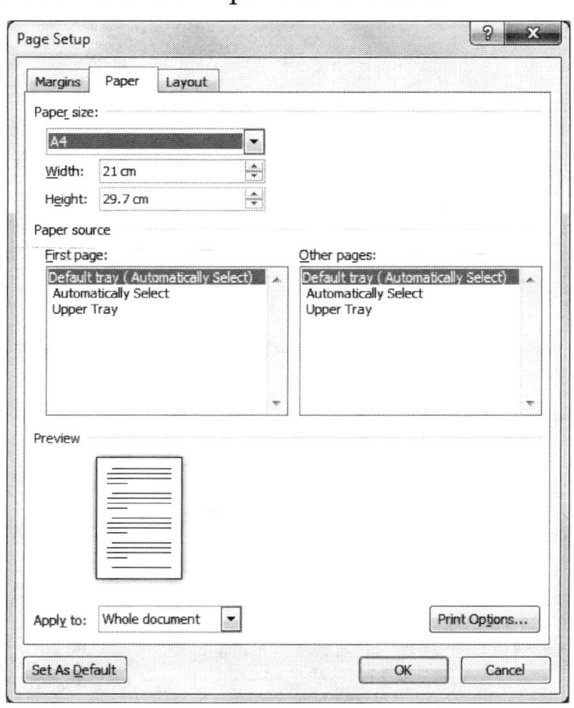

2. Click on the option required for the **First page**.
3. Click on the option required for the **Other pages**.
4. Click on **OK**.

> ***As an aside*** *... Options available in this dialogue box depend on the capabilities of the printer you are connected to. To change options for all new documents that you create, set your requirements then click on* ***Set As Default****. Respond* ***Yes*** *to the question that follows.*

Hands-on exercise 50

In this exercise you practise creating a document which requires a different orientation, page size and paper source.

First, you set the document orientation, paper size and source.

- Create a **new** blank document.
- Display the Page Layout ribbon, click on the **Orientation** button (Page Setup group), then click on **Landscape**.

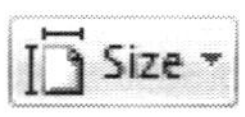

- Click on the **Size** button (Page Setup group). Select **A5**.
- Click on the **Size** button, then click on **More Paper Sizes** (Page Setup group). The Page Setup dialogue box is presented. Ensure the Paper tab is active.
- Set the **Paper Source**: **First page** to an option of your choice, i.e. Default Tray or Upper Paper Tray (if available).
- Click on **OK**.

Next, you create an invitation.

- Type the following attractively formatted using your own selection of fonts/sizes/paragraph spacing. Add a page colour and border.

- **Save** your document as *Invitation*.
- Leave your document open for the next exercise.

Setting tab stops

Tab stops are another useful document layout technique. By setting tab stops you can align text on a page in vertical columns. Setting tab stops is useful for short, simple columns of text (larger, more complex layouts should be aligned using the Tables feature.

There are four main types of tab stop *alignment* as illustrated below: **Left**, **Center**, **Right** and **Decimal**.

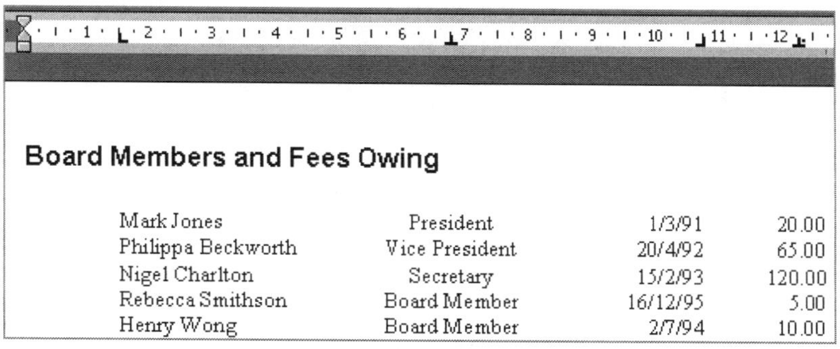

Board Members and Fees Owing

Mark Jones	President	1/3/91	20.00
Philippa Beckworth	Vice President	20/4/92	65.00
Nigel Charlton	Secretary	15/2/93	120.00
Rebecca Smithson	Board Member	16/12/95	5.00
Henry Wong	Board Member	2/7/94	10.00

A short list of information aligned using tabs: left, centre, right and decimal.

Default tab stops are already available in your document. These can be seen as dark grey markers on the grey bar running beneath your horizontal ruler (positioned approximately every centimetre). (If your ruler is not visible see **How to display your ruler** on next page.)

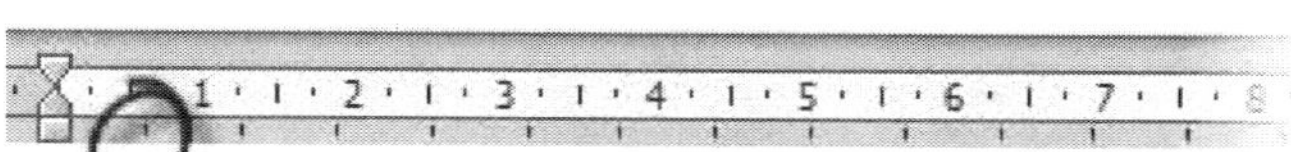

You can set your own tab stops, and the default tab stops are cleared.

To move to or align to a tab stop, you press **Tab** to produce a tab character.

How to: Display your ruler

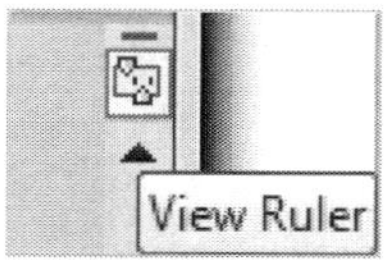

1. Click on the **View Ruler** icon at the top of the vertical scroll bar *~or~*
2. Display the View ribbon, then click on the **Ruler** option (Show/Hide group). (Both are on/off features.)

How to: Set tab stops using the ruler

1. Position the insertion point in the required paragraph *~or~* Select the required paragraphs.

2. Click on the **Tab** button on the far left of the horizontal ruler until the required tab is displayed.

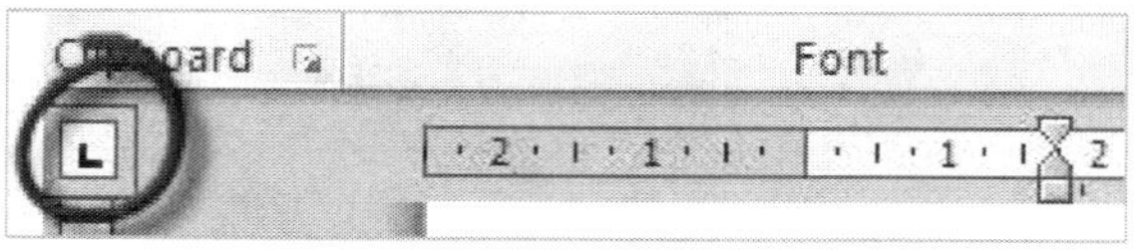

Tab stops

Left Tab	Text aligns to the left of the tabbed column.
Center Tab	Text aligns to the centre of the tabbed column.
Right Tab	Text aligns to the right of the tabbed column.
Decimal Tab	Text aligns to the decimal point in the tabbed column.

1. Click on the horizontal ruler at the measurement where the tab stop is required.
2. Repeat as necessary.

How to: Move a tab stop

1. Select the required paragraphs.
   (The tab settings are contained in each paragraph mark ¶.)
2. Drag the tab to a new position on the horizontal ruler.

As an aside ... *To clear a tab stop, select the required paragraphs and drag the tab marker off the ruler into the document area and release.*

Hands-on exercise 51

In this exercise you practise setting and moving tabs.

- Create a **new** blank document.
- Ensure the ruler is displayed.
- Remove any spacing after paragraphs.
- Type the following text: *Telephone list*
- Press Enter twice.
- Click on the **Tab** button on the far left of the horizontal ruler until the **Center Tab** displays.
- Click on the ruler at approximately **4**.
- Click on the **Tab** button on the far left of the horizontal ruler until the **Right Tab** displays.
- Click on the ruler at approximately **7**.
- Type the following: *Name*
  Press Tab
- Type the following: *Department*
  Press Tab
- Type the following: *Extension*
  Press Enter
- Complete the list as follows:
  (Press Enter after each line.)

Name	Department	Extension
Alessandra	Finance	2234
John	Personnel	2239
Sarah	Marketing	234

- Select the paragraphs of the tabbed list (including the headings).
- Keeping the paragraphs selected, drag the **Right Tab** along the ruler from **7** cm to approximately **8** cm.
- **Save** your document as *Telephone list.*
- **Close** your document.

Setting leader characters

Leader characters 'lead up' to tab stops. They can be used in a variety of ways including questionnaires and forms.

For example ...

Flight	**From**
QF4589	Sydney
AN5940	Sydney
AN5678	Sydney
AN533	Ballina

~or~

Where will you be going on your summer vacation this year? ....

Where did you go last year? ....

Leader characters can be dots, lines or dashes.

For example ...

Where will you be going on your summer vacation this year? ______________________

Where did you go last year? ____

Leader characters can also be used across the entire page.

....

(Tear off at the dotted line.)

To create leader characters you use the Tabs dialogue box.

How to: Set leader characters

1. Set your basic tabs using the ruler.
2. Position the insertion point in the required paragraph *~or~*
   Select the required paragraphs.
3. Display the Home ribbon, locate the **Paragraph** group, then click on the dialogue box launcher.
   The Paragraph dialogue box is displayed. Click on **Tabs**.
   The Tabs dialogue box is presented displaying any existing tab settings.

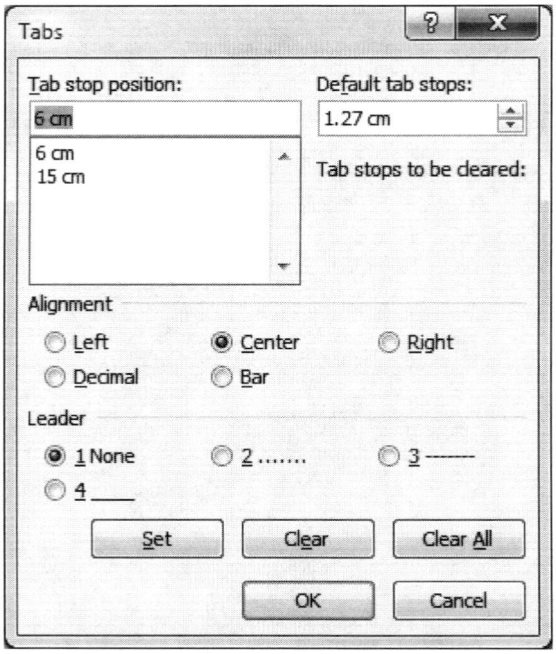

4. Click on the required **Tab stop position**.
5. Click on the **Leader** option of your choice.
6. Click on **Set**.
7. Repeat steps 5-7 as necessary.
8. Click on **OK**.

***As an aside** … You can also double-click on any existing tab stop on the ruler to display the Tabs dialogue box.*

Hands-on exercise 52

In this exercise you practise working with decimal tabs and leader characters.

- Create a **new** blank document.
- Remove any spacing after paragraphs.
- Type the following text: *Price information*
- Press Enter twice.
- Click on the **Tab** button on the far left of the horizontal ruler until the **Center Tab** displays.
- Click on the ruler at approximately **5.5**.

- Click on the **Tab** button on the far left of the horizontal ruler until the **Right Tab** displays.
- Click on the ruler at approximately **11**.
- Click on the **Tab** button on the far left of the horizontal ruler until the **Decimal Tab** displays.
- Click on the ruler at approximately **14**.
- Type the following: *Travel Number*
  Press Tab
- Type the following: *Destination*
  Press Tab
- Type the following: *Ticket Number*
  Press Tab
- Type the following: *Price*
- Press Enter
- Complete the list as follows (pressing Enter after each line):
  (Note how the decimal points line up with the Decimal Tab.)

Travel Number	Destination	Ticket Number	Price
XT2345	Canberra	345678-8	$234.89
ST378	Perth	789-9	$978.56
DF8900	Coolangatta	45678-8	$99.00
FT569	Sydney	1224-4	$239.77

Next, you add leader characters to the final tab stop (this could also have been set up before the information was typed).

- Select the data of the list (excluding the headings).
- Double–click any existing tab stop on the ruler.
  The Tabs dialogue box is presented.
- Click on the final **Tab stop position** (14 cm approximately).
- In the **Leader** section of the dialogue box, click on option **2**.
- Click on **Set**.
- Click on **OK**.
  This has set leader characters prior to the final tab stop.
- Select the first line of the list (that contains the headings Travel Number etc.).
- Drag the **Decimal Tab** along the ruler to approximately **14.5**.
- **Save** your document as *Price information*.

Finally, you set a tab with a solid leader to create a line.

- At the end of your document, press Enter twice.
- Double-click any existing tab stop on the ruler.

- Click on **Clear all** to remove all previously set tabs from the new paragraph.
- In **Tab stop position** type: *14*
- In the **Alignment** section, click on **Right**.
- In the **Leader** section, click on option **4**.
- Click on **Set**.
- Click on **OK**.
  This has set your tab at 14 cm with a leader character.
- Type: *How many holidays do you take each year?*
- Press [Tab]
- Press [Enter] twice.
- Type: *What is your favourite destination?*
- Press [Tab]

How many holidays do you take each year?_______________________________________

What is your favourite destination?____

- **Save** your changes.
- **Close** your document.

Consolidation task 12

In this task you create a letter using an organisational standards document as your guide.

- Print out the following document: *Org style guide – letter standard.*
- In a new blank document, type the following letter. Follow your style guide for the letter layout. Check you have setup the following as requested:
  - Margins and page size.
  - Font and font size.
  - Line spacing.
  - Space before/after paragraphs.

12 October 2010

Mr Simon Jones
The Manager
Harper and Watson Pty Ltd
54-56 Grange Road
CASULA NSW 2170

Dear Sir

Returned product

Please find enclosed the product discussed in our telephone conversation of today's date. I think you will agree that the quality for this product is not satisfactory and that it requires your immediate attention.

I would bring your attention to the following:

- defective seal
- poor quality finish
- damaged wrapping.

Please can you advise as soon as convenient the steps you will be taking to ensure that quality standards are maintained in the future.

Thank you for your assistance in this matter.

Yours faithfully

Kate Jackson
Senior Engineer
ABC Engineering Pty Ltd

KJ/sak

- Save your document as *Letter to Simon Jones*.
- Spell and grammar check your document.
- Preview your document.
- Print your document and proofread, correcting any errors.
- Save any changes.
- Close your document.

After this Consolidation task, do you feel confident... tick the appropriate box:

	Following a style guide
	Changing margins/page size
	Changing line/paragraph spacing
	Proof reading a document

Consolidation task 13

In this task you create an attractive flyer.

- In a new blank document, create the following flyer. Choose your own font/font size/paragraph and line spacing. (AutoCorrect will format the web address as a hyperlink.
- Set all margins to 2.54 cm. Start in a portrait orientation.

NZ Touring

Email: nztouring@provider.com

You can have the holiday of a lifetime touring around beautiful New Zealand! No timetables, no accommodation worries, just pristine countryside and spectacular scenery.

We offer a range of services starting from booking your flights, collecting you at the airport and setting you up in your own motor home.

We also offer:

- ✓ full insurance
- ✓ food starter pack
- ✓ van site or accommodation booking
- ✓ ski bookings.

We also provide free maps.

For more information on our holidays, contact us at:

100 Hilltop Road, SYDNEY NSW 2000 – Phone 02 1234 5000

- Set your orientation to landscape.
- Set your left and right margins to 5 cm, and then centre your text vertically on the page.
- Add a page border. Add a page colour.
- Save your document as *NZ flyer*.
- Spell and grammar check your document.

- Preview your document.
- Print your document and proofread, correcting any errors.
- Save any changes.
- Close your document.

After this Consolidation task, do you feel confident... tick the appropriate box:

	Changing orientation
	Changing margins
	Adding a page border

Consolidation task 14

In this task you create another flyer featuring Clip Art.

- In a new blank document, create the flyer on the following page. Choose your own font/ font size/paragraph and line spacing/Clip Art. Set a left margin of 5 cm. Use a tab stop to align the contact details at the bottom of the flyer.
- Save your document as *PA flyer*.
- Spell and grammar check your document.
- Preview your document.
- Print your document and proofread, correcting any errors.
- Save any changes.
- Close your document.

After this Consolidation task, do you feel confident... tick the appropriate box:

	Inserting Clip Art
	Changing margins
	Inserting tab stops

Virtual PA Services

Make magic happen!

Your Solution to Administrative, Secretarial and Organisational Problems

If you don't know which way to turn you need **Virtual PA Services** to help. Whether it's a 'one-off' situation or an occasional overload we're here to help.

Virtual PA Services
100 Hilltop Road
SYDNEY NSW 2000

Phone: 02 1242 4888
Fax: 02 1242 4887
Email: virtualpa@provider.com.au

Topic 10 – Inserting shapes & SmartArt

Word provides an extensive range of preconfigured shapes that you can insert into your documents. You can choose from a range of basic shapes, or more complex designs using SmartArt

Inserting basic shapes

These include squares, circles, lines and arrows, flowchart symbols and callouts.

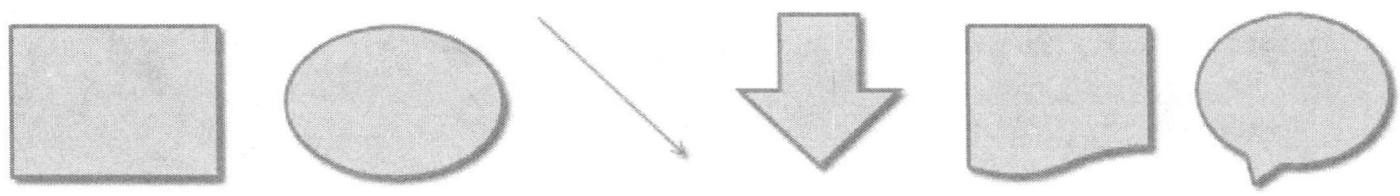

How to: Draw a shape

1. Display the Insert ribbon, then click on the **Shapes** button (Illustrations group). The Shapes gallery is presented.
2. Click on the shape you want to insert.
   Your mouse pointer becomes a cross +
3. Drag diagonally to create your shape.
   Note the Drawing Tools added on a new Format ribbon.
4. To **resize** a shape, select and drag on a sizing handle at the end or corner.
5. To **move** a shape, point to it and drag.
6. To **copy** a shape, press Ctrl and drag.
7. To **delete** a shape, select and press Delete.
8. To **rotate** a shape, select and drag the green rotate handle 

How to: Change a shape fill colour

1. Double-click on a shape to select (and display the Format ribbon).

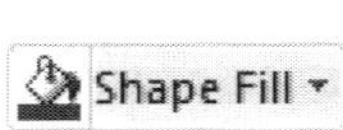

2. Click on the **Shape Fill** down-arrow (Shape Styles group), then click on the required colour.

How to: Change a shape outline

1. Double-click on a shape to select (and display the Format ribbon).

2. Click on the **Shape Outline** down-arrow (Shape Styles group), then click on the required colour.

How to: Change a shape effect

1. Double-click on a shape to select (and display the Format ribbon).

2. Click on the **Shape Effects** down-arrow (Shape Styles group), a list of options is presented. Point to the required category, then sub-category and click to select.

How to: Change a shape style

1. Double-click on a shape to select (and display the Format ribbon).
2. Click on the **More** button in the **Shape Styles** gallery (Shape Styles Group), click to select.

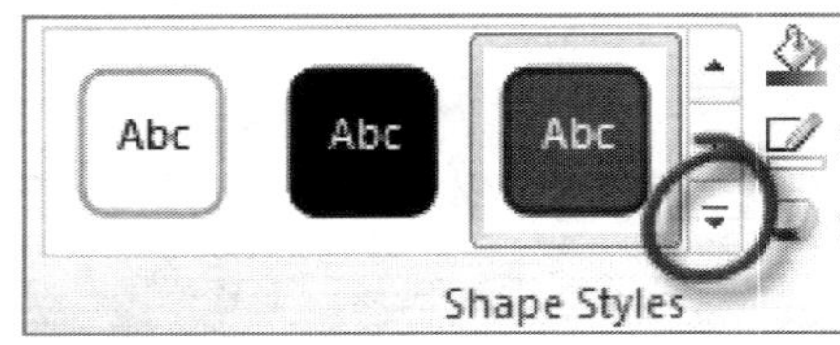

How to: Add text to a shape

1. Right-click on a shape, then click on **Add Text**.
2. Type the required text.

Hints & tips

What if I want to draw a square or a circle?

Press Shift as you draw with a Rectangle shape to draw a square.

Press Shift as you draw with the Oval shape to draw a circle.

What if I cannot keep my lines straight as I draw?

Press Shift as you draw a line to keep it straight.

What if I see an additional yellow sizing handle on an object?

Some of the shapes have an additional yellow adjust handle(s). Point to the handle and drag to change the depth or angle.

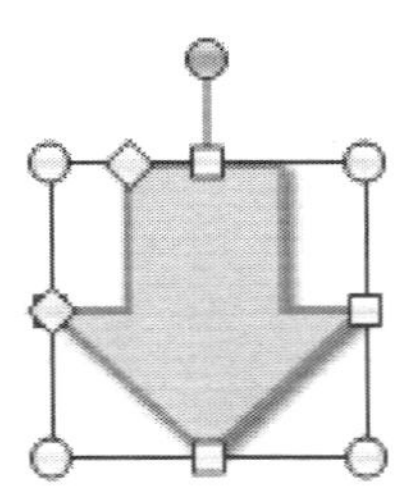

Hands-on exercise 53

In this exercise you practise creating shapes.

- Create a **new** blank document.
- Display the Insert ribbon, then click on the **Shapes** button (Illustrations group). The Shapes gallery is presented.
- Click on a rectangle.
  Your mouse pointer becomes a cross +
- Drag diagonally to create your shape.
  Note the Drawing Tools added on a new Format Ribbon.
- Draw some lines, rectangles, ovals, circles, squares, block arrows and callouts.

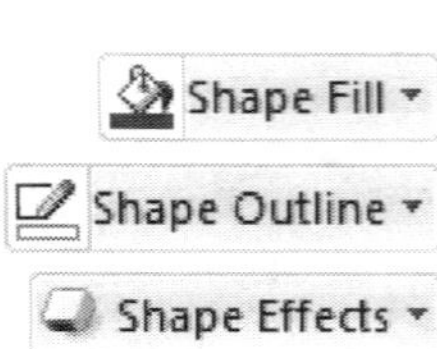

- Experiment with **Shape Fill**, **Shape Outline** and **Shape Effects**.
- Draw a star.

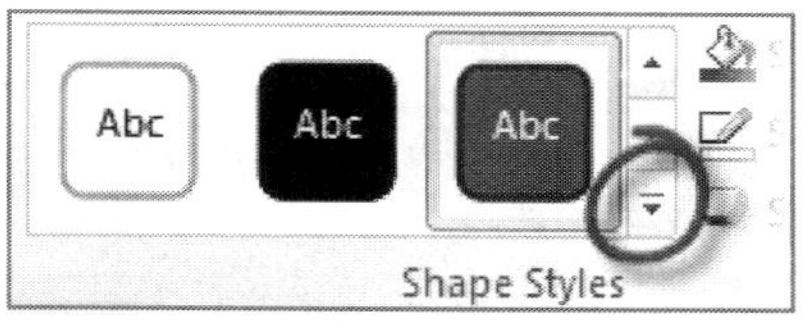

- Click on the **More** button in the **Shape Styles** gallery (Shape Styles Group), Click to select.
- Right-click on the star, then click on **Add Text**. Type: *Star buy!*
- **Save** your document as *Shapes example.*
- **Close** your document.

Selecting and working with multiple objects

You can work with several objects at the same time, e.g. to save time when applying colour or effects. You can also select several objects together in order to align or group them.

How to: Select multiple object

1. Click on the first object, then press Shift and click on subsequent objects.

How to: Align multiple objects

1. Select the required objects.

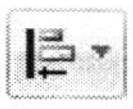

2. Display the Format ribbon, then click on the **Align** button (Arrange group), then click on the required alignment, e.g. Align Top.

How to: Group objects

1. Select the required objects.

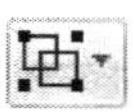

2. Display the Format ribbon, then click on the **Group** button (Arrange group), then click on **Group**.

***As an aside** … To ungroup, click on the **Ungroup** option, then click away from the group before you select an individual shape.*

Hands-on exercise 54

In this exercise you practise grouping objects.

- Create a **new** blank document.
- Create a star, circle and square. Make each object slightly smaller than the previous object.

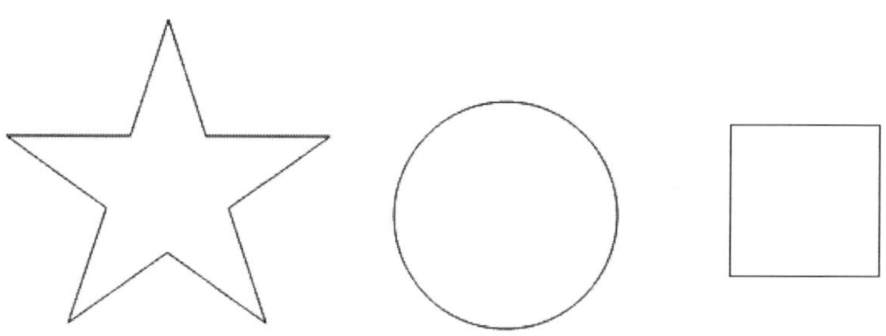

- **Save** the document as *Logo example.*

- Fill each object with a different colour.
- Select the three objects using the Shift key.
- Display the Format ribbon, then click on the **Align** button (Arrange group), then click on **Align Center**.
  Repeat and **Align Middle**.
- Keeping all the objects selected, click on the **Group** button (Arrange group), then click on **Group**.
- Next, you copy your group to another document.
- Keeping the group selected, click on the **Copy** button.
- **Open** the supplied document *Design*.
- Click on the **Paste** button.
- **Position** the group in the top left of the document.
- **Save** your changes.
- **Close** all open documents, saving if prompted.

Hints & tips

*To change the order of objects before grouping in the previous exercise, click on an object then click on the **Bring Forward**, **Send Backward** buttons (Arrange group).*

*Note also in the Arrange group the **Rotate** button, to rotate for flip objects.*

*In the Align list, the **Distribute Horizontally**, and **Distribute Vertically** options are useful to align objects in a row.*

Creating a text box

You can create text boxes to organise information, draw attention to important text, or attractively display headings. Word provides a simple text box or a number of pre-set alternatives.

How to: Insert an empty text box

1. Display the Insert ribbon, then click on the **Text Box** button (Text group). A gallery of options is presented.
2. Click on the required option. The text box is inserted into your document.
3. The text box appears surrounded with sizing handles and new Text Box Tools are available on the Format ribbon.
4. To enter text into your text box, simply begin typing. Format your text as required. You can also use the **Shape Fill/Outline/Effects** buttons (Format ribbon) to format your text box.

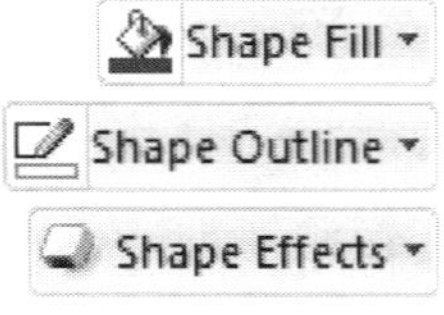

5. Drag on a sizing handle to re-size the box.
   To move the text box, simply point to *the border* and drag it to a new location.

Hands-on exercise 55

In this exercise you practise creating text boxes.

- **Open** the document *Book reviews2*.

- Display the Insert ribbon, then click on the **Text Box** button (Text group). A gallery of options is presented.
- Scroll down and click on the option **Tiles Sidebar**. The text box is inserted into your document.
- The text box appears surrounded with sizing handles and new Text Box Tools are available on the Format ribbon.
- Type the following text: *Three leadership books to kick start your thinking.*
- Keeping the text box selected, click on the **Shape Fill** button (Text Box Styles group), and select a different colour.

Next, you enter a simple text box to bring together a picture and caption.

- Click anywhere in the first body paragraph of text. (To ensure you don't insert a new text box inside the existing.)
- Click on the **Text Box** button (Text group).
  A gallery of options is presented.
- Click on the option **Simple Text Box**. The text box is inserted into your document.
- Keeping the text box selected, insert a **Clip Art** picture of a book (in reality this could be the actual book).
- Keeping the picture selected insert a caption which reads:
  Maverick!
- Resize the text box appropriately.
- Centre the caption in the text box.
- Point to the border of the text box and drag it beneath the Maverick! Heading.
- Apply a square text wrapping.
- Adjust the text box size as appropriate.
- Remove the **Shape Outline**.
- Review your document in Print Preview.
- Press Esc to exit **Backstage** view.
- **Close** the task pane.
- **Save** your changes.
- **Close** your document.

Creating an organisation chart using SmartArt

An organisation chart can be quickly and effectively incorporated into your document using **SmartArt**. SmartArt helps you to illustrate information and ideas with shapes, e.g. an organisation chart, steps in a process, cyclical information. Here you concentrate on an organisational chart.

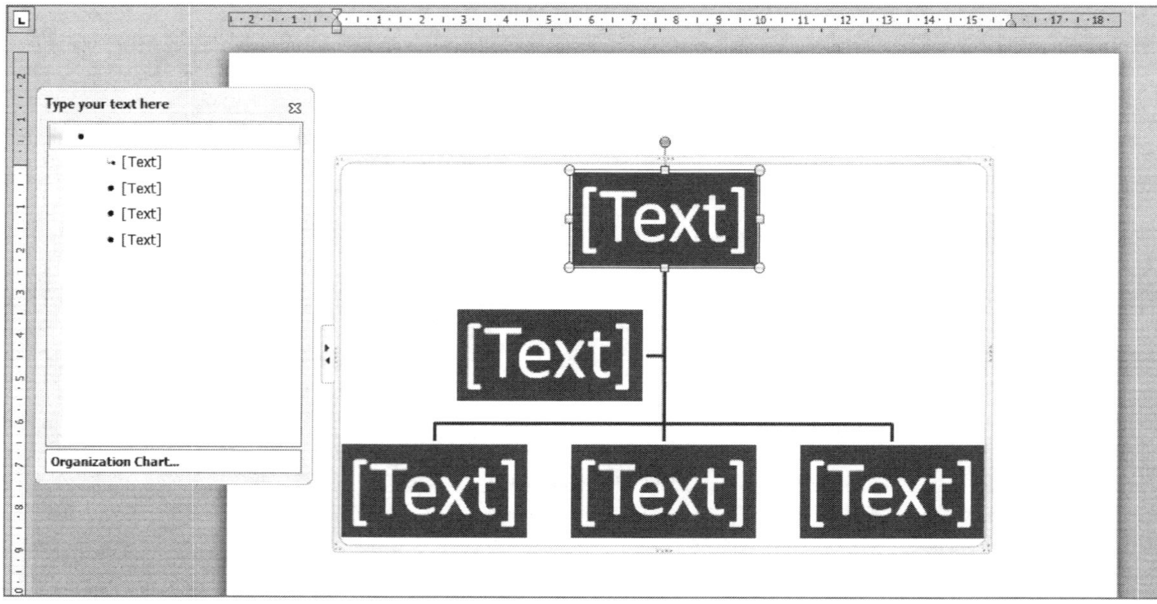

Organization Chart SmartArt with Text Pane to the left

How to: Insert an organisation chart

1. Click where you require the organisation chart.
2. Display the Insert ribbon, then click on the **SmartArt** button (Illustrations group). The Choose a SmartArt Graphic dialogue box is presented.
3. Click on the **Hierarchy** option in the left pane, then click on **Organization Chart** (first option) from the **List** in the right pane.

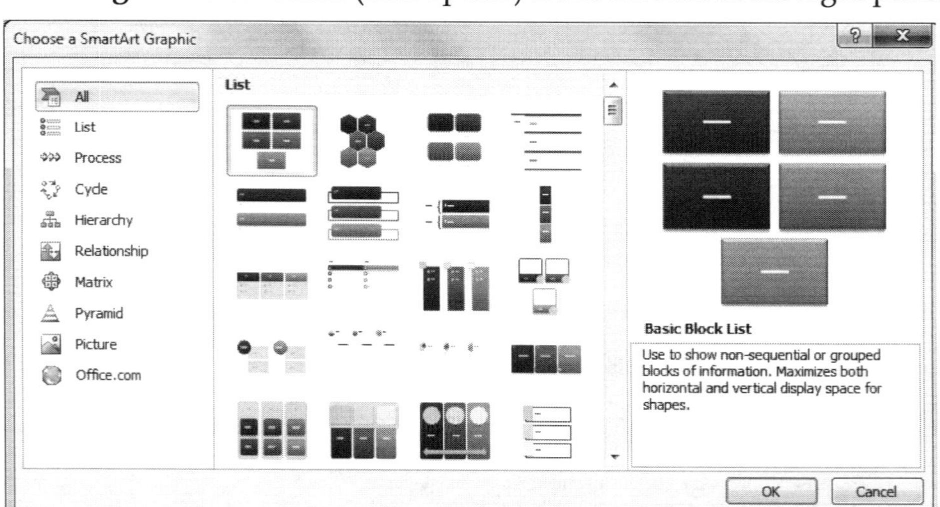

4. Click on **OK**.
   The SmartArt shape is inserted into your document. Alongside the shape is the Text Pane, which can help when entering text. Two new ribbons are displayed with SmartArt Tools (Design and Format). The Design ribbon is active.

How to: Add text

1. Click in a shape and begin typing *~or~*
   Click in the **Text Pane** against a bullet point and begin typing. (Your font size adjusts based on the text entered).

> ***As an aside** … If you close the Text Pane you can re-open by clicking on the **Text Pane** button (Create Graphic group, Design ribbon). You can drag the Text Pane around using the Title bar.*

How to: Insert a shape

1. Click on the shape you want to insert before/after, etc.

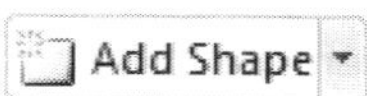

2. Click on the Design ribbon, then click on the **Add Shape** down-arrow (Create Graphic group).
3. Click on the required option, e.g. Add Shape After.

How to: Adjust the branch layout

1. Click on the required shape.

2. Click on the **Layout** button (Create Graphic group).
3. Click on the required option, e.g. Standard.

How to: Delete a shape

1. Click on the shape you want to delete, then press 

How to: Change the chart style

1. Double-click on the chart.
2. On the Design ribbon, point to any option in the **SmartArt Styles** gallery to see the design effect previewed on your chart. Click on the **More** button to display the full gallery of styles.

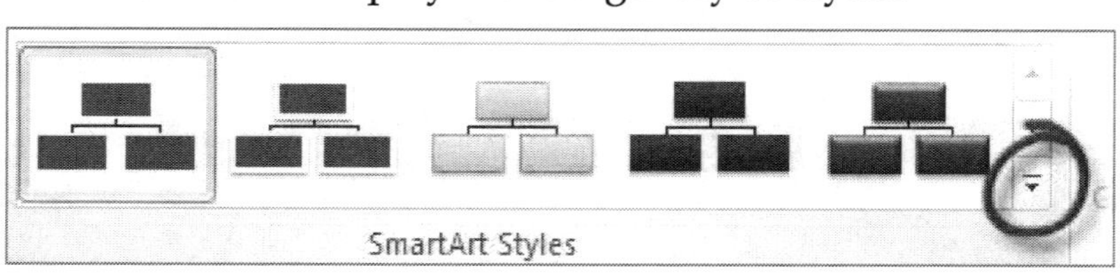

3. Click on the required style to apply.

How to: Change chart colours

1. Double-click on the chart.
2. On the Design ribbon, click on the **Change Color** button, then click on a colour of your choice.

How to: Position a chart

1. Double-click on the chart.
2. Drag the chart by the border (to another paragraph marker) *~or~*
   Display the Format ribbon, click on the **Arrange** button, then click on **Position**.

3. Click on the required position.

Hands-on exercise 56

In this exercise you practise creating an organisation chart in a document.

- Create a **new** blank document.
- Change the document to a landscape orientation.

- Display the Insert ribbon, then click on the **SmartArt** button (Illustrations group). The Choose a SmartArt Graphic dialogue box is presented.
- Click on the **Hierarchy** option in the left pane, then click on **Organization Chart** (first option) from the **List** in the right pane.
- Click on **OK**.
  The SmartArt shape is inserted into your document.
- Click in the first shape and type: *Richard Mortimer*
  Press Shift Enter then type the title: *Managing Director*
- Click in the shape on the next level and type: *Joseph Hope*
  Press Shift Enter then type the title: *Special Projects*
- Click in the first shape on the next level and type: *Tim Wallis*
  Press Shift Enter then type the title: *Finance Manager*
- Click in the next shape across and type: *Susan Hong*
  Press Shift Enter then type the title: *Production Manager*
- Click in the next shape across and type: *James Harris*
  Press Shift Enter then type the title: *Logistics Manager*
- **Save** your document as *Management structure*.

Hands-on exercise 57

In this exercise you practise adding to the organisational chart. First, you add further Production employees.

- Using the presentation *Management structure,* click on the **Logistics Manager**.

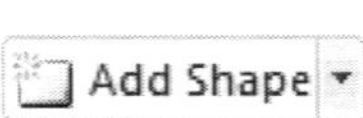

- Click on the Design ribbon, then click on the **Add Shape** down-arrow (Create Graphic group).
- Click on the option **Add Shape After**.
- In the new shape, type: *Sally Lynam*
  press Shift Enter then type the title: *Sales Manager*
- Click on the **Finance Manager**.
- Click on the **Add Shape** down-arrow, then click on **Add Shape Below**.
- In the new shape, type: *Charles Shimmer*
  press Shift Enter then type the title: *Project Accountant*
- Click on the **Finance Manager** again.
- Click on the **Add Shape** down-arrow, then click on **Add Shape Below**.

- In the new shape, type: *Jennifer Bridges*
  press Shift Enter then type the title: *Project Accountant*
- Click on the **Finance Manager** again.
- Click on the **Layout** button, then click on **Standard**.
- To change the chart style, point to any option in the **SmartArt Styles** group (Design ribbon) to see the design effect previewed on your chart. Click on the **More** button to display the full gallery of styles.

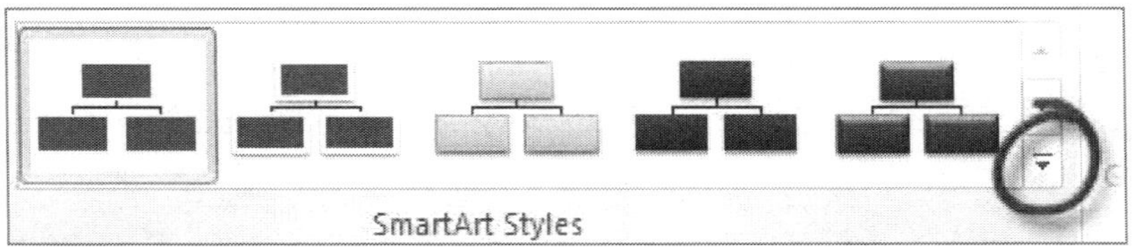

- Click on the style **3-D Polished**.
- To change the chart colour, click on the **Change Color** button and click on a colour of your choice.

- To position the chart, click on the **Arrange** button, then click on **Position**, then click on the middle centre option.
- **Save** your changes.
- **Close** your document.

Hints & tips

You can use these SmartArt skills to create different SmartArt graphics. Investigate the Lists group and the Pictures group for instance.

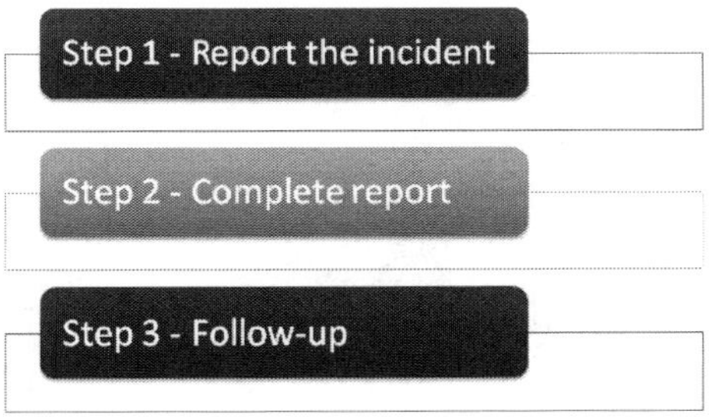

Graphics created from the List group

Graphics created from the Picture group

Consolidation task 15

You have been asked to create an organisational chart to display the new company structure and who is responsible.

- In a new blank document, create the following organisational chart (Hint: Name and title organisational chart).
- Choose your own font and change the colour of the chart.
- Save your document as *Organisational Chart*.
- Spell and grammar check your document.
- Print your document and proofread, correcting any errors.
- Save any changes.
- Close your document.

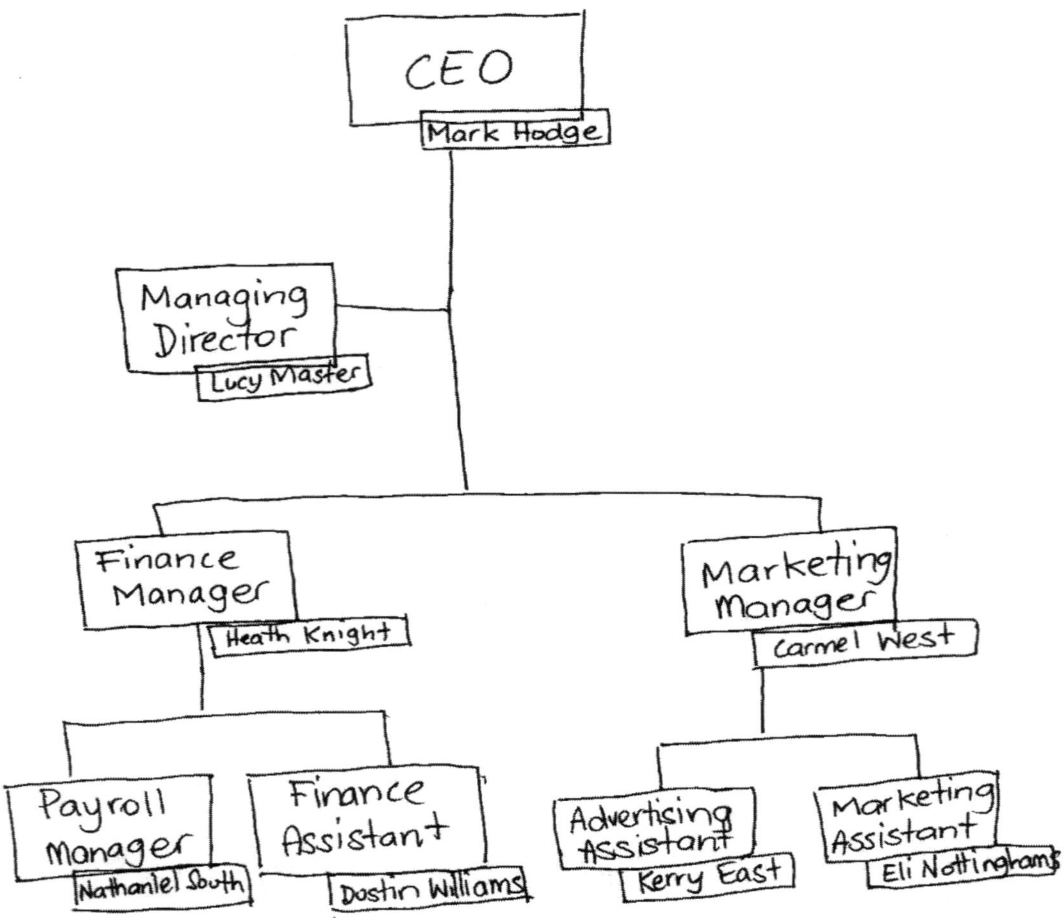

After this Consolidation task, do you feel confident... tick the appropriate box:

	Inserting SmartArt to create organisational charts
	Adding levels
	Adding text to SmartArt
	Changing colours

Terms & concepts review

- How do you add text to a shape?

  ____

  ____

- How do you draw a **square**?

  ____

  ____

- How do you draw a **straight** line?

  ____

  ____

- How do you select **multiple** objects?

  ____

  ____

- What feature do you use to create an **organisational chart**?

  ____

  ____

Topic 11 – Creating newsletter layouts

Text for newsletters is often best presented in **newspaper-style** columns. In these columns text flows continuously from the bottom of one column to the top of the next.

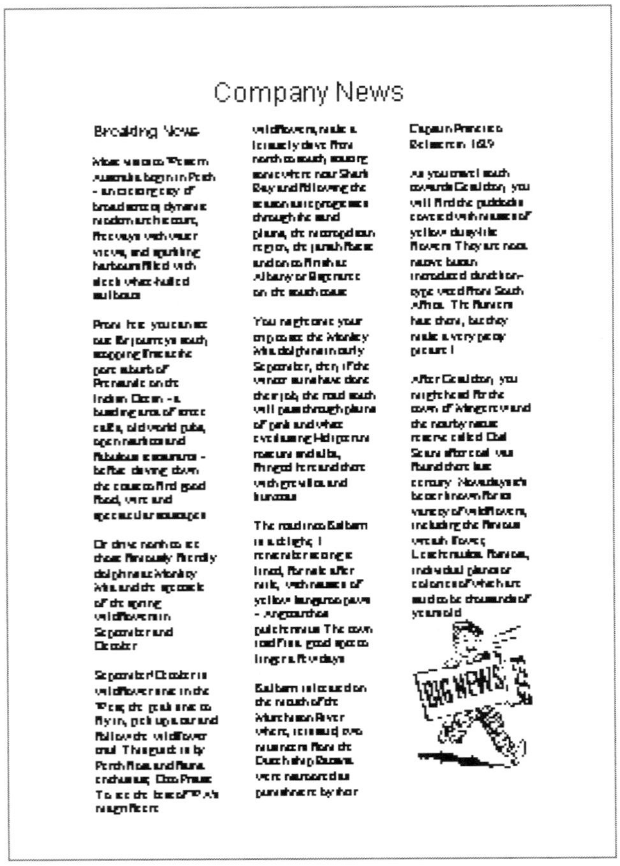
Company News

A three-column newsletter layout

Creating newspaper-style columns

Creating columns is a very simple process, and you can easily change your mind about how many columns you use.

How to: Create columns of equal width

1. Display the Page Layout ribbon, then click on the **Columns** button (Page Setup group).
2. Click on the required number of columns from the list presented.

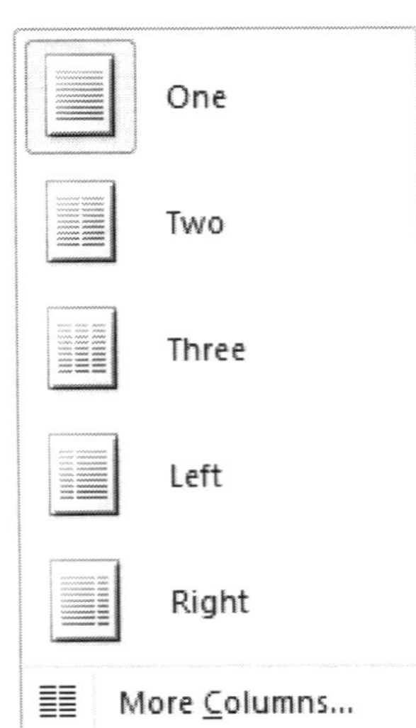

Hands-on exercise 58

In this exercise you create a recycling newsletter.

- **Open** the document *Recycling news.*
- Display the Page Layout ribbon, then click on the **Columns** button (Page Setup group).
- Click on the **Two** from the list presented.
- **Zoom** your document to view a single page. This is a useful way to review your column layout.
- Click on the **Columns** button, then change to **Three** columns.
- Change your **Zoom** back to **100%**
- Click on the **Columns** button, then change back to **Two** columns.
- **Save** your changes.

Breaking a column

As mentioned earlier, text in newspaper-style columns flows continuously from the bottom of one column to the top of the next. However, you may want to adjust the point in the text where one column ends and the next column begins.

> ***For example ...*** *A sub-heading may appear at the bottom of a column with its associated text at the top of the next column. It would look more attractive if a column break forced the sub-heading to the top of the next column.*

How to: Insert a column break

1. Position your insertion point where the column break is required.
2. Display the Page Layout ribbon, click on the **Breaks** button (Page Setup group), then click on **Column**.

Column break Ctrl Shift Enter

How to: Delete a column break

1. Click on the **Show/Hide** button (Home ribbon), to display non-printing characters.
2. Click on the Column Break marker, then press Delete.

Hands-on exercise 59

In this exercise you insert a column break to improve the presentation of your newsletter.

- Using the document *Recycling news,* position your insertion point before the heading: Disposal of Other Waste (bottom of first column).
- To force a column break , press Ctrl Shift Enter
  The column break forces the paragraph to the top of the next column.
- Click on the **Show/Hide** button.
- Scroll to the bottom of the page and note the Column Break marker.
- Click again on the **Show/Hide** button.
- **Zoom** your document to view a single page.
- Change your **Zoom** back to **100%**.
- **Save** your changes.
- **Close** your document.

As an aside *... When working with columns, ensure you use paragraph spacing (before/after) to space paragraphs. This avoids stray paragraph markers appearing at the tops of columns.*

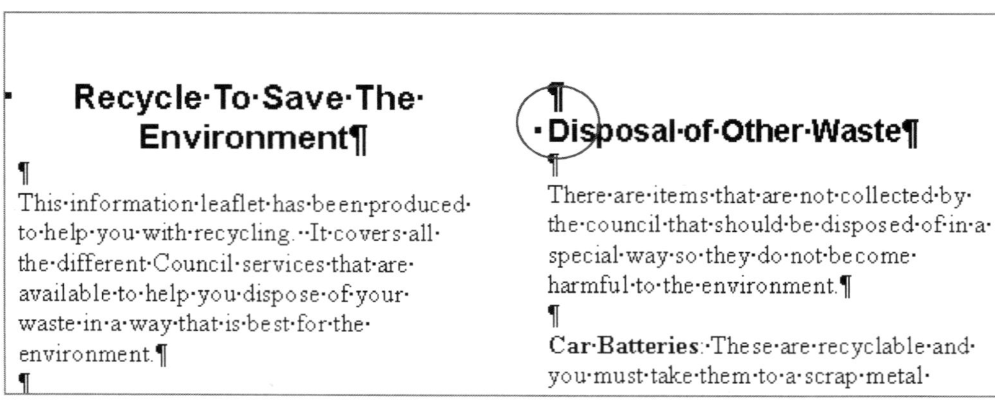

Recycle·To·Save·The·Environment¶

¶
This·information·leaflet·has·been·produced·to·help·you·with·recycling.··It·covers·all·the·different·Council·services·that·are·available·to·help·you·dispose·of·your·waste·in·a·way·that·is·best·for·the·environment.¶
¶

¶
Disposal·of·Other·Waste¶
¶
There·are·items·that·are·not·collected·by·the·council·that·should·be·disposed·of·in·a·special·way·so·they·do·not·become·harmful·to·the·environment.¶
¶
Car·Batteries:·These·are·recyclable·and·you·must·take·them·to·a·scrap·metal·

Creating unequal columns

You are not limited to columns of equal width. You can create columns of unequal width. You can also specify exact column width measurements.

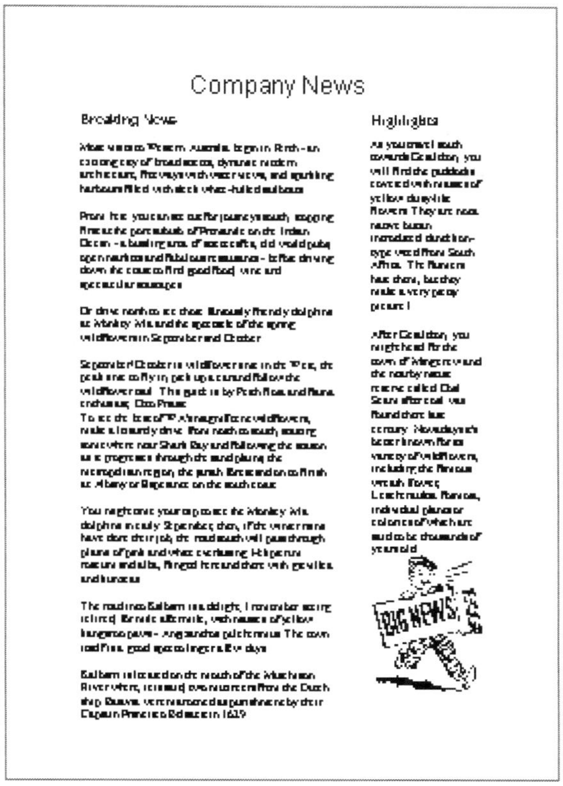
Company News

Breaking News

Highlights

Columns of unequal width (one is wide, the other is narrow)

How to: Create columns of unequal width

1. Display the Page Layout ribbon, click on the **Columns** button (Page Setup group), then click on **More Columns**.
   The Columns dialogue box is presented.

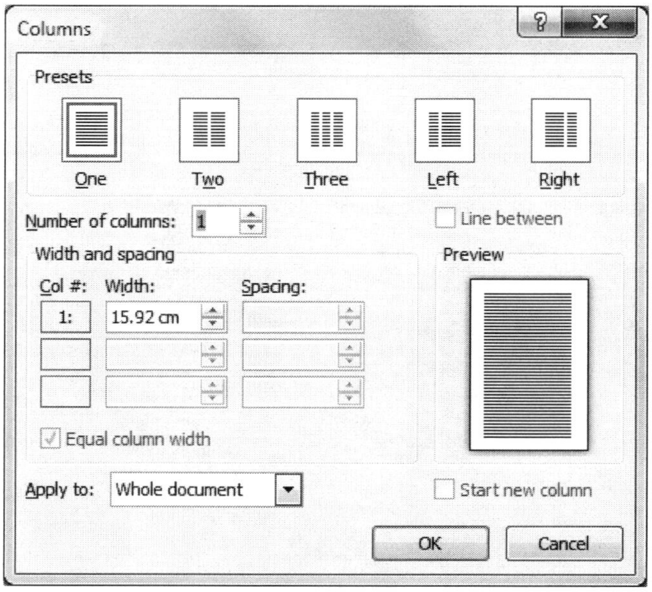

2. Click on a column format under **Presets** *~or~*
   Type the **Number of columns** and their **Width and spacing**.
3. Click on **OK**.

> ***As an aside ...*** *Columns can also have a vertical line between them. This can make your text easier to read, especially if there is limited white space between the columns. Click on the option* ***Line between*** *in the Columns dialogue box.*

Hands-on exercise 60

In this exercise you change the layout of your newsletter to include columns of uneven widths, and a line between the columns.

- Using the document *Recycling news*, ensure you are at the top of the document.
- **Zoom** your document view a single page.

- Display the Page Layout ribbon, click on the **Columns** button (Page Setup group), then click on **More Columns**. The Columns dialogue box is presented.
- Under **Presets**, click on the column format **Right**.
- Click on the option **Line between**.
- Click on **OK**.
- Insert a column break before the heading: Ways to Reduce Waste
  The column break forces the paragraph to the top of the next column (which is on the next page).
- Change your view to two pages.
- Return the document to an equal two-column layout.
- Change your **Zoom** back to **100%**.
- Delete the column break prior to the heading:
  Ways to Reduce Waste
  (show your non-printing characters first).
- Switch off your non-printing characters.
- **Save** your changes.

Changing columns for part of a document (Section breaks)

You may be required to change the number of columns displayed mid-way through a document.

> ***For example ...*** *The following page changes from a two-column layout to a three-column layout.*

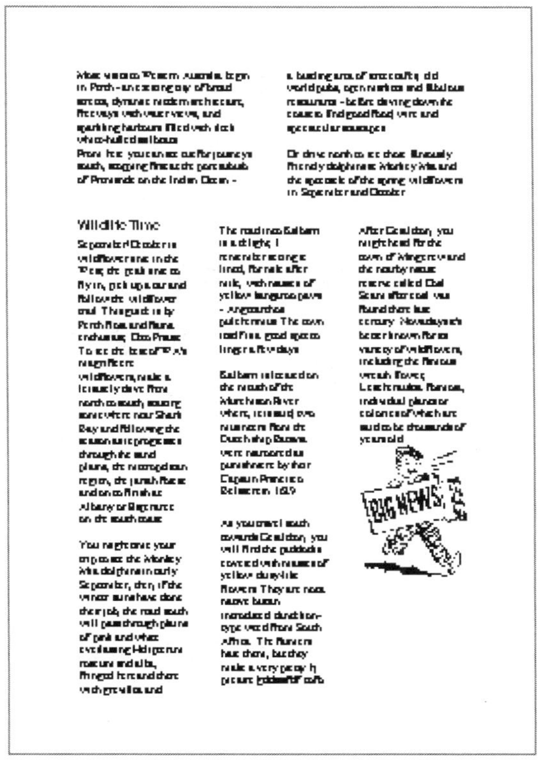

To change the number of columns mid-way through a document, you need to divide the document into **sections** by inserting **section breaks**.

In a document containing no section breaks, all document formatting (e.g. number of columns, margins, page orientation, headers and footers, etc.) flows through the entire document. By inserting section breaks, you create 'compartments' that can contain different document formatting, e.g. you can have a two-column layout in one section, followed by a three-column layout in the next section.

A section break displays as a double-dotted line when the **Show/Hide¶** button is activated.

There are four different types of section break: **Next page**, **Continuous**, **Even page** and **Odd page**.

A **Continuous** section break starts the new section on the same page. This is most commonly used for multiple column layouts.

The **Next page, Even page** and **Odd page** section breaks force the next section onto the next page. **Next page** is most commonly used where the following page has a different page layout, e.g. landscape orientation. **Even page** and **Odd page** section breaks are most commonly used for books, where new chapters must start on a particular odd or even page.

When creating sections it is a good idea to display section numbers on the Status bar.

How to: Display section numbers on the Status bar

1. Right-click on the Status bar. The Customize Status bar list is presented.
2. Click on **Section** in the list presented. The section number is added to the start of the Status bar.
3. Click anywhere in the document to close the list.

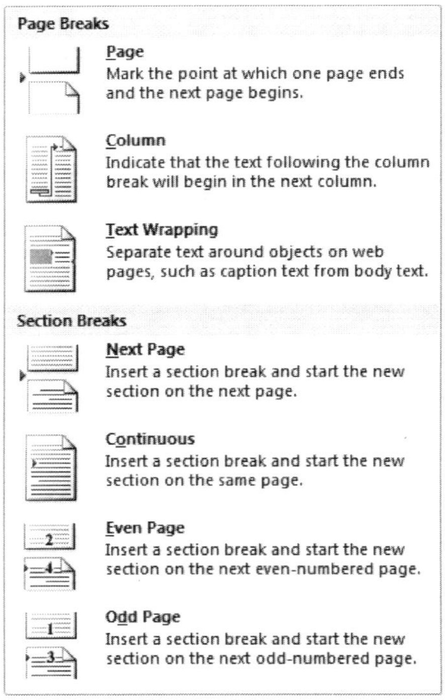

How to: Insert a section break

1. Position your insertion point where you want the new section to begin.
2. Display the Page Layout ribbon, then click on the **Breaks** button (Page Setup group).

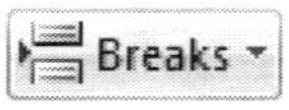

3. Under Section Breaks in the list presented, click on a section break option.

How to: Change the number of columns

1. Divide your document with **Continuous** section breaks.
2. Click in a section.
3. Click on the **Column** button, and select the number of columns for that section.

Hands-on exercise 61

In this exercise you create document sections, each section containing a different number of columns.

- Using the document *Recycling news*, right-click on the Status bar. The Customize Status bar list is presented.
- Click on **Section** in the list presented. The section number is added to the start of the Status bar.
- Click anywhere in the document to close the list.
- Position your insertion point at the start of the heading: Recycling Collection

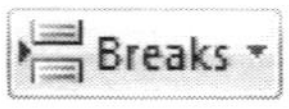

- Display the Page Layout ribbon, then click on the **Breaks** button (Page Setup group).
- Under Section Breaks in the list presented, click on the **Continuous** section break option.
- Show your non-printing characters. Note the location of the double dotted line.

Next, you change the number of columns in the second section.

- Ensure your insertion pointer is located in the second section of the document. (Check that the Status bar at the bottom of your screen reads Section 2.)

- Click on the **Columns** button and select **Three** columns.

- **Zoom** your document to a single page.
- Change your **Zoom** back to **100%**.

Next, you require the document heading to extend across all the columns. (This is sometimes referred to as a **banner** or **headline**.)

- Return to the top of the document.
- Click your insertion point beneath the document heading, at the start of the paragraph: This information leaflet …

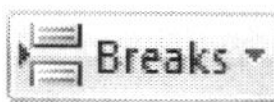

- Click on the **Breaks** button and insert a **Continuous** section break. You now have three sections.
- Click anywhere in Section 1. (Check the Status bar.)
- Click on the **Columns** button and select **One** column.
  The heading now appears in its own one-column section and the centre formatting applied to the heading text means that it is centred above the columns.

Finally, you insert another column break.

- Click to position your insertion point prior to the text in the first section commencing: The Council is committed…

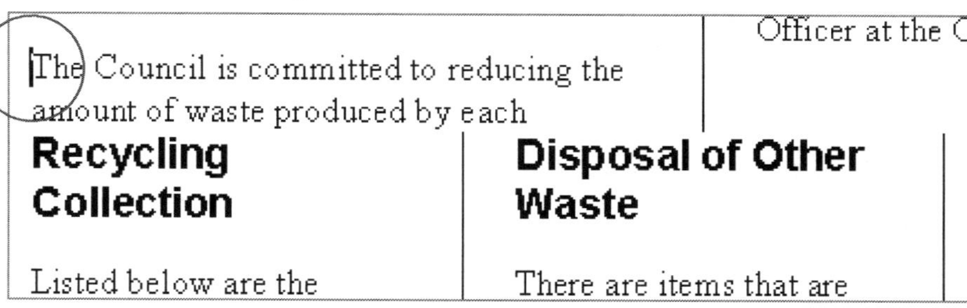

- Insert a **Column** break.
- Hide your non-printing characters.
- **Save** your changes.

Hints & tips

You may be left with a final column that is only partially filled. To overcome this, simply insert a continuous section break at the end of the final column. This will 'balance' the text across all the columns. This can also be used to balance text in a section.

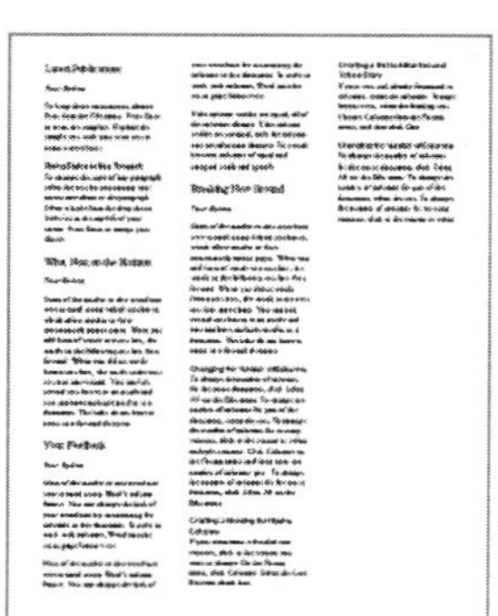

Text before balancing

Text after balancing

Deleting a section break

Sections breaks can be removed - just like page breaks - if they are no longer required. However, it is useful to be aware of how section formatting is stored before attempting to delete a section break.

A section break stores the formatting for the section **above** the break. If you remove a section break, the section takes on the formatting of the section **below** it.

> ***For example ...*** *Your document is formatted into two sections; the first containing a two-column layout, the second a three-column layout. If you delete the section break separating the two sections, your document will be left in a three-column layout.*

How to: How to: Delete a section break

1. Display your non-printing characters.
2. Click on the section break (double dotted line).
3. Press Delete

Hands-on exercise 62

In this exercise you delete section breaks to observe how these breaks store formatting for a section.

- Using the document *Recycling news,* display your non-printing characters.
- Return to the top of the document.
- If you were to delete the section break under the heading: Recycle to Save the Environment
  - How many columns would the first section have?

  ____

Now, you try it.

- At the top of your document, click on the section break *after* the heading: Recycle to Save the Environment (may actually display alongside the heading).
- Press Delete
  Notice that the heading section (Section 1) adopts the formatting of the section below, i.e. a two-column format.
- If you were to delete the section break before the heading: Recycling Collection:
  - How many columns would the first section have?

  ____

  - How many columns would the second section have?

  ____

Now, you try it.

- Click on the section break *before* the heading: Recycling Collection

- Press Delete
  Your entire document is now in a three-column layout.
- Delete the two column breaks.
- Create a two-column layout.
- Hide your non-printing characters.
- Insert a column break prior to the heading: Disposal of Other Waste
- **Save** your changes.
- **Close** your document.

Terms & concepts review

- Why might you need to use a **column break**?

  ____

- What do you need to **insert** to change the number of columns mid-way through a document?

  ____

- How do you display **section numbers** on the Status bar?

  ____

  ____

Consolidation task 16

In this task you create an attractive newsletter.

- Open the document *Canberra spring*.
- Format the document with a two-column layout
- Apply **Heading 1** style to the document heading.
- Apply **Heading 2** style to the headings:
  Floriade Packages
  Winter Packages
  A Night with the Stars
- Apply **Heading 3** style to the headings:
  Three-in-one ticket
  Park Hotel
- The paragraphs in the document are currently formatted with the style **Body Text**. Update this style to create justified text.
- Save your changes.
- Display your non-printing characters.
- Insert a continuous section break beneath the document heading. (Click before the **S** of the text 'Spring is Floriade …'.)
- Click in Section 1 and format the section as a one-column layout. Centre align the text in the column.
- Go to the end of the document, press Enter and type your name. Press Enter again.
- Insert a continuous section break to balance the columns on the final page.
- Review your document in Print Preview.
- Print your document.
- Save your changes.
- Close your document.

After this Consolidation task, do you feel confident... tick the appropriate box:

	Inserting columns
	Updating styles
	Inserting section breaks
	Inserting continuous breaks

Topic 12 – Working with multi-page documents

When working with documents that consist of many pages, you will want these documents to be both attractive and easy to read. Readability can be enhanced by using:

- headers & footers
- section breaks
- cross-references
- footnotes and endnotes.

Adding a basic header & footer

One of the most powerful Word features available when working with multi-page documents is headers and footers. These can be used for further information and to direct the reader, e.g. using page numbers. Word offers a variety of pre-designed layouts for headers and footers, or you can create your own and align text using pre-existing tab stops at the centre and far right.

How to: Add a pre-set header & footer

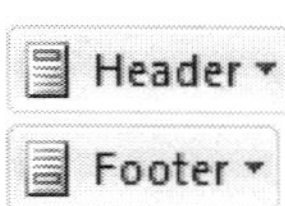

1. Display the Insert ribbon, then click on the **Header** or **Footer** button (Header & Footer group). A gallery of options is presented.
2. Click on the required option. Your header/footer is displayed. The insertion point is located in an area of your document reserved for your header/footer, and the body of the document appears greyed. A new Design ribbon is displayed with Header and Footer Tools.
3. Click on any of the '**Type text**' markers and insert your own text.

4. Click on the **Go to Header/Go to Footer** buttons (Navigation group) to move between header/footer.
5. Click on the **Header/Footer** buttons to re-display the gallery options (Header & Footer group - start of ribbon).
6. Click on the **Close Header and Footer** button to exit.

How to: Add your own header & footer

1. Display your document and double-click on the header or footer area (even if blank).
2. Your header/footer is displayed. The insertion point is located in an area of your document reserved for your header/footer, and the body of the document appears greyed. A new Design ribbon is displayed with Header and Footer Tools. Type or insert your details.

3. Click on the **Go to Header/Go to Footer** buttons (Navigation group) to move between header/footer.
4. Click on the **Close Header and Footer** button to exit.

As an aside *...You can also double-click in the document area to exit a header or footer.*

How to: Display/edit a header & footer

1. Display the Insert ribbon, then click on the **Header** or **Footer** button (Header & Footer group).
2. Click on the **Edit Header/Edit Footer** option.
   Your header/footer is presented and the Design ribbon displayed.

As an aside *...You can also double-click on an existing header and footer area to edit.*

How to: Insert a page number

1. Display the header or footer and position your insertion point.
2. Click on the **Page Number** button (Design ribbon, Header & Footer group). A number of position options are presented.
3. Point to the required position, e.g. Bottom of Page, then click on the required option.

How to: Remove a header & footer

1. Display the Insert ribbon, then click on the **Header** or **Footer** button (Header & Footer group).
2. Click on the **Remove Header/Remove Footer** option.
   Your header/footer is removed.

As an aside *... To remove you can also display, select any text and press* Delete

Hands-on exercise 63

In this exercise you practise inserting a pre-set header and footer.

- **Open** the document *Superfood annual report.*
- Display the Insert ribbon, then click on the **Header** button (Header & Footer group). A gallery of options is presented.
- Click on the option **Blank (Three Columns)**. Your header with markers is displayed. The insertion point is located in the header and the body of the document appears greyed. A new Design ribbon is displayed with Header and Footer Tools.
- Click on the first '**Type text**' marker and type: *SuperFood*
  Click on the second '**Type text**' marker and press Delete.
  Click on the third '**Type text**' marker and type: *Annual Report*
- Click on the **Close Header and Footer** button to exit.
- Double-click on the header to return for editing.
- Click on the **Go to Footer** button (Navigation group).
- Click on the **Footer** button (Header & Footer group – start of ribbon).
- Click on the option **Conservative**. Your footer is displayed.
- Click on the **Close Header and Footer** button to exit.
- Review your pages in Print Preview.
- **Save** your changes.

***As an aside** … Your header/footer text is based on a style called Header or Footer, so is easy to update.*

Inserting fields for more information

More information can be added to headers and footers by working directly with **fields**. Fields are used as placeholders for data that might change in a document. If changes occur an update is made automatically.

***As an aside** … The page number you have already inserted is a field.*

How to: Insert the date and/or time

1. Display the header or footer and position your insertion point (use pre-set tab stops for quick alignment).

2. On the Design tab (Header & Footer Tools), click on the **Date & Time** button (Insert group). The Date & Time dialogue box is presented.

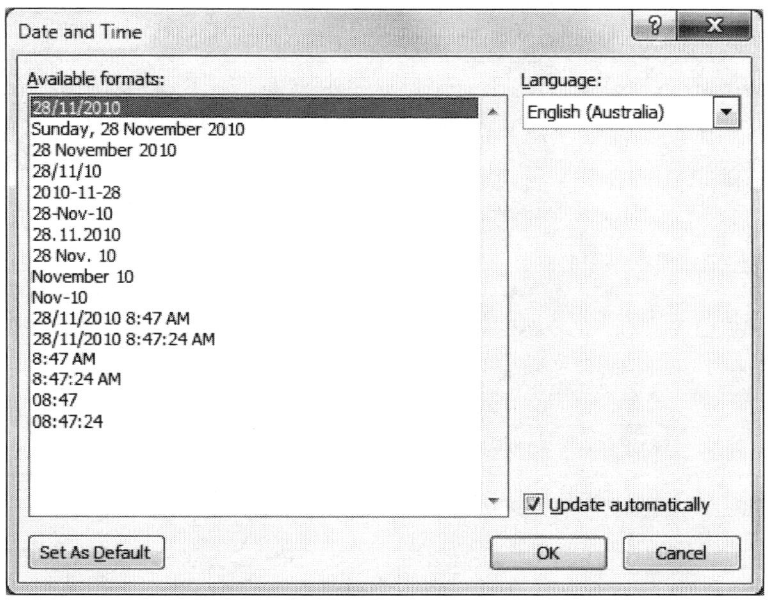

3. From the **Available formats** list, select the required date/time format.
4. Click on **Update automatically** if you would like the date to update each time the document is opened/printed.
5. Click on **OK**.

How to: Insert a filename field

1. Display the header or footer and position the insertion point.
2. On the Design tab (Header & Footer Tools), click on the **Quick Parts** button, then click on **Field** (Insert group).
The Field dialogue box is presented.

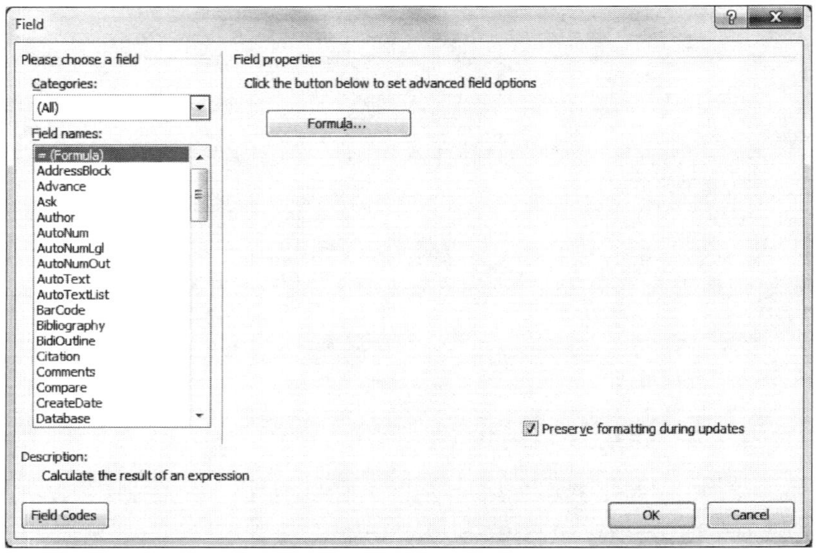

3. Scroll down the **Field names** list and click on **FileName**. Note the **Description**.
4. Click on a **Format**, and click on **Add path to filename** if required.
5. Click on **OK**.

> ***As an aside*** *... Other useful fields to insert include CreateDate, PrintDate, SaveDate, Page and NumPages.*

Altering a header & footer position

You can alter the position of the header and footer in relation to the edge of the page.

How to: Alter header & footer position

1. Display the header or footer.
2. On the Design tab (Header & Footer Tools), adjust the **Header from Top**, **Footer from Bottom** positions (Position group).

> ***As an aside*** *... You can use the* ***Insert Alignment Tab*** *button (Position group) to quickly add new tab stops if you accidentally remove any.*

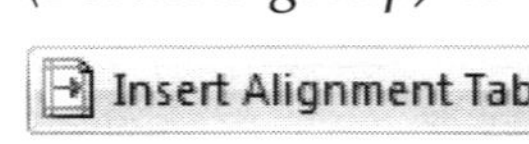

Hands-on exercise 64

In this exercise you practise inserting fields into your document footer.

- Using the document *Superfood annual report*, double-click on the footer to open it for editing.

- Click on the **Footer** button (Header & Footer group), then click on the **Remove Footer** option. Your footer is removed.

- Click on the **Page Number** button (Header & Footer group). A number of options are presented.
- Point to **Bottom of Page**, then click on the option **Bold Numbers 2** (you need to scroll some way down through options).
- Double-click in the document area to close the footer.
- Review your pages in Print Preview, exit Print Preview.

- Display the document footer.
- Delete the existing document footer (select and press Delete).
- Press Tab to align text to the centre of the document.

- Click on the **Date & Time** button (Design ribbon, Insert group). The Date & Time dialogue box is presented.
- From the **Available formats** list, select the first date format.
- Select **Update automatically**.
- Click on **OK**.
- Note the date in your footer.
- Delete the date.

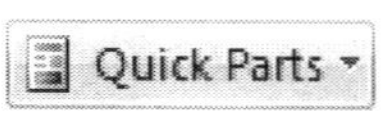

- On the Design tab (Header & Footer Tools), click on **Quick Parts**, then click on **Field** (Insert group). The Field dialogue box is presented.
- Scroll down the **Field name** list and click on **FileName**. Note the **Description**.
- Click on the **Format** Lower case, and select **Add path to filename**.
- Click on **OK**.
- Reduce the size of the font is necessary to fit the text on one line.
- Click on the **Center** align button (Home ribbon).
- Adjust the **Header from Top**, **Footer from Bottom** positions (Position group) to **1 cm**.
- Close your footer.
- Review your document in Print Preview.
- **Save** your changes.
- **Close** your document.

Different headers & footers for document sections

In a longer document you may have areas that require a different header and/or footer.

> ***For example ...*** *A different header and/or footer for the executive summary before the body of the report. A different header and/or footer for the marketing pages, finance pages and personnel pages.*

To achieve different headers and footers in different areas of a document you need to separate your document into sections. This is achieved by inserting **section breaks** to create separate 'compartments'. Once section breaks have been inserted, you can **unlink** the sections that require a different header and/or footer and enter the new information (or leave blank as required).

How to: Insert a section break for headers & footers

1. Position your insertion point in the text where you want the new section to begin.

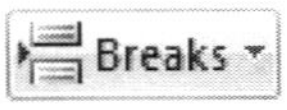

2. Display the Page Layout ribbon, then click on the **Breaks** button (Page Setup group).
3. Under Section Breaks in the list presented, click on the **Next Page** option.
4. Display the header or footer. Once sections are inserted, a marker appears on the left of the header or footer indicating the section number, e.g. Header – Section 1.

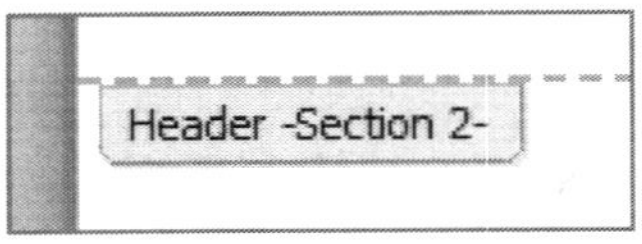

5. Click on the **Show Next** / **Show Previous** buttons to move between the sections (Design ribbon, Navigation group).

How to: Unlink a section header/footer

1. Display the header or footer.
2. When a header or footer is linked to the previous section, Word displays the **Same as Previous** marker on the right of the header or footer area.

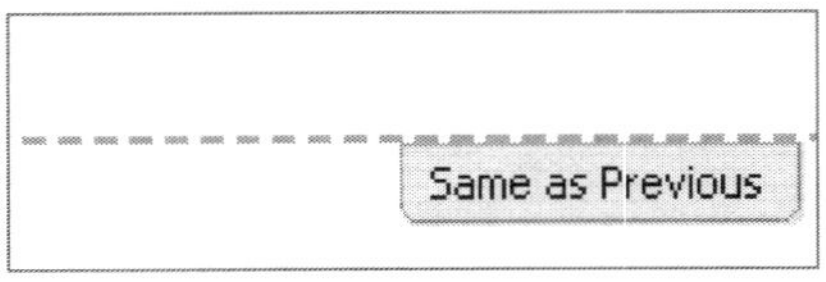

3. Click on the **Link to Previous** button (Design ribbon, Navigation group). (This button is lit up (active) until the section is unlinked.)
4. The **Same as Previous** marker is removed.
5. Your new header or footer information can now be entered without affecting the previous header/footer.

***As an aside** ...You need to unlink a header and footer separately.*

How to: Restart page numbering

1. Display the header or footer.
2. Click on the **Page Number** button, then click on **Format Page Numbers** (Header & Footer group). The Page Number Format dialogue box is presented.

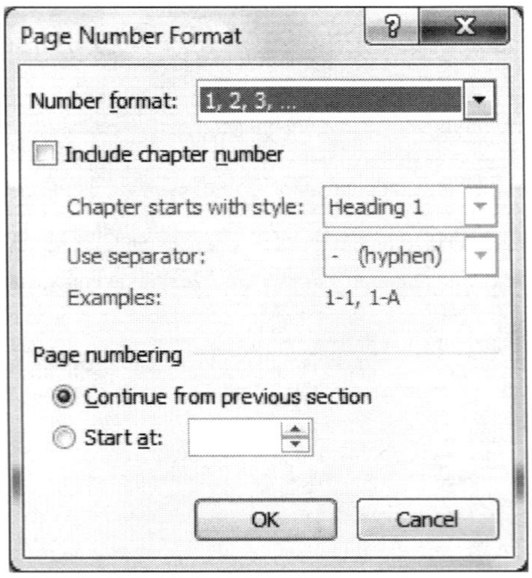

3. Click on the option **Start at**, and ensure the number is set to **1**.
4. Click on **OK**.

> ***As an aside*** *... Also use this dialogue box to change the format of your numbers, e.g. to roman numerals.*

Hands-on exercise 65

In this exercise you practise dividing a document into three sections, where each section requires different header and footer information.

- **Open** the document *Superfood annual report 2*.
- Review your document in Print Preview.
  The document has 6 pages; a title page, followed by copyright information, then the body of the report.
  Currently it has no headers or footers.
- Exit Print Preview.

First, you separate the document into two sections. The title page and copyright are the first section, then the body of the report.

- Position the insertion point before the heading on page 2:
  The Managing Director's Report
- Display the Page Layout ribbon, then click on the **Breaks** button (Page Setup group).
- Under Section Breaks in the list presented, click on the **Next Page** option. Your document now has 2 sections.
  Note the information in the Status bar.
  Section 2 commences on page 3.
- Return to the top of the document.
- Review page 2 in Print Preview, exit Print Preview.

Next, you create the headers for each section. No header is required in the first section which contains the title page and the copyright.

- Return to the top of the document.
- Double-click on the blank Header area on the first page to open it.
  Note it says Header - Section 1.

- Click on the **Show Next** button to display the Section 2 header.
- Word displays **Same as Previous** on the right of the header.
  This indicates that the Section 2 header is linked to the Section 1 header, and that any change here will also affect the Section 1 header.

- Click on the **Link to Previous** button (Design ribbon, Navigation group). (This button is lit up (active) until the section is unlinked.)
- The **Same as Previous** marker is removed.
- Type the text: *SuperFood Annual Report*
- Align to the right.

Next, you insert a footer for Section 2.

- Click on the **Go to Footer** button (Design ribbon, Navigation group).
- Ensure the Section 2 footer is displayed.
- Click on the **Link to Previous** button (Navigation group).
  (This button is lit up (active) until the section is unlinked.)

- The **Same as Previous** marker is removed.
- Click on the **Page Number** button (Header & Footer group).
  A number of options are presented.
- Point to **Bottom of Page**, then click on the option **Bold Numbers 3** (you need to scroll some way down through options).
- Double-click in the document area to close the footer.
- Review your pages in Print Preview.
  Note that the page numbering starts in the body of the document at 3.
- Exit Print Preview.

Finally, you need to change the page numbering so that it commences at 1 in the body of the report.

- Display the Section 2 footer.
- Click on the **Page Number** button, then click on **Format Page Numbers** (Header & Footer group).
  The Page Number Format dialogue box is presented.
- Click on the option **Start at**, and ensure the number is set to **1**.
- Click on **OK**.
- **Close** your footer.
- Note how the page numbers read 1 of 7 (total pages of the report). You may require the footer to read the total pages of the section only.
- Return to the Section 2 footer.
- Delete the **7** from the footer.
- On the Design tab (Header & Footer Tools), click on **Quick Parts**, then click on **Field** (Insert group). The Field dialogue box is presented.
- Scroll down the **Field name** list and click on **SectionPages**.
  Note the **Description**.
- Click on **OK**.
  Apply bold to the 5 so it matches the 1.
- Double-click in the document to exit the footer.
- **Save** your changes.
- **Close** your document.

Hands-on exercise 66

In this exercise you practise dividing a document into three sections, where each section requires different header and footer information. Currently, there are no sections or headers and footers.

- **Open** the document *Ski NZ*.

First, you separate the document into three sections.

- Position the insertion point before the heading on page 2:
  South Island Skiing
- Insert a **Next Page** section break.
- Position the insertion point before the heading on page 4:
  North Island Skiing
- Insert a **Next Page** section break.
- Your document now has 3 sections.
  Note the information in the Status bar.
- Return to the top of the document.

Next, you create the headers for each section. No header is required in the first section as it contains only the title page and copyright information page.

- Return to the top of the document.
- Display the header.
- Click on the **Show Next** button to move to the Section 2 header.
- Click on the **Link to Previous** button to remove the link.
- Type the text: *South Island Skiing*
  Align the text to the right.
- Click on the **Show Next** button to move to the Section 3 header.
- Click on the **Link to Previous** button to remove the link.
- Change the text to: North Island Skiing

Next, you insert a footer required in Sections 2 and 3 only.

- Click on the **Go to Footer** button to move to your footer.
- Click on the **Previous Section** button to display the Section 2 footer.
- Click on the **Link to Previous** button to remove the link to Section 1 (Sections 2 and 3 remain linked).
- Click on the **Page Number** button (Header & Footer group).
  A number of options are presented.
- Point to **Bottom of Page**, then click on the option **Bold Numbers 2**.

Finally, you fix the page numbering so that it commences at 1.

- Ensure the Section 2 footer is displayed.
- Click on the **Page Number** button, then click on **Format Page Numbers** (Header & Footer group).
  The Page Number Format dialogue box is presented.

- Click on the option **Start at**, and ensure the number is set to **1**.
- Click on **OK**.
- Display the footer for Section 1.
- Insert in the footer the pre-set page number **Plain Number 2**.
- Format the number as small roman numerals.
- **Close** your footer.
- Review your document in Print Preview.
- **Save** your changes.
- **Close** your document.

> ***As an aside ...*** *If not already displayed on your Status bar, display the* ***Formatted Page Number*** *as well as the* ***Page Number****. This shows printed v. physical page number. (To display on the Status bar, right-click on the bar, then click on the required item.)*

Changing margins and orientation with section breaks

Sections breaks have other uses in multi-page documents, e.g. if you need to change margins or page orientation mid-way through a document you need a section break.

> ***For example ...*** *The second page of a letter is printed on different stationery so requires a different top margin. Insert a next page section break when you have finished typing the first page. Then a separate 'compartment' is created and you can change the top margin.*

Hands-on exercise 67

In this exercise you practise adding a section break in a letter to enable the use of a different top margin and orientation.

- **Open** the document *New mortgage letter*.
- Go to the end of the document. Press Enter
- Type the following: *Enc*
  Press Enter
- Insert a **Next Page** section break.
  Page 2 is now a new section.
- Set a custom top margin of **2 cm**.
- Type the following: *Happy Homes Mortgage Services Staff*
- Ensuring your insertion point is still in Section 2, change the page orientation to landscape. Note how these changes only affect Section 2.
- Create the following SmartArt organisation chart.

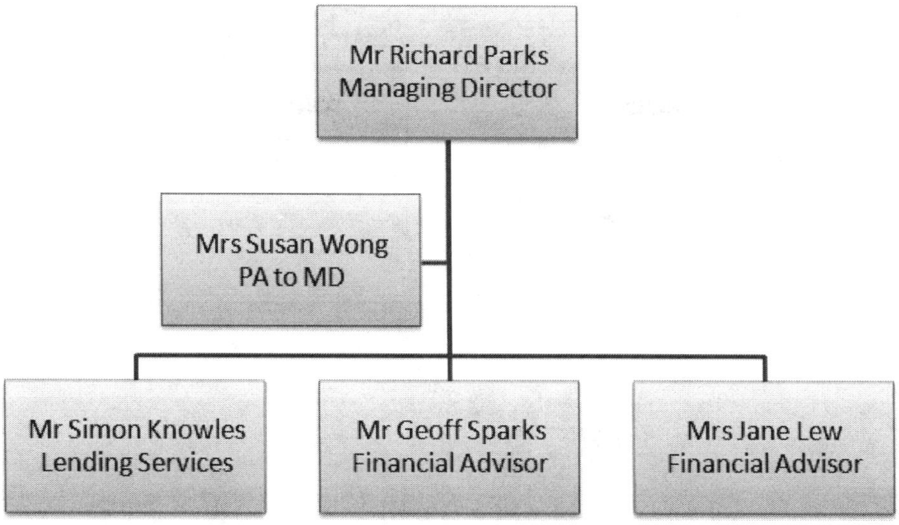

- **Position** the chart in the middle centre of the page.
- Format the page heading in a larger font and align to the centre.
- Review in Print Preview.
- **Save** your changes.
- **Close** your document.

Inserting cross-references

A cross-reference refers to an item in another part of a document.

> ***For example ...*** *For further information see page 3.*

In the above example the page number is inserted using a cross-reference, which is a field.

If you use a cross-reference and the information is later moved to a different page, the page reference is automatically updated.

There are many different ways to incorporate cross-references into your documents. Here you look at just a few examples.

Cross-referencing heading text

To add a page number cross-reference to a heading, the headings need to be formatted with Heading Styles (Heading 1, 2, 3 etc.).

How to: Insert a page number cross-reference to a heading

1. Position your insertion point where the cross-reference is required.

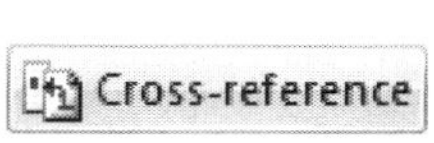

2. Display the Insert ribbon, then click on the **Cross-reference** button (Links group). The Cross-reference dialogue box is presented.
3. Click on the **Reference type** down-arrow, then click on **Heading**. The Headings in the document (those formatted with Heading styles 1, 2, 3, etc.) are displayed.

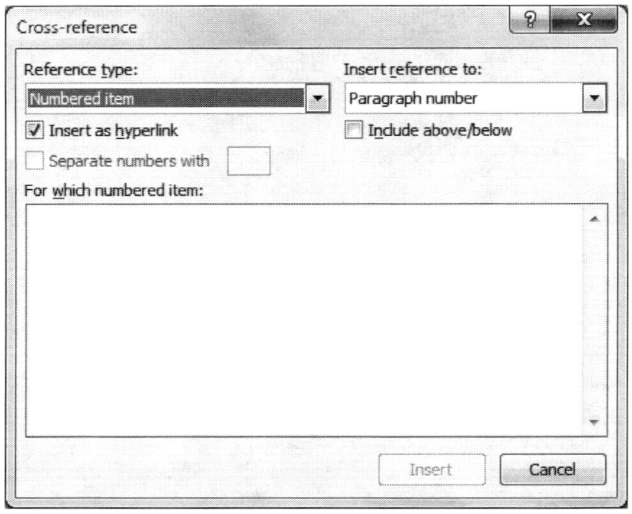

4. Click on the **Insert reference to** down-arrow, then click on **Page number**.
5. In the **For which heading** list, click on the required heading.
6. Click on **Insert**.
   A cross-reference field is inserted into your document.
   The dialogue box remains open for you to add a further cross-reference if required.
7. When your cross-references are complete, click on **Close**.

> ***As an aside ...*** *Word automatically updates all cross-references (indeed all fields) when you print your document or view in Print Preview. However, for an immediate update, select all of your text, then press* F9.

Hands-on exercise 68

In this exercise you practise adding page number cross-references to headings.

- **Open** the document *Leadership characteristics*.
  (You must have completed Consolidation Tasks 1 and 2 to apply Heading Styles.)
- Position your insertion point above the heading **Decision making**.

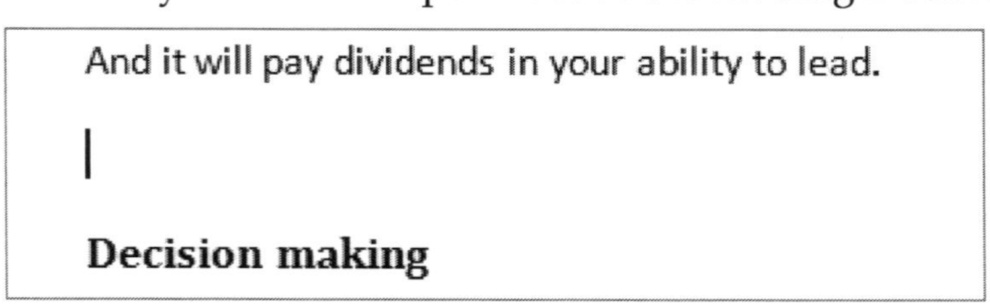

- Type: *For further details on Communication see page*

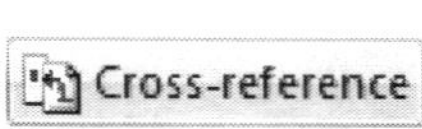

- Display the Insert ribbon, then click on the **Cross-reference** button (Links group). The Cross-reference dialogue box is presented.
- Click on the **Reference type** down-arrow, then click on **Heading**.
  The Headings in your document are display, i.e. the ones with Heading Styles applied.
- Click on the **Insert reference to** down-arrow, then click on **Page number**.

- In the **For which heading** list, click on the heading: Communication
- Click on **Insert**.
  A page number cross-reference field is inserted into your document.
- Click on **Close**.
  Complete the punctuation with a full stop.
- Locate the Communication heading on page 3.
- Insert a page break before it so that the heading and following text is now on page 4.
- Select the paragraph with the page number cross-reference field. Press F9 to update. (Printing would also update.)
- **Save** your changes.

Hints & tips

Other useful cross-references include a cross-reference to Heading Text, so that if a heading is changed the cross-referenced heading text also changes. Using the above example, the heading could also have been referenced – a cross-reference field to Heading Text.

Cross-referencing bookmarked items

If there is text in your document that you need to refer to, and it is not a heading, you can bookmark the text first, then add a cross-reference to the bookmark.

How to: Insert a bookmark

1. Select the text to be bookmarked, i.e. the text to be referred to.

2. Display the Insert ribbon, then click on the **Bookmark** button (Links group). The Bookmark dialogue box is presented.

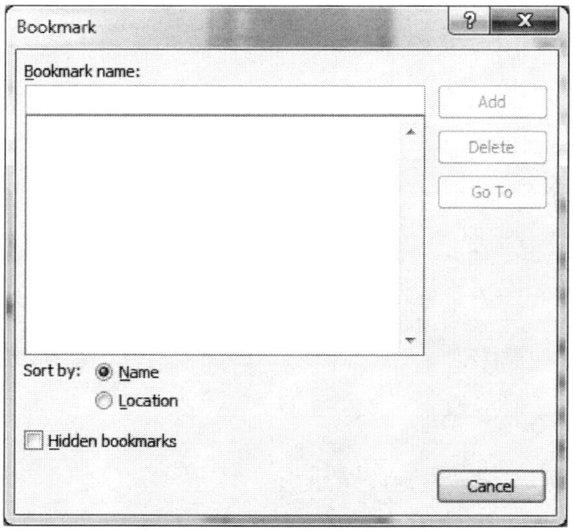

3. Type a **Bookmark** name (no spaces).
4. Click on **Add**.

How to: Insert a page number cross-reference to a bookmark

1. Position your insertion point where the cross-reference is required.
2. Display the Insert ribbon, then click on the **Cross-reference** button (Links group). The Cross-reference dialogue box is presented.

3. Click on the **Reference type** down-arrow, then click on **Bookmark**. The bookmarks in the document are displayed.
4. Click on the **Insert reference to** down-arrow, then click on **Page number**.
5. In the **For which bookmark** list, click on the required bookmark.
6. Click on **Insert**.
   A cross-reference field is inserted into your document.
   The dialogue box remains open for you to add a further cross-reference if required.
7. When your cross-references are complete, click on **Close**.

Hands-on exercise 69

In this exercise you practise inserting a page number cross-reference to a bookmark.

- Using the document *Leadership characteristics*, go to the top of the document.

First, you bookmark the text to be cross-referenced.

- Find the text: Ernest Shackleton.
  Select the paragraph ready for book marking.
- Display the Insert ribbon, then click on the **Bookmark** button (Links group). The Bookmark dialogue box is presented.
- Type the following **Bookmark** name: *EShack*
- Click on **Add**.
- Go to the bottom of the document.
- Start a new paragraph and type: *For more information on Ernest Shackleton, see page*
- Click on the **Cross-reference** button (Links group). The Cross-reference dialogue box is presented.
- Click on the **Reference type** down-arrow, then click on **Bookmark**. The bookmarks in the document are displayed.
- Click on the **Insert reference to** down-arrow, then click on **Page number**.
- In the **For which bookmark** list, click on the bookmark **EShack**.
- Click on **Insert**.
  A cross-reference field is inserted into your document.
- Click on **Close**.
  Complete the punctuation with a full stop.

- **Save** your changes.

Hints & tips

In the exercise above the bookmarked text could also have been included as a reference – a cross-reference field to Bookmark Text.

For more information on Ernest Shackleton, see page 1.

Cross references can also be made to Captions (Figures and Tables). Note that a caption must not be housed in a text box for the cross-reference to work.

Inserting footnotes

Footnotes explain or provide references for text that appears in the body of a document. They are displayed at the bottom of the page where they appear. A footnote consists of two linked parts, the footnote reference in the body text [1], and the corresponding footnote text at the bottom of the page (see below example).

Endnotes operate in the same way but the corresponding endnote text is located at the end of the document.

How to: Insert a footnote

1. Click your insertion point where you want to insert the footnote reference.
2. Display the References ribbon, then click on the **Insert Footnote** button (Footnotes group).
3. The footnote reference is inserted and you are positioned in the Footnote area at the bottom of the page. Type your footnote text, then click in the document to continue.

How to: Insert an endnote

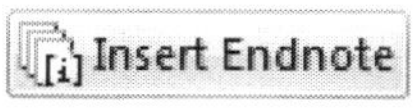

1. Click your insertion point where you want to insert the endnote reference.
2. Display the References ribbon, then click on the **Insert Endnote** button (Footnotes group).
3. The endnote reference is inserted and you are positioned in the endnote area at the end of the document. Type your endnote text, then click in the document to continue.

How to: Locate the next footnote

1. Display the References ribbon, click on the **Next Footnote** button (Footnotes group).

---

[1] This is an example of footnote text. It is displayed above the footer but under the body text on the page.

How to: Locate the next footnote

1. Display the References ribbon, click on the **Next Footnote** down-arrow, then click on **Next Endnote** (Footnotes group).

	Insert a footnote	Alt Ctrl F
	Insert an endnote	Alt Ctrl E

What if I want to delete a footnote or endnote?

Delete the footnote/endnote reference in the body text. This also deletes the footnote/ endnote text.

Hands-on exercise 70

In this exercise you practise inserting footnotes and endnotes in a document.

- Using the document *Leadership characteristics*, go to the top of the document.
- Click your insertion point after the following text:
  Here's my view on some of the important characteristics.

- Display the References ribbon, then click on the **Insert Footnote** button (Footnotes group).
- The footnote reference is inserted and you are positioned in the Footnote area at the bottom of the page. Type the following:
  All views expressed are solely those of the author.
- Click after the paragraph: The dictionary definition of 'ruthless' is 'Have no pity', and that doesn't sound like a nice characteristic to have, does it?
- Click on the **Insert Footnote** button.
- The footnote reference is inserted and you are positioned in the Footnote area at the bottom of the page. Type the following:
  Macquarie Dictionary.
- Position your mouse pointer over any footnote reference in the body of the document and your footnote text will be displayed in a box with a note icon.

Next, you delete a footnote.

- Go to the top of the document.
- Select the first footnote reference, then delete it.
  The reference and its associated text are removed.
- Click on the **Next Footnote** button.
  The remaining footnote is renumbered.

Finally, you add an endnote.

- Click after the author name: Ernest Shackleton.
- Click on the **Insert Endnote** button. Insert Endnote
- The endnote reference is inserted and you are positioned in the Endnote area at the end of the document (page 4). Type the following: *Shackletons Way by Margot Morrell & Stephanie Capparell.*
- **Save** your changes.
- **Close** your document.

As an aside *...Double-click on a footnote/endnote reference to go to the linked text.*

Terms & concepts review

- What do you need to **insert** to create a document with different headers and footers? ____

  ____

- By default, are headers and footers in different sections of a document **linked** or **unlinked**?

  ____

- Name two items in a document that you can **cross-reference**?

  ____

  ____

- Where do **footnotes** appear in a document?

  ____

  ____

- Where do **endnotes** appear in a document?

  ____

  ____

Consolidation task 17

In this task you add a variety of header and footer information to a multi-page document.

- Open the document *The Great Ocean Road.*
- Insert a **Next Page** section break prior to the heading on page 2: The Great Ocean Drive.
- In Section 1 of this document, you require no header or footer information. In Section 2 of this document you require a header that reads: The Great Ocean Road, and a footer that displays the page number. Insert the required header/footer information.
- Ensure that the page numbering in the Section 2 footer starts at 1.
- Click in the Copyright heading (on page 2).
- Add a space before paragraph measurement of 600 pts.
- Add a Clip Art picture on the title page.
- Review your document in Print Preview.
- Save your changes.
- Close your document.

After this Consolidation task, do you feel confident... tick the appropriate box:

	Inserting Next Page section break
	Assigning different header and footer for sections
	Adding Clip Art

Topic 13 – Generating merged documents

When you want to send the same basic letter or information to a number of people, but you want each letter individually addressed or personalised, you can save time and effort by using the mail merge feature.

Mail merge for form (standard) letters

Merging involves bringing together two files: a file that contains the standard text of a letter, and a file that contains the address information of the multiple recipients. The letter is known as the **main document**, and the address file is known as the **data source**.

In order that the address information is inserted into each letter, the **main** document (i.e. the letter) includes **merge fields**. These fields correspond to the information held in the data source. These fields appear surrounded by << >> brackets.

***For example** … The letter below has the merge fields highlighted.*

3 July 2011

«Title» «Fname» «Lname»
«Street»
«Suburb» «State» «Pcode»

Dear «Fname»

Congratulations! You have won a deluxe chocolate hamper. Please bring this letter to a participating store to redeem your prize.

Yours sincerely

Andrew Mars
Chocolates R US

The corresponding data source, stores the variable information for the fields. Each column is a merge field (headed by a merge field name); each row is a merge record.

Title	Fname	Lname	Street	Suburb	State	Pcode
Ms	Jackie	Glover	100 Red Street	SYDNEY	NSW	2000
Mr	Tom	Storey	5 Hill Street	PERTH	WA	6000
Mr	Jake	Woods	220 Harbour Street	SYDNEY	NSW	2000

When the two files are brought together, or **merged**, a third document is produced. This third document holds all of the (form) letters that are generated.

There are several ways that merging can be achieved in Word. In this course you are shown a process where merge fields are added directly to your main document using the **Mailing ribbon**. Word does also offer a Step by Step Mail Merge Wizard.

What is most important at this stage is to understand the concept of merging two files to create a third.

Creating a main document

For form letters the **main document** is simply the letter that you want to mail out. It contains only the standard text that everyone receives. Variable information is left out at this stage, e.g. name, address. This is a standard document that can contain formatting, headers, footers, fields (date), etc.

Hands-on exercise 71

In this exercise you practise creating a standard letter (from a handwritten draft) to advise clients of a price increase. This document is your **main document**.

- Print out the following document for reference:
  Org style guide – letter standard.
- In a **new** blank document, type the following letter.
  Follow your style guide for the letter layout.
  Check you have setup the following as requested:
  - Margins and page size.
  - Font and font size.
  - Line spacing.
  - Space before/after paragraphs.
  - Note a footer is required.

Date

Dear

Your satisfaction is important to us. In order to produce a high-quality product we have recently installed new high-speed, high-definition printing presses. This, along with the increased price of paper, has forced us to increase our prices by 10% effective October 1st.

Thank you for your understanding in this matter. We feel that these increases will still allow you to sell your products at competitative prices. We hope you will let us know immediately if there is any way we can serve you better

Sincerely

Sally Jones
Director

- Spell and grammar check your document.
- **Save** your document as *Price increase letter*.

Creating a data source

The **data source** can simply be a document that holds a **table** of data. The table can hold all of your name, address and additional details efficiently.

When creating a data source using a Word table, the first row of the table contains your **merge field names**, i.e. labels for your variable data such as FirstName, LastName.

> ***As an aside** ... When creating your own data source it is recommended that you do not include spaces in the merge field names.*

Each row of the table then becomes a merge record: one row being used for each form letter created as part of the merge process.

> ***Additional info** ... You should avoid adding any formatting to the table being used as a data source. Let the text wrap naturally in the cells, e.g. do not press* Enter *between the words just because your column width is narrow.*

Hands-on exercise 72

In this exercise you create your data source using a table.

- Create a **new** blank document.
- **Insert** a table of seven columns and seven rows.
- Type the following text into the table. Let the text wrap naturally in the cells, i.e. do not press **Enter** between the words in the Company or Street names.
- As this is a data source you should avoid adding any formatting to the table.
- **Save** your document as *Price increase data*.
- **Close** your document.

FirstName	LastName	Company	Street	Suburb	State	Postcode
Jane	Low	JP Printing	2 Red Lane	PALM BEACH	QLD	4221
Tom	Stubbs	ICS Pty Ltd	44 Port Street	INGHAM	QLD	4850
Tessa	Stuart	Nerrina Press	28 Robert Street	NERRINA	VIC	3350
Susan	George	My card Distributors	56 Gilmour Road	MANLY	NSW	2095
Margaret	Kelly	Tilde Pty Ltd	6 Botany Bay	ROSEBERRY	NSW	2018
James	Dawson	Castel Pty Ltd	7 Harbour Road	WEST PERTH	WA	6005

Commencing the merge

Once you have created your main document and data source you can begin the merge process. Using the Mailing ribbon you:

Step 1 – nominate your letter as a form letter

Step 2 – attach your data source

Step 3 – insert your merge field

Step 4 – preview your merge letters

Step 5 – merge your letters.

How to: Nominate your letter

1. Display your main document.
2. Display the Mailings ribbon, click on the **Start Mail Merge** button, then click on **Letters** (Start Mail Merge group).

How to: Attach your data source

1. Display your main document.
2. Display the Mailings ribbon, click on the **Select Recipients** button, then click on **Use Existing List** (Start Mail Merge group).
   The Select Data Source dialogue box is presented.
3. Select the storage location of your data source.
   Click on the data source, then click on **Open**.
   The data source is attached to your main document.

How to: Insert merge fields

1. Position your insertion point where you need a merge field.
2. Display the Mailings ribbon, click on the **Insert Merge Field** down-arrow, then click on the required field (Write & Insert Fields group). Remember to put punctuation as required around fields, e.g. leave a space between first name and surname.

   «FirstName» «LastName»
   «Company»
   «Address1»
   «Suburb» «State» «PostCode»

   Dear «FirstName»

3. **Save** your main document after you have inserted the merge fields.

Hands-on exercise 73

In this exercise you practise Steps 1-3 of the merge process (nominate your letter, attach your data source and insert merge fields).

- Display your main document (*Price increase letter*).

First, you nominate your letter.

- Display the Mailings ribbon, click on the **Start Mail Merge** button, then click on **Letters** (Start Mail Merge group).

Next, you attach your data source.

- From the Mailings ribbon, click on the **Select Recipients** button, then click on **Use Existing List** (Start Mail Merge group).
  The Select Data Source dialogue box is presented.
- Locate and select your data source *Price increase data*, then click on **Open**. The data source is attached to your main document.

Next, you insert your merge fields.

- Position your insertion point where the address is required.

- From the Mailings ribbon, click on the **Insert Merge Field** down-arrow, then click on the **FirstName** field (Write & Insert Fields group).
  If the fields are not available then the data source has not been attached.
- Press the Spacebar
- Click on the **Insert Merge Field** down-arrow, then click on the **LastName** field.
- Press Enter
- Repeat this process to add the remaining address fields. Remember your punctuation.
- Position your insertion point after Dear and insert the **FirstName** field.

  Dear «FirstName»

- **Save** your changes.

Completing your merge

Finally, you are ready to merge together the main document and the data source. You can preview your output to ensure the letters to be produced are as expected, then you can merge to a file for later printing or merge directly to the printer. It is recommended that you merge to a file to allow final checking or individual tweaking, and to allow you to print off larger merge files in smaller chunks (to minimise printer hiccups).

How to: Preview your merge output

1. Display the Mailings ribbon, then click on the **Preview Results** button (Preview Results group).
2. Note the first record from your data source is displayed in the letter.
3. To view other records, click on the **Next Record** , **Previous Record**  buttons.

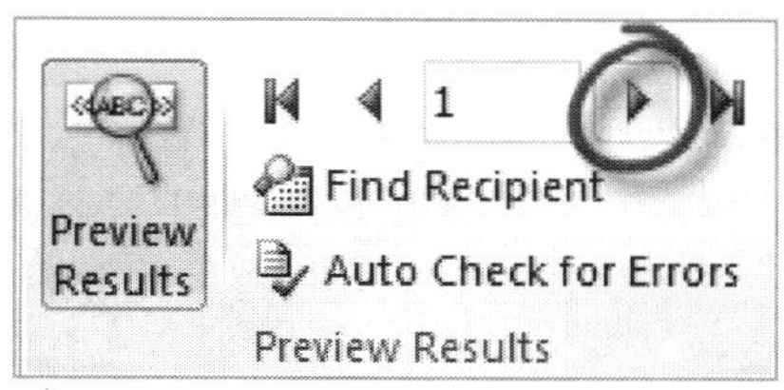

4. Click again on the **Preview Results** button to switch off the preview feature.

How to: Merge to a new document

1. Display the Mailings ribbon, click on the **Finish & Merge** button, then click on **Edit Individual Documents** (Finish group).
   The Merge to New Document dialogue box is presented.

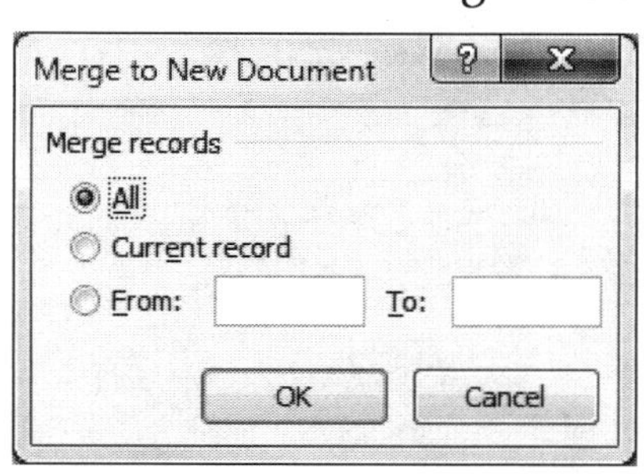

2. Click on **All** to merge all records in the data source; click on **Current Record** to merge only the previewed record; or click on **From/To** and type required merge record numbers (i.e. rows in the data source table).
3. Click on **OK**.
   A new document is presented with your merged letters.
   The document is called *Letters1*.
4. Scroll through the letters presented.

Hands-on exercise 74

In this exercise you practise Steps 4-5 of the merge process (preview and merge).

First, you preview your merge result.

- Ensure your letter is displayed.
- Display the Mailings ribbon, then click on the **Preview Results** button (Preview Results group).
- Note the first record from your data source is displayed in the letter.
- To view other records, click on the **Next Record** ▶, **Previous Record** buttons ◀.
- Click again on the **Preview Results** button to switch off the preview feature.

Next, you merge to a new document, i.e. bring together the letter and data into a third document (the output).

- From the Mailings ribbon, click on the **Finish & Merge** button, then click on **Edit Individual Documents** (Finish group). The Merge to New Document dialogue box is presented.

- Click on **All** to merge all records in the data source.
- Click on **OK**.
  A new document is presented with your merged letters.
  The document is called *Letters1*.
- Scroll through the letters presented.
- **Close** your output document without saving.
- **Save** and **close** your main document *Price increase letter*.

> ***As an aside** … When you save and close your main document, the connection to the data source is saved with it. On re-opening the main document the following message will appear: Click on* ***Yes****.*

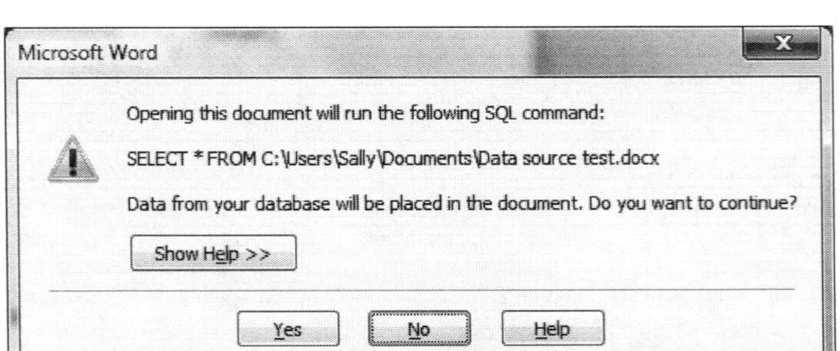

Hands-on exercise 75

In this exercise you again practise mail merge. This time you add additional merge fields to the body of a memo.

- Print out the following document for reference:
  Org style guide – memo standard.
- In a **new** blank document, create the following memo.
  Follow your standards guide for the memo layout.
  Check you have setup as requested before you start the document:
  - Margins and page size.
  - Font and font size.
  - Line spacing.
  - Space before/after paragraphs.
  - Row height, column width.
  - Alignment of text in table.
  - Note a footer is required.
  - Note also an additional row for email details is required.
  - Leave two spaces for the number of days leave.

MEMORANDUM

To

Department

From (Your Name)

Department Human Resources

Date (Date)

Subject Annual Leave

At the end of this financial year you had ... days of annual leave accrued. Please remember that all annual leave applications must be signed by your Manager before you send it to the Payroll Office.

- Spell and grammar check your document.
- **Save** your document as *Annual leave memo.*

Next, you create a new data source.

- Create a **new** blank document.
- Insert the following table.

FirstName	LastName	Department	AnnualLeave
Tom	McEwan	Sales	10
Jerry	Atkin	Accounts	8
Sarah	Tan	Sales	12
Cindy	Jones	Administration	5

- **Save** your document as *Annual leave data.*
- **Close** your data source.
- Ensure you are displaying your letter, then start a mail merge for **Letters** using this document as the main document (Mailing ribbon, **Start Mail Merge**).
- Select the existing data source *Annual Leave Data* (**Select Recipients**).
- Insert merge fields into the main document for the To, Department and days in the body (between the two spaces).
- **Preview** your output.
- Merge all records to a new document.
- Scroll though the letters created.
- **Close** your output document without saving.
- **Save** and **close** your main document *Annual leave memo.*

Merging to produce envelopes and labels

Mail merge can also be used to produce envelopes or labels to accompany your mail merge letters.

How to: Merge to envelopes

1. Create a **new** blank document. This is your main document.

2. Display the Mailings ribbon, click on the **Start Mail Merge** button, then click on **Envelopes** (Start Mail Merge group).
   The Envelope Options dialogue box is presented.
3. Enter your envelope options. Click on **OK**.
4. Your (blank) envelope is presented. Click in the lower half of the envelope and a text box is activated with your insertion point flashing inside.

5. Click on the **Select Recipients** button, then click on **Use Existing List** (Start Mail Merge group). The Select Data Source dialogue box is presented.
6. Locate the storage location of your data source.
   Click on the data source, then click on **Open**.
   The data source is attached to your main document.

7. Ensuring your insertion point is located in the text box, click on the **Insert Merge Field** down-arrow, then click on the required field (Write & Insert Fields group). Remember to put punctuation as required around fields, e.g. leave a space between first name and surname.

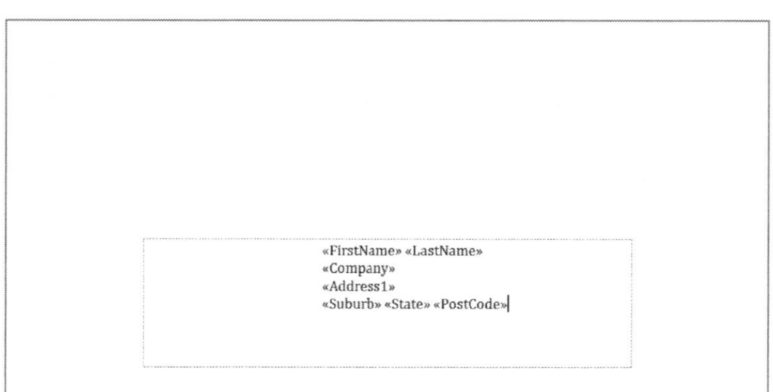

8. **Save** your main document after you have inserted the merge fields.
9. Preview and merge as previously (your output document will be *Envelopes1*).

How to: Merge to labels

1. Create a **new** blank document. This is your main document.
2. Display the Mailings ribbon, click on the **Start Mail Merge** button, then click on **Labels** (Start Mail Merge group).
   The Label Options dialogue box is presented.
3. Enter your label options. Click on **OK**.
4. Your (blank) labels document is presented with a table layout.

5. Click on the **Select Recipients** button, then click on **Use Existing List** (Start Mail Merge group). The Select Data Source dialogue box is presented.
6. Locate the storage location of your data source.
   Click on the data source, then click on **Open**.
   The data source is attached to your main document and the <<Next Record>> field is inserted in each label except the first.

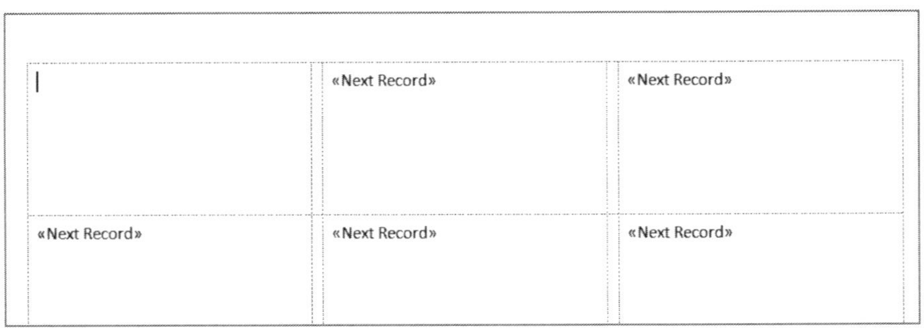

	«Next Record»	«Next Record»
«Next Record»	«Next Record»	«Next Record»

7. Ensuring your insertion point is located in the first label, click on the **Insert Merge Field** down-arrow, then click on the required field (Write & Insert Fields group). Remember to put punctuation as required around fields, e.g. leave a space between first name and surname.

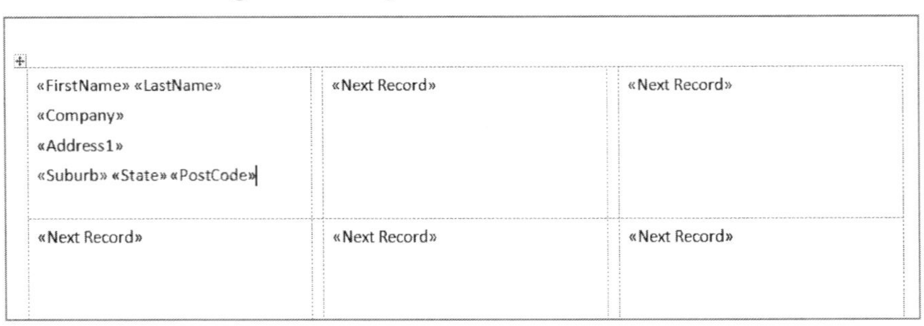

«FirstName» «LastName» «Company» «Address1» «Suburb» «State» «PostCode»	«Next Record»	«Next Record»
«Next Record»	«Next Record»	«Next Record»

8. From the Mailings ribbon, click on the **Update Labels** button (Write & Insert Fields group). The merge fields are replicated in each label.

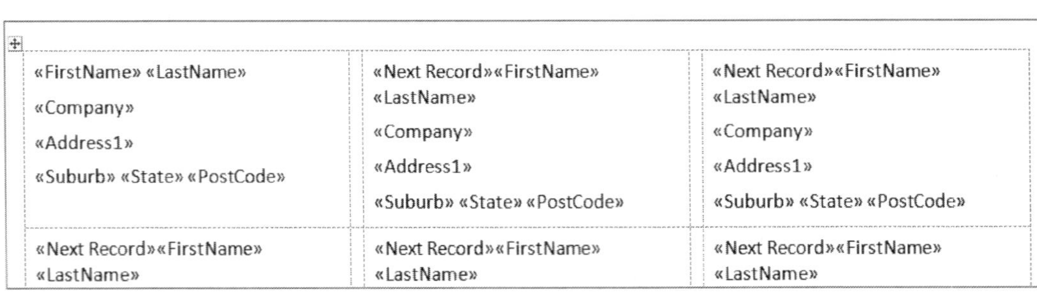

«FirstName» «LastName» «Company» «Address1» «Suburb» «State» «PostCode»	«Next Record»«FirstName» «LastName» «Company» «Address1» «Suburb» «State» «PostCode»	«Next Record»«FirstName» «LastName» «Company» «Address1» «Suburb» «State» «PostCode»
«Next Record»«FirstName» «LastName»	«Next Record»«FirstName» «LastName»	«Next Record»«FirstName» «LastName»

9. **Save** your main document after you have inserted the merge fields and updated.

10. Preview and merge as previously (your output document will be *Labels1*).

Hands-on exercise 76

In this exercise you practise merging to produce envelopes.

- Create a **new** blank document. This is your main document.
- Display the Mailings ribbon, click on the **Start Mail Merge** button, then click on **Envelopes** (Start Mail Merge group). The Envelope Options dialogue box is presented.
- Select the **Envelope size** DL, then click on **OK**.
- Your (blank) envelope is presented. Click in the lower half of the envelope and a text box is activated with your insertion point flashing inside.
- Click on the **Select Recipients** button, then click on **Use Existing List** (Start Mail Merge group). The Select Data Source dialogue box is presented.
- Locate and select the file *Price increase data*, then click on **Open**. The data source is attached to your main document.
- From the Mailings ribbon, click on the **Insert Merge Field** down-arrow, then click on the **FirstName** field (Write & Insert Fields group).
- Press the Spacebar
- Click on the **Insert Merge Field** down-arrow, then click on the **LastName** field.
- Press Enter
- Repeat this process to add the remaining address fields. Remember your punctuation.
- **Save** your main document as *Price increase envelopes*.
- Preview and merge all records as previously (your output document will be *Envelopes ...*).
- **Close** your output document without saving.
- **Save** and **close** your main document (*Price increase envelopes*).

Hands-on exercise 77

In this exercise you practise merging to produce labels.

- Create a **new** blank document. This is your main document.
- Display the Mailings ribbon, click on the **Start Mail Merge** button, then click on **Labels** (Start Mail Merge group). The Label Options dialogue box is presented.
- Enter your label options: **Label vendor** Avery A4/A5 labels and **Product number** J8159. Click on **OK**.
- Your (blank) labels document is presented in a table layout.

- Click on the **Select Recipients** button, then click on **Use Existing List** (Start Mail Merge group). The Select Data Source dialogue box is presented.
- Locate and select the file *Price increase data*, then click on **Open**. The data source is attached to your main document and the <<Next Record>> field is inserted in each label except the first.
- Ensuring your insertion point is located in the first label, click on the **Insert Merge Field** down-arrow, then click on the **FirstName** field.
- Press the Spacebar
- Click on the **Insert Merge Field** down-arrow, then click on the **LastName** field.
- Press Enter
- Repeat this process to add the remaining address fields. Remember your punctuation.
- Select the table and remove any paragraph spacing.

Update Labels

- From the Mailings ribbon, click on the **Update Labels** button (Write & Insert Fields group). The merge fields are replicated in each label.
- **Save** your main document as *Price increase labels*.
- Preview and merge all records as previously (your output document will be *Labels ...*).
- **Close** your output document without saving.
- **Save** and **close** your main document (*Price increase labels*).

Hints & tips

If you need to delete a merge field drag over the merge field and press Delete.

You can select and apply formatting to merge codes, e.g. font, font size, etc.

Unless you make individual changes to letters in your merge output, there is no need to save the output. It can always be regenerated from your main document and your data source. The main document retains the connection with your nominated data source. It might be worth keeping the output from a large merge until the documents are in the post!

*If you don't see table gridlines separating the labels, display the Layout ribbon, then click on **View Gridlines** (Table group).*

If you need a return address on an envelope before you start display the Mailings ribbon. Click on the Envelopes button (Create group), and enter a return address. Please don't save a return address during this course so a clean install is available for the next student.

*In your main document, click on the **Highlight Merge Fields** button (Write & Insert Fields group) to shade the merge fields. This is helpful to locate merge fields.*

*You can use **Edit Recipients List** to exclude records from your merge.*

If your merge fields look like this you are viewing the field code rather that the field name.

```
{ DATE \@ "dd MMMM yyyy" }


{ MERGEFIELD FirstName } { MERGEFIELD LastName }
{ MERGEFIELD Company }
{ MERGEFIELD Address1 }
{ MERGEFIELD Suburb } { MERGEFIELD State } { MERGEFIELD PostCode }

Dear { MERGEFIELD FirstName }
```

Press Alt F9 *to re-display the field names.*

Terms & concepts review

- Is the merge letter known as the **main document** or the **data source**?

- Is the address file known as the **main document** or the **data source**?

- What do **merge fields** do?

Consolidation task 18

In this task create a mail merge to send thank you letters to supporters of your charity who have recently made donations.

- In a new blank document, type the following letter using your standards:

Date

Dear

The United Benefit for Community Improvement would like to thank you for your generous contribution to this year's campaign. Your contribution of $ was very welcome and will definitely help us to meet our goal of $2 million.

You are to be commended for your generosity. Thank you again for your support.

Yours sincerely

Lorraine Miller
Campaign Chairperson

- Save your letter as *Charity letter*.

Next, you create the data source.

- In a new blank document, create a table of seven columns and five rows.
- Add the following information as the field names in the first row:
  - *FirstName*
  - *LastName*
  - *Street*
  - *Suburb*
  - *State*
  - *PostCode*
  - *Donation*
- Add information for four friends. Include a fictitious amount for the donation.

- **Save** your data source as *Donations data.*
- Close your document.
- Display your letter and insert appropriate merge fields.
- Merge all the records to a new document.
- Review your merged letters, then **close** without saving.
- Save and close your main document (*Charity letter*).

Next, you create labels.

- Create labels to accompany your letters.
- Review your labels, then close without saving.
- Save your main document as *Donations labels.*
- Close all open documents.

After this Consolidation task, do you feel confident... tick the appropriate box:

	Creating a data source
	Merging documents
	Creating labels

Topic 14 – Automating standard documents

Memos, faxes and other standard documents can be automated so that they prompt for information.

For example ... *You can prompt for the To, From, and Subject details to be entered into a memo or fax as it is created.*

This can ensure that required details are entered into documents, and that the details are placed in the correct positions.

A special Word field called a **Fill-in** field is used to prompt for information. A Fill-in field generates a dialogue box. The dialogue box can be used to request information to be placed into a document in place of the Fill-in fields.

Shown below is first an example of a Fill-in field, then the dialogue box it generates.

Note the question in the field appears in the dialogue box

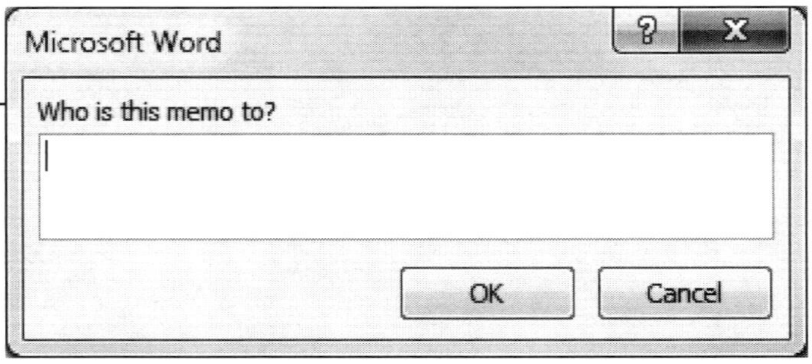

Dialogue box created by the Fill-in field

Fill-in fields need to be **updated** to produce a dialogue box. If Fill-in fields are placed in a **template** the update happens automatically as the new document is produced from the template. So, to automate your document production, you need to create a template which includes Fill-in fields.

In this topic you learn how to create your own automated memo template. These are the steps you will follow:

Step 1 – you create a standard layout for a memo in a document;

Step 2 – you save the document as a template;

Step 3 – you open your template for editing;

Step 4 – you edit the template to include Fill-in fields.

As an aside ... *If you are displaying file extensions on your computer (when file names are listed) you will notice that Word templates in 2010 have a file extension of .dotx (XML file format).*

Step 1 – Creating the memo layout

To create the memo layout, you simply type a standard document.

Hands-on exercise 78

In this exercise you create your memo layout in a document.

- Create a **new** blank document.
- Create the following memo layout using a table.

Memorandum

To	
Cc	
From	
Department	
Email	
Date	
Subject	

- Select the table and set a row height of **0.6 cm** and align the text **Align Center Left.** Set a first column width of 3.5.
- Remove all borders. Select the bottom row and apply a bottom border.
- Leave the memo open on your screen without saving.

Step 2 – Saving your memo as a template (Review)

The next step is to save your document as a template so that it can be further automated. These steps assume you are working with a new document, but basically you need to display the Save As dialogue box.

How to: Save a new document as a template

1. Click on the **Save** button (Quick Access Toolbar).
   The Save As dialogue box is presented.
2. Type a **File name**.
3. Click on the **Save as type** down-arrow, then click on **Word Template**.
4. Scroll to the top of **Navigation pane** and click on **Microsoft Word**.

5. Double-click on the **Templates** folder displayed.

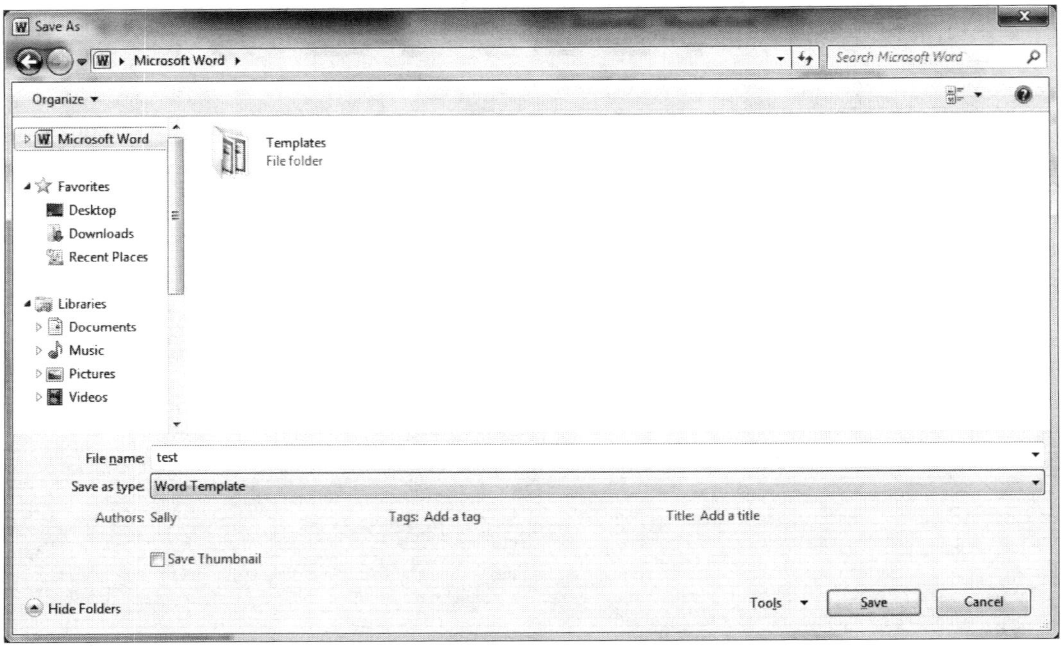

6. Note the path displayed in the **Address Bar**.
   This is where your templates are stored. For example,

7. Click on **Save**.

Hands-on exercise 79

In this exercise you save your memo as a template.

- Using your memo document, click on the **Save** button (Quick Access Toolbar).
- Type a **File name** of *Company memo*.
- Click on the **Save as type** down-arrow, then click on **Word Template**.
- Scroll to the top of **Navigation pane** and click on **Microsoft Word**.
- Double-click on the **Templates** folder displayed.
- Note the path displayed in the **Address Bar**.
  This is where your templates are stored (make a note at the bottom of the page).
- Click on **Save**.
  Note the name of the template is now displayed at the top of the screen
  in the Title Bar.
- **Close** your template.

As an aside *… Make a note here of your template storage location:*

____

Hands-on exercise 80

Your template is not yet automated, but let's first check that you can create a new document based on your template.

- Display **Backstage** view, click on **New**, then click on **My Templates**. The New dialogue box is presented.
- Click on the *Company memo* template, then click on **OK**.
- A new *document* is presented based on your memo template. Note in the Title Bar it says *Document ....*
- **Close** your document (without saving).

Step 3 – Editing your memo (Review)

The next step is to open your *template* for editing so you can add the required Fill-in fields for automation. Opening a template for editing is exactly the same as opening a document, except when selecting the template you must remember it has a different file type and generally it is stored in a template folder away from your other documents.

In this step you practise locating and opening your template before you add the Fill-in fields.

How to: Open a template for editing

1. Click on the **Open** button.
2. Navigate to your template storage location.
3. Double-click on your template to open it. Check for the correct name in the Title bar

As an aside ... *If your template is not displayed check files of type is 'All Files'.*

Hands-on exercise 81

In this exercise you first locate and open your template for editing.

- Display the **Open** dialogue box.
- Navigate to your template storage location, e.g. *C:\Users\Username\AppData\Roaming\Microsoft\Templates.*
- Double-click on the *Company memo* template to open it.
- Leave your template open for the next activity.

Step 4 – Editing your memo to include Fill-in fields

To automate your template you need to include the Fill-in fields. As described earlier Fill-in fields produce dialogue boxes which prompt for information. The template needs to be open for editing, or of course you could have added the fields as you created the template. These steps have been developed to reinforce all aspects of working with templates and fill-in fields.

How to: Insert the Word field: Fill-in (into your template)

1. Open your **template** for editing.
2. Position your insertion point where you want the dialogue box to prompt for information, e.g. To, From.

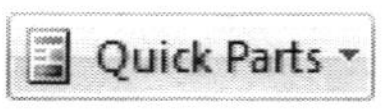

3. Display the Insert ribbon, click on **Quick Parts**, then click on **Field** (Text group). The Field dialogue box is presented.
4. Scroll down the **Field name** list and click on **Fill-in**.
   Note the **Description**.

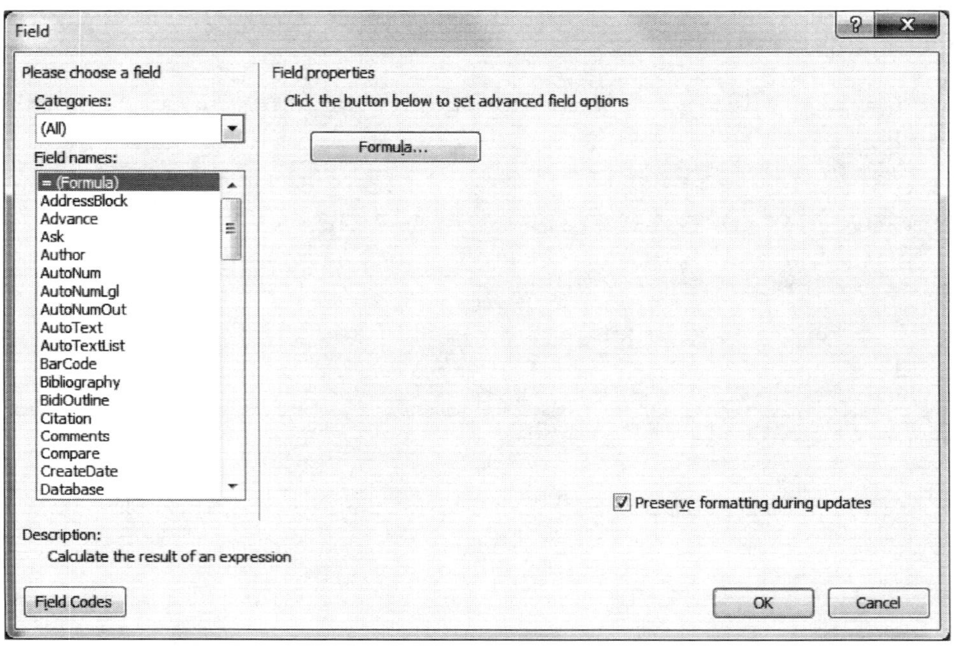

5. Click in the **Prompt** field and type your text, e.g. *Who is this memo to?*
6. Click on **OK**.
   The created dialogue box is presented. Click on **OK**.
7. Reposition the insertion point and repeat the above steps for all the required prompts.

As an aside *... Press* Alt F9 *to see field codes, and press again to return to text.*

Hands-on exercise 82

In this exercise you practise inserting Fill-in fields to automate your template.

First, you modify your template, inserting a variety of fields.

- Using your *Company memo* template, click your insertion point beside the **To** cell, i.e.

Memorandum

To	|
Cc	
From	
Department	
Email	
Date	
Subject	

Quick Parts

- Display the Insert ribbon, click on **Quick Parts**, then click on **Field** (Text group). The Field dialogue box is presented.
- Scroll down the **Field name** list and click on **Fill-in**.
- Click in the **Prompt** field and type the following: *Who is memo to?*
- Click on **OK**.
  The created dialogue box is presented. Click on **OK.**
- Press Alt F9 to see the inserted field.
- Click your insertion point beside the **Cc** cell.
- Click on **Quick Parts**, then click on **Field**. The Field dialogue box is presented.
- Scroll down the **Field name** list and click on **Fill-in**.
- Click in the **Prompt** field and type the following: *Who will receive a copy?*
- Click on **OK**.
  The created dialogue box is presented. Click on **OK.**
- Click your insertion point beside the **From** cell.
- Click on **Quick Parts**, then click on **Field**. The Field dialogue box is presented.
- Scroll down the **Field name** list and click on **Fill-in**.
- Click in the **Prompt** field and type the following: *Who is memo from?*
  Click in the field **Default response to prompt** and type: *Your Name.*
- Click on **OK**.
  The created dialogue box is presented. Click on **OK.**
- Complete the rest of the fields. Use a default for Department and Email (make something up), and use a Date field against the Date.
- Press Alt F9 to hide the field codes.
- **Save** your changes, then **close** your template.

Next, you create a new *document* based on this template.

- Display **Backstage** view, click on **New**, then click on **My Templates**. The New dialogue box is presented.
- Click on the *Company memo* template, then click on **OK**.
- A new *document* is presented based on your memo template and the first dialogue box is presented asking the question "Who is memo to?".
- Type a name, and then click on **OK**. The next dialogue box is presented.
- Type a name, and then click on **OK**. The next dialogue box is presented.
- Respond to all prompts, press Enter to accept defaults.
- **Save** your completed document as *Memo test* (with your other exercise files). Note the date of the memo is today's date.
- **Close** your document.

Hints & tips

You can copy and paste a field. But edit with care.

*Syntax of the fill-in field. Fields are surrounded by curly brackets, then comes the field name, then in the case of the fill-in field the prompt surrounded by double quote marks. The default text is preceded by a \d, then the default text (again with double quote marks). The \d is called a switch. Fields creating using the Field dialogue box automatically include the switch *MERGEFORMAT. This ensures that any formatting applied is retained when an update occurs.*

Terms & concepts review

- What is the name of the Word **field** used to prompt with dialogue boxes?

  ____

- Why are **fill-in fields** used in a template?

  ____

  ____

  ____

Consolidation task 19

In this task you produce an automated fax template.

- Create a new blank document.
- Create the following fax layout:

Facsimile

To
From
Department
Email
No of pages
Date
Subject

- Save your document as a **template** called *Company fax*.
  Leave the template open.
- Insert Fill-in fields to prompt for the information you require in your template. Ensure your insertion point is positioned before you insert a field. If a field is incorrectly positioned, drag over the entire field and press Delete
- Save your changes.
- Close your template.
- Create a new document from your template.
- Complete the required details in the dialogue boxes displayed.

After this Consolidation task, do you feel confident... tick the appropriate box:

	Creating template
	Inserting Fill-in fields
	Completing Fill-in fields

Topic 15 – Adding comments, tracking changes & comparing content

When collaborating on a document it can be useful to leave **comments** as you go, explaining why you have made changes or suggesting places where additions might be necessary.

To ensure that changes to a document are clearly identified, you can **track** changes, i.e. mark where you have added, deleted or modified text. These changes can then be reviewed (perhaps by your manager) and accepted or rejected.

If tracking was not switched on, and you wanted to know what changes had been made to a document, you can **compare** two versions of a document.

Adding comments to your document

Comments can easily be added, reviewed and deleted.

How to: Add a comment

1. Select the text that you want to comment on.
2. Display the Review ribbon, then click on the **New Comment** button (Comments group). A Markup Area opens. Note your initials in the comments balloon (as shown under Word *Options/General*).

Markup Area

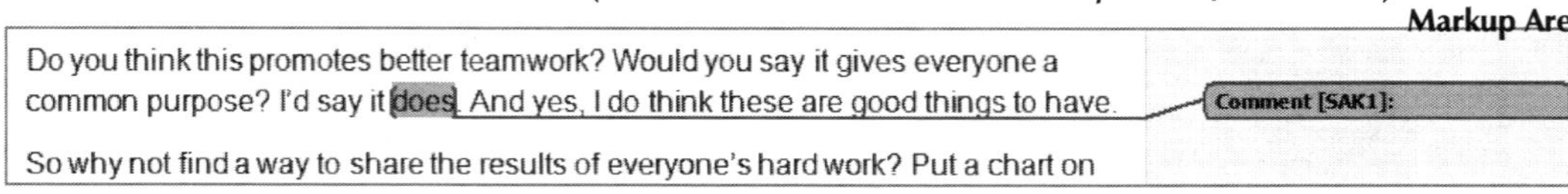

3. Type your comment into the comments balloon.

How to: Review your comments

1. Display the Review ribbon, then click on the **Next Comment/ Previous Comment** buttons (Comments group).

How to: Show/Hide your comments

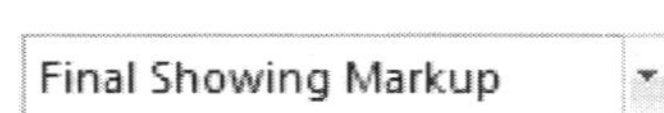

1. Display the Review ribbon, then click on the **Display for Review** down-arrow (Comments group).
2. Click on **Original Showing Markup/Final**.

How to: Delete a comment(s)

1. Show your comments

2. Right-click on a comment balloon, then click on **Delete Comment** *~or~*

   Display the Review ribbon, click on the **Delete** down-arrow (Comments group), then click on **Delete All Comments**.

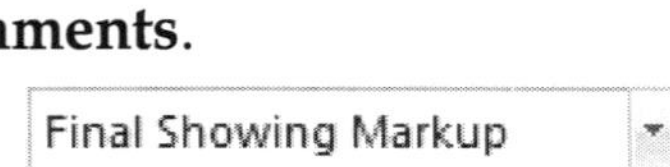

How to: Change your view

1. Display the Review ribbon, click on the **Display for Review** down-arrow (Comments group), then click on the required view.

Hands-on exercise 83

In this exercise you practice working with comments.

- **Open** the document *Developing a team*.
- Select the document heading.
- Display the Review ribbon, then click on the **New Comment** button (Comments group). A Markup Area opens. Note your initials in the comments balloon.

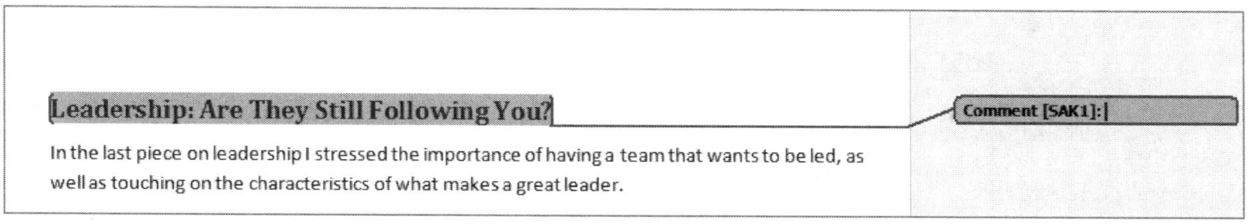

- Type the following comment into the comments balloon: *Can we reduce the following paragraphs?*
- Select the heading: Common Purpose
- Click on the **New Comment** button (Comments group).

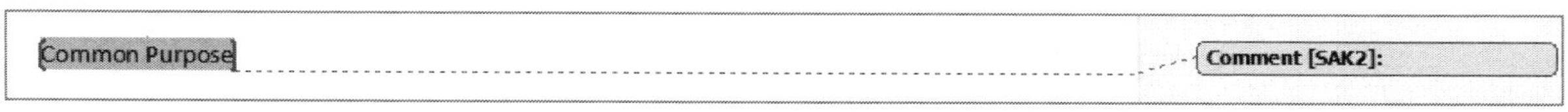

- Type the following comment into the comments balloon: *Can we expand the following paragraphs?*
- Go to the final page.
- Select the text as follows, and click on the **New Comment** button:

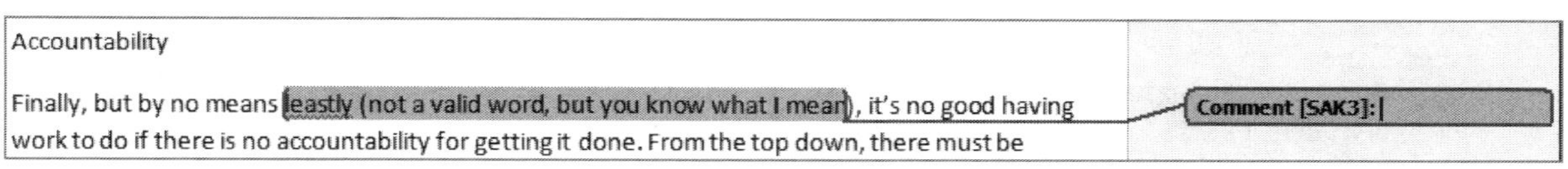

- Type the following comment into the comment balloon: *This needs rewording*.
- Go to the top of the document.

- Click on the **Next Comment** button to display each comment. Click on **OK** to the final message.
- Click on the **Display for Review** down-arrow (Comments group), then click on **Final**. Your document is displayed in its final state.
- Click on the **Display for Review** down-arrow, then click on **Final: Showing Markup**. Your document is displayed in its final revision state but with the comments showing.

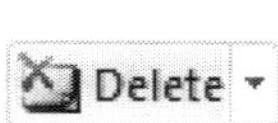

- Right-click on the first comments balloon, then click on **Delete Comment**.
- **Save** your changes.

Tracking document changes

If your manager asks you to review a document, but they want to see the changes you have made and decide whether to accept or reject them before the final document is distributed, then tracking is the feature to use.

How to: Turn tracking on/off

1. Display the Review ribbon, then click on the **Track Changes** button (Tracking group). The button is highlighted.
2. Make your changes to the text. Altered text is marked and changes are noted in the Markup Area.

3. To switch tracking off, click back on the **Track Changes** button. The highlight is removed from the button.

How to: Accept revisions

1. Ensure you are displaying markups.

2. Display the Review ribbon, then click on the **Accept and Move to Next** button (Changes group) *~or~*
   Click on the **Accept** down-arrow, then click on **Accept All Changes in Document**.

How to: Reject revisions

1. Ensure you are displaying markups.

2. Display the Review ribbon, then click on the **Reject and Move to Next** button (Changes group) *~or~*
   Click on the **Reject** down-arrow, then click on **Reject All Changes in Document**.

How to: Move between revisions

1. Display the Review ribbon, then click on the **Next Change/ Previous Change** buttons (Changes group).

Hands-on exercise 84

In this exercise you practise tracking.

- Using the document *Developing a team*, click on the **Track Changes** button (Tracking group). The button is highlighted.
- Select the paragraph at the top of the document commencing: In the last piece on leadership … .
- Delete this paragraph. Note the text is displayed in a colour with a line through. Note the line in the left margin.
- Select the following paragraph and apply **Bold**. The change is noted in the Markup Area. Note the line in the left margin.
- Click on the **Display for Review** down-arrow (Comments group), then click on **Original Show Markup**. Note how formatting changes are not displayed in this view, just detailed in the Markup area.

- Return to the view **Final Showing Markup**.
- Delete the comment attached to the heading Common Purpose.
- Type the following text beneath the existing paragraph:

  So in business, will it be helpful if everyone in the team has a common view of what they are trying to achieve? Does that need an answer?

  The altered text is shown in a colour and underlined (with a solid underline).
- Go to the final page.
- Delete the comment.
- Delete the following text:

> Finally, ~~but by no means leastly (not a valid word, but you know what I mean),~~ it's no good having work to do if there is no accountability for getting it done. From the top down, there must be consequences if things don't get done. This could mean slower progression, reduced responsibility, smaller pay rises, or it could just mean that someone actually gets upset about it (as opposed to nothing happening).

- Note the revision marks.
- Keeping this edit in view, click on the **Display for Review** down-arrow (Comments group), then click on **Original**. Note the original text without revision is displayed.
- Click on the **Display for Review** down-arrow, then click on **Final**. Your document is displayed in its final state.
- Click on the **Display for Review** down-arrow, then click on **Final with Markup**.

Next, you now work through accepting or rejecting the revisions.

- Go to the top of the document.

- Click on the **Next Change** button (Changes group).

- Click on the **Accept and Move to Next** button (Changes group). The text marked for deletion is removed.
- Click on the **Accept and Move to Next** button.
- Click on the **Accept and Move to Next** button.
- Click on the **Accept and Move to Next** button.
- Click on **OK**.

Finally, you switch off tracking.

- Click on the **Track Changes** button (Tracking group). The highlight is removed from the button.
- **Save** your changes.
- **Close** your document.

Comparing and merging content

If tracking was not switched on, and you needed to know what changes had been made to a document, you can **compare** two versions. Compare allows you to **merge** the differences between two documents into a single new document, reviewing each change. The documents being compared are not altered.

> ***As an aside** … Compare documents is best used when the original and revised documents do not contain tracked changes, as tracked changes are treated as accepted.*

How to: Compare two documents

1. Display the Review ribbon, click on the **Compare** button, then click on **Compare** (Compare group). The Compare Documents dialogue box is presented.

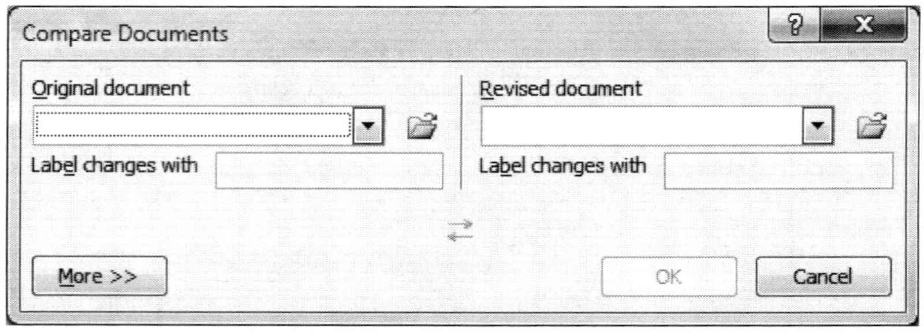

2. Select your **Original document**. (Use the folder icon to Browse.)
3. Select your **Revised document**. (Use the folder icon to Browse.)
4. Click on **OK**.

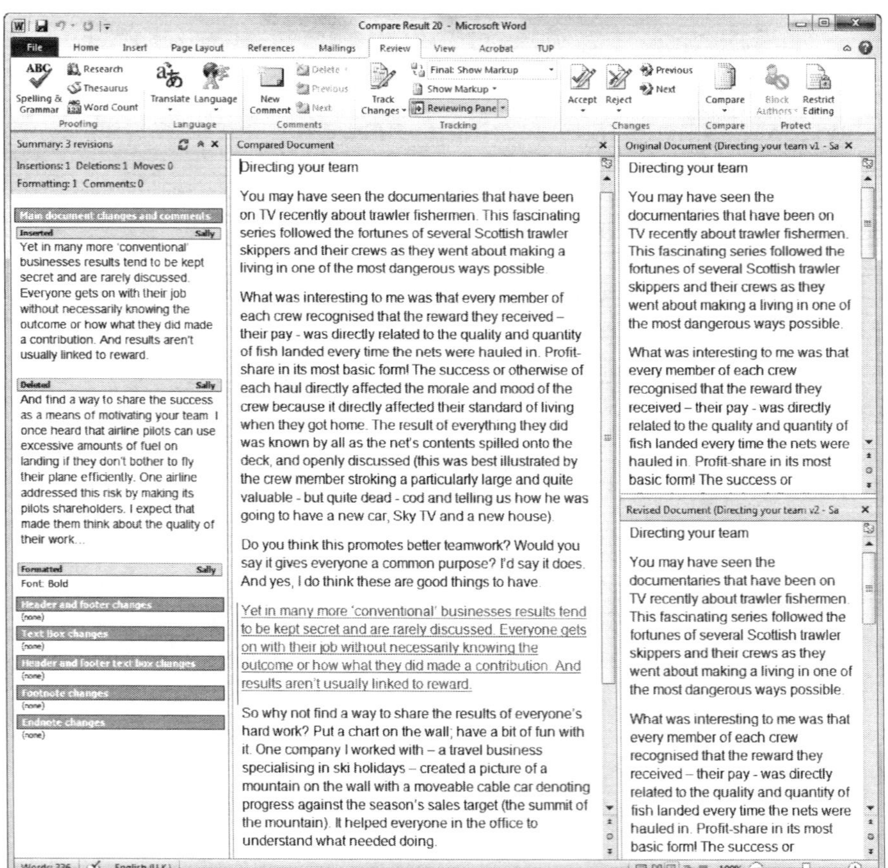

A new document is opened *Compare Results ...*
The Reviewing Pane is opened on the left of the screen.
At the top of the Reviewing Pane the differences are summarised (between the original and the revised version).
On the right of the screen are your two document versions (Original Document and Revised Document).
The new Compared Document is in the middle.

5. Use your **Accept/Reject/Next** and **Previous** buttons (Changes group) to view and accept or reject changes.
6. **Save** your new compared document.

Hands-on exercise 85

In this exercise you practise comparing two documents.

- **Open** the document *Directing your team v1*.
- Display the Review ribbon, click on the **Compare** button, then click on **Compare** (Compare group). The Compare Documents dialogue box is presented.
- Select *Directing your team v1* as your **Original document**.
(Use the folder icon to Browse. Click on **Open**.)
- Select *Directing your team v2* your **Revised document**.
(Use the folder icon to Browse. Click on **Open**.)
- Ensure the names of your selected documents are displayed.

  Click on **OK**.
  A new document is opened *Compare Results ...*
  The Reviewing Pane is opened on the left of the screen.
  At the top of the Reviewing Pane the differences are summarised (between the original and the revised version).
  On the right of the screen are your two document versions (Original Document (top) and Revised Document (bottom).
  The new Compared Document is in the middle.

- Click on the **Next Change** button.
You are taken to the first change.
Note the information in the Reviewing Pane (**Inserted -** and by whom).

- Click on the **Accept and Move to Next Change** button.
- You are taken to the next change.
Note the information in the Reviewing Pane (**Deleted**).
- Click on the **Accept and Move to Next Change** button.
- You are taken to the next change.
Note the information in the Reviewing Pane (**Bold**).
- Click on the **Accept and Move to Next Change** button.
- Click on **OK** to the message re comments and tracked changes.
- **Save** your new document as *Final version – Directing your team*.

- **Close** your document.
- Also **close** *Directing your team v1.*
- Re-**open** *Final version – Directing your team.* Ensure it is displayed in Print Layout view.
- **Close** your documents.

> ***As an aside*** *... Compare is used when comparing two documents. Combine is used when comparing two or more documents. If tracking is present these appear as tracked changes in the combined document.*

Hints & tips

To add a Track Changes indicator on the Status bar, right-click on the Status bar and click on Track Changes in the list presented.

*To prevent you from inadvertently distributing documents that contain tracked changes and comments, Word displays tracked changes and comments by default. (**Final Showing Markup** is the default option in **Display for Review**.)*

Terms & concepts review

- Why use **comments**?

  ____

  ____

- What does **tracking** create in a document?

  ____

  ____

  ____

- What happens when you **compare** two documents?

  ____

  ____

  ____

Workplace scenarios

These Workplace Scenarios have been developed as a set of tasks within a fictitious child care centre called the **Acorns Nursery**. To complete the scenarios you will need to refer to the following files which are stored with your exercise documents. Print out each file to refer to (you may have already printed some). Ask your instructor if you need assistance to locate these files:

- *OH&S guide* (PDF)
- *Org style guide - letter standard* (Word document)
- *Org style guide - memo standard* (Word document)
- *Acorns Nursery DocProc* (Word document).

First, you need to create a folder on the **C:** drive called **Acorns Nursery - HR - Your Initials**, e.g. **Acorns Nursery - HR - SAK***. You will store all your documents here. Within this folder create a sub-folder called **General Documents**, i.e. **C:\Acorns Nursery - HR - SAK\General Documents**.

* The initials are simply to distinguish the folder if several people are sharing one computer. Omit if unnecessary. You may also be directed to save this on your flash/USB drive.

Workplace scenario 1

You work for a fictitious child care centre called the **Acorns Nursery**. You have been asked to ensure that a Nursery Prospectus has an attractive and consistent look.

- First, using the *OH&S guide*, check your workstation setup.
- Open the document *Nursery prospectus* and review the text (located with your exercise files).
- Save this document into your **General Documents** folder, referring to the naming conventions specified in the document procedures guide *Acorns Nursery DocProc*.
- Referring again to your document procedures guide, review the Other Publications section.
- Improve the appearance of this document using paragraph styles with text characteristics as required by the guide. Also use a suitable character style to enhance readability. This document does not require a footer.

Workplace scenario 2

You have been asked to standardise the department's monthly report documents and ensure that in the future they follow a consistent layout and style.

- Create a new monthly report template which includes the following title information attractively formatted:

  Acorns Nursery Monthly Report
- Create a style for this heading called MainTitle.
- Include in the template a style to be used for Heading levels 1, 2, and 3, and body text. (Refer to your procedures guide for text characteristics.)
- Include a footer as per the procedures guide.
- Save your template using a suitable file name, then close.
- Create a new document based on your monthly report template and test the styles it contains. Close without saving.
- Re-open the template and add a blue colour to the MainTitle style.
- Save and close your template.
- Create a new document based on your revised monthly report template and review the updated style. Close without saving.

Workplace scenario 3

You have been asked to create an interview record form for new nursery staff. This form will be used on an on-going basis and therefore should be created as a template.

- Create the following:

Interview Record	
Vacancy	
Name	
Job Title	
Grade	
Salary	Office Use Only

Interview notes:

- **Save** your template using a suitable file name, then close.
- Create a new document based on the template.
- Close your document, without saving.

Workplace scenario 4

You have been asked to complete an Activity Sheet created for the nursery classes.

- The Activity Sheet has been commenced in a document called *Activity sheet*. Open and review, ensuring you review in Print Preview.
- Save this document into your **General Documents** folder, referring to the naming conventions specified in the document procedures guide.
- Insert three appropriate headings and Clip Art pictures in the blank squares on the right, e.g. jigsaws, pre-maths skills, drawing, story time, cooking. (Leave the Shapes square blank for now.)
- Insert the picture *Anne* into the square marked 'Your teacher'. This is a photograph.
- Add a border around the photograph.
- In the remaining Shapes square add three shapes of your choice with fill colour. Group your shapes.

Workplace scenario 5

You need to send out standard letters to all applicants for a newly created staff position. Interviews will be held on the same day, but candidates are each allotted a separate time. A document is available containing the candidates' names and time slots.

- Referring to your *Org style guide - letter standard*, create the following letter. (Note that <time> is a merge field that you will insert later.)

> Date
>
> Dear
>
> Thank you for applying for the position of Nursery Supervisor.
>
> I have reviewed your Curriculum Vitae and was impressed. Please arrange to attend for interview on 15th January at <Time>.
>
> If this time is not convenient, please contact the Human Resources Department on (extn.) 234 to make alternative arrangements.
>
> Yours sincerely
>
> Jane Pinkerton
> Human Resources Director

- Save this document into your **General Documents** folder, referring to the naming conventions specified in the document procedures guide.
- **Open** and review the document *Nursery applicants*.
  This is your data source. Also save this document into your **General Documents** folder, referring to the naming conventions specified in the document procedures guide.
- **Close** your data source document.

- Ensure you are displaying your letter, then create a mail merge for letters with appropriate address information.
  Don't forget the <Time> merge field in the body of the document.
- Merge all records to a new document.
- **Save** the main document.
  You do not need to save any output documents.
- Create **labels** to accompany the letters, again with suitable address information. Refer to your document procedures guide.

Workplace scenario 6

You have been asked to create a number of templates, with styles, to ensure that all the communications from the Acorns Nursery are consistent.

- Referring to the *Org style guide - letter standard*, create a letter template for the Acorns Nursery. Include two Quick Part items, one for Yours sincerely...James Pinkerton, Director, one for Yours faithfully... .
- Referring to the *Org style guide - memo standard*, create a memo template for the Acorns Nursery.
- Ensure you test your templates.

Skills challenges & Assessment tasks

Skills challenges are undertaken by a student on his or her own, providing further practice and challenges. *Assessment tasks* are suitable to assess competency in the unit.

Creating a working area

Throughout this part of the course you create a number of files. To ensure these are efficiently organised, you need to have a suitable location in which to store them.

In the student exercise files downloaded at the beginning of this book, you will find a folder named: *Challenges and Assessment task files*. Within this folder you will find all necessary files for these Challenges and Assessment tasks. The files and folder structure are set up so it feels like you are on a business intranet. You will be instructed to open, edit and save into these files to prepare you for a workplace folder structure.

If you find you need more assistance with creating folders, refer to the *Managing files and folders* topic in *Tilde Publishing and Distribution's Using Business Technology*. Create these folders before you begin the next section.

Information used in the assessments section was originally provided by Earth Sanctuaries Limited (ESL). Environmental Challenges Australia (ECA) and Commetz Pty Ltd are fictitious organisation.

OH&S

Re-check your workstation setup using your printout of the supplied *OH&S guide* before you continue.

Skills challenge 1

Environmental Challenges Australia are setting up a new office in NSW. You have been recruited as an assistant to two managers with responsibilities in Personnel (including Health and Safety) and Communications (including public liaison).

Your first task is to read the company style and procedures guide from the company files. This document has been password protected for changes, but read-only access is available.

- Locate your student exercise folder.
- Open (read-only) *Advanced style and procedures guide.doc* (Found in *1 About this Organisation/ Standard files*).
- Print and review the company style and procedures guide. (You will refer to this document throughout the course for organisation requirements relating to document style and image.)
- Close your document.

> ***As an aside*** *... Many organisations have their own requirements for the presentation of documents, e.g. size and style of text used and document layout. Standards are usually presented in a company Style Guide or Procedures Manual.*

Skills challenge 2

Your next task is to attractively format a document using styles to ensure a consistent appearance as the document develops.

- The Communications Manager has left you the following voicemail:

> Some information has been saved into a document which will be the basis for a handout I am developing. Can you open it for me and format attractively (within company guidelines)? I will be developing this document over the next few days.
>
> Thanks

- Open the document: *Australian wildlife.doc* (*2 Keeping Members Informed/Educational Material*).
- Apply the Heading 1 style to the document heading.
- Apply the Heading 2 style to the headings: *Southern Brown Bandicoot; Tammar Wallaby; and Woylie.* (Apply to the text above the pictures only.)
- Apply the Heading 3 style to the headings: *Scientific name; Where to see them*; and *Status*. (These headings are repeated 3 times.) (Only apply to the headings, not the text under it.)
- Save your changes.

Having reviewed the corporate style guide, you realise you need to modify a number of styles. You will also create some new styles.

- Modify the Heading 1, 2 and 3 styles so that they reflect the corporate style requirements.
  Ensure all headings are updated throughout the document.

- Return to the top of the document and select the first picture.
- Apply a centre alignment and a space after paragraph measurement of 4 pts.
- Create a new style from the selected picture called: *Picture*
- Apply the new style to all pictures in the document.
- Return to the top of the document and select the text under the first picture: *'Southern Brown Bandicoot'*.
- Apply a centre alignment, italics, and a font colour of green.
- Create a new style from the selected text called: *Picture Captions*
- Apply the new style to all captions beneath pictures.
- Create an italicised style for all scientific names called *Latin Names*. Apply as required throughout the document.
- Modify the Latin Names style to incorporate the font colour orange. Ensure all Latin text is updated throughout the document.
- Modify the Normal style to reflect the corporate style requirement (Basic font and font size). Also, add a space after paragraph measurement of 12 pts.
- Modify the Picture style so that it is followed automatically by the Picture Captions style.
- Modify the Picture Captions style so that it is followed automatically by the Heading 3 style.
- Insert a next page break on page 1 before the heading: *Tammar Wallaby*.
- Review your document in Print Preview, then print it.
- Save your changes and close your document.

Skills challenge 3

You receive the following email from the Communications Manager.

> I have noticed that fax cover sheets produced by various departments are not following the company standard closely enough. I understand that you have the knowledge and skills to create Word templates. Please can you create a template for a fax which follows the guidelines provided in the corporate style and procedures document. I would also like to know where the templates we create are stored.
>
> Thanks.

- You begin by finding out where your templates are stored.
- Review your template storage locations and note down your location for User templates.

____

As an aside ... *If you do not have access to this area, refer to your instructor or Systems Administrator. In a standard installation of Office 2010 on Windows 7, the Templates folder is in the AppData\Roaming\Microsoft\Template folder within your user folder. Office 2010 on Windows XP is generally in the C:\Documents and Settings\User Name\Application Data\Microsoft\Templates.*

- Create a template for a fax cover sheet that follows the corporate layout requirements. (Consider indents, tab settings or a table layout, and a paragraph/table border.)
- Save using a suitable name and close your template.
- Create a new document from your fax template.
- Close the document without saving.
- Open the fax template (check your title bar to ensure you are working in the template).
- Add a footer in a suitable font/size/position which reads:
  Environmental Challenges Australia
  Tel: 02 9976 0843 Fax: 02 9977 1221
- Save your changes and close your template.
- Create a new document from your fax template.
- Close the document without saving.
- Present your newly created template to your teacher or assessor.

Skills challenge 4

You receive a follow-up email from the Communications Manager.

> The fax template is great – well done! Can you also create a report template? What I am most concerned about here is that the correct text style is used for headings. Again, if you refer to the corporate style and procedures document you will find the company requirements outlined.
>
> Many thanks.

- Commence a new template from scratch.
- Check the report margins to the company style guidelines.

Next, you edit the built-in Heading styles (Heading 1, 2, 3) to reflect the company style guidelines.

- With the template open, display the Modify Style dialogue box for each heading style and modify as required.
  (Note you have gone straight to the modify dialogue box rather than amending the style using a selection of text as no text is used in the template.)
- Modify the Normal style as required for a report.
- Save using a suitable name and close your template.
- Create a new document from your report template.
- Test the heading and normal styles by typing paragraphs of dummy text.
- Close the document without saving.
- Open the report template (check your title bar to ensure you are working in the template).
- Add a footer in a suitable font/size/position which provides page information as follows: Page *x*
- Add an entry for Environmental Challenges Australia Ltd to the AutoCorrect list for the *report template*.
- Add 3 AutoText entries to the *report template* as follows:

Fnrep	ECA Financial Report
mkrep	ECA Marketing Report
Perep	ECA Personnel Report

  (In this instance type the text into the template in order to create the AutoText, then delete before you save.)

- Save your changes and close your template.
- Create a new document from your report template.
- Test your AutoCorrect and AutoText entries.

- Close the document without saving.
- Present your newly created template to your teacher or assessor.

Skills challenge 5

You receive the following voicemail:

> "We now seem to have a good suite of templates. There is a company letter template available on the intranet we should also have. Can you download and store it with the others. You will need to amend it with our office details.
>
> Thanks"

- Open the template for editing *Letter template.dot* (*1 About this Organisation/Standard files*).
- Add the office telephone, fax and address details as follows.

  Environmental Challenges Australia Ltd
  Challenges House
  Wildlife Lane
  Manly NSW 2095

  Tel: 02 9976 0843
  Fax: 02 9977 1221
- Save your changes and close your template.
- Create a new document from your letter template and check the added details.
- Close the document without saving.
- Present your amended template to your teacher or assessor.

Skills challenge 6

The Personnel Manager has asked you to create a form for recording employment details. She has sketched out her ideas.

Employment Record	Employee Number
Name:	
Department:	
Date employment commenced:	
Grade:	
Starting salary:	
Comments:	For Office Use Only

- Create the form in a landscape, A5 document.
  Margins: Top/bottom: 2 cm; Left/right 2.5 cm.
- The required table should fill the page.

> ***As an aside** … Remember, don't worry if the rows etc are uneven at first. Use the Distribute Rows/Columns Evenly button to address this once the basic design is in place.*

- Save the document into your *Communications* folder using a suitable filename (refer to the company style and procedures guide for file naming conventions).
- Perform a spelling and grammar check on your document.
- Preview, print and proof read your document for accuracy. (Print on A4 paper if A5 not available.)

After reviewing your initial draft, the Personnel Manager has requested the following changes:

Employment Record	
Name:	For Office Use Only
Department:	
Date employment commenced:	
Grade:	
Starting salary:	

- Make the required changes.
- Preview, print and proof read your document for accuracy.
- Close your document.

Skills challenge 7

The Communications Manager has asked you to create the following table of share price data.

ECA	Last	$ +/-	Bid	Offer	Open	High	Low	Vol
	ECA – Environmental Challenges Australia							
	0.200	0.020	0.170	0.200	0.180	0.200	0.180	5,200

- Create the table in a landscape document.
- Ensure you align the decimal data with decimal tabs (the **Vol** heading and data are right-aligned).
- Save the document into your *Communications* folder using a suitable filename (refer to the company style and procedures guide for file naming conventions).
- Perform a spelling and grammar check on your document.
- Preview, print and proof read your document for accuracy.
- Close your document.

Skills challenge 8

You have received the following voicemail from the Communications Manager:

> Can you quickly open for me the list of awards. It's not quite in the format I need. Is it possible to sort the list by category within year and add an attractive heading?
>
> Thanks

- Open the document *Awards.doc* (2 *Keeping Members Informed/ News*).
- Sort the list by category within year (ascending).
- Add an attractive heading to the table (in a new row) that reads: Environmental Awards Received 2008 - 2011
- Save your changes.
- Print and close your document.

Skills challenge 9

You have received the following email from the Communications Manager.

> Do you remember the Australian Wildlife document I was creating? Well I've eventually got round to having another look. I've noted down some requirements and layout ideas. Can you pop into my office when convenient so I can talk them through with you?
>
> Thanks.

You meet with the Communications Manager and from that meeting you have a list of points to be addressed.

- Open the document *Australian wildlife* created earlier.
- Add a table to hold information at the top of the document as follows (no borders):

Australian Wildlife at **Environmental Challenges Australia**	

Southern Brown Bandicoot

Southern Brown Bandicoot

Next, in the empty cell of the table you add a picture.

- Insert the picture *Quoll young at Warrawong* into the empty cell. The picture is saved in 2 *Keeping Members Informed/ Photos*.
- Reduce the size of the downloaded picture and centre align it in the cell.

Next, you add a Clip Art picture in a new cell at the front of the table.

- Add a new column to the front of the table.
- Add a suitable 'nature' Clip Art into the new cell.
- Size and align the picture appropriately.
- Centre the text in the middle cell.

Next, you download the company logo from the intranet and insert it into the document.

- Insert the picture file *ECA logo.jpg* (*1 About this Organisation/ Standard files)* into the footer of your document, making it right-aligned.
- Reduce the logo to fit appropriately.
- Change the text wrapping on the picture to In Front of Text.
- Add a text box alongside with the text:
  Environmental Challenges Australia
- Draw the following AutoShape at the top of the page.

- Insert a text box and rotate to align with the AutoShape. Add the following text:
  Open Day 12th March
- Add a lime green fill colour.
- At the top of the document, delete the caption under the picture Southern Brown Bandicoot.

- Cut and paste the picture to the beginning of the descriptive paragraphs below:

Status

Endangered

The Southern Brown Bandicoot is in critical trouble. Their numbers have crashed across Australia. What has gone wrong?

- Change the text wrapping on the picture to Tight.
- Make this change to all three pictures in the document.
- Paginate the document so that each animal appears on a new page.

Finally, you insert a text file of further information.

- Display your *Australian wildlife* document.
- Go to the end of the document.
- Insert a page break
- Insert the *Ringtail Possum* file (*2 Keeping Members Informed/Educational Material*).
- Rework the text to match the previous pages.
- Review your document in Print Preview.
- Save your changes.
- Print and close your document.

Skills challenge 10

The Communications Manager has asked you to create a newsletter from some of the information available on the publicly-accessible web site.

You meet with the Communications Manager and from that meeting you have a list of points to be addressed.

- In a new document create three (equal) newspaper columns.
- Import the file *Warrawong Earth Sanctuary webpage*. (*2 Keeping Members Informed/Educational Material*).
- Save the file into your *Communications* folder with an appropriate title.

Next, you modify a number of the styles associated with the imported text.

- Modify the style **Normal (Web)** to Times New Roman 12 pt, space after paragraph 12 pt, and single line spacing.
- Modify the style **title_sub1** to Arial 14 pt, bold.
- Modify the style **title_sub2** to Arial 12 pt, bold.
- Add column breaks before the two headings: Accommodation and Guided Tours.

Next, you create a new section with a different layout.

- At the top of the document, insert a continuous section break.
- Format the new section as one column.
- Type the heading: *Environmental Challenges Australia News*
- Format with the heading with the style Heading 1.
- Modify the style to incorporate a centre alignment and a space after paragraph of 24 pts.

Finally, you add a picture taken from the web site.

- Insert the picture *Rufous Bettong at Warrawong* (*2 Keeping Members Informed/Photos*) into the document.
- Add wrapping and drag the picture to the centre of the first page.
- Review your column breaks and adjust any as necessary.
- Balance the columns on the final page.
- Save your changes.
- Preview, print and proof read your document for accuracy.
- Close your document.

Skills challenge 11

You have received further feedback on the Australian wildlife document created earlier. You need to add a title page and a copyright page, and then adjust the document footer.

- Open the document *Australian wildlife* created earlier.
- At the top of the document, insert a page break followed by a next page section break. This will create a section of two pages.
- Move the heading (entire table) from page 3 onto page 1.
- Move the table further down the page by dragging on the table move handle ⊞.
- Go to the top of page 2.
- Change the vertical alignment of the text to bottom.
- Type the following text:

Copyright

Text copyright © <*insert current year*> by Environmental Challenges Australia.
Illustration, layout and design copyright © <*insert current year*> by Environmental Challenges Australia.

- Save your changes.

Next, you change the footers in the two different sections of the document.

- Go to section 2.
- View the document footer.
- Unlink the footer from section 1.
- Delete the footer in section 1.
- Use an appropriate view to review the layout of your document.
- Save your changes.
- Print your document.
- Close your document.

Skills challenge 12

You have received the following email from the Communications Manager.

> Can you download the latest Director's report from the intranet, and then come see me. I would like to make a few changes to the layout before distribution within the department.
>
> Thanks.

- Open the document: *Directors report.doc* (*1 About this Organisation/ Standard files*).

You meet with the Communications Manager and from that meeting you have a list of points to be addressed.

- Use an appropriate view to review the document. It is comprised of five pages, all in one section.
- You have been asked to add the following footer on pages 3-5 only (aligned left, centre and right):

  Confidential, Page #, Date
- Ensure the page numbering (from page 3) starts at 1. Format appropriately.

Next, you add a page number cross reference to a heading.

- Go to page 3.
- Add the following text beneath the list of names (aligned to the left margin):

  For further information on the Directors of Environmental Challenges Australia, see page
- Create a page number cross reference to the heading:

  Information on Directors
- Also on page 3, add a paragraph **above** the heading Principal Activities which reads:

  For further information on the Directors' remuneration policy, see page
- Create a page number cross reference to the heading: Remuneration Policy

Finally, you add footnotes.

- Also on page 3, click your insertion point after the text:

  Miles M. Cummings (resigned 15/6/02)
- Insert a footnote at the bottom of the page that reads:

  Alternate for Alison G. Besley.
- Find the text:

  $500,000 for the financial year
- Click your insertion point after this text.

- Insert a footnote at the bottom of the page that reads:

  Representing a gain of 1 cent per share.
- Use an appropriate view to review your document.
- Save your changes.
- Print your document.
- Close your document.

Skills challenge 13

You have been asked to create a mail merge to send thank you letters to supporters of your organisation who have recently made donations. You also need to create accompanying labels.

First, you create the data source to be used for your standard letters and labels.

- Create a data source document containing the following information on supporters who have made donations:
  - First Name
  - Last Name
  - Street
  - Suburb
  - State
  - Post Code
  - Donation
- Add information for four fictitious contacts. Also include an amount for the donation.
- Save the document into your *Communications* folder using a suitable filename.
- Print and proof read the data for accuracy.

Next, you create your standard letter.

- Create the following letter using your letter template:

> Date
>
> Earth Challenges Australia would like to thank you for your generous contribution to our environmental work. Your donation of $ was gratefully received.
>
> Thank you again for your support.
>
> Yours sincerely
>
> Mark Harrison
> Communications Manager

- Save the document into your *Communications* folder using a suitable filename.
- Perform a spelling and grammar check on your document.
- Preview, print and proof read your document for accuracy.

Next, you perform your merge.

- Commence a merge and merge this letter with your data source. Insert merge fields in the letter in the appropriate places. The Donation field is required in the body of the letter.
- Merge the letter to a new document. After viewing your output, you do not need to save the document created.
- Close all open documents, ensuring you save your letter layout if prompted.

Next, you create labels to accompany your letters.

- Create a new document to hold your label layout.
- Commence a mail merge for labels.
- Ensure you select all the required options for your labels – refer to the company style and procedures guide for label conventions.
- Use your table of supporters as your data source document.
- Ensure all suitable fields are included on the label layout.
- Merge to a new document and review.
- Close the label output without saving.
- Save the label layout document into your Communications folder using a suitable filename.
- Close all open documents.

Assessment tasks

This section of the topic contains realistic Assessment tasks. They are designed to provide a final check of your competency of this text in documents through a number of real world scenarios.

Output from Assessment tasks should be submitted to your teacher or assessor for review. Consult with your teacher or assessor as to how and when they require completed work to be submitted, i.e. emailed as attachments or in a printed format.

Assessment task 1

The Personnel Manager says that a document has been posted on the company intranet re health and safety standards which she wants you to review.

- Open the document: *Company health and safety policy.doc (1 About this Organisation/ Standard files)*.
- Print and review the document. Ensure that your workspace and work organisation meet company standards, and that you remind yourself of energy and resource conservation techniques.

Assessment task 2

You have received the following email from the Communications Manager.

> Can you design a weekly report template to be used by all the secretaries? Ensure the presentation compliments other report templates and follows the corporate style guidelines. Include a heading at the top which says Environmental Challenges Australia. This will be the main heading. Add a date beneath, right-aligned, then add a secondary heading of Weekly Management Report. I will often type a bulleted list and want to make sure this is typed consistently. I will also often type the following text:' to be carried forward to the next meeting'. It would be useful if this could be entered quickly each time. Also, can you include the company logo somewhere (ECA logo.jpg).
>
> Thanks

- Check with your teacher or assessor for the timeline on this task.
- Create a template that contains all the required items mentioned in this email. Ensure the resulting document follows good document design and layout principles.
- Save the document into an appropriate folder using a suitable filename.
- Ensure the document is accurate and error free.
- Present the functionality of your newly created template to your teacher or assessor.

Assessment task 3

The Communications Manager calls you into his office to discuss an agenda he is working on. He has sketched out a layout and has asked you to create the document, ensuring it fits in with the corporate style guidelines.

Agenda

Project Manager's Meeting

Date:	26/05/11	Time:	8:00 am–9:30 am	Location:	Meeting Rm 1
Participants:	XYZ Project Team				
Purpose:	Weekly Project Manager's (PMs) meeting				

Order of Business

1.	Opening of meeting.		
2.	Apologies.		
3.	Approval of previous minutes.		
4.	Agenda Items:		
	Unsupported items	SAK	20 mins
	Standard project plan	HGP	15 mins
	Departmental status report	RIR	15 mins
5.	Any other business.		
6.	Closing of meeting.		

Agenda Distribution

Participants; RYT.

- Check with your teacher or assessor for the timeline on this task.
- Create a document that contains all the necessary information. Ensure the resulting document meets the task requirements and corporate guidelines.
- Save the document into your *Communications* folder using a suitable filename.
- Ensure the document is accurate and error free.
- Submit your completed document to your teacher or assessor for assessment.

Assessment task 4

You have received the following voicemail from Mark Harrison, the Communications Manager.

> I need to send a letter to a student who enquired about some information on bilbies. Send them a reply saying: Many thanks for your enquiry regarding information on bilbies for your school project. Please find attached details that I hope you will find useful. Please ensure that my name and title appears as the letter signatory.
>
> Then, insert the Bilby file.
>
> The student's details are: Miss Alison Quong, 23 Jack Street, Rydalmere, NSW 2115.
>
> Thanks

- Check with your teacher or assessor for the timeline on this task.
- Create the letter as required in the above voicemail, then start a new page and insert the file *Bilby.doc* (*2 Keeping Members Informed/ Educational Material*).
- Save the document into your *Communications* folder using a suitable filename.
- Reformat the text headings and body text appropriately. (Information in tables can be left as is.)
- Use a suitable view to review your document.
- After page one, remove the document header and change the top margin to 2.5 cm.
- Paginate appropriately.
- Ensure the document is accurate and error free.
- Submit your completed document to your teacher or assessor for assessment.

Assessment task 5

The Personnel Manager asks you to generate a letter to staff of Environmental Challenges Australia advising them of their pay increase. A document already exists which can be used as the data source.

- Check with your teacher or assessor for the timeline on this task.
- Open the document *Pay increase* (*1 About this Organisation/ Staff files*) to review.
  It has a password for security. The password in 1357a.
  (Passwords are case sensitive.)
- Create an appropriate letter to be used as the main document in your letter merge. You need to include the name, department and location (as an address). You also need to include the amount of the increase in the body of the letter. The letter is being sent by: Susan Harris, Personnel Manager.
- Save your letter into an appropriate folder using a suitable filename.
- Ensure your letter is accurate and free of errors.
- Pass-on/email your letter to your teacher or assessor for comments on content and presentation. Amend as necessary.
- Generate a letter to each staff member. The letters produced need to be sorted by Dept. Print your letters.
- Generate a label to accompany each letter. The labels also need to be sorted by Dept. Print your labels.
- Submit your completed documents to your teacher or assessor for assessment.

Assessment task 6

The Communications Manager has asked you to download a document he needs to review.

- Open the document *Catalogue of wildlife* (*2 Keeping Members Informed/ Educational Material*).
- After reviewing the document, he sends you the following email.

> I will be adding lots more information to this document. Can you ensure that the main headings in this document (Southern Brown Bandicoot, Tamar Wallaby, etc) always start on a new page? I know you use a style. Can you add something to the style to ensure this happens?
>
> Thanks.

- Amend your style to include the required pagination (page break before). If required, use Word's Help feature to determine how to control pagination.
- Demonstrate the solution to this request to your teacher or assessor.

Appendix I

Keyboard shortcuts: Direct key combinations

Fundamentals

New document	Ctrl N	Open document	Ctrl O
Close document	Ctrl W	Print	Ctrl P
Save document	Ctrl S	Save as	F12
Undo	Ctrl Z	Redo	Ctrl Y
Cut	Ctrl X	Copy	Ctrl C
Paste	Ctrl V	Find	Ctrl F
Replace	Ctrl H	Go to	Ctrl G
Return to last edit	Shift F5	Repeat	F4
Spell check	F7	Thesaurus	Shift F7

Character formats

Bold	Ctrl B	Italics	Ctrl I
Underline	Ctrl U	Remove character formats	Ctrl Spacebar
Font	Ctrl Shift F	Font size	Ctrl Shift P

Paragraph formats

Centre	Ctrl E	Align left	Ctrl L
Align right	Ctrl R	Justify	Ctrl J
Single line spacing	Ctrl 1	Double line spacing	Ctrl 2
1½ line spacing	Ctrl 5	Remove paragraph formats	Ctrl Q

Page/line/word division

Manual (hard) page break	Ctrl Enter	New line (not a new paragraph)	Shift Enter
Non-breaking space	Ctrl Shift Spacebar		

Extra movement keys - text

Beginning of line	Home	End of line	End
Top of document	Ctrl Home	End of document	Ctrl End
Top of previous page	Ctrl Page Up	Top of next page	Ctrl Page Down
Select browse object	Alt Ctrl Home		

Extra movement keys - tables

Previous cell	Shift Tab	First cell in row	Alt Home
Last cell in row	Alt End	First cell in column	Alt Page Up
Last cell in column	Alt Page Down		
Tab in a table cell	Ctrl Tab		

Styles

Normal	Ctrl Shift N	Heading 1	Alt Ctrl 1
Heading 2	Alt Ctrl 2	Heading 3	Alt Ctrl 3
Apply Styles task pane	Ctrl Shift S		

Field codes

Insert field brackets	Ctrl F9	Update fields (Manually)	F9
Display fields (All)	Alt F9	Display fields (Selected)	Shift F9
Move to next field (useful for editing)	F11	Move to previous field	Shift F11

Index, footnotes and endnotes

Insert a footnote	Alt Ctrl F
Insert an endnote	Alt Ctrl E

Selecting

Press the Shift key with movement keys to select as you move, e.g. Shift End to select to the end of the line.

To mark a large block of text, click to mark the start of the block. Scroll with the scroll bar, then press Shift and click to mark the end of the block.

Keyboard shortcuts: Word 2010 access keys

New to Word 2010, you can use an alternative set of key strokes to access ribbons and commands.

How to: Activate access keys

1. Press Alt. Letter badges appear against each tab.

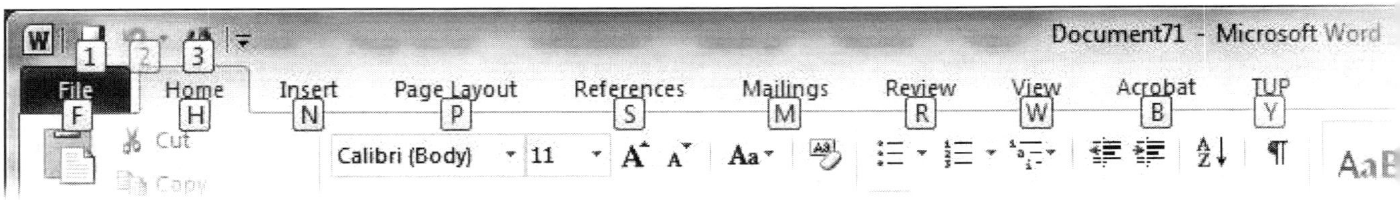

2. Press the required letter to activate a ribbon, e.g. N to activate the Insert ribbon. The selected ribbon is presented with more badges.

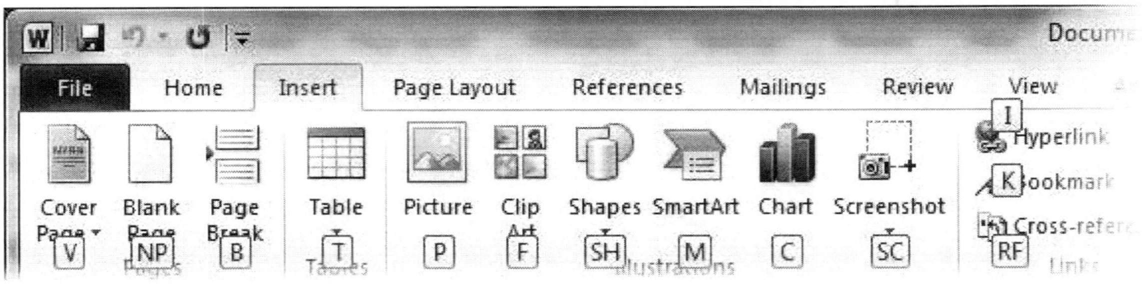

3. Press the required letter for a command, e.g. B for Page Break. The command is executed and the badges disappear.
4. Once you have memorised these commands, you can simply type them in sequence, e.g. Alt, N, B.

As an aside *… Press Esc to hide the badges if you display them accidentally.*

Appendix II

Customising the Quick Access Toolbar

You may find that you have several frequently-used commands that you require quicker access to. Command buttons can easily be added to the Quick Access Toolbar.

How to: Customise the Quick Access Toolbar

1. Right-click on a command button, then click on **Add to Quick Access Toolbar** *~or~*
   Click on the **Customize Quick Access Toolbar** button, then click on the additional commands required from the list presented.

How to: Remove buttons from the Quick Access Toolbar

1. Right-click on a command button added to the Quick Access Toolbar, then click on **Remove from Quick Access Toolbar**.

Using Help

No matter how good your knowledge of Word, there will be times when you need to look for further information. When you request help, if you are connected to the internet you are connected to online help. If you are not connected to the internet (offline), help files stored on your computer are searched. Online help provides access to extended facilities including tutorials and the latest downloads.

How to: Use Help

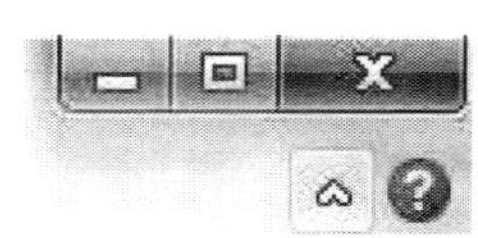

1. Click on the **Microsoft Word Help** button.
   The Word Help window is presented.

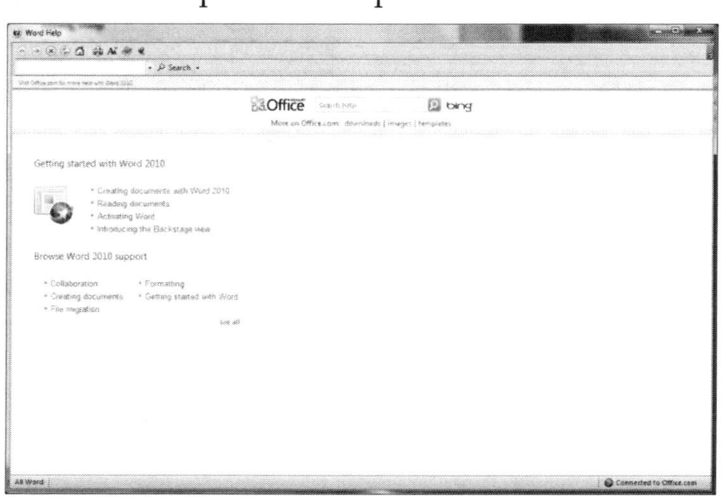

2. Note in the bottom-right corner of the window whether you are connected to the internet for your help (Connected to Office.com) or

whether you are Offline. (Click on this option if you want to change where you go for help – online or offline.)

3. Click on one of the links in the Help window, e.g. **Formatting** ~*or*~ Type a search word or phrase in the **Search list**,

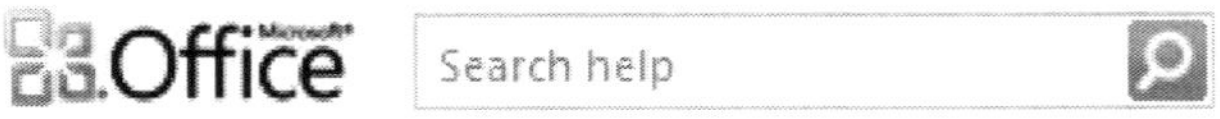

then press Enter

4. If topics are found they are presented in the Help window (as links).
5. Follow the link on the most relevant topic.
6. The following buttons are particularly useful.

	Back
	Forward
	Print

7. Click on **Close** to exit the Help window.

Inserting hyperlinks

A hyperlink is text formatted to jump or link to related information when you hold Ctrl and click on the link. Hyperlinks normally appear in blue text and underlined to help you easily identify them. The linked document can be located on your desktop, an intranet, a network, or the Internet. A hyperlink might also go to an email address or to another area within the same document.

> ***As an aside ...*** *If you type a web address directly in your document, Word will automatically format it as a link.*

How to: Insert a hyperlink

1. Select the text you want to appear linked.
2. Display the Insert ribbon, then click on the **Hyperlink** button (Links group). The Insert Hyperlink dialogue box is presented.

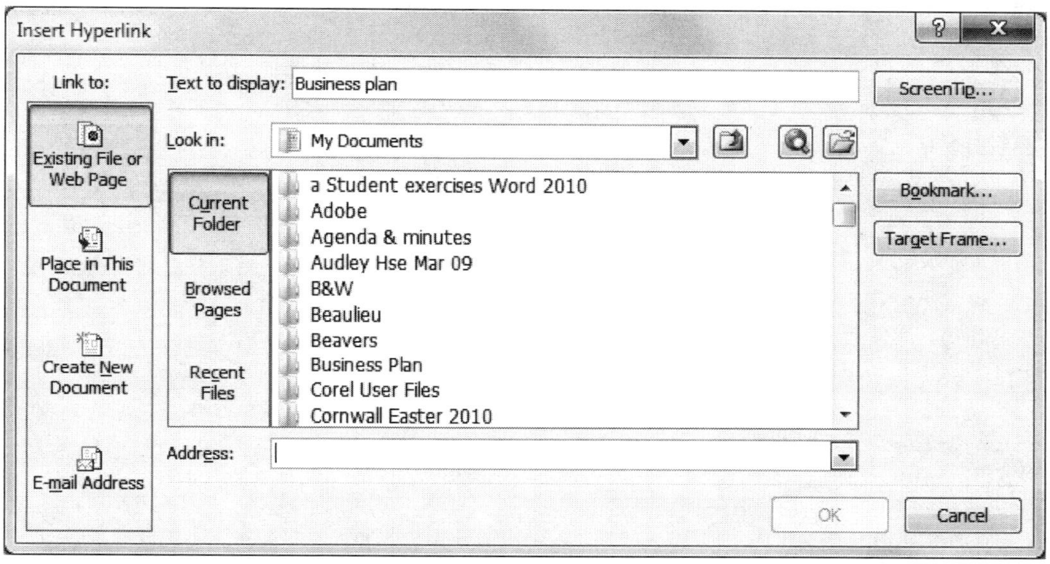

3. Enter the file to which you want the hyperlink to jump to in **Address**.
4. Click on **OK**.

Index

SPITFIRE

THE HISTORY OF

BRITAIN'S MOST FAMOUS

WORLD WAR II FIGHTER

SPITFIRE

THE HISTORY OF BRITAIN'S MOST FAMOUS WORLD WAR II FIGHTER

ROBERT JACKSON

Parragon

Bath · New York · Singapore · Hong Kong · Cologne · Delhi · Melbourne

This edition published by Parragon in 2010

Parragon
Queen Street House
4 Queen Street
Bath BA1 4HE, UK

Editorial and design by
Amber Books Ltd
Bradley's Close
74–77 White Lion Street
London N1 9PF
www.amberbooks.co.uk

ISBN 978-1-4075-9404-0

Printed in China

CONTENTS

CHAPTER ONE

Ancestral Lines

The name 'Spitfire' has become a household word in the English language, not just by identification with a particularly beautiful fighter aircraft, but also as a symbol of defiance from the darkest days of World War II. Mention the word Spitfire to anyone, even all these years later, and it will be greeted with a smile of understanding.

Mention the name Supermarine Baby, on the other hand, and it will probably be greeted with a blank look. The Baby was the first British fighter flying boat. Only one example was built, but the concept led to the development of two more designs, the Sea King and the Sea Lion; and all three aircraft were the first links in a chain of development that would lead directly to the Spitfire.

The Sea King, powered by a 119kW (160hp) Beardmore engine, attracted a lot of interest but no customers. The Sea Lion, with a 224kW (300hp) Hispano-Suiza powerplant, was entered in the 1919 Schneider Trophy contest and performed well, despite the fact that its hull got holed and the pilot lost himself in fog. In the 1922 contest, Supermarine entered the Sea Lion II, which was the original Sea Lion rebuilt as a racing flying boat and powered by a 336kW (450hp) Napier Lion engine. Piloted by Captain H.C. Biard, the Sea Lion II won the contest with comparative ease, completing the 370km (200nm) course in 1 hour 34 minutes and 54 seconds at an average speed of 234.4km/h (145.7mph) and beating three Italian entries.

Talented

The Sea Lion II was the brainchild of a talented young designer named Reginald Mitchell. Mitchell joined Supermarine in 1916 as assistant to Hubert Scott-Paine, chief engineer and designer (the company had been founded in 1912 by the pioneer aviator Noel Pemberton-Billing, who had built his first flying boat in 1913, and was based at Woolston, on the Itchen river near Southampton). In 1920, Scott-Paine appointed Mitchell chief engineer and designer on projects that were mainly concerned with military flying boats.

The key to the whole task of producing a successful high-speed aircraft was the powerplant, and it was their technical skill in building high-performance aero-engines which enabled the

Opposite: HM King Edward VIII inspects K5054, the Supermarine Spitfire prototype, at Martlesham on 8 July 1936. R.J. Mitchell is standing next to the propellor.

Below: Staff of the Supermarine Aviation Works, Southampton, with HRH the Prince of Wales in 1924. R.J. Mitchell, designer of the Spitfire, is third from the right, front row.

Above: **Against the background of the setting sun, Supermarine S6 N248 is manoeuvred to her moorings. Her sister aircraft, N247, won the 1929 Schneider Trophy contest.**

Americans and French to establish a commanding lead in the years immediately after World War I. In 1920-23 racing variants of the Nieuport-Delage 29 fighter, fitted with a 239kW (320hp) Hispano-Suiza engine, improved on the world absolute air speed record seven times, as well as capturing numerous trophies, while Curtiss CR-3 biplanes powered by 298kW (400hp) Curtiss D12 engines achieved first and second places in the Schneider Trophy contest.

These foreign successes prompted the leading British aero-engine manufacturers to re-examine their engine design philosophy. As a result Rolls-Royce produced the Kestrel, which represented a considerable advance over the Curtiss D12 and was selected to power the Hawker Hart light bomber and Hawker Fury fighter. The Kestrel in its ultimate form – the Kestrel V – later developed into the PV12, the prototype of the engine that was to play such an enormous part in World War II, the Rolls-Royce Merlin.

Destroyed

But in the early 1920s Rolls-Royce were not yet in a position to combine engine reliability with high performance, and in 1925 it was a 522kW (700hp) Napier Lion engine that powered Reginald Mitchell's entry for that year's Schneider Trophy contest, the Supermarine S4. Unfortunately, the aircraft crashed and was totally destroyed on the day before the race, Henry Biard narrowly escaping with his life. A 653kW (875hp) Napier Lion was also selected to power the Supermarine S5 in the 1926 contest, but the engine was not delivered in time for the aircraft to take part and the race was won by an Italian Macchi M.39. The S5 was ready in time for the 1927 contest, and won it with an average speed of 453.282 km/h (281.49mph), setting up a new 100km closed circuit world seaplane speed record into the bargain.

For the 1927 competition, held in Venice, the British entry was an all-RAF affair, a special unit known as the High Speed Flight having been formed for the occasion. There was no contest in 1928, but the High Speed Flight's development work continued at Felixstowe, and in February 1929 the Air Ministry once again decided to enter a team. This time, Rolls-Royce were asked to provide the engine for Mitchell's latest racing design, the Supermarine S6. To cut a few corners, as time was running short, Rolls-Royce decided to modify an existing engine, the 615kW (825hp) Buzzard (virtually a scaled-up Kestrel). The engine that emerged was the 'R' type, strengthened and fitted with a large double-sided centrifugal supercharger. These improvements increased the engine's power at sea level to a massive 1380kW (1850hp).

Above: Supermarine S6B S1595 being pre-flight checked prior to its uncontested winning of the 1931 Schneider Trophy outright for Britain. The aircraft was powered by a Rolls-Royce 'R' engine.

Technical challenges

While Rolls-Royce worked to overcome some fuel problems that had arisen during development of the 'R' type, Reginald Mitchell had been tailoring his S6 seaplane design to fit around the new engine. His estimate was that the aircraft would be capable of a speed in the order of 644km/h (400mph), and his figures included a level speed of 563km/h (350mph), a diving speed of 842km/h (523mph) and a rate of climb of 1525m (5000ft) per minute. In fact, these estimates were to reappear as the design characteristics for the Spitfire.

Despite a number of technical problems the Supermarine S6, flown by Flt Lt H.R.D. Waghorn, went on to win the 1929 Schneider Trophy contest at Spithead with a speed of 531.20km/h (330mph). On 12 September one of the other High Speed Flight pilots, Sqn Ldr A.H. Orlebar, flew the aircraft to a new world seaplane speed record of 575.53km/h (357.7mph) over a 100km closed circuit. These were phenomenal speeds for their time, and should have encouraged the British Government to invest in further development of both aircraft and engine. But the Government announced that it was no longer prepared to subsidize RAF participation in the contest (which was now held over two years) on grounds of cost, and economic uncertainty.

The news was received with bitter disappointment by all concerned, because Britain had won two consecutive contests – if the British could win a third, they could keep the coveted trophy permanently. It was only thanks to the intervention of Lady Houston, a great patriot and philanthropist, who donated £100,000, that the

Below: The Supermarine Type 224, K2890. Designed to meet the requirements of F7/30, it was not a success, one of the problems being the steam-cooled Rolls-Royce Goshawk engine.

situation was rescued. Instead of taking up a new design, as time was now short, Mitchell set about modifying the two existing S6s by fitting them with enlarged floats and re-designating them S6As. He then built two new machines, based on the existing airframe but incorporating much more powerful Rolls-Royce 'R' engines developing 1753kW (2350hp). The new aircraft were designated S6B.

Suddenly, the British found themselves with no competitors. The Italians could not produce an aircraft in time, and the French entry had crashed during trials, killing the pilot. Nevertheless, the 'contest' went ahead, and on 13 September 1931 Flt Lt J.W. Boothman flew S6B S1595 over the seven laps of the 50km course at an average speed of 547.188km/h (340.08mph). That same afternoon, Flt Lt G.H. Stainforth set up a new world speed record of 609.89km/h (379.05mph) in the other S6B, S1596. Later, on 29 September, Stainforth pushed the world speed record up to 655.66km/h (407.5mph).

Peril

Both S6As are preserved today, one (S1595) in the Science Museum, London, and the other (S1596) at Southampton. They brought the Schneider Trophy back to Britain for all time, but more importantly, they and their progenitors made a contribution to the development of high-speed aerodynamics and high-powered engines that, within a decade, would help the nation to survive her hour of greatest peril.

In the autumn of 1930 the Air Ministry issued specification F7/30, which called for a single-seat monoplane day and night fighter with a speed of at least 314km/h (195mph), exceptional manoeuvrability, long endurance, a low landing speed, high initial rate of climb and excellent all-round view. It was to be armed with four 7.7mm (0.303in) Vickers guns, and R/T equipment was to be fitted. F7/30 was the most important specification issued so far, because it attempted to sweep aside the inadequacies of the contemporary generation of biplane fighters. Supermarine, Westland, Blackburn, Bristol and Gloster all tendered designs to meet it.

The aircraft developed by Supermarine (named the Type 224) was an all-metal monoplane with a thick inverted gull wing and short cantilever undercarriage, the aerodynamic design having been subjected to much wind tunnel testing. It was powered by a Rolls-Royce Goshawk engine. The F7/30 was Mitchell's first attempt to apply the aerodynamic knowledge derived from the Supermarine Schneider racers to a land-based fighter design, and he was far from happy with the result. Nevertheless, the aircraft was built, and on 19 February 1934 it was flown by Supermarine test pilot J. 'Mutt' Summers, after which it went to Martlesham Heath for competitive trials. It was not a success, and nor were the designs from Supermarine's competitors. The Air Ministry were left with no alternative but to adopt the Gloster Gladiator, another biplane fighter.

Gunnery target

Despite the failure of the Supermarine entry Mitchell continued working on it, making improvements that included a retractable undercarriage and straight, thinner wings. With such refinements, he calculated that he could raise the F7/30's maximum speed to 265mph. This improved version was never built, but in concept it was much closer to the aircraft that would become the Spitfire. The original Type 224 F7/30 went to RAE Farnborough in 1935

Below: **The first Spitfire, K5054. The aircraft featured a tail skid rather than a wheel. The shape of the fin and rudder was later altered.**

and from there back to Martlesham in 1937, eventually ending its days as a gunnery target on Orfordness ranges.

On 16 November 1934, the Air Ministry issued specification F5/34 in connection with the proposed monoplane fighter. Reginald Mitchell and his design team had already seen a draft of this specification in October, and at that time the Air Ministry suggested that it might be met by the revised F7/30 with a Napier Dagger engine, a proposal that was rejected. In November the Vickers-Supermarine Board, under the chairmanship of Sir Robert McLean, authorised Mitchell to proceed with an entirely new fighter design as a private venture. It was to be powered by the Rolls-Royce PV12, with Rolls-Royce contributing £7500 toward the cost of building a prototype.

On 1 December 1934, Supermarine received an Air Ministry contract for the redesigned fighter prototype, which was allocated the Company Type No 300. It was covered by specification F37/34; another specification, F36/34, covered a monoplane fighter design by Hawker, later to become the Hurricane.

Poetic

The aircraft that took shape on Mitchell's drawing board was a long way removed from the Type 224, even in its revised version. Whereas the latter had been angular in appearance, with a wing design resembling that of the Hurricane, the Type 300 could only be described as beautiful, its lines blending into one another in a way that was almost poetic. The wing was elliptical in plan, a shape that Mitchell had selected once before in a 1929 project for a six-engined flying boat.

It is not clear why Mitchell chose the elliptical shape. It was difficult to engineer, and calculations showed that it offered an aerodynamic performance at high speed less than one per cent better than a wing with a straight taper, but there is no doubt that it was successful. In the original design the wing was perfectly elliptical, but it was redesigned to produce the familiar Spitfire wing shape, with a greater flare to the curve of the trailing edge. The concept was not new. The Heinkel He 70, which had first flown in December 1932 and had been designed for high-speed communication and mail transport, had featured an elliptical wing; as did the early-model He 111 bomber.

Shrew and Shrike

The prototype Supermarine 300, which gradually took shape in the company's Woolston factory in the course of 1935, had yet to receive a name. Sir Robert McLean, chairman of Vickers-Supermarine, suggested that it should begin with 'S' and sound venomous. Shrew and Shrike had been suggested for the F7/30, and according to some sources so had Spitfire. McLean particularly liked the latter name, although neither Mitchell nor the Air Ministry did. Mitchell, in fact, is reported to have called it 'bloody silly'. But it stuck, and it was formally adopted after the Type 300's maiden flight.

Early in January 1936 the airframe of the Supermarine 300 was at last complete, having undergone a considerable number of modifications in its development phase. It was given the serial number K5054. The engine had been fitted the previous November, and all was set for the first flight. This took place on the morning of 5 March 1936, and 'Mutt' Summers was the pilot. The flight was made from Eastleigh airport and the Type 300, painted a pale blue-grey, took off 35 degrees across wind. This was because experience with the racing seaplanes had revealed a strong tendency to swing to port due to the high torque (the force exerted on the airframe by the rapid rotation of the propeller). Summers found that although there was indeed a tendency to swing, it was easily checked by the application of opposite rudder. The aircraft seemed to drift into the air, and the maiden flight, which was made with the undercarriage locked down, was effortless. When Summers landed, he told the Supermarine designers not to touch anything.

In fact, the only thing that was touched was the propeller. For the maiden flight K5054 had been fitted with a fine-pitch propeller to give the pilot more rpm and therefore more power on take-off. This propeller was replaced by a normal-pitch one for the second and subsequent flights, and Supermarine test pilots George Pickering and Jeffrey Quill joined Summers for the flying programme.

Gun platform

In addition to high power and refined aerodynamics, the other key factor was armament. The fighter aircraft had to be an effective gun platform. For 15 or more of the 20 years that separated the two world wars, the concept of the

Left: This splendid Charles Brown photograph shows K9787, the first production Spitfire Mk I, flown here by Jeffrey Quill in May 1938. The Spitfire remained in production throughout WWII.

traditional fighter layout died hard. In the early 1930s the world's leading air arms were still equipped with open-cockpit biplane or parasol-wing fighters, armed with two rifle-calibre machine guns mounted to fire through the propeller disc. The only large-calibre machine gun in general use in the later 1930s was the 12.7mm (0.50in) gun mounted in some American fighters and its 12.7mm or 13mm equivalents fitted in a few Continental designs like the Italian Fiat CR.32.

The problem of air armament was well summarized by Squadron Leader Ralph Sorley of Flying Operations 1 (FO1) in the British Air Ministry, leader of a campaign that led to the RAF's new monoplane fighters, the Spitfire and Hurricane, being fitted with eight 0.303in machine guns.

'The choice' (Sorley wrote later) 'lay between the 0.303 gun, the 0.50 gun and a new 20mm Hispano gun which was attracting the attention of the French, and in fact of other countries in Europe who could obtain knowledge of it from them. During 1934 this gun was experimental and details of its performance and characteristics were hard to establish. On the other hand, designs of better 0.303 guns than the Vickers had been tested over the preceding years with the result that the American Browning from the Colt Automatic Weapon Corporation appeared to offer the best possibilities from the point of view of rate of fire. Our own development of guns of this calibre had been thorough but slow, since we were in the throes of economizing, and considerable stocks of old Vickers guns still remained from the first war. The acceptance of a new gun in the numbers likely to be required was a heavy financial and manufacturing commitment. The 0.50-inch on the other hand had developed little, and although it possessed a better hitting power the rate of fire was slow and it was a heavy item, together with its ammunition, in respect of installed weight...the controversy was something of a nightmare during 1933-34. It was a choice on which the whole concept of the fighter would depend, but a trial staged on the ground with eight 0.303s was sufficiently convincing and satisfying to enable them to carry the day.'

While the RAF opted for an armament of eight 0.303 guns (which would be replaced by four 20mm Hispano cannon from 1941) the Americans adopted a standard armament of up to six 0.50in guns in their new generation of monoplane fighters. The Germans, Italians, Russians, French and Japanese all settled for a mixed armament of cannon and machine guns, a pattern that would be maintained throughout much of World War II. But eight 0.303in guns packed a powerful punch; harmonized so that the bullets converged at 228m (250 yards), they could place a cone of fire into an area about 0.60m (2ft) in diameter at the rate of 8000 rounds per minute, a one-second burst hitting the target with a punishing 4.5kg (10lb) of metal.

Reflector gunsight

By September 1937 the Spitfire prototype K5054 had been fitted with its eight-gun armament and had been brought up to Spitfire Mk I production standards. Other refinements included the fitting of a Barr and Stroud Type GD5 reflector gunsight and a G22 camera gun. The original Rolls-Royce Merlin C engine had been replaced by a Merlin F, producing 780kW (1045hp). By this time the Spitfire was in full production, Supermarine having received an initial order for 310 aircraft on 3 June 1936. The first Spitfire Mk I to be delivered, serial number K9789, flew on 4 August 1938, and two days later it was delivered to No 19 Squadron at Duxford, Cambridgeshire – the first Spitfire to be taken on charge by RAF Fighter Command. Sadly, Reginald Mitchell never lived to see his creation in RAF squadron colours. He died of cancer on 11 June 1937, only 42 years old – the disease had been diagnosed four years earlier. There is no doubt that Mitchell's refusal to rest while he was at work on the Spitfire design hastened his end. But before he died he was already at work on other projects, including the Type 317; a long-range, four-engined bomber.

Slow delivery

Because of the many problems associated with mass production, and the necessity of much sub-contracting, initial deliveries were slow, averaging only one aircraft per week. The other fighter squadron at Duxford, No 66, received its first Spitfire (K9802) on 31 October 1938. By the end of the year 45 aircraft had been delivered, which meant 19 and 66 Squadrons were at full strength. But the production schedule for the initial batch had slipped badly. It had been due for completion in March 1939, and was not fulfilled until August. As well as the problems of slow delivery, the Spitfire's introduction into service was marred by many accidents. Most of the pilots were used to flying fixed-undercarriage biplanes, and the transition to monoplanes with retractable landing gear, 100mph faster than their predecessors, was often not easy.

The initial order for 310 Spitfire Mk Is was followed by three more: two batches of 200 aircraft and one of 450. At the outbreak of war on 3 September 1939, nine RAF squadrons had fully rearmed with Spitfires and a tenth, No 609, was just beginning. In September No 603 Squadron, based at Turnhouse near Edinburgh, also began to receive Spitfires. It was the two Scottish Auxiliary Air Force squadrons, Nos 602 and 603, that were the first to make contact with the Luftwaffe over the United Kingdom.

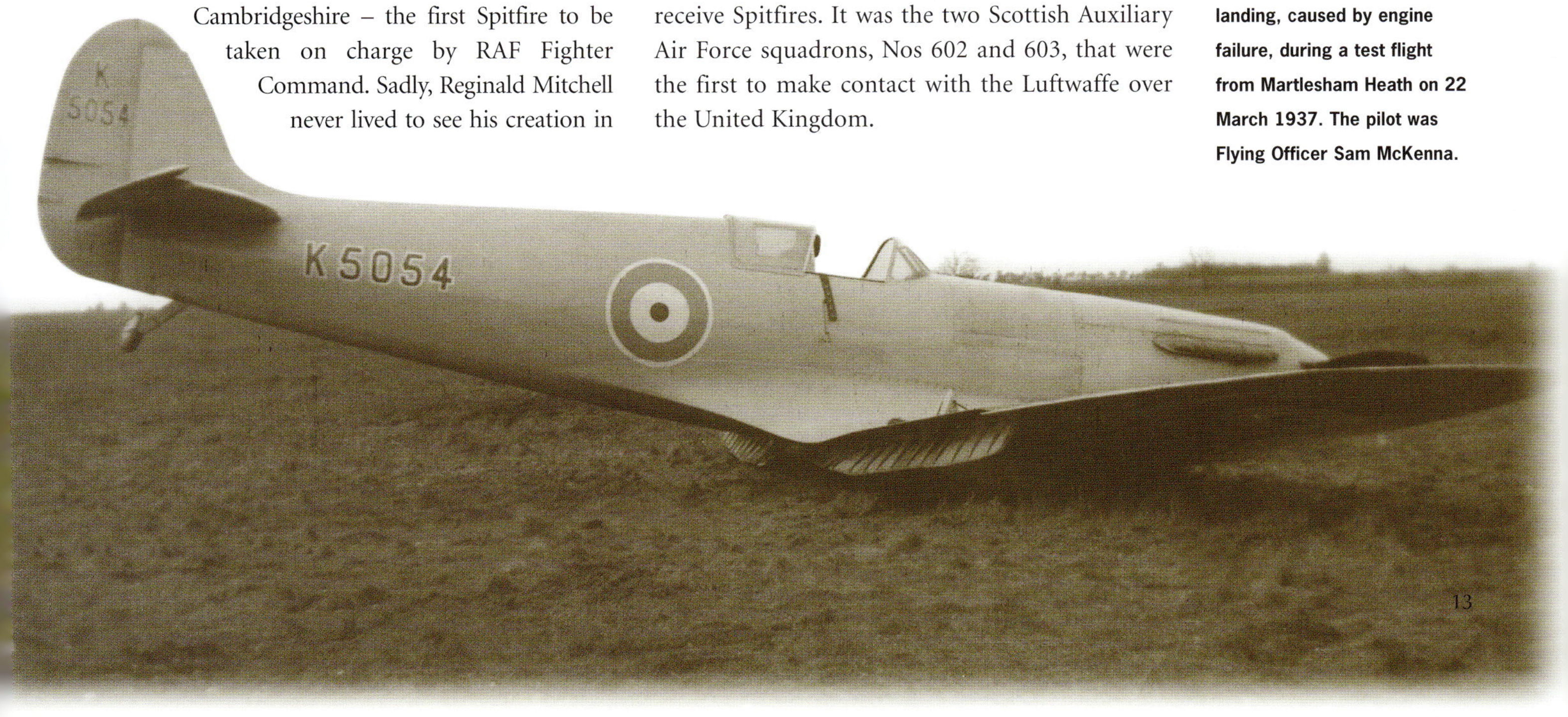

Below: **K5054 looking somewhat sorry after a forced landing, caused by engine failure, during a test flight from Martlesham Heath on 22 March 1937. The pilot was Flying Officer Sam McKenna.**

ZH T

CHAPTER TWO

Their Finest Hour: The Battle of Britain

In October 1939 the Luftwaffe was fresh from its victories in Poland. But the Spitfire was to teach the German flyers the sharp lesson that daylight operations over the British Isles could not be carried out with impunity.

On the morning of 16 October Junkers Ju 88 bombers of I/KG30 set out from Westerland, on the north German island of Sylt, to attack naval targets in the Firth of Forth. The Germans believed that the RAF had only a handful of Gloster Gladiator biplane fighters in the area, but they were wrong. The Spitfires of Nos 602 and 603 Squadrons were based at Drem and Turnhouse, while the Hurricanes of No 607 were at Usworth, near Sunderland, also in a position to cover the Firth. Two Ju 88s were shot down, one by Sqn Ldr E.E. Stevens of No 603 Squadron and the other by Flt Lt G. Pinkerton of No 602.

This was Fighter Command's first action of World War II. Although there had been plenty of false alarms in the first weeks of the war (one of which had ended in tragedy when Spitfires of No 74 Squadron shot down two Hurricanes in error in what became known as the 'Battle of Barking Creek'), the anticipated German bombing onslaught had not materialized. The Auxiliary Air Force squadrons in the north had several more encounters with the Luftwaffe in the weeks following 16 October, but it was not until 9 February 1940 that they scored their next success when a Heinkel He 111 was brought down near North Berwick by Sqn Ldr A.D. Farquhar of No 602 Squadron.

Prisoners

While the Scottish-based Spitfire squadrons carried out their primary task of defending the Royal Navy's bases during the first months of the war, those based south of the border, at Acklington in Northumberland and Catterick in North Yorkshire, also saw some early action. On 17 October 1939, three Spitfires of No 41 Squadron from Catterick caught a reconnaissance Heinkel He 111 25 miles off Whitby and shot it down into the sea. The pilot and navigator survived and were rescued from their dinghy at dawn the next day – the first German prisoners to be landed on English

Opposite: **Spitfire Mk IIa of No 266 Squadron, RAF Hornchurch, Essex, in September 1940. This squadron operated Spitfires until the beginning of 1942, when it converted to Hawker Typhoons.**

Below: **Pilots of No 65 Squadron simulate a 'scramble' at RAF Hornchurch, Essex, in May 1939. The aircraft is a Spitfire Mk I.**

Right: **The Hawker Hurricane was the Spitfire's partner in the Battle of Britain. This photograph shows PZ865, the last Hurricane ever built, which featured in several films.**

soil in World War II. Although most of the enemy aircraft destroyed off north-east England during this phase fell to the Hurricanes of Nos 43 and 111 Squadrons, the Spitfires had their share. On 3 February 1940, for example, three Spitfire pilots of No 152 Squadron, Acklington, destroyed a Heinkel off the coast.

Below: **This photograph of an armourer at work on the machine guns shows the Spitfire's elliptical wing shape to good advantage. The wing tips, secured by two bolts, could be detached.**

Lucky escape

One Spitfire pilot, Flt Lt Norman Ryder of No 41 Squadron, Catterick, had a very lucky escape. On 3 April 1940, Ryder shot down a Heinkel 111 between Redcar and Whitby, but his Spitfire was hit in the engine by return fire and he was forced to ditch in very rough seas close to a trawler. The impact with the water knocked him unconscious, and when he came to he was already some way below the surface in an aircraft that was sinking rapidly. He recalled later:

'I remember sitting in the cockpit and everything was a bright green. I was very fascinated by the stillness of it all – it was amazing, and I recall watching a lot of bubbles running up the windscreen before my nose and parting as they got to the front. I sat there fascinated by the sight and not a bit afraid. The calm was so restful after the noise. The green colour around me was lovely, but it turned to blackness before I got out. I started to get out by undoing my straps. I stood on my seat and just when I thought I was clear I found my parachute had caught under the sliding hood, and I could not move. I got partially into the cockpit again and at this point noticed that it was getting very much darker as the aircraft sank. I was again nearly hooked up by my parachute, but I wriggled and got clear. By now it was very black and I just saw the silhouette of the tailplane pass my face. I still had on my parachute which hampered my movement, but I managed to dog paddle my way upward.'

After considerable difficulty, Ryder freed himself from his parachute harness and, completely exhausted by his efforts, was picked up by the trawler crew. He had the dubious distinction of being the first Spitfire pilot to be shot down by the Luftwaffe, a fact compensated for to some extent by the award of the Distinguished Flying Cross.

Dunkirk battles

The first large-scale battles between the RAF's Spitfire and Hurricane squadrons and the Luftwaffe took place in May 1940, during the evacuation of the British Expeditionary Force from France via the port of Dunkirk. Since Dunkirk and the other ports were within easy reach of fighter bases in southern England, the German bombers could expect strong opposition. The Junkers Ju 87 Stuka dive-bombers, which were to suffer appalling losses in the Battle of Britain, had a foretaste of things to come on 25 May when a group of 15 of them were attacked by Spitfires over Calais and four were shot down. The day after that the Luftwaffe carried out its first major attacks on Dunkirk itself. Constant defensive patrols were maintained by 16 Spitfire and Hurricane squadrons of No 11 Group, RAF Fighter Command, whose pilots claimed 20 victories in the course of the day.

In the air battles that raged over and around the beaches during the nine days of the Dunkirk evacuation the RAF lost 177 aircraft, and the Luftwaffe sustained a comparable loss. Although these losses were roughly similar on paper, the fact was that the Luftwaffe had, for the first time, lost the air superiority it had enjoyed since its attack on Poland the year before. The British fighter pilots had dealt them a psychological blow – but an altogether more damaging one was to come in the skies over southern England before long.

Night combat

The defeat of France in June 1940 was followed by a growing number of incursions into British air space by enemy aircraft at night. Many of these raids were intercepted both by single-seater day fighters and by

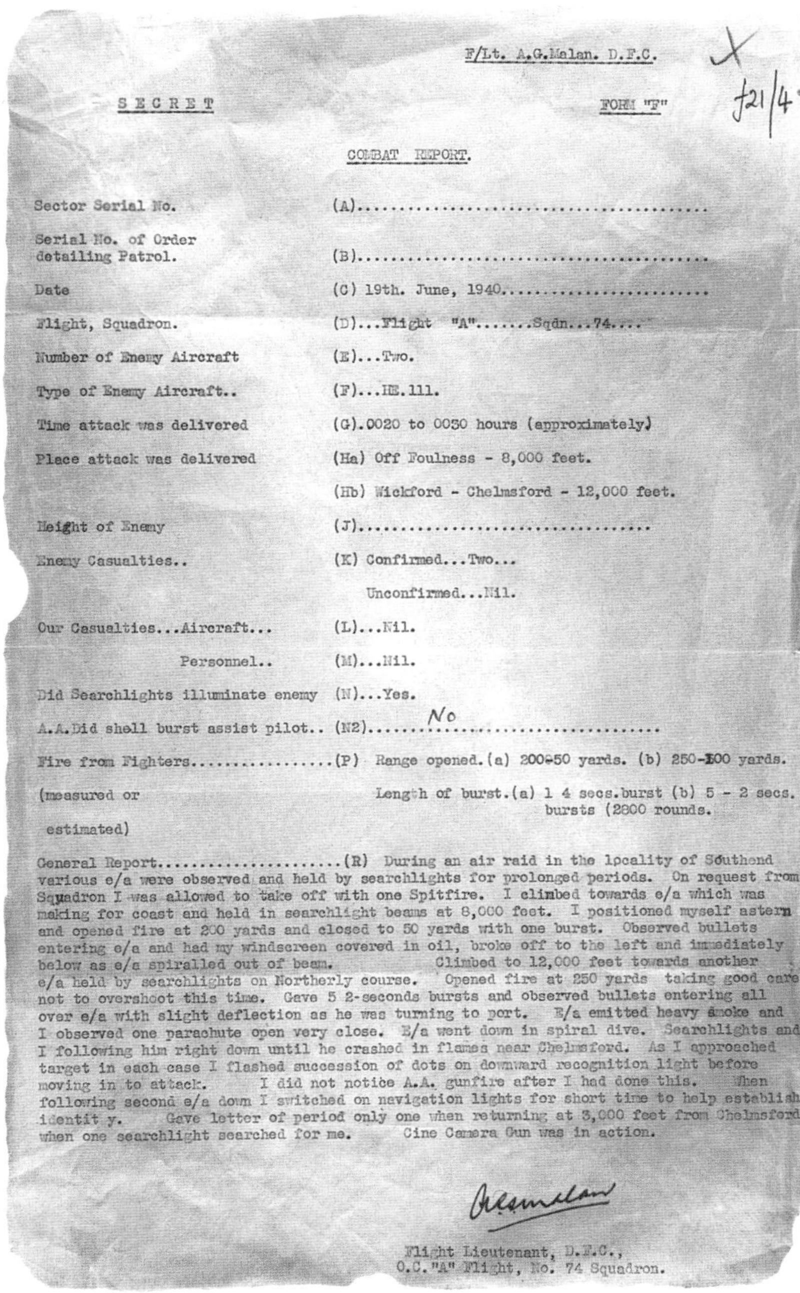

F/Lt. A.G.Malan. D.F.C.

X f21/4.

SECRET FORM "F"

COMBAT REPORT.

Sector Serial No. (A)..

Serial No. of Order detailing Patrol. (B)..

Date (C) 19th. June, 1940........................

Flight, Squadron. (D)...Flight "A".......Sqdn...74....

Number of Enemy Aircraft (E)...Two.

Type of Enemy Aircraft.. (F)...HE.111.

Time attack was delivered (G).0020 to 0030 hours (approximately)

Place attack was delivered (Ha) Off Foulness - 8,000 feet.

(Hb) Wickford - Chelmsford - 12,000 feet.

Height of Enemy (J)....................................

Enemy Casualties.. (K) Confirmed...Two...

Unconfirmed...Nil.

Our Casualties...Aircraft... (L)...Nil.

Personnel.. (M)...Nil.

Did Searchlights illuminate enemy (N)...Yes.

A.A.Did shell burst assist pilot.. (N2).........No.........................

Fire from Fighters.................(P) Range opened.(a) 200-50 yards. (b) 250-100 yards.

(measured or estimated) Length of burst.(a) 1 4 secs.burst (b) 5 - 2 secs. bursts (2800 rounds.

General Report.......................(R) During an air raid in the locality of Southend various e/a were observed and held by searchlights for prolonged periods. On request from Squadron I was allowed to take off with one Spitfire. I climbed towards e/a which was making for coast and held in searchlight beams at 8,000 feet. I positioned myself astern and opened fire at 200 yards and closed to 50 yards with one burst. Observed bullets entering e/a and had my windscreen covered in oil, broke off to the left and immediately below as e/a spiralled out of beam. Climbed to 12,000 feet towards another e/a held by searchlights on Northerly course. Opened fire at 250 yards taking good care not to overshoot this time. Gave 5 2-seconds bursts and observed bullets entering all over e/a with slight deflection as he was turning to port. E/a emitted heavy smoke and I observed one parachute open very close. E/a went down in spiral dive. Searchlights and I following him right down until he crashed in flames near Chelmsford. As I approached target in each case I flashed succession of dots on downward recognition light before moving in to attack. I did not notice A.A. gunfire after I had done this. When following second e/a down I switched on navigation lights for short time to help establish identit y. Gave letter of period only one when returning at 3,000 feet from Chelmsford when one searchlight searched for me. Cine Camera Gun was in action.

A.G.Malan

Flight Lieutenant, D.F.C.,
O.C."A" Flight, No. 74 Squadron.

Above: Combat report submitted by Flt Lt A.G. 'Sailor' Malan on 19 June 1940. It describes a night combat with a Heinkel He 111; at that time the RAF had no dedicated night fighters.

Blenheim night fighters (the latter had already registered some successes as intruders during the Battle of France). At 0050 on 19 June, for example, Flt Lt R.M.B Duke-Woolley in a Blenheim of No 23 Squadron shot down a Heinkel He 111H-4 of 2/KG54 into the sea off the Norfolk coast. The German crew were captured. On the same night two Heinkels of 4/KG4 were also destroyed, both at 0115. Flt Lt A.G. ('Sailor') Malan in a Spitfire of No 74 Squadron destroyed the first off Felixstowe. The second was shot down jointly by a Spitfire of No 19 Squadron and a Blenheim of No 23 Squadron at Fleam Dyke, Cambridgeshire. Unfortunately the Spitfire pilot, Flying Officer Petra, was forced to bale out after his aircraft was hit; and the Blenheim pilot, Sqn Ldr O'Brien, baled out after losing control. Both the other Blenheim crew members were killed. Flying Officer G.E. Ball of No 19 Squadron, who shot down a Heinkel 111H of 6/KG4 into the sea off Margate, achieved the third victory of the night at 0215.

Three more Heinkels were destroyed in the early hours of 26 June. The first, a Heinkel He 111P-2 of 3/KG4, was shot down into the sea off Hull by Pilot Officers R.A. Smith and R. Marples at 0017, while two He 111H-3s of 3/KG26 were shot down by pilots of Nos 602 and 603 Squadrons off the Scottish coast. Interceptions like these were aided by the perfect visibility of the summer nights.

Convoy attacks

In June 1940, while the Battle of France still raged, the Luftwaffe began to turn its attention to 'fringe' targets, like ports on the English coast. This was a prelude to the larger-scale attacks that began early in July on shipping in the English Channel – the aim being to probe Fighter Command's defences and reaction times, and to tempt out and inflict damage on the British fighter squadrons. The convoy attacks continued through July and the first week of August.

Although there were several major air battles in this phase, mainly in the Dover area, the enemy formations were usually intercepted by only half a dozen British fighters, and were often able to carry out their attacks and head for home before any British fighters arrived. This was because Air Chief Marshal Sir Hugh Dowding, C-in-C Fighter Command, was husbanding his valuable fighter resources. He had earlier turned down repeated requests to send more RAF fighter squadrons to France, knowing that the decisive battle would be fought over the British Isles. The fighters available to him at the beginning of July 1940 numbered about 600 aircraft – 29 squadrons of Hurricanes, 19 of Spitfires, seven of Blenheim fighters (mostly assigned to night defence) and two of Boulton Paul Defiants. One of the Defiant squadrons, No 141, lost six aircraft in an encounter with Bf 109s on 19

Below: A bullet-riddled He 111 of KG26 in a field near Haddington, Lothian, Scotland, after being forced down by Spitfires of Nos 602 and 603 Squadrons on 29 November 1939.

Left: **This painstakingly rebuilt Me 109G was the only one flying with the original DB601 engine. It was a later model than the 109E that fought in the Battle of Britain.**

Below: **Harmonizing the guns of a 609 Sqn Spitfire. The fighter's eight machine guns could be aligned so that their cone of fire converged at a spot 220 yards ahead of the attacker.**

July, and after that the Defiants played no further part in the daylight phase of the battle.

Dowding's approach was essentially a scientific one; he believed that Britain's air defences should have the benefit of the very latest technological developments. This was reflected in Fighter Command's operations rooms, linked with one another by an elaborate system of telephone and teleprinter lines to provide an integrated system of control. This enabled fighter aircraft to be passed rapidly from sector to sector and from group to group, wherever they were most needed. It was No 11 Group, in the crucial south-east of England, that would bear the brunt of the fighting throughout the battle; 29 of Dowding's squadrons were based there. Another 11 squadrons were in No 12 Group north of the Thames, and 17 in No 13 Group, covering northern England and Scotland.

Radar battle

Nowhere was modern technology more apparent in Britain's defences than in the use of radar, or radio direction finding (RDF) as it was then known. Developed by Robert Watson-Watt from earlier experiments in thunderstorm detection by the use of radio waves, the use of radar as an integral part of the British air defence system was largely the fruit of Dowding's initiative. He had worked with Watson-Watt in the 1930s and had quickly recognized the potential of the new invention. The Germans knew all

about the British radar warning system, and the destruction of the radar stations on the south coast of England was included in their plans as a necessary preliminary to the main air offensive against England.

Planning for the German offensive was completed by 2 August 1940. Air Fleets (Luftflotten) 2 and 3 were to attack simultaneously, their main tasks being to bring the RAF's fighters to combat, to destroy their airfields and the coastal radar stations, and to disrupt the RAF's ground organization in southern England. The attacks on the south coast radar stations began on 12 August. The station at Ventnor on the Isle of Wight was damaged beyond repair, but although others suffered damage they were operational again within hours. It turned out that the Germans did not fully understand the importance or the method of operation of the British radar, or its crucial value to the whole structure of the British air defence system. Attacks on radar sites were sporadic, and were soon abandoned – the Germans believed the radar sites' operations rooms were in bomb-proof underground bunkers and were therefore invulnerable. In fact, they were mostly in flimsy huts above ground.

Eagle attack

On 13 August 1940 the Luftwaffe launched the full weight of its air offensive against Britain with what they called the Adler Angriff (Eagle Attack). Its initial objective was to neutralize RAF Fighter Command by striking at its airfields, and by drawing the fighter squadrons into combat. H-Hour at 0730 was postponed because of bad weather, but the Dornier Do 17s of KG2 failed to receive the order and set out over the Channel without fighter escort. They were attacked over the

Spitfire Mk I

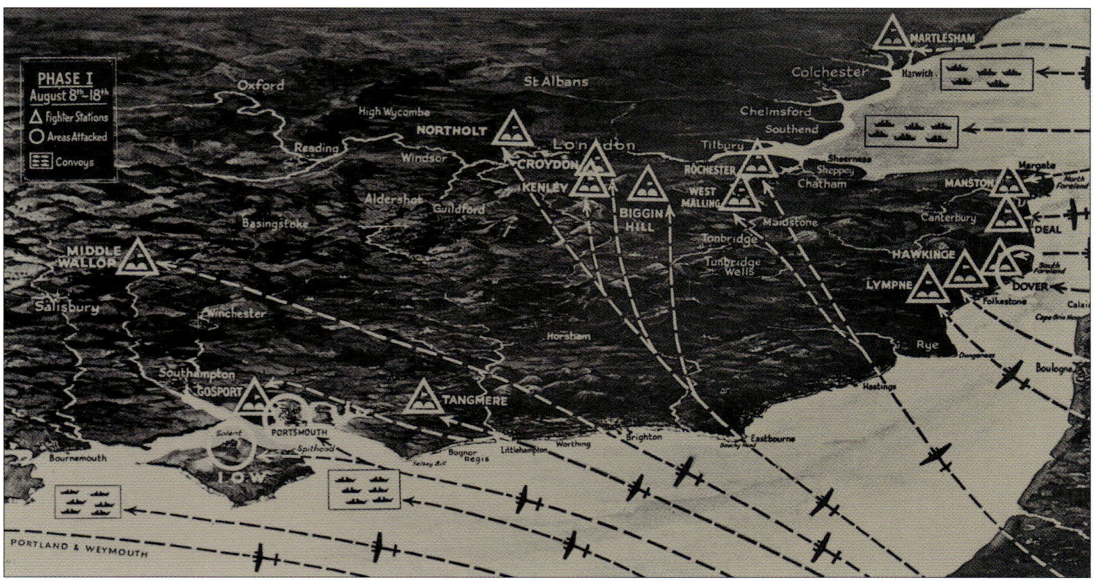

Right: **Diagram showing the RAF airfield and merchant convoy targets assigned to the German Luftflotten at the beginning of the attack on England.**

SPITFIRE Mk I

Type: single-seat interceptor fighter

Powerplant: one Rolls-Royce Merlin II or III rated at 1030hp (768Kw) at 16,250ft (4953m)

Performance: maximum speed 346mph (557km/h) at 15,500ft (4724m); maximum range 630 miles (1014km); range at maximum cruising speed 415 miles (668km); time to climb 6 minutes 51 seconds to 15,000ft (4572m); service ceiling 30,500ft (9296m)

Dimensions: span 36ft 10in (11.23m); length 29ft 11in (9.12m); height 12ft 8in (3.86m); wing area 242sq ft (22.48m^2)

Below: **A rather fanciful scoreboard displayed beside a Spitfire of No 92 (East India) Squadron in February 1941. Claims were almost always greatly exaggerated in the heat of battle.**

Thames Estuary and five bombers were shot down, though the remainder caused heavy damage to Sheerness and Eastchurch. In the afternoon Ju 87s of Stukageschwader 2, escorted by Bf 109s of JG53, set out to attack airfields in the Portland area. They were engaged by Spitfires of No 609 Squadron and four Stukas were shot down. In all, the Luftwaffe lost 34 aircraft on 13 August. The RAF lost 12 Hurricanes, which had borne the brunt of the fighting, and one Spitfire.

Enemy attacks were disrupted by bad weather on 14 August, but the next day was to be the climax of the battle. Although 15 September, when heavy daylight attacks on London took place, was later designated as Battle of Britain Day, the heaviest fighting in fact took place on 15 August. It began in mid-morning, when 40 Stukas of Fliegerkorps II, escorted by a similar number of Bf 109s, were despatched to attack the airfields of Lympne and Hawkinge. The raid was intercepted over the coast by the Spitfires of No 54 and the Hurricanes of No 501 Squadrons, but while these took on the fighter escort, the Stukas broke through to hit Lympne, putting the airfield out of action for two days.

Attack on the north

At the same time aircraft of Luftflotte 5 from Norway and Denmark launched their first (and only) major daylight attack on the north of England. The two units involved, KG26 and KG30, had to fly 640 and 725km (400 and 450 miles) respectively from their bases at Stavanger and Aalborg to reach their targets on the north-east coast between Tyne and Humber. The first to approach over the North Sea were the 63 Heinkel 111s of KG26, escorted by 21 Messerschmitt Bf 110s of ZG76. 12 Spitfires of No 72 Squadron from Acklington intercepted them off the Farne Islands.

As it turned out, the size of the raid had been greatly underestimated by the British radar, which in fact had been tracking a formation of 20 He 115 seaplanes, sent towards the Firth of Forth as a diversion. The German plan had been to cross the north-east coast south of the Tyne and then fly south to their objectives, the airfields of Dishforth and Linton on Ouse, in Yorkshire. But the enemy had made a serious navigational error – they had made their landfall 100 miles too far north, and their track took them right across that of the diversionary seaplanes. So instead of the '30 plus' advised by radar, the 12 pilots of No 72 Squadron found themselves confronted with over 80 German aircraft.

Below: Inside the cockpit of a Spitfire. The cockpit was small and compact, with the standard instrument panel as shown in the photograph.

Fortunately the Spitfires were quickly joined by the Hurricanes of No 79 Squadron, also from Acklington, and under the determined attacks of the two fighter squadrons the enemy formation was quickly disrupted. The bombers continued southwards, searching for their targets. The first wave, harried by the Hurricanes of 79 Squadron and some belonging to 605 Squadron, unloaded its bombs more or less at random between Newcastle and Sunderland. The second wave, attacked by the Spitfires of No 41 Squadron from Catterick and the Hurricanes of No 607 from Usworth, also dropped its load randomly and turned for home. Between them the two waves had lost eight Heinkels and six Bf 110s. The RAF lost only one aircraft, a 605 Squadron Hurricane which crashed while attempting a forced landing. The pilot was unhurt.

Meanwhile the 40 Ju 88s of KG30 were approaching the Yorkshire coast near Flamborough head. Radar detected them while they were still a long way out to sea, and Air Vice-Marshal Trafford Leigh-Mallory, commanding No 12 Group, ordered 18 Spitfires and Hurricanes of Nos 616 and 73 Squadrons up from Church Fenton to intercept them. Six Ju 88s were shot down, but the majority got through to the RAF airfield at Driffield, where their bombs destroyed four hangars and several Whitley bombers.

Southern battle

While the fighters of Nos 12 and 13 Groups were engaging Luftflotte 5 in the north-east, battle was joined again in the south. At 1500, a big radar plot began to build up as the Dornier 17s of KG3 assembled over their Belgian airfields and set course

Above: **Spitfire Mk IIs in the final stages of assembly at the Castle Bromwich 'shadow factory', where all the Mk IIs were built. This photograph shows the sheer scale of the plant.**

over the Channel with a massive fighter escort of Bf 109s. Eleven fighter squadrons were scrambled to intercept, but such was the variety, number and complexity of the incoming raid plots that the fighters were shuttled to and fro by the sector controllers with no real co-ordination. KG3 broke through to bomb the airfields of Eastchurch and Rochester, and the fighter airfield at Martlesham Heath was heavily damaged by bomb-carrying Messerschmitts of Erprobungsgruppe 210 (a special unit which had been involved in attacks on the south coast radar stations on 12 August) and put out of action for 36 hours.

Heavy losses

Two hours later, a mixed formation of Ju 87s and 88s of Luftflotte 2, again under heavy escort, took off from their airfields in the Cherbourg area. It took them a long time to assemble, and it was not until 1800 that the armada of 200 aircraft set course for the English coast. By then the Germans had thrown away their tactical advantage. The time that had elapsed since the earlier raids had enabled Air Vice-Marshals Keith Park and Quintin Brand (commanding 11 and 10 Groups respectively) to

Below: **Messerschmitt Bf 109Es of 8/JG2 Richthofen at an airfield in France, 1940. The Bf 109E was Fighter Command's principal opponent in the battle.**

Right: A flight of Messerschmitt Bf 109s over the English Channel near Dover. Note the classic 'finger four' formation, developed by the Luftwaffe in the Spanish Civil War.

Below: Spitfire Mk Is of No 65 Squadron. The nearest aircraft is flown by Flying Officer (later Wing Commander) Robert Stanford Tuck, who became a noted wing leader in 1941.

take adequate counter-measures, and they were able to put up 14 fighter squadrons to meet the enemy assault. The Spitfires and Hurricanes engaged the bombers over the coast and concentrated on the Stukas, which were soon fighting for their survival. Other Spitfires pounced on the Ju 88s of Lehrgeschwader 1, which were trying to slip through to their targets, and inflicted heavy losses on them. Out of 15 aircraft of II/LG1, for example, only three managed to reach their objective, the Fleet Air Arm base at Worthy Down; the others were forced to jettison their bombs. The worst hit was IV/LG1, one flight of which lost five aircraft out of seven.

The day's fighting was by no means over. At 1935, 15 Bf 110s and eight Bf 109s of Erprobungsgruppe 210 set out to attack Kenley, south of London, but they made a navigational error and bombed Croydon by mistake, destroying 40 training aircraft. The Messerschmitts were engaged by the Hurricanes of Nos 32 and 111 Squadrons, and four Bf 110s were shot down. As the rest ran for the Channel, they were intercepted by the Spitfires of No 66 Squadron, which destroyed two more Bf 110s and a 109. This brought the Luftwaffe's combat losses for the day to 71 aircraft to the RAF's 30, of which 12 were Spitfires. The day's fighting had demonstrated that it was the Bf 109 that was causing the Spitfire and Hurricane squadrons their biggest problems. The twin-engined Bf 110 'Destroyer', intended as a long-range escort fighter, had shown itself markedly inferior to the British fighters, and no fewer than 31 had been destroyed in the course of the day. The Bf 110 would continue to suffer unacceptable losses throughout the battle.

Brief respite

Although the Germans struck hard at eight RAF airfields in the morning of 16 August, in the afternoon bad weather frustrated the Luftwaffe's attempts to make further attacks. Nevertheless, air combats that day, mostly in the morning, cost the Luftwaffe 44 aircraft and the RAF 26, 11 of them Spitfires. Five of the downed Spitfires were from No 266 Squadron from Hornchurch, 'bounced' by Bf 109s over Canterbury.

Poor weather again prevailed on 17 August, bringing a brief respite for the hard-pressed RAF fighter squadrons, but on the 18th the Luftwaffe launched a series of heavy attacks on the important sector stations of Kenley and Biggin Hill. Kenley was badly hit, and its operations room was put out of action. In the afternoon a strong force of Stukas attacked the airfields at Ford, Gosport and Thorney Island without adequate fighter escort. They were engaged by the Hurricanes of No 43 and the Spitfires of Nos 152 and 602 Squadrons, and 18 Stukas were destroyed. The Luftwaffe lost 60 aircraft in the day's fighting, the RAF 34. The Hurricane squadrons had taken a terrible mauling, losing 29 fighters, some in airfield attacks, with 13 more damaged. The Spitfire squadrons escaped relatively lightly, with five aircraft destroyed and 14 damaged.

Defensive shield

The weather improved steadily in the last week of August, and the Luftwaffe stepped up its airfield attacks, striking hard at the fighter bases that formed a defensive shield around London. The attacks were to last for two weeks, and marked a crucial phase in the battle. Both sides had used the bad weather to recoup their strength. The Germans moved the fighters of Luftflotte 3 to reinforce those of Luftflotte 2 in the Pas de Calais, while the RAF took delivery of replacement fighters – including 60 much-needed Spitfires in the period 19–24 August.

Most of these new Spitfires were Mk IIs, produced by the Nuffield factory at Castle Bromwich. The differences between the Mk I and Mk II were minor, the principal one being that the Mk II had a Merlin XII engine that

Below: **Spitfire Mk Is of No 19 Squadron, the first unit to receive the type, pictured at RAF Duxford before the outbreak of World War II.**

ran on 100 octane fuel and used a Coffman cartridge starter instead of a trolley-accumulator. The Mk II also had 33kg (73lb) of armour plate fitted on the production line, whereas the Mk I's armour had been fitted retrospectively in service. Other modifications included bullet-proof windscreens, not fitted previously. Dowding famously commented that, if Chicago gangsters could protect themselves with bullet-proof glass, his pilots should too.

Exhaustion

The replacements came just in time, for losses were beginning to mount. Six Spitfires were lost on 24 August and eight on the 25th; and on the following day No 616 Squadron, in the thick of the fighting, lost no fewer than seven Spitfires – though five of the pilots were saved. By mid-week, every squadron in No 11 Group was suffering seriously from exhaustion. Some units were down to half strength, and they had to be withdrawn from the battle and sent north into No 13 Group's area for a rest. On 30 August, the vital sector station of Biggin Hill was completely wrecked by bombing, and it was attacked again the following afternoon, along with Hornchurch. Fighter Command lost 11 Spitfires on the 30th, and 14 more on the 31st. Three of these belonged to No 19 Squadron, which had been carrying out trials with 20mm cannon with little success.

Losses

Of the 328 Spitfires delivered to Fighter Command since the beginning of July, 163 had been destroyed and 161 damaged, though the latter were repairable. As yet, the squadrons of No 12 Group north of the Thames had not been committed in strength to the battle, but of necessity that would soon change. Fighter Command's situation was now very serious indeed. In the space of the fortnight from 24 August to 6 September the RAF lost 103 pilots killed and 128 badly wounded – this represented almost a quarter of the available trained fighter pilots. Maintaining the flow of replacement pilots was becoming a serious problem. Some were being sent to front line squadrons with as little as 20 hours' flying experience on Spitfires and Hurricanes, and many of the fighter pilots joining their squadrons early in

Below: **Spitfire Mk IIa of the Battle of Britain Memorial Flight pictured at Duxford during the annual Battle of Britain Air Display.**

Left: **Polish pilots of No 303 'Kosciusko' Squadron, which operated from Northolt in the Battle of Britain from the beginning of August until October.**

September 1940 did not survive their first sortie, such was their lack of experience. Others managed to hang on and found themselves catapulted from the lowly status of new boys to section and even flight commanders in record time.

By 3 September, for the first time in the battle, Luftwaffe crews were returning to base and reporting that they had encountered no opposition. It was beginning to look as if the collapse of Fighter Command were imminent. But a chain of events was about to bring a dramatic and unexpected change in enemy policy. On the night of 24 August, a few German bombers made a navigational error and dropped some bombs on London, and on the following night RAF Bomber Command retaliated by attacking Berlin. Provoked by this, Hitler pressed the Luftwaffe C-in-C, Hermann Göring, to switch the main bombing offensive away from the airfields, to London. This plan was bitterly opposed by General Hugo Sperrle, commanding Luftflotte 3, who believed (probably rightly) that if the airfield attacks were kept up for another few days the Luftwaffe would achieve air superiority over south England, opening up the possibility of an invasion.

Safer bases

On the other hand, the Luftflotte 2 commander, General Albert Kesselring, thought that the RAF

Below: **Spitfire Mk IA R6800 of No 66 Squadron at Gravesend. This aircraft was shot down by the German ace Werner Mölders on 17 October 1940.**

Above: **Pilots of No 610 Squadron, Biggin Hill, at readiness in September 1940. No 610 Squadron, an Auxiliary Air Force unit, operated Spitfires throughout the war.**

was about to evacuate its fighters from the hard-hit 11 Group airfields and withdraw them to safer bases to the north and west of London, out of range of the German fighter escorts. His belief was that an all-out assault on London would force the RAF to throw its last fighter reserves into the defence of the capital. Göring was persuaded by Kesselring's argument, and the attacks on London were authorized. Meanwhile on 5 September, 22 German bomber formations attacked RAF airfields and the oil storage tanks at Thameshaven, the Luftwaffe losing 23 aircraft and Fighter Command 20. For once, Spitfire losses exceeded Hurricanes by 13 aircraft to seven. About a third of these were suffered by No 41 Squadron, which had recently arrived in the combat area from Catterick. The heaviest combat losses in this period were sustained by squadrons newly rotated back to 11 Group after being rested elsewhere – another indication of the vulnerability of the replacement pilots.

Bitter combats

The Thameshaven attack was a prelude to the main assault on London, which began at 1500 on 7 September and lasted throughout the night. The London docks were pounded by 625 bombers, escorted in the daylight hours by 617 fighters. The civilian death toll was 448, with many more injured, and the severity of the attacks was such that the codeword Cromwell – signifying 'invasion imminent' – brought the British defences to their highest level of readiness. Of the 23 RAF fighters lost in the bitter combats of 7 September, eight were Spitfires. The Luftwaffe lost 38 aircraft.

The attacks continued and on 11 September, for the first time, the RAF suffered more heavily than the Luftwaffe, losing 27 aircraft to 22. Eight Spitfires were destroyed and ten damaged. After a spell of bad weather, eight more Spitfires were destroyed on 14 September. Then on 15 September the Luftwaffe threw 200 bombers against London in two waves. When the first wave attacked, the RAF had no more fighter squadrons in reserve; if the second wave had come immediately, the Spitfires and Hurricanes would have been caught on the ground as they refuelled and rearmed, allowing the enemy to bomb without opposition. But it was two hours before the second wave attacked, and by that time the fighter squadrons were once more ready for it. A total of 148 bombers got through to attack London, but 56 were shot down and many more limped back to their bases with severe battle damage. To the Luftwaffe, 15 September was remembered as 'Black Sunday'. Fighter Command's loss was 29, of which 22 were Hurricanes – once again, the Spitfire squadrons had escaped comparatively lightly.

Towards the end of September, dense cloud cover stretched over much of the British Isles, and the Luftwaffe's tactics underwent a complete change. The large daylight formations were abandoned. Instead the Luftwaffe began to send over small groups of aircraft, including bomb-carrying Messerschmitts, at high altitude. The Luftwaffe had clearly failed to achieve its objectives in daylight, but from the beginning of November it began to step up its night attacks on London and other targets. The Battle of Britain had ended in victory for Fighter Command, but the ordeal of Britain's cities was only just beginning.

Of the 742 Spitfires delivered to the RAF between 1 July and 31 October 1940, 361 were lost and 352 damaged. In the same period, 565 Hurricanes were lost and 455 damaged.

The importance of the Luftwaffe's failure over Britain rests in the fact that the island could later be used as a base for the Allied air offensive against Germany and for the Allied invasion of the European continent, which decided the war in the West. But it was fighter strength that decided the Battle of Britain – that, and the sacrifice of 537 young fighter pilots. The two fighter aircraft they flew, the Spitfire and the Hurricane, both became immortal in the heart of the British nation; but it was the Spitfire that became the legend.

Above: **'The swirling vortex of invisible battle'; a dogfight in progress over Maidstone, Kent. Pilots, as yet, had no idea what caused condensation trails.**

Below: **The sole Spitfire Mk III, intended as an air superiority fighter, saw a good deal of experimental flying and yielded much information which was used in the design of later marks.**

F ZD

CHAPTER THREE

In Action Over Northwest Europe, 1941–43

The Battle of Britain was over. Hitler had postponed indefinitely the plan for the invasion of Britain, Operation Sea Lion, and it was time for RAF Fighter Command to turn from defence to attack. On 20 December 1940 two Spitfires of No 66 Squadron, flown by Flight Lieutenant G.P. Christie and Pilot Officer C.A.W. Brodie, took off from Biggin Hill and set course across the Channel under a low cloud base. Crossing the enemy coast at Dieppe, they swept down on Le Touquet airfield and strafed several installations. There was no opposition from either flak or fighters, and both Spitfires returned safely to base.

Opposite: A splendid Charles Brown photograph of a Spitfire Mk V of No 222 Squadron, which operated this mark from North Weald in 1941. The squadron converted to Hawker Tempests late in 1944.

Over the next few days Spitfires and Hurricanes from various squadrons, operating in twos and threes, made short forays into enemy territory, again without meeting opposition. Encouraged, Fighter Command decided to try something bigger, and on 9 January 1941, in brilliant sunshine and perfect visibility, five fighter squadrons penetrated 50km (30 miles) into France. There was no sign of enemy movement, either on the ground or in the air. The next morning, six Blenheims of No 114 Squadron, escorted by six squadrons of Spitfires and Hurricanes, attacked ammunition and stores dumps in the Forêt de Guines. A few enemy fighters were encountered and there was some skirmishing, in the course of which one Hurricane was shot down. Two battle-damaged Spitfires crash-landed on return to base, and one of the pilots was killed. It was an inauspicious end to the RAF's first combined daylight bombing raid and fighter sweep, known as Circus No 1. Nevertheless, offensive sweeps were carried out whenever the

Below: Spitfire Mk VB AB910 of the Battle of Britain Memorial Flight, seen in the markings of No 92 Squadron. During WWII, this aircraft made one circuit of an airfield with a WAAF hanging on its tail; she survived.

weather permitted during the early weeks of 1941, and Luftwaffe opposition gradually increased.

Spitfire V

By March 1941, fighter sweeps over the Continent were becoming tightly-organized affairs, with the Spitfire and Hurricane squadrons operating at wing strength. A Fighter Command wing consisted of three squadrons, each of 12 aircraft. There were Spitfire wings at Biggin Hill, Hornchurch and Tangmere, mixed Spitfire and Hurricane wings at Duxford, Middle Wallop and Wittering, and Hurricane wings at Kenley, Northolt and North Weald. The Hurricane wings would soon be rearmed with Mk V Spitfires, which first came into service that same March.

Converted from the Mk I airframe, the Mk V was to be the main production version of the Spitfire. 6479 Mk V Spitfires were built in total. The majority of Spitfire Vs were armed with two 20mm cannon and four machine guns, packing a more powerful punch, particularly against armour plating. The Mk V was powered by a Rolls-Royce Merlin 45 engine, developing 1056kW (1415hp) at 5000m (16,400ft) compared with the 858kW (1150hp) of the Merlin XII fitted in the Mk II.

But the Mk V was essentially a compromise aircraft, rushed into service to meet an urgent requirement for a fighter with a performance superior to that of the latest model of Messerschmitt – the Bf 109F. The debut of the Spitfire V came just in time, because the Bf 109F began to arrive with the Luftwaffe fighter units in May 1941 (the new Messerschmitt had suffered from technical problems in its development phase, but these had now been resolved). On 11 May, a

Below: A neat formation of Spitfire IXs of No 611 Squadron, RAF Biggin Hill, photographed early in 1943. Note the wing blisters over the 20mm cannon breeches.

Above: **Spitfire Vs of No 485 (New Zealand) Squadron, formed at Driffield, Yorkshire, in March 1941. It later converted to Typhoons.**

group of bomb-carrying Bf 109Fs attacked Lympne and Hawkinge, one being shot down by a Spitfire. But the Spitfire V failed to deliver the overall superiority Fighter Command needed so badly. At high altitude, where a high proportion of the decisive combats took place, it was found to be inferior to the Bf 109F on most counts, and several squadrons equipped with the Mk V took a severe mauling during that summer.

'Sailor' Malan

In the spring and summer of 1941 the Biggin Hill Wing was made up by Nos 72, 92 and 609 Squadrons, all of which had achieved impressive records in the Battle of Britain. It was led by Wing Commander A.G. Malan, a South African with 18 confirmed victories, a DSO and two DFCs. Known by his nickname of 'Sailor' because of his pre-war service in the Merchant Navy, he was one of the RAF's foremost air combat tacticians, and his famous 'Ten Rules of Air Fighting' were displayed on dispersal hut walls throughout Fighter Command.

The pilots of the Biggin Hill Wing were proud to belong to what was generally regarded as an elite formation. One of them was Sergeant (later Flight Lieutenant) Jim Rosser of No 72 Squadron, who flew his first fighter sweeps in the spring of 1941. One of his early experiences was typical:

'We would cross the Channel in sections, line astern, climbing all the time. We always climbed into the sun, which was absolute hell; your eyes felt as though they were burning down into your head and within a few minutes you were saturated in sweat. I will never forget my first operation; 72 Squadron was flying top cover and I was "Yellow Two", in other words the number two aircraft in Yellow Section. Quite honestly, I hadn't a clue what was going on. We flew a sort of semi-circle over France, still in sections line astern, and then came out again. I never saw a single enemy aircraft, but we must have been attacked, because when we got home three of our Spits were missing.'

Seven 109s

No 72 Squadron's commanding officer was an Australian, Squadron Leader Desmond Sheen, who had begun his operational career with the squadron

Below: **Spitfire VB of No 316 (Warszawski) Squadron, a Polish unit formed at Pembrey, Wales, in February 1941. It was originally armed with Hurricanes.**

before the war. In April 1940 he had been posted to No 212 Squadron (the only Spitfire squadron to operate from French soil during the Battle of France) and in the next few weeks he flew photo-reconnaissance sorties all over Europe in specially-modified Spitfires, returning to No 72 Squadron just in time to take part in the Battle of Britain.

Sheen was to lead the squadron in sweeps over occupied Europe for eight months, from March to November 1941. Sheen's opposite number in No 92 Squadron was Squadron Leader Jamie Rankin, a Scot from Portobello, Edinburgh, who had originally joined the Fleet Air Arm but later transferred to the RAF. When he was appointed to command No 92 Squadron in March 1941 it was the top-scoring unit in Fighter Command, and its score steadily increased under Rankin's leadership. Rankin himself opened his score with No 92 by destroying a Heinkel He 59 floatplane and damaging a Bf 109 on 11 April. This was followed by another confirmed 109 on the 24th, and in June, a month of hectic air fighting over France, he shot down seven more 109s and claimed another probably destroyed.

Douglas Bader

Douglas Bader commanded the Tangmere Wing (Nos 145, 610 and 616 Squadrons, all flying Spitfire Vs). Bader's reputation was near-legendary, partly because he flew with artificial legs as the result of a pre-war flying accident. By the end of July 1941 his personal score stood at 22 enemy aircraft destroyed. He had an aversion to cannon armament, believing that it encouraged pilots to open fire at too great a range, so his personal aircraft was a Spitfire VA with an armament of eight machine guns.

Below: Ground crew rearming and refuelling a Spitfire under simulated gas attack conditions. Poison gas was considered a credible threat.

Handling the large fighter formations that were being pushed across the Channel in the summer of 1941 called for a high level of skill on the part of the controllers. By July 1941 Circus operations were very large affairs, with as many as 18 squadrons of fighters covering a small force of bombers. Getting six wings of Spitfires airborne, to the rendezvous at the right time and place, and shepherding them into and out of enemy territory, was something of a nightmare for everyone concerned. It began on the ground. Three squadrons of Spitfires – 36 aircraft – made an impressive sight as they taxied round the perimeter of an airfield, but with propellers revolving dangerously close to wingtips and tails it was all too easy to make a mistake. A late starter would add to the problems as the pilot edged around the outside of the queue, trying to catch up with the rest of his squadron.

The rendezvous with the bombers, usually over Manston, was another critical moment. A Spitfire's tanks held only 85 gallons of petrol, and every minute spent in waiting for the Blenheims to turn up reduced a pilot's chances of getting home safely if he found himself in trouble over France. Over enemy territory the Luftwaffe always seemed to have the advantage. No matter how high the Spitfires climbed, the 109s usually managed to climb higher, ready to pounce on the 'tail-end Charlies' of the fighter formations and pick them off. There was no dog-fighting in the original sense of the word; the Messerschmitts fought on the climb and dive, avoiding turning combat with the more manoeuvrable Spitfires wherever possible. The difference between life and death was measured in mere seconds.

Biggest sweep

One of the biggest fighter sweeps of 1941, Circus 62, was mounted on 7 August, when 18 squadrons of Spitfires and two of Hurricanes accompanied six Blenheim bombers in an attack on a power station at Lille. The whole force made rendezvous over Manston, with the North Weald Wing (made up of the Hurricanes of No 71 Squadron and the Spitfires of Nos 111 and 222 Squadrons) providing close support for the bombers. Behind and above, as

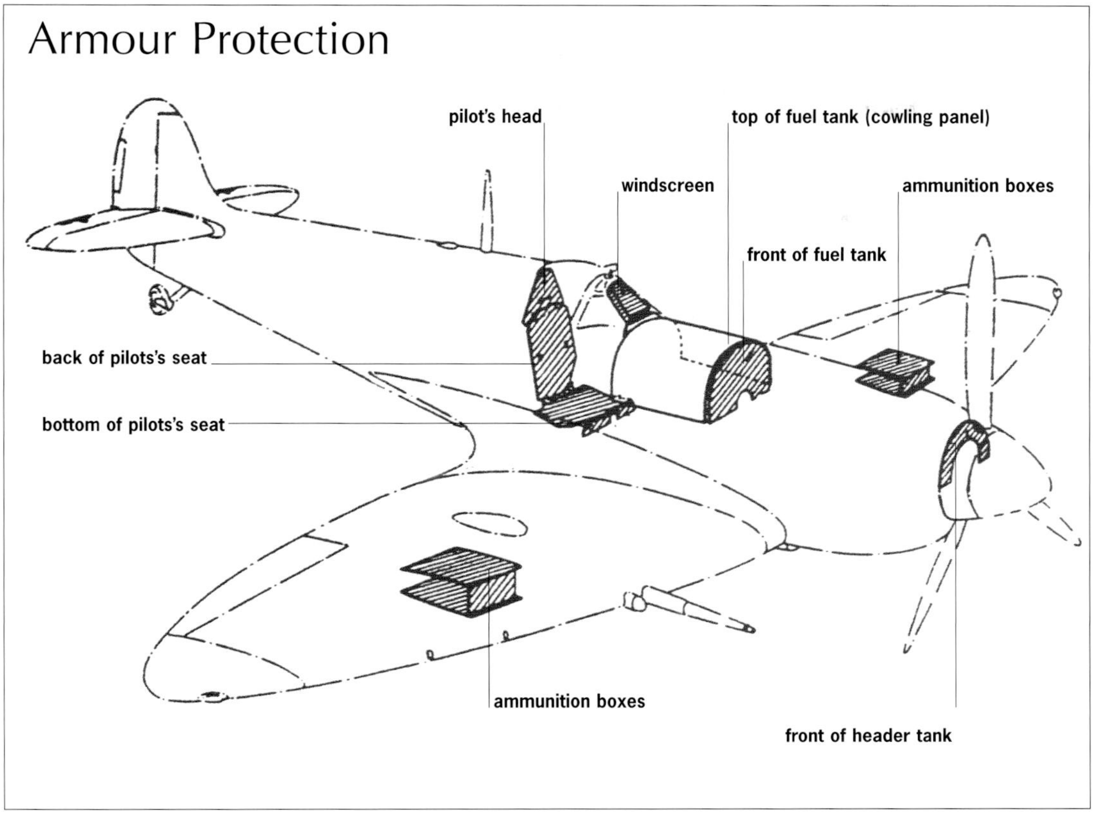

Left: **Diagram showing the position of the armour protection in a Spitfire VB. Spitfires did not have bullet-proof windscreens until the Battle of Britain.**

immediate top cover, came the three Spitfire squadrons of the Kenley Wing: Nos 452 (Australia), 485 (New Zealand), and 602. High above this 'beehive' of nearly 80 fighters and bombers came the three target support wings, flying at 8200m (27,000ft). They were the Biggin Hill Wing, with Nos 72, 92 and 609 Squadrons; the Hornchurch Wing, with Nos 403 (Canadian), 603 and 511 Squadrons; and Douglas Bader's Tangmere Wing, with Nos 41, 610 and 616 Squadrons. The target support force's task was to assure air superiority over and around Lille while the attack was in progress.

On this occasion, however, the Luftwaffe refused to be drawn into battle in large numbers. Six weeks earlier, the Germans had invaded the Soviet Union, and many fighter units had been transferred from the Channel area to the Eastern Front. Those that remained, seriously outnumbered in the face of Fighter Command's growing strength, had been ordered to conserve their resources. The 109s stayed well above the Spitfire formations, shadowing them. From time to time, small numbers of Messerschmitts broke away, darting down to fire on a straggler, always disengaging when the rest of the Spitfires turned on them. The 109s shot down one of No 41 Squadron's flight commanders in this way.

The bombers meanwhile had found Lille obscured by cloud, so had turned back towards the Channel to attack a concentration of barges at Gravelines. A fierce air battle was already in progress over the coast, where two Polish squadrons of the Northolt Wing, Nos 306 and 308, had been waiting

Below: **His Majesty King George VI examining the cockpit of a Spitfire. King George and Queen Elizabeth made frequent visits to RAF bases.**

Right: **Spitfire VBs of No 243 Squadron over northern England in the summer of 1942. The squadron left for North Africa in November.**

to cover the Blenheims during the final phase of their withdrawal. 308 Squadron was suddenly bounced by about 18 Messerschmitts, and lost two Spitfires. The Blenheims made their escape, but the rear support wing, comprising Nos 19, 257 and 401 Squadrons, was attacked and lost two Spitfires and a Hurricane. The RAF had therefore lost six aircraft, an outcome which, set against a claim of three Bf 109s destroyed, could hardly be considered favourable.

Right: **The type of gyro gunsight fitted to a Spitfire. The switch could be turned so that an illuminated graticule corresponded with the wingspan of an enemy aircraft type.**

Isolated

Another large operation, Circus 63, was mounted two days later on Saturday 9 August. This time the Blenheims' objective was a supply dump in the Béthune area. Once again, Bader's Tangmere Wing formed part of the target support force, but things went wrong from the start when No 41 Squadron failed to rendezvous on time. The remainder, unable to wait, carried on across the Channel. For a while all was peaceful; then just a few miles short of the target, the 109s hit them hard. Bader's pilots were hard put to hold their own, the wing becoming badly dislocated as the Messerschmitts pressed home determined attacks. Bader himself misjudged an attack on a 109 and found himself isolated. Six enemy fighters closed in on him but by superb flying he destroyed two. The end came soon afterwards, when another 109 collided with him and severed his Spitfire's fuselage just behind the cockpit. Bader managed to struggle clear of the plunging aircraft, leaving one of his artificial legs still trapped inside. His parachute opened, and he floated down to a painful landing and captivity.

As August gave way to September, some senior Air Staff officers began to have serious doubts about the value of Circus operations. Fighter Command losses were climbing steadily, and the results achieved hardly seemed to justify them. The new

AOC of 11 Group, Air Vice-Marshal Trafford Leigh-Mallory, claimed that between 14 June and 3 September 1941 his pilots had destroyed 437 German fighters, with another 182 'probables'. As the Luftwaffe never had more than 260 single-engined fighters in France and the Low Countries at any one time during this period, this claim later proved to be wildly exaggerated – the actual figure was 128 destroyed and 76 damaged. Fighter Command lost 194 pilots in those three months. The RAF's claim for the six and a half months from 14 June to 31 December 1941, 731 enemy aircraft destroyed, was equally exaggerated. The actual German loss was 154, including 51 not attributable to combat. Fighter Command's losses came to 411.

Focke-Wulf 190

A growing proportion of the RAF's losses were attributable to a single new factor. In September 1941, Polish pilots of No 315 Squadron, returning to base after Circus 101, reported being attacked by 'an unknown enemy aircraft with a radial engine'. RAF Intelligence concluded correctly that the Luftwaffe's latest fighter, the Focke-Wulf 190, had arrived in France. The first unit to receive the aircraft on the Channel coast was Jagdgeschwader 26, closely followed by JG2, and by October 1941 the RAF were running into more and more of them. Within weeks, the Fw 190 had established air superiority east of the Channel, outclassing the Spitfire VB at all altitudes and in every respect except radius of turn. On the personal orders of Winston Churchill, Fighter Command's sweeps over France were halted in November. No 118 Squadron, flying Spitfire VBs from Ibsley, participated in one of the last, flown on 15 November 1941. The Squadron War Diary tells the story:

'It was decided in the afternoon to carry out a most ill-conceived scheme, designated Rodeo 5, in which the Middle Wallop Wing rendezvoused with the Whirlwinds of 263 Squadron and carried out a sweep of the Channel Islands area.' (No 263 was one of two squadrons equipped with the twin-engined Westland Whirlwind, armed with four 20mm cannon. Designed as a long-range escort fighter, it was later used as a fighter-bomber.) 'The whole sortie seems to have been one long muddle. The Whirlwinds led the Spits much too far south and

Below: The Focke-Wulf Fw 190 was the Spitfire's most formidable opponent. Seen here is an Fw 190A of JG54.

Right: **Close-up of the nose of a Spitfire Mk IXLF, showing the Merlin 66 engine and Rotol four-bladed propeller, stripped of its spinner.**

Below: **The first high-altitude Spitfire Mk VI, fitted with a pressurized cockpit and a Merlin 47 engine, seen at Hucknall. Note the extended wingtips.**

then returned right over the flak area. 501 Squadron were sent out to deal with a few Huns that put in an appearance when we were on the way back. 118 went back to help, but 501 were not located. The net result was at least three planes damaged by flak and enemy aircraft, and one shot down, and all we could claim was one enemy aircraft damaged.'

Mk IX

Meanwhile, development of the Spitfire design had been moving forward. To counter the activities of high-flying German reconnaissance aircraft the Spitfire Mk VI was produced, with a long, tapered wing and a pressurized cockpit; the aircraft was assigned to a specialized flight of a home defence squadron. The Mk VII, also with a pressurized cockpit, was powered by a Rolls-Royce Merlin 60 engine, a two-stage, two-speed, inter-cooled powerplant that took the development of the Merlin to its ultimate level of performance. Early in 1942, Air Staff were intending to produce both the Spitfire Mk VII and the Spitfire Mk VIII (in much larger numbers). The Mk VIII was to be an unpressurized version of the Mk VII, intended for low-level air superiority operations as a counter to the Fw 190.

But the Mk VIII design needed a lot of refinement, including a general strengthening of the fuselage, which meant that production would be delayed for an unacceptably long time. The Air Staff therefore turned to an interim solution: a Mk V Spitfire airframe combined with a Merlin 61 engine. The resulting combination was the Spitfire Mk IX, which for a stop-gap aircraft turned out to be a resounding success. Deliveries to the RAF began in June 1942 and 5665 were built, more than any other version apart from the Mk V.

Circus resumed

Meanwhile by March 1942 Circus operations had been resumed, albeit on a reduced scale. The vulnerable Blenheims of Bomber Command's No 2 Group were replaced by the faster, more modern Douglas Boston. The number of Bostons involved in these operations was never more than 30 but they were often escorted by up to 27 squadrons of Spitfires, nearly half Fighter Command's available strength. On one occasion, on 30 April 1942, no fewer than 38 squadrons of Spitfires were involved in escorting 24 Bostons on four separate operations. Only six Bostons were lost in April but Spitfire losses were heavy as the Fw 190s (and, to a lesser extent, the Bf 109Fs) continued to show their superiority over the Spitfire V. For example, 11 Spitfires failed to return on 4 April, 15 on 12 April, and 12 on 25 April. Spitfire losses for the whole of the month were 59 aircraft.

The sternest test for Fighter Command in 1942 was the Dieppe operation of 19 August (Operation Jubilee), one object of which was to bring to battle all the forces of the Luftwaffe in northern France and the Low Countries. Control of the RAF part of the operation was given to Air Vice-Marshal Trafford Leigh-Mallory of No 11 Group. 56 squadrons of Spitfires, Hurricanes and Typhoons were placed at his disposal, as well as five Blenheim and Boston squadrons of No 2 Group and four Mustang squadrons of Army Co-operation Command. The story of that ill-fated venture, and of the gallantry of the Canadian troops who suffered appalling casualties in the landing, is well known. Dieppe was a disaster for the RAF, too – in the day's operations the RAF lost 106 aircraft to the Luftwaffe's 48. Of the RAF losses, 88 were fighters, and the majority were Spitfires.

American Eagles

Tuesday 29 September 1942 was a significant day for the officers and men of Nos 71, 121 and 133 Spitfire Squadrons. Known as the Eagle Squadrons,

Below: **Spitfire Mk IX in the markings of No 316 (Polish) Squadron. The code SZ was carried by this squadron from February 1941 until December 1946, when it disbanded.**

these three units had been formed from a nucleus of American volunteer pilots in 1940–41. Now based together at Debden in Essex, they were formally handed over to VIII Fighter Command, United States Army Air Force to become the 334th, 335th and 336th Fighter Squadrons of the 4th Fighter Group. From now on the primary task of the pilots would be bomber escort to the Boeing B-17s that had become operational with the Eighth AAF in the United Kingdom that summer. The pilots of No 133 Squadron had already had an unfortunate taste of this type of mission on 4 September, when 12 brand new Spitfire IXs accompanied a formation of B-17 Fortresses in an attack on Morlaix. A serious navigational error, compounded by bad weather, had resulted in 11 of the 12 Spitfires running out of fuel over the Brest peninsula on the return flight. Four pilots were killed, and the rest were taken prisoner. The 4th Fighter Group continued to fly Spitfires until March 1943, when it rearmed with Republic P-47 Thunderbolts.

Escort missions

The following extract from the War Diary of No 118 Squadron, flying its Spitfire VBs from Coltishall in Lincolnshire, well illustrates the typical activity of a Spitfire squadron early in 1943. It describes an operation flown on 21 January:

Below: **Pilots of the 4th Fighter Group, USAAF, scramble for the benefit of the press at Debden in 1942. The 4th FG exchanged its Spitfires for P-47s in March 1943.**

SPITFIRE Mk IX

Type: fighter
Powerplant: one 1565hp Rolls-Royce Merlin 61 or 1650hp Merlin 63 12-cylinder V-type
Max speed: 655km/h (408mph) at 7320m (24,000ft)
Service ceiling: 12,105m (43,000ft)
Max range: 1576km (980 miles)
Wing span: 11.23m (36ft 10in)
Length: 9.46m (31ft)
Height: 3.85m (12ft 7¾in)
Weights: empty 2545kg (5610lb); max take-off 4309kg (9500lb)
Armament: two 20mm cannon and four 7.7mm (0.303in) MG (Mk IXe)

Spitfire Mk IX

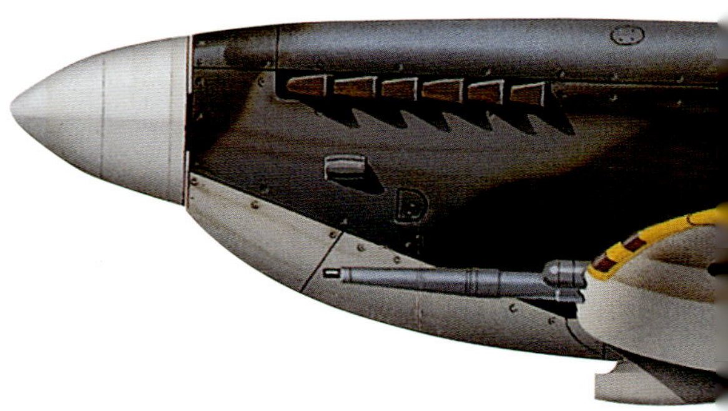

Left: **Comforts for the troops: a Spitfire Mk IXE en route to Normandy with two 18-gallon (81-litre) beer barrels attached to its underwing shackles.**

'Misery (the Squadron Intelligence Officer) went on a 48 (hours' leave) and of course things happened: there were four flights by 27 aircraft in fine weather. In the morning there was drogue towing, air-to-air and air-to-sea firing, camera gun practice, camera tests and in the afternoon a sweep over Ijmuiden... In the afternoon the Squadron made rendezvous with 167' (another Spitfire V squadron, whose personnel were mainly Dutch) 'and 12 Venturas over Mundesley and flew at sea level to within a few miles of the Dutch coast, then climbed to 9000ft over Ijmuiden. As we crossed the coast four Fw 190s were seen breaking cloud below at 2000 feet. Our allotted task was to give top cover to the bombers which, instead of bombing immediately, went inland for ten minutes then turned round and bombed from east to west on an outward heading. Squadron Leader Wooton decided not to go down for the 190s until the bombers had carried out their task, or while they were still in danger of being attacked. While the bombers and escorts were making their manoeuvre the 190s climbed up and were joined by others, but before they could attack the bombers 118 Squadron engaged them. In the following dog-fight, of which no one seemed to have a very clear picture, Sgt Lack destroyed a Fw 190 which he followed down to sea level and set on fire; it was eventually seen to crash into the sea by (Sgt) Hallingworth.

'Hallingworth was attacked and his aircraft hit, and he in turn claimed a 190 damaged. The CO, who engaged the leading Fw 190, also claimed one

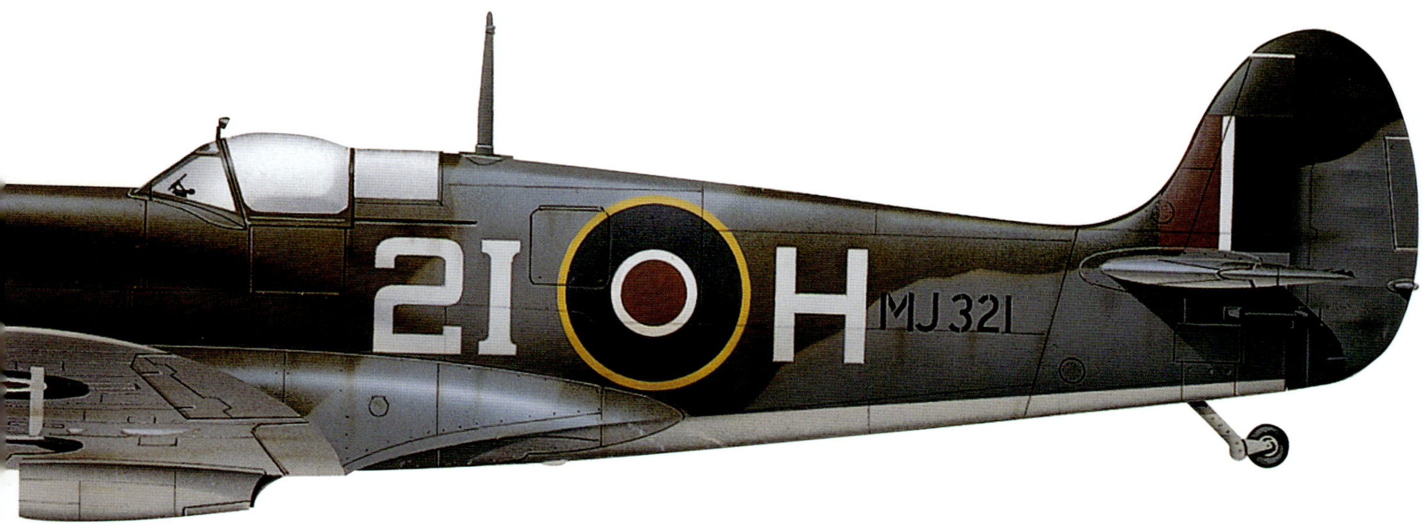

Right: **Spitfire Mk II P8131 of No 276 Squadron was one of 50 converted for air-sea rescue work to drop survival equipment from flare chutes.**

damaged, the enemy aircraft breaking away after being hit by cannon fire and going down followed by Sgt Buglass, who lost sight of it. Shepherd went to Hallingworth's rescue when he was being attacked, and was himself fired at head-on by two Fw 190s. Flight Sergeant Cross is missing from this engagement; no one saw what happened to him, but as he was flying number two to Shepherd it is believed that he must have been hit during the double attack on his section leader. The Squadron got split up during the engagement, seven aircraft coming back together and the other four in two pairs. No one saw Cross crash. He was a very nice, quiet Canadian and will be very much missed.'

Below: **Spitfire Mk IXC preparing for take-off on a night intruder sortie. Note the under-fuselage auxiliary tank.**

Deep penetration

From the spring of 1943 the fighter wings of No 11 Group equipped with the Spitfire IX were also assigned to escort duties with the US Eighth Army Air Force, which began deep-penetration missions into Germany in March. The Spitfires' limited range meant that escort could only be provided for part of the way, leaving the bombers to continue unescorted into Germany. The Luftwaffe soon shattered the illusion that large formations of heavy bombers could operate deep inside enemy territory without fighter escort, relying entirely on their defensive armament. Some of the heaviest fighting took place over Holland, a main route into Germany for the Allied bomber squadrons. By the summer of 1943 almost all the Spitfire squadrons had rearmed with the Mk IX, and for escort missions the fighters were given auxiliary fuel tanks. A 30-gallon 'slipper' type belly tank was fitted, which could be jettisoned before combat. Although unsatisfactory in many respects it served its purpose, and some 300,000 were produced for use by the Spitfire squadrons.

Repeated attacks

Pilots were content with the Spitfire Mk IX, which many considered to be superior to the Focke-Wulf 190 at medium and low level. One pilot, Squadron Leader D.G. Andrews, showed what the aircraft could do in skilled hands when faced with superior numbers. His squadron was escorting USAAF B-26 Marauders on a raid to Woensdrecht when, having turned back because of bad weather, the Spitfires were attacked by more than a dozen Fw 190s over the island of Walcheren. One Spitfire was shot down and the squadron became scattered.

Andrews was subjected to repeated attacks from ahead, abeam and astern, which damaged his Spitfire in several places and put the R/T out of action. Unable to call for help, Andrews lost height almost to ground level near Walcheren in an attempt to shake off his pursuers, though he now had to face ground fire as well. Gradually, the number of enemy aircraft decreased until only four attackers were left, although Andrews could make little homeward progress because of the need to take constant evasive action. Up to this point Andrews had had no opportunity to fire his guns, but by the time he was ten miles west of Walcheren, having shaken off another two Focke-Wulfs, he was in a position to turn against the remaining enemy fighters. This unexpected move caused one of the enemy to fly directly into Andrews' concentrated fire; the Fw 190 dived into the sea with a tremendous splash and the other immediately disengaged, leaving Andrews free to return to his base at Manston.

Frustrating time

Despite the provision of auxiliary fuel tanks, the Spitfire's limited range meant that it could only provide bomber escort to a point midway across the Netherlands. Its main usefulness therefore lay in meeting the bombers as they returned, when they were at their most vulnerable, short of ammunition

Below: Ground crew preparing a Spitfire VB of No 322 (Norwegian) Squadron for a sortie from RAF Catterick, Yorshire, in 1942.

Right: **This Spitfire Mk IX, BF274, never officially existed. It carried the wrong serial number throughout its service life, for reasons that were never explained.**

and with their crews exhausted. For the Spitfire pilots it was a frustrating time.

Despite serious losses sustained in the summer of 1943, particularly during the so-called 'anniversary raids' of August, General Eaker, commanding the US VIII Bomber Command, was determined to maintain the daylight offensive. Early in October it was judged that the Eighth Air Force was ready to resume its deep-penetration attacks. But when the US bombers did so, the lessons of August were soon rammed home even more forcibly. In one week between 8 and 14 October, when the Americans attacked Bremen, Marienburg, Danzig, Münster and once again Schweinfurt, they lost 148 bombers and nearly 1500 aircrew. In the Schweinfurt raid of 14 October, which became known as Black Thursday, the Luftwaffe flew over 500 sorties and destroyed 60 of the 280 bombers taking part – over 20 per cent.

Wing Commander J.E. 'Johnnie' Johnson, then the Kenley Wing Leader (he was to become the RAF's top-scoring Spitfire pilot with 38 victories), commanded a formation of Spitfires heading out to escort the returning bombers. He described the aftermath of this terrible encounter:

'It was a clear afternoon, and we first saw their contrails many miles away, as well as the thinner darting contrails of the enemy fighters above and on either flank. As we closed the gap we could see that they had taken a terrible mauling, for there were gaping holes in their precise formations. Some Fortresses were gradually losing height, and a few

Below: **Pilots of No 340 'Ile de France' Squadron practise a scramble at Westhampnett in 1942.**

Above: A Spitfire of No 453 (Canadian) Squadron being prepared for D-Day operations on 5 June 1944. The aircraft wears black and white 'invasion' stripes.

stragglers, lagging well behind, were struggling to get home on three engines.

'We swept well behind the stragglers and drove off a few 109s and 110s, but the great air battle was over, and what a fight it must have been, because more than half the bombers we nursed across the North Sea were shot up. One or two ditched in the sea, and many others, carrying dead and badly injured crew members, had to make crash-landings. How we longed for more drop tanks, so that some of the many hundreds of Spitfires based in Britain could play their part in the great battles over Germany…'

Favourite prey

Among the hundreds of other Spitfire pilots who flew bomber escort missions was Pierre Clostermann, a French fighter ace flying with the RAF, who wrote in his book *The Big Show*:

'Behind the formation were the stragglers, making for the coast, for the haven of refuge of an advanced air base on the other side of the Channel, flying only by a sublime effort of will… You could imagine the blood pouring over the heaps of empty cartridges, the pilot nursing his remaining engines and anxiously eyeing the long white trail of petrol escaping from his riddled tanks. These isolated Fortresses were the Focke-Wulf's favourite prey. Therefore the squadrons detached two or three pairs of Spitfires, charged with bringing each one back safe: an exhausting task as these damaged Fortresses often dragged along on a third of their total power, stretching the endurance of their escort to the limit… In many cases it was only the moral support of the presence of a pair of Spitfires that gave them the courage to hold out to the end, to resist the temptation of baling out and waiting for the end of the war in some Oflag or other.'

As the end of 1943 approached, many of the UK-based Spitfire squadrons were preparing for a different role. In June 1943 the Second Tactical Air Force was formed to provide tactical support for the 1st Canadian and 2nd British Armies in the forthcoming invasion. By June 1944, 32 Spitfire squadrons were assigned to Second TAF, while 22 more were retained in the UK for air defence. In November 1943, Fighter Command was renamed Air Defence of Great Britain; a year later there was an about-face, and it became Fighter Command again – to much rejoicing among its personnel.

CHAPTER FOUR

The Griffon-engined and Photo-recce Spitfires

Another development of the Rolls-Royce 'R' engine, which had powered the Supermarine S6 racing seaplane series, was the '37', built in 1939. Named Griffon, after the mythical bird, it produced 1294kW (1735hp) and weighed 900kg (1980lb). Although it had a larger frontal area than the Merlin, fitting it to a Spitfire airframe was a logical next step.

***Opposite*: The Battle of Britain Memorial Flight Spitfire Mk XIX, the last of the PR Spitfires, in D-Day recognition stripes.**

***Below:* The underside of a Spitfire was not a particularly pretty sight. Seen here is a Mk XII, the first of the Griffon-engined Spitfires.**

The Griffon was under development for naval aircraft, and it was the IIB version that first became available for installation in a Spitfire. The airframe selected was that of the Spitfire Mk IV prototype, DP845 (not to be confused with the PR IV, which was unconnected). Trials proved satisfactory and an order for 750 Mk IVs was placed, but this was later cancelled and it was not until 1942 that 100 Spitfires, designated Mk XIIs, were converted to Griffon engines.

These aircraft had been either Mk Vs in the process of being converted to Mk IX standard, or Mk VIIIs which were still on the production line. The Mk XII was given extra length and the fuselage was strengthened to compensate for the extra weight and power of the Griffon. As a result of its greater frontal area, the engine cowling had to be given two pronounced bulges to cover the cylinder banks. The propeller was a four-blade Rotol. The Griffon propeller shaft rotated in the opposite direction to that of the Merlin, and this produced a strong swing to the right on take-off. About half of the Mk XIIs produced had retractable tailwheels, depending on whether the individual aircraft was converted from a Mk V/IX or Mk VIII airframe. The Mk XII had clipped wings, as it was intended for use only as a low-level interceptor. Armament was two cannon and four machine guns, like that of the Mk VIII and Mk IX. Maximum cruising speed was a fast 585km/h (364mph), but this gave a short range of only 529km (329 miles). The Mk XII could reach 1500m (5000ft) in a little over a minute after take-off, but it needed 6.7 minutes to reach 6100m (20,000ft). Maximum speed at 1680m (5500ft) was 598km/h (372mph), rising to 632km/h (393mph) at 5490m (18,000ft).

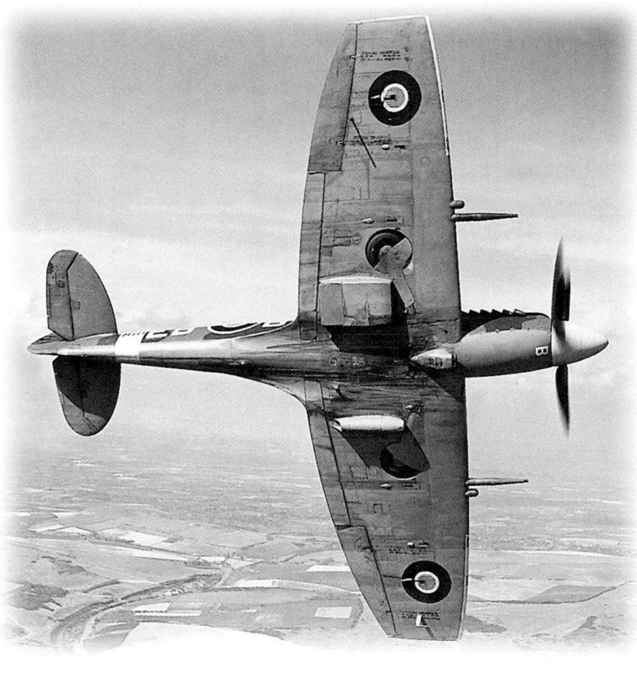

Low-level attacks

The Mk XII was developed specifically to counter low-level attacks on the English south coast by German fighter-bombers, which were becoming increasingly troublesome in the first half of 1942.

The principal Luftwaffe units involved in attacks on the south coast at this time were Jagdgeschwader 2 and 26. Armed with the Messerschmitt Bf 109F-4/B fitted with racks for a 250kg (550lb) bomb, they specialized in low-level intruder operations. Often taking off in poor visibility from their well-defended airfields at Abbeville, Ligescourt, Poix or St Omer, they would hug the ground and head out over the Channel at wave-top height. Favourite targets were the towns of Dover, Brighton, Folkestone, Worthing and Newhaven. JG2 (based to the south around Evreux and Caen) concentrated its attacks on Channel shipping, while JG26 attacked the coastal towns.

Pure luck

This type of attack was hurried and literally hit-or-miss, but it kept the RAF's fighter defences in a state of constant alert. Once the fighter-bombers had made their attack, defending Spitfires stood little chance of catching them on the homeward run, and it was a matter of pure luck if a patrol intercepted them on the way in. The situation became even worse from June 1942, when the fighter-bomber Geschwader on the Channel coast began to rearm with the Focke-Wulf Fw 190A-3, which could carry a 500kg (1100lb) bomb. Enemy attacks, usually carried out by a Schwarm of four aircraft, reached new levels of success, and it was fortunate for the British that JG2 and 26 never had more than about 20 Fw 190s available for operations at any one time. In an attempt to redress the situation the RAF's latest fighter, the Hawker Typhoon, was rushed into action; but the Typhoon was suffering from a series of development problems, and so the deployment of the Spitfire XII was accelerated.

Daylight raid

On 20 January 1943 the third Spitfire XII, EN223, flew to Manston in Kent from the Air Fighting Development Unit at Duxford, where it had been undergoing trials. At this time the Typhoons of No 609 Squadron were based at Manston, and the lone Spitfire's arrival coincided with a daylight raid on London by 28 Fw 190s and Bf 109s. The Manston fighters were scrambled in time to intercept the raiders as they left the target area and they destroyed four Fw 190s and three Bf 109s, one of the Focke-Wulfs being shot down by Squadron Leader R.H. Harris of No 91 Squadron, flying the Spitfire XII.

The first squadron to equip fully with the Spitfire XII, in February 1943, was No 41

Below: **Bomb-carrying Spitfire XII HB878 of No 41 Squadron, one of three units to be equipped with the type.**

Spitfire Mk XIVE

SPITFIRE MK XIVE

Type: single-seat fighter-bomber
Powerplant: one Rolls-Royce Griffon 65 or 66 Vee-12 piston engine rated at 1517kW (2035hp) at altitude
Performance: maximum speed 721km/h (448mph) at 7925m (26,000ft); range with internal fuel 740km (460 miles); service ceiling 13,100km (43,000ft)
Dimensions: span 11.23m (36ft 10in); length 9.96m (32ft 8in); height 3.87m (12ft 8in); wing area 22.67m^2 (244 sq ft)

Squadron, which shot down its first FW 190 on 27 April, while operating from Hawkinge. The second unit to re-equip with the Mk XII, No 91, destroyed five enemy fighter-bombers in a running battle over the Channel on 25 May 1943. In June 1943, following a marked decline in enemy fighter-bomber activity, and with the Typhoons now well able to cope with the situation, the two Spitfire XII-equipped squadrons moved to Westhampnett to form a bomber support wing.

Right: **Fine study of a Spitfire XII. The type was rushed into service to counter enemy fighter-bombers intruding at low level.**

Right: **Supermarine Spitfire LF.Mk XVI SL721. The aircraft was used as the personal transport of Air Marshal Sir James Robb, AOC-in-C RAF Fighter Command, 1945–47.**

No 41 Squadron shepherded 60 B-17s home from Le Mans on 26 June, and with the arrival of No 91 Squadron a couple of days later the Wing began escorting the medium bombers of No 2 Group and also Typhoon fighter-bombers. Nos 41 and 91 Squadrons were the only operational units to be armed with the Spitfire XII, although a few examples were used by No 595 Squadron for anti-aircraft co-operation duties at Aberporth, Wales, from December 1944 to July 1945.

Large-scale production

The next Griffon-engined Spitfire variant was Mk XIV. Based on a Mk VIII airframe, it was the first Griffon-engined Spitfire variant to go into large-scale production, a total of 957 being built. The first aircraft were issued to No 322 (Netherlands) and No 610 Squadrons in March and April 1944. The Mk XIV's most distinctive feature was a five-blade Rotol propeller, driven by a 1517kW (2035hp) Griffon 65. The Mk XIV had a maximum speed of 720km/h

(448mph) at 7930m (26,000ft) and 670km/h (417mph) at 3660m (12,000 ft), which made it a very fast aircraft indeed. Together with the Spitfire XII, it was pressed into service to combat the V-1 flying bombs, the first of which fell on British soil on 12 June 1944.

The Mks XII and XIV both performed well against the V-1. 14 pilots of No 91 Squadron flying the Mk XII destroyed five or more flying bombs apiece, and five pilots had scores of over ten. Both 41 and 91 Squadrons exchanged their Mk XIIs for Mk XIVs before the V-1 offensive was over. Spitfire squadrons also carried out many dive-bombing attacks on V-1 launching sites in the Pas de Calais; these continued until September 1944, when the sites were overrun. The Spitfire XIV's speed also gave it a good chance of catching Me 262 jet fighters, several of which were destroyed by the Spitfires of No 127 Wing based in Belgium in the latter part of 1944 and in 1945.

Final development

The Spitfire Mk XVIII was the last Griffon-engined development of the original Spitfire airframe and was almost identical in appearance to the Mk XIV, except that the latter's 'universal' Spitfire wing was replaced by a specially designed one. The first 100 aircraft were completed as fighters, and a further 200 as FR.XVIII fighter-reconnaissance aircraft. Production aircraft were not available before the middle of 1945 and so the type did not see operational service in WWII, although a few examples reached the Far East before the end of hostilities. But the FR.XVIII did see action in Malaya against communist insurgents in 1948, while operating with No 81 Squadron. The type also equipped Nos 11, 28, 32, 60 and 208 Squadrons, all serving in the Middle and Far East.

Above: **Spitfire Mk XIV of No 322 (Netherlands) Squadron, which was formed at Woodvale in June 1943 and which operated Spitfires until October 1945.**

Above: **Spitfire F XIV RB140 seen here in its early form. The first six aircraft were converted from Mk VIII airframes at Rolls-Royce's Hucknall factory.**

New wing

The next Griffon Spitfire was the F.21, which represented a major redesign of the Spitfire airframe. In fact, the F.21 bore so little resemblance to the original Spitfire that at one point the name Victor was mooted for it. Although thousands were on order before the end of WWII, only 120 examples were actually produced. The F.21 had a new, strengthened wing, with provision for four cannon. The day of the airborne machine gun was over, in the RAF at least. An increase in weight made it necessary to reposition the undercarriage, which when retracted was fully enclosed by wheel flaps. The tail wheel was also retractable and the aircraft had a new, broad-chord vertical tail unit. Metal-covered elevators and rudder and 86kg (190lb) of armour plating contributed to an empty weight of 3244kg (7160lb), making this the heaviest Spitfire so far.

The F.21 was nevertheless a handsome aircraft, and entered service at the end of 1945. Powered by the Griffon 61, the F.21's maximum speed was 724km (450mph) at heights from 5795m (19,000ft) to 7930m (26,000ft), 676km/h (420mph) at 3660m (12,000ft) and 627km/h (390mph) at sea level. Its internal fuel capacity of 120 gallons gave it a range of 788km (490 miles) at 458km/h (285mph), the range being boosted to 1415km (880 miles) with maximum auxiliary fuel. The Spitfire 21 equipped eight squadrons, three of them Auxiliary Air Force units.

Another Spitfire variant, the F.22, came off the production line at the same time as the F.21. Apart from a cut-down fuselage, a revised

SPITFIRE PR.Mk XIX

Type: single-seat reconnaissance aircraft

Powerplant: one Rolls-Royce Griffon 65 Vee-12 piston engine rated at 1528kW (2050hp) at altitude

Performance: maximum speed 721km/h (448mph) at 7472m (24,500ft); maximum range l 745km (1085 miles); service ceiling 13,565m (44,500ft)

Dimensions: span 11.23m (36ft 10in); length 9.96m (32ft 8in); height 3.87m (12ft 8in); wing area 22.67m^2 (244 sq ft)

Left: **The Spitfire XIV prototype, JF318, was converted from a Mk VIII airframe. It was a more powerful fighter at all altitudes than the low-level Mk XII.**

cockpit canopy and a 24-volt electrical system instead of the F.21's 12-volt, there were no differences between the two. Production of the F.22 began in March 1945 and 260 were built, the original order for 627 having been reduced. The Spitfire F.22 equipped 13 squadrons, all but one being Auxiliary units. The exception was No 73 Squadron, which used its F.22s at Ta' Qali, Malta, until 1948.

Last Spitfire

The last of the long line of Spitfires, and according to some the most beautiful of them all, was the F.24. Only 81 F.24s were produced, which were in effect modified F.22s. The only squadron to be armed with the type was No 80, at Kai Tak, Hong Kong; this unit maintained a high state of alert during the Chinese Civil War and also during the early months of the Korean War. Occasionally, its aircraft made fast incursions into Chinese air space to monitor airfields and military installations.

On Battle of Britain Sunday, 1951, before handing over its aircraft to the Hong Kong Auxiliary Air Force, No 80 Squadron carried out a

Spitfire PR.Mk XIX

***Right:* Painting showing the destruction of a V-1 flying bomb by a Spitfire XIV of No 130 Squadron. The airflow from the fighter's wingtip has toppled the bomb over.**

memorial flypast. It was the last time that a Spitfire squadron performed this tribute.

Photo-reconnaissance

The Spitfire performed the vital task of photographic reconnaissance throughout World War II. The first two aircraft – Spitfire Is N3069 and N3071 – were delivered to Heston, Middlesex, where the RAF's embryo PR organization was based, on 13 October 1939. In November, stripped of all non-essential equipment and fitted with an F.24 camera, the second of these aircraft deployed to Seclin near Lille, and on the 18th of that month it carried out the first Spitfire PR flight, over Aachen. The Spitfire's limited range was a problem, but the provision of extra fuel tanks extended this to around 1200km (750 miles). The modified aircraft were designated Spitfire PR.IB.

In January 1940 the PR organization at Heston was renamed the Photographic Development Unit (PDU), and the Special Survey Flight (the cover name for the unit responsible for clandestine reconnaissance flights before the war) became No 212 (PR) Squadron. By spring 1940 the Spitfires had photographed almost the entire Ruhr and, together with the PR Blenheims also used by the squadron, had located all the major surface vessels of the German fleet. In July 1940 the PDU was designated No 1 Photographic Reconnaissance Unit (PRU).

Zeiss camera

The next PRU to be formed, on 16 November 1940, was No 3 at RAF Oakington near Cambridge. It had an initial establishment of six Spitfires and two Wellingtons. The first Spitfire sortie, to Cologne, was flown on 29 November. Ironically the aircraft was fitted with a Zeiss

***Below:* A pilot prepares for a sortie in a Spitfire XIV. Note the massive five-bladed constant-speed Rotol propeller.**

Left: **Spitfire XIV of No 350 (Belgian) Squadron. The first Belgian-manned RAF fighter squadron, No 350, was formed at Valley, Anglesey, in November 1941.**

Below: **Spitfire LF.XVI bearing the code letters of the Central Gunnery School. Flying Training Command units carried four-letter identity codes in 1946.**

camera taken from a Junkers Ju 88 of a Luftwaffe reconnaissance unit, 4(F)121, forced down at Oakington with engine trouble on 19 September. No 2 PRU, formed in June 1941, was based at Heliopolis, Egypt, but did not receive Spitfires until 1942, having been equipped until then with Hurricanes and a Lockheed Model 12A. The Spitfires were PR Mk IVs, which were converted Mk Vs. The conversion involved sealing the wing torsion box forward of the main spar to form integral fuel and oil tanks. No armament was fitted and instead 300-litre (66-gallon) fuel tanks were incorporated, giving the aircraft sufficient radius of action to take it as far as Greece. The

Above: **Spitfire F.21 of the Central Fighter Establishment. The F.21 was used in a wide variety of training roles in the post-war years.**

total fuel capacity was 977 litres (215 gallons), giving a range of 2250–2400km (1400–1500 miles). No 4 PRU was formed to provide photographic intelligence before and during the Allied landings in North Africa in November 1942 and subsequently operated from Maison Blanche, Algeria.

Armed version

The Spitfire PR.VII, which was also a Mk IV conversion, was basically an armed version of the PR.IV, having an 'A' type armament of eight machine guns and an extra fuel tank only in the rear fuselage. Inevitably, it was not long before the superior high-altitude performance of the Spitfire Mk IX, with its Merlin 61 engine, led to the development of a

Right: **Head-on view of the Spitfire F.22, a variant that equipped many Auxiliary Air Force units in the years after the war, before jet equipment arrived.**

photographic reconnaissance version, the PR.XI. Paradoxically, the aircraft that was developed from the PR.XI, and followed it, was designated Mk X; it featured a pressurized cockpit and was not a success, only 16 aircraft being produced. These were used from July 1944 to April 1945 by No 542 Squadron, based at Benson in Oxfordshire.

The PR.XIII was designed for low-level work; 18 Mk V airframes were converted and fitted with the Merlin 32 engine. The PR.XIII was the last of the Merlin-engined Spitfires, being followed by the Griffon-engined PR.XIX. Basically, the latter was a late production Mk XIV airframe fitted with a bowser wing (a wing adapted as a fuel tank), with a universal camera installation based on that of the PR.IV/XI. It was developed early in 1944 to give greater range, speed and ceiling than existing PR Spitfires, both to elude the German defences, whose methods of detection and interception had steadily improved, and to meet the requirements of operations in the Far East.

The first of 225 Mk.XIXs was delivered in May 1944. It was intended that the type would be replaced on the production line by a PR version of the Spiteful, but prolonged delays in the development of this aircraft ultimately led to its cancellation. Due to the increased weight of the Griffon, together with petrol-filled wing leading edges, the PR.XIX was more nose-heavy than any other Spitfire type, and particular care had to be exercised when taxiing before take-off. The PR.XIX remained in service in the Far East until 1954, performing valuable photographic work with No 81 Squadron during the Malayan Emergency, and was used for meteorological tasks until 1957.

Substantial size

By the end of 1943 ten specialist PR squadrons, seven of them equipped with Spitfires, had been formed at home and overseas within the framework of the PRUs, which had now grown to a substantial size. The first Spitfire PR squadrons were Nos 541 and 542, formed respectively from B and F, and A and E Flights of No 1 PRU at Benson. A third squadron, No 543, also formed at Benson in October 1943. Overseas, No 680 Squadron formed at Matariya in North Africa on 1 February 1943, and on the same day No 682 Squadron formed at Maison Blanche from No 4 PRU. On 8 February 1943 No 683 Squadron formed from B Flight of No 69 Squadron at Luqa, Malta. In the meantime, No 3 PRU had deployed to the Far East, where No 681 Squadron was formed from it in January 1943 at Dum Dum, Calcutta. Also in 1943, No 106 Group was established at Benson to control all RAF PR training, operations and photographic interpretation.

This expansion meant that PR Spitfires operated in all theatres, from Burma to the Arctic. In August 1942, following the destruction of the Russia-bound convoy PQ17, three Spitfire PR.IVs of No 1 PRU deployed to Vayenga, North Russia, to keep watch on enemy surface raiders. The Spitfires carried Soviet markings and the first operation was flown over Altenfjord, Norway, on 10 September. The detachment returned to the UK in November and a second one went to Vaenga in April 1943. This maintained surveillance on the *Tirpitz*, and as a result of the PR activity the German battleship was badly damaged when she was attacked in her anchorage by midget submarines on 22 September.

Below: A Spitfire Mk 22 displaying its graceful lines. The laminar-flow wing surface is marred only by the blisters over the four cannon.

Above: **Apart from some equipment changes, there was no difference between the Spitfire F.22 and the F.24, seen here. F.24s served in Hong Kong into the 1950s.**

It was a PR Spitfire, too, that located *Tirpitz*'s sister ship, *Bismarck*, heading for the North Atlantic via a Norwegian fjord in May 1941, beginning a pursuit that ended with the battleship's destruction several days later.

Perils

In North Africa, the commanding officer of No 4 PRU was Wing Commander (later Air Marshal Sir) Alfred Ball, who later provided an interesting insight into the perils faced by a PR pilot:

'In Tunisia at the end of '42 we had a lot of large area photography to do, mostly front-line mapping for First Army. It was very costly and on one occasion we lost four aircraft in three days from a squadron of nine. The difficulty was the great concentration of Fw 190s and Me 109Gs and standing patrols in the battle area (our own fighters were having a bad time just then, December '42 and January '43). In this case the problem was solved by the replacement of our Mk IV Spitfires by Mk XIs while our fighter squadrons got Mk IXs.

Left: **Spitfire F.22 PK312, with F.21 LA232 behind, poses for the camera of renowned aviation photographer Charles E. Brown.**

'Let me outline an experience in a Spitfire Mk IV at 24,000 feet (a bad height for the Spitfire but ideal for the Fw 190) near Tunis. I was just completing some 45 minutes of front line photography when I spotted four Fw 190s some three to four miles away and about 1000 feet below going in the opposite direction. They turned to me shortly after I saw them and I opened up to full throttle and dived slightly to gain speed as quickly as possible. Within a very few minutes, however, they were on to me and the first of eight attacks took place. My only chance lay in out-turning them. In the event I was hit by the very first burst of fire – having left my turn (maximum possible)

Below: **Spitfire F.22 of No 602 'City of Glasgow' Squadron, Royal Auxiliary Air Force, pictured at Abbotsinch in 1948. The squadron used F.22s until 1951.**

a fraction too late – but although the aircraft was hit in a number of interesting places, the damage was not catastrophic. This one-sided combat went on for five to ten minutes until the Focke-Wulfs broke off, either out of ammunition or short of fuel.'

Early sighting

'I have touched on interception risks but not on the capabilities of PR Spitfires and enemy fighters – Me 109Es and Fs until mid-1942, then increasingly Gs and Fw 190s. Until the end of 1942 we were still flying the old Mk IVs with Merlin 45 engines. We could match the Es in speed and cope with the Fs too, provided we saw them in time, for we could out-turn them, but we

Above: **Spitfire PR.IV BR416 spent most of its operational career based in Palestine. The PR.IV was the first variant to adopt the Type D wing, all armament being replaced by extra fuel.**

Right: **Last of the Spitfires. In this superb shot, a Spitfire Mk.22 is flanked by two Mk.21s. Compare the wing shape with that of earlier Spitfires.**

could not afford to lose much height as they could always outdive us. It was another story with the 109Gs and 190s. They were both faster, but the 190's best height was around 24,000 feet and provided we could stay at 30,000 feet, we had a chance at full throttle, but it depended on an early sighting of the enemy fighters, and preferably well before they saw you. The 109G had a better ceiling than the 190 but we could out-turn them both, so an experienced pilot could get away with it so long as he got his time to turn just right, but it was touch and go until we received the Spitfire Mk XI in early 1943.'

As a result of these developments, the PR loss rate, which was just about acceptable during the first two years of the war, became quite serious in the last six months of '42 and in early '43, particularly over north-west Germany, where experienced pilots only were allowed to operate, and in Tunisia, where there was that unusual concentration of 190s and 109Gs covering Rommel's last stand against Montgomery in North Africa. For the remainder of the war, however, Mk XI (Merlin 60 Series engine) and, later, Mk XIX (Griffon engine) Spitfires were able to range freely over Germany, and indeed worldwide, with acceptable losses, even when they came up against the jet-engined Me 262 and the Me 163 rocket-powered fighter.

It is for its contribution to the RAF's victory in the Battle of Britain that the Spitfire is best remembered. But the contribution made by a relatively small number of PR Spitfires to the overall Allied victory was truly outstanding.

Above: **Supermarine Spitfire PR.XIX PM665 of the Central Photographic Development Unit, which continued to operate this mark into the early 1950s.**

Left: **Spitfire PR.XIX pictured early in 1945, fitted with a long-range fuel tank. The PR.XIX was intended to cope with more advanced enemy air defences.**

PS915

Left: Spitfire PR.XIX PS915 of the BBMF flying over Warton, Samlesbury and Fylde on 19 March 1987. It was delivered to the RAF in April 1945.

CHAPTER FIVE

Spitfires Abroad

From 11 June 1940, the day after Italy declared war on the Allies, the strategically vital island of Malta came under almost constant air attack. The initial attacks on the island by the Regia Aeronautica were opposed at first by a trio of Gloster Sea Gladiators and a handful of Hurricanes, and it was the latter aircraft that bore the brunt of the enemy onslaught for 18 months – until the first Spitfires arrived.

On 7 March 1942, in an operation code-named Spotter, 15 Spitfires flew off the aircraft carriers *Eagle* and *Argus* at extreme range. All the aircraft arrived safely in Malta, as did nine more on 21 March (Operation Picket I) and seven more on 29 March (Operation Picket II). The newcomers were divided among the three Hurricane squadrons defending the island, Nos 126, 185 and 249 (which had only 30 serviceable aircraft between them). The arrival of the Spitfires enabled the air defences to hold out for another month or so, but after that the position once again became desperate.

On 20 April 1942 Operation Calendar was mounted, in which 47 more Spitfires reached the island after flying from the aircraft carrier USS *Wasp*. But their arrival had been detected by the Germans, and within hours the airfields were under attack. By the end of the next day, after further heavy raids, only 18 of the original 47 Spitfires were still airworthy. For the first time, Operation Calendar involved the deployment of a complete Spitfire squadron to Malta; this was No 603, transferred to the island from its base at Peterhead in Scotland. 603 had been one of the first Spitfire squadrons to engage the Luftwaffe, right at the start of the war.

Climax of the raids

On 9 May the USS *Wasp* returned with HMS *Eagle*, and between them the carriers flew off 64 more Spitfires, which went into action almost immediately. The following day saw a major air battle over the island when the Lufwaffe made a determined effort to sink the minelayer HMS *Welshman*, which had docked in Valletta harbour laden with supplies and ammunition. Between them the island's Spitfires and

Opposite: **A Spitfire Mk VC (Trop) pictured against a background of palm trees in Tunisia in 1943. The Mk V was the 'workhorse' Spitfire.**

Below: **A Spitfire Mk VB, equipped with long-range tank, about to leave the aircraft carrier USS *Wasp* for Malta on 9 May 1942.**

Above: **Seafire III of No 807 Squadron comes to grief on the escort carrier HMS *Hunter*. A great many Seafires were written off in accidents of this kind.**

Hurricanes flew 124 sorties that day, destroying 15 enemy aircraft. Three Spitfires were lost, but two of the pilots survived. Seventeen more Spitfires arrived later in May and deliveries of fighter aircraft continued throughout the summer months of 1942. HMS *Eagle* alone delivered 182 Spitfires before she was sunk by a U-boat on 11 July. Most of the ferry work was undertaken by HMS *Furious*, which flew off 37 Spitfires on the day HMS *Eagle* went down, followed by 27 more on 7 August. Several RAF pilots distinguished themselves in the summer of 1942 – one of them was Canadian-born Pilot Officer George F. Buerling, who scored 27 victories while flying Spitfires over the island. He survived the war only to be killed while ferrying an aircraft to Israel in 1948.

Last reinforcement

The last Spitfire reinforcement to Malta, Operation Train, took place on 25 October when HMS *Furious* flew off 31 aircraft, of which 29 reached the island. The enemy raids continued, reaching their climax in November 1942, when the Germans subjected Malta to a furious round-the-clock bombardment that lasted ten days. The defenders remained unbroken, and the offensive against the supply convoys ferrying desperately needed supplies and reinforcements to the German and Italian forces in North Africa went on almost unchecked. The battle for Malta was over; by the end of the year most of the Luftwaffe units in Sicily had been withdrawn for service on other fronts. In the early months of 1943 Malta was turned into a major supply base as the Allies built up their resources for the offensive that would take them across the narrow straits to Sicily

Below: **Spitfires of No 601 Squadron, Tunisia, in company with AB502, the personal aircraft of Wing Commander Ian Gleed, OC 224 Wing, who was shot down and killed by a Bf 109 on 16 April 1943.**

and, ultimately, the Italian mainland. It was in Malta that the Spitfire was first used as a fighter-bomber, attacking enemy airfields on Sicily. It was a role that Reginald Mitchell had never envisaged for it, but one in which it was to prove very successful.

Desert Spitfires

The first Desert Air Force Spitfire squadron to become operational in North Africa was No 145, which embarked for the Middle East in February 1942 and set up at Heliopolis in Egypt in April. The following month it equipped with Spitfire Mk VBs fitted with Vokes tropical filters and moved up to Gambut, from where it flew its first mission, an escort for Hurricane fighter-bombers, on 1 June. In the next few weeks No 145 was joined by two more Spitfire squadrons deployed from the United Kingdom, Nos 92 and 601, which formed No 244 Wing of No 211 Group together with the Hurricanes of No 73 Squadron.

One of the most important benefits of the Spitfire's arrival in North Africa was that it seriously disrupted the enemy's air reconnaissance activities over the Canal Zone, which was being constantly monitored by high-flying Ju 86Ps operating from Crete. Flying at altitudes of up to 12,800m (42,000ft), these aircraft went unchallenged until personnel at the Aboukir Aircraft Depot modified a pair of Spitfires to deal with them. Two Spitfire VCs were stripped of all non-essential equipment, including armour plating. New four-bladed Rotol propellers were fitted, and the Spitfires' Merlin 46 engines were tuned to produce more power at high altitude. The usual armament of two 20mm cannon and four 7.7mm (0.303in) machine guns was also removed and replaced by two 12.7mm (0.50in) machine guns. Within a month, in August-September 1942, the modified Spitfires destroyed three Ju 86Ps, bringing an abrupt halt to overflights of the Canal Zone.

Spitfires at sea

It was in the North African theatre that the Spitfire's naval version, the Seafire, made its combat debut. Between the two world wars the Royal Navy's carrier-borne aircraft evolved at a much slower pace than their land-based counterparts. With the outbreak of WWII the RN found a partial solution to the problem of its outdated fighters by adapting land-based aircraft like the Hawker Hurricane for carrier operations, and in late 1941 it was decided to adapt the Spitfire in similar fashion under the name of Seafire. The main variants were the Seafire Mk IB (166 conversions from Spitfire VB airframes); Mk IIC (372 aircraft intended for low- and medium-altitude air combat and air reconnaissance); 30 Mk III (Hybrid) aircraft with fixed wings, followed by 1220 examples of the definitive Seafire Mk III with folding wings; and the Seafire Mks XV, XVII, 45, 46 and 47, these being Griffon-engined variants.

The Seafire saw much action in the Mediterranean in the summer of 1943 and in the Pacific in 1945. The Seafire 47, operating from HMS *Triumph*, took part in air strikes against terrorists in Malaya and against North Korean forces in the early

Below: **Cactus palms and Spitfires; local people lend a hand as RAF ground crew service their aircraft at a forward operating base in Tunisia, 1943.**

weeks of the Korean War. Although far from ideal for carrier operations because of its narrow-track undercarriage and long nose, the Seafire performed well and was used by RN Reserve Air Squadrons until 1954. In November 1942, two Seafire squadrons, Nos 801 and 807, provided air cover for the Allied landings in North Africa (Operation Torch), and on 8 November Lt G.C. Baldwin of No 801 Squadron scored the Seafire's first kill, shooting down a Vichy French Dewoitine D520.

American Spitfires

Spitfires also took part in Operation Torch, Nos 72, 81, 93, 111, 152 and 242 Squadrons deploying to the newly-captured Algerian airfield of Maison Blanche. In addition the USAAF's 31st Fighter Group, equipped with Spitfire VBs and operating from Gibraltar, provided air cover for US ground forces approaching the airfield of Tafaraoui, Oran. Armed with Spitfires since its arrival in England in May 1942, and originally assigned to the Eighth Air Force, the 31st FG had seen action over Dieppe in August. Now assigned to the Twelfth Air Force, it operated Spitfires until April 1944, when it re-equipped with P-51 Mustangs.

In December 1942 some Spitfire IXs were deployed to North Africa to counter the threat posed by the Fw 190, which had made its appearance in the theatre. Attached to No 145 Squadron, these aircraft were flown by a highly experienced group of Polish fighter pilots led by Squadron Leader Styanislaw Skalski and collectively known as the Polish Fighting Team, or more popularly as 'Skalski's Circus'. During an eight-week period in January and February 1943, they destroyed more enemy aircraft than any other Polish unit in the whole of that year, and the pilots were subsequently offered appointments as commanding officers of other RAF fighter squadrons. Skalski, who shot down two Bf 109s and a Ju 88 over Tunisia, became the first Pole to command an RAF fighter squadron, No 601. In 1944 he was promoted to Wing Commander and led No 2 (Polish) Wing for the rest of his career, flying Mustangs. He ended the war with a score of 19 enemy aircraft destroyed, four of them over his native Poland in 1939.

Slaughtered

In February 1943 enough Spitfire IXs had arrived in North Africa to equip No 72 Squadron, just in

Right: A Seafire Mk XV, showing the folding wing arrangement. The Seafire XV was the first Griffon-engined example of the naval fighter.

Right: **These Spitfire VBs, seen at the Persian Gulf port of Abadan in April 1943, are undergoing a pre-delivery inspection prior to being handed over to the USSR.**

time for the Allied offensive that would end on 7 April with the link-up of the US II Corps and the British Eighth Army in Tunisia. At the same time the Allied air forces launched a series of heavy attacks on enemy airfields on Sicily and in southern Italy, where fleets of transport aircraft were being assembled for a desperate, last-ditch effort to send reinforcements and supplies to the crumbling and demoralized Afrika Korps.

The Junkers Ju 52 and Messerschmitt 323 transport aircraft that survived the airfield attacks and attempted to fly to the German-held airfields in Tunisia were caught by formations of Allied fighters, often while still far out to sea, and slaughtered. On 18 April 1943, for example, 47 P-40 Warhawks of the US Ninth Air Force, together with 12 Spitfires of No 92 Squadron RAF, intercepted a formation of 90 Ju 52s escorted by 50 German and Italian fighters and destroyed 77 of them for the loss of six Warhawks and a Spitfire. This great air battle, called the Palm Sunday Massacre, resulted in the destruction of more enemy aircraft than the RAF shot down in one day at the height of the Battle of

Below: **A Seafire XV hooks the wire on the escort carrier HMS** ***Pretoria Castle*** **in August 1945, at the very end of the Pacific war.**

Britain. On 22 April RAF Spitfires followed up this success by shooting down 21 massive Me 323 six-engined transports, all heavily laden with troops. It was the end. On 13 May 1943 the remnants of the Afrika Korps finally surrendered.

Sicily

Having had their first taste of action in Operation Torch in November 1942, the Fleet Air Arm's Seafires featured prominently in the Allied invasion of Sicily on 9 July 1943. Aircraft of Nos 807, 880, 885 and 899 Squadrons operated from the fleet carriers *Formidable* and *Indomitable* to provide air cover over the beachheads. On 13 July the Spitfire squadrons of No 244 Wing deployed to the Sicilian airfield of Pachino from Malta, and on the same day the Spitfires of the USAAF's 31st Fighter Group flew into Agrigento. The arrival of more Spitfire units in the days that followed ensured full air support for the Allied ground forces in their conquest of the island.

On 3 September British forces landed at Reggio di Calabria on the Italian mainland, and on the 9th a second Allied landing was made at Salerno. Combat air patrols were flown by Seafires, operating from five escort carriers; 60 Seafires were lost in five days, the majority in landing accidents. On the credit side, only two enemy fighter-bombers were shot down and four damaged, a poor result attributed to the fact that the Seafire was not fast enough to catch the Messerschmitt 109F. The surviving Seafires were deployed to an airstrip at Paestum, where they were joined by the Spitfires of No 324 Wing. In the months that followed the Spitfire squadrons flew many ground attack sorties against pinpoint targets in Italy like railway and road bridges with considerable success, alternating these operations with bomber escort. On 30 January 1944, the Spitfires of No 7 Wing South African Air Force, which had crossed the Apennines to support the US Fifth Army's offensive, escorted 215 B-17s and B-24s in an attack on four enemy airfields. The bombers dropped 29,000 fragmentation bombs,

Below: Seafire Mk.17s ranged on the deck of HMS *Triumph* in 1948.

Left: **Spitfire VCs of No 43 Squadron at Comiso airfield, Sicily, after the island was captured in July 1943. ES352 was stricken in April 1944.**

causing much damage among enemy fighters assembling to intercept American bombers operating from Foggia against targets in Austria and southern Germany.

German fighters put in only occasional appearances during this period, but they were frequent enough to make bomber escort a necessity, and there were a number of combats. On 24 April 1944, for example, No 451 Squadron RAAF, which had arrived at Poretta in Corsica with its Spitfire Vs a week earlier, was escorting 25 B-25 Mitchell medium bombers in an attack on Orvieto when it was engaged by ten Fw 190s and four Bf 109s. No Spitfires were lost and the Germans were beaten off, although no claims were made by the Australians. On 25 May, No 451 Squadron destroyed three Fw 190s near Roccalbegna.

Balkan Air Force

The three Spitfire squadrons of No 7 Wing SAAF plus that of No 451 Squadron RAAF were assigned to Operation Dragoon, the Allied invasion of

Below: **Spitfire Mk VIII JF880 of No 417 (City of Windsor) Squadron, RCAF, at Fano, Italy, on 29 December 1944.**

Above: **Spitfire IXs of No 241 Squadron against the majestic backdrop of Mount Vesuvius in the spring of 1944.**

southern France, which took place in August 1944. Other Spitfire squadrons involved in this operation were Nos 237, 238 and 253, all former Hurricane units. Several Spitfire squadrons were also included in the Balkan Air Force, created to support partisan operations in Yugoslavia and Greece; among them were Nos 335 and 336 (Hellenic) and 351 and 352 (Yugoslav) Squadrons, all formed previously in North Africa. In November 1944 the two Greek Spitfire squadrons moved to Greece, while the Yugoslav squadrons continued to operate from Italian airfields, sending detachments to the Adriatic island of Vis in order to fly fighter sweeps over Yugoslavia. In April 1945 both squadrons moved to the captured airfield of Prkos, in Yugoslavia itself.

In the summer of 1944 some of the Spitfire squadrons in Italy rearmed with the Mk IX, and 53 Mk Vs were released for service with the Italian Co-Belligerent Air Force, which was fighting on the side of the Allies. The Spitfires were somewhat war-weary and only 33 could be made serviceable, serving with the Gruppo 20 of Stormo 51 alongside the unit's Macchi C202s and C205s. The Italian Spitfires flew their last mission of World War II on 5 May 1945, when two aircraft made a reconnaissance of the Zagreb area.

Spitfires against the Japanese

On 19 February 1942 the Japanese 1st Carrier Air Fleet launched a heavy attack on the North Australian harbour of Port Darwin. Attacks on Darwin and other strategic targets in northern Australia continued throughout the year, and were opposed by P-39s and P-40s, neither of which was a match for the Mitsubishi Zero fighter. At the request of the Australian government two UK-based RAAF Spitfire squadrons, Nos 452 and 457, were disbanded to re-form in Australia as a Spitfire Wing, together with No 54 Squadron RAF. The personnel were in place

Right: **Spitfire IXB of No 242 Squadron taxiing on a Corsican airstrip between March and August 1944.**

Above: **Spitfire VC of Squadron Leader E.M. Gibbs, OC No 54 Squadron, being pushed back into its camouflaged bay at Darwin, 22 June 1943.**

by August 1942, but the slow delivery of Spitfires (Mk VCs, many of which had been diverted to the Middle East) meant that it was the middle of January 1943 before all three squadrons of No 1 Fighter Wing and their radar-equipped Mobile Fighter Sector HQ were operational in the Darwin area. No 1 Fighter Wing was commanded by Wing Commander Clive Caldwell, a highly skilled and experienced fighter pilot with 20 victories.

By the end of May 1943 the Spitfires had destroyed 24 enemy aircraft, but ten Spitfires had also been lost in combat, with others destroyed in forced landings. A change of tactics produced better results, and the Spitfires, which had been subjected to much criticism by the Australian media, began to inflict more serious punishment on the enemy. By the middle of the year 247 Spitfire VCs had been delivered to Australia, but such was the rate of attrition in No 1 Fighter Wing that no spare aircraft were available to form new squadrons until the Japanese air attacks began to lose momentum in late 1943, when No 79 Squadron RAAF was able to re-equip for operations in New Guinea.

In April 1944 the Australian Spitfire squadrons began to receive the more effective Mk VIII, which also equipped two more RAF squadrons, Nos 548 and 549 Squadrons, formed in Australia for air defence duties. Both became operational in April 1944. While the three RAF squadrons remained responsible for air defence, Nos 452 and 457 Squadrons moved forward to Morotai in the Moluccas in December 1944 and February 1945 as part of the First Tactical Air Force, RAAF, being followed by No 79 Squadron. The RAAF Spitfire squadrons disbanded shortly after the end of hostilities in August 1945. The RAF squadrons disposed of their aircraft in September and their personnel embarked for the UK in the following month. Only No 54 Squadron was destined to re-form as a fighter unit in the post-war years.

The Burma campaign

The first Spitfires (Mk VCs) in the Burma–India theatre became operational with Nos 136, 607 and 615 Squadrons (all former Hurricane units) in September 1943, and quickly made their mark by destroying four Mitsubishi Dinah fast reconnaissance aircraft within a month. On 31 December, No 136 Squadron destroyed 12 Japanese bombers and fighters of a force that was attempting to attack shipping off the Arakan coast. By this time two more Spitfire squadrons had arrived in India;

these were Nos 81 and 152, equipped with the Spitfire Mk VIII. By the beginning of 1944 there were six Spitfire squadrons on Eastern Air Command's order of battle; these were Nos 136 and 607 (No 165 Wing) at Ramu, still with Spitfire VCs; No 615 Squadron, also with VCs, at Dohazari with No 166 Wing; Nos 152 and 155 Squadrons at Bargacchi and Alipore, with Mk VIIIs; and No 81 Squadron at Tulihal, also with Mk VIIIs, responsible for covering the Imphal sector. In January 1944 the Spitfire squadrons claimed 24 enemy aircraft destroyed for the loss of seven Spitfires in air combat; their most numerous opponent was the Nakajima Ki-43 Hayabusa, known as Oscar to the Allies. But they were also encountering increasing numbers of the Mitsubishi A6M3 Model 32 fighter, an improved clipped-wing version of the Zero known as the Hamp.

Imphal

The arrival of the Spitfires was timely, for early in 1944 the Japanese launched a major offensive with the objective of breaking through to India. The fortified position of Imphal came under a siege that was to last for 80 days, during which time the Spitfire squadrons, operating from within the perimeter, kept enemy fighters away from the transport aircraft that were bringing in supplies to the besieged troops. The plan was to keep three Spitfire squadrons available at Imphal at any one time, with a fourth in immediate support, and it worked well.

In general, the Spitfire pilots took advantage of the Mk VIII's superior performance at altitude to position themselves above enemy fighters, attack at speed out of the sun, then climb away hard out of range; these were much the same tactics that the Spitfire squadrons used in the defence of northern Australia. The Japanese Oscars, the only enemy fighter type encountered at Imphal, were more manoeuvrable than the Spitfire, had greater endurance, and were generally present in greater numbers, so the Spitfire pilots avoided turning combats wherever possible. Proof that the tactics were effective lay in the fact that in the entire 80-day siege, the enemy managed to shoot down only three transport aircraft.

By July 1944 there were ten Spitfire squadrons on the Burma front, Nos 17 and 273 Squadrons having been transferred there. The total included a PR squadron, No 681. Two of the squadrons, Nos 81 and 136, were withdrawn to Ceylon in July and August 1944. No 81 Squadron disbanded in June 1945, but No 136 deployed to the Cocos Islands

Below: **Spitfire VIIIs of No 136 Squadron and the squadron pilots lined up (more or less, in the case of the latter) for inspection on Cocos Island, September 1945.**

in March and, after the Japanese surrender in September, went to Kuala Lumpur in Malaya. It remained there until May 1946, when it moved to Bombay and was re-numbered as No 152 Squadron.

Of the other squadrons, No 615 went to Calcutta for air defence duties in August 1944, returning to Burma in February 1945 to operate in the tactical role with Nos 67, 152, 155 and 607 and Nos 1, 2, 3, 4, 6, 7, 8, 9 and 10 Squadrons of the Indian Air Force, now combat-ready and armed with the Spitfire VIII. All provided support for the Fourteenth Army in the closing phase of the Burma Campaign.

Above: **This resplendent-looking Seafire, SW847, was one of 110 Mk XVs delivered to the Royal Navy, the majority of an original order for 500 being cancelled.**

Far Eastern Seafires

In October 1943, the escort carrier HMS *Battler* arrived in the Indian Ocean to form the nucleus of an anti-submarine group.

Her air group consisted of a single squadron, No 834, which included a flight of Seafire Mk IIs. A few weeks later, a complete Seafire squadron, No 889, deployed to the theatre aboard the escort carrier HMS *Atheling*. But it was not until March 1945 that the Seafire reached the Indian Ocean in strength, three squadrons – Nos 807, 809 and 879 – being embarked on the escort carriers *Hunter*, *Stalker* and *Attacker*. These joined Royal Navy Hellcats in flying 180 combat air patrol (CAP) sorties in the course of Operation Dracula, the Allied amphibious landings in the Rangoon area. No Seafires were lost in combat, but six were written off in landing accidents.

Seafire ace

Seafires also served with the British Pacific Fleet, which operated under US command as Task Force 57, and made their first combat claims in the theatre on 1 April 1945. On that day Sub-Lieutenant R. Reynolds of No 894 Squadron, who had already destroyed two Blohm & Voss Bv 138 flying boats over the Atlantic, shot down three Zeros to become the only Seafire 'ace'. In their initial two-month operational deployment, the aircraft of Task Force 57 destroyed some 200 enemy aircraft, 98 in air combat and the rest in strafing attacks; most of the air combat victories were achieved by Corsairs and Hellcats, either over enemy territory or while flying on the outer CAP screen.

The Seafire's role was very much a secondary one, its lack of combat radius restricting it to operations in close proximity to the task force. But on the relatively few occasions when it did engage the enemy, it performed well. On 15 August 1945, for example, Seafires of Nos 887 and 894 Squadrons shot down eight Zeros in the Tokyo area; these were probably the last British air combat victories of World War II.

Below: **The powerful Seafire 46 was the equivalent of the RAF's Spitfire F.22. Twenty-four were delivered, but none served on an aircraft carrier.**

CHAPTER SIX

Foreign Spitfires and Spitfire Variants

In the immediate post-war years there was a thriving market for Spitfires in Europe and the Middle East, as many aircraft became surplus to RAF requirements. Spitfires served as first-line equipment with the air arms of some 20 countries, and played their part in several conflicts, most notably in the Arab-Israeli war of 1948–49, in which Spitfires fought Spitfires.

Belgium

At the end of WWII there were two Belgian-manned Spitfire squadrons, Nos 349 and 350. These passed to the control of the Belgian Government in October 1956, together with 51 Spitfire Mk IXs and 25 Mk XVIs. The latter were on loan pending the delivery of Mk XIVs, ordered by the Belgians from Britain under the terms of the Western Union (the precursor of NATO). The Belgian Air Force took delivery of 132 Spitfire Mk XIVs between 1948 and 1951.

Burma

In 1951 the Union of Burma Air Force took delivery of 20 de-navalized Seafire Mk XVs, and in 1955 also received 30 Mk IXs from Israel.

***Opposite*: Last and most powerful of the single-engined naval fighters, the Supermarine Seafang prototype shows its paces above the clouds.**

***Below:* One of 51 Spitfire IXs handed over to the Belgian Air Force after World War II, this aircraft carries the civil registration OO-ARA.**

Czechoslovakia

At the end of WWII there were three Czechoslovak Spitfire squadrons, Nos 310, 312 and 313. In August 1945 these flew to Czechoslovakia and were formally disbanded as RAF squadrons in 1946, forming the nucleus of a reconstituted Czech Air Force. They flew 75 Spitfire LFIXs, but these were retired when the country came under communist domination two years later. Many were purchased by Israel.

Denmark

In 1947-48 the Royal Danish Air Force took delivery of 41 Mk IX Spitfires and one Mk XI, the aircraft equipping three Eskadrille. The Spitfires were phased out between 1949 and 1955 as the RDAF's tactical fighter squadrons rearmed with Gloster Meteors and F-84 Thunderjets.

Egypt

The Royal Egyptian Air Force received 37 Spitfire Mk IXs between August and September 1946. Some of these saw action in the Arab-Israeli war of 1948-49, the only conflict in which Spitfire fought Spitfire (see under Israel). Twenty refurbished Spitfire F22s were also sold to Egypt in 1950, to be replaced later by Vampire FB5s.

Eire

Twelve de-navalized Seafire Mk IIIs, refurbished and returned to Spitfire VC standard, were delivered to the Irish Air Corps in 1947. The IAC also took delivery of six Mk IX trainers.

France

Six French-manned Spitfire squadrons served with the RAF in World War II. Between October 1945 and March 1946, 172 Spitfire Mk IXs were delivered to the Armée de l'Air from surplus RAF stocks, and many of these were immediately deployed to North Africa and French Indo-China. France also took delivery of 70 Mk Vs, most of which were used for training, and in 1948 the French Naval Air Arm received some Seafires, Mks III and XV, for service on the aircraft carrier *Arromanches* (formerly HMS *Colossus*).

Greece

At the end of the war in Europe, the operational component of the Royal Hellenic Air Force comprised Nos 335 and 336 Squadrons, armed with Spitfire Vs. A third Spitfire squadron, No 337, was formed shortly afterwards, and in 1947 the Spitfire Vs

Below: **An Egyptian Air Force Spitfire LF.IX shot down during the War of Independence. It was later used for spare parts.**

Left: **Formerly a Seafire III, this unfortunate Spitfire was one of 12 brought up to VC standard before delivery to the Irish Air Corps in 1947.**

were replaced by Mk IXs. Deliveries of 74 of these aircraft were completed in 1949; they were followed by 55 Mk XVIs, which remained in service until 1955. One Spitfire PR Mk XI was also delivered.

India

In 1946 the Royal Indian Air Force was invited to deploy one of its Spitfire VIII squadrons, No 4, to Japan as part of the British Commonwealth Occupation Force. It was the last operational deployment of a RIAF Spitfire squadron, the others being in the process of conversion to the Tempest II. The last two Spitfire squadrons to receive Tempests, Nos 7 and 8, completed their conversion by the end of 1947, but two other squadrons, Nos 14 and 101, did not relinquish their Spitfires (Mks XVIII and PR.XIX) until 1955. No 14 Squadron rearmed with the Vampire FB9, while No 101 converted to a photo-recce version of the Vampire T55.

Below: **Converted from a Mk IX, this Spitfire T.9 two-seat trainer was one of several delivered to the Indian Air Force.**

Above: This Spitfire LF.IXE was flown by Ezer Weizmann, an experienced pilot who later rose to command the Israeli Air Force.

Israel

In 1948 the newly-created State of Israel purchased 50 Spitfire LF.IXs from Czechoslovakia, which was disposing of its stocks prior to rearming with Russian types. Nine more Spitfires were sent by the Czechs later, along with a substantial quantity of spares. Of the 59 Spitfires, 56 reached Israel and entered service. Prior to this, two Spitfires had been assembled from parts salvaged from abandoned British and crashed Egyptian aircraft, and these were put into service with No 101 Squadron, which took the ex-Czech Spitfires on charge as they arrived. The first kill was achieved by Jack Doyle, a Canadian WWII fighter pilot, who shot down an Egyptian Spitfire in an air battle over the Negev on 21 October 1948. Doyle destroyed a second Egyptian aircraft, a Fiat G.55, over Faluja on 28 December. Three days later, other 101 Squadron pilots destroyed two G.55s on the ground at Bir-Hama and a third in air combat. The fighting on Israel's southern frontier came to an end on 7 January 1949, but in a series of unfortunate incidents that day four RAF Spitfire FR.XVIIIs and a Tempest were shot down by 101 Squadron Spitfires, having infringed Israeli air space. Two of the British pilots were killed.

By the end of the War of Independence the Israeli Air Force had 26 Spitfires on strength, and 26 more aircraft were in the process of assembly, having arrived by sea. With more aircraft becoming available, a second Spitfire squadron, No 105, was established in August 1950. In 1953, 30 Spitfire IXs were acquired from Italy. A third Spitfire squadron, No 107, formed at the beginning of 1953 with aircraft released by No 101 Squadron, which was re-equipping with P-51D Mustangs. By 1955 all the surviving Spitfires were concentrated in No 105 Squadron, the last being withdrawn in February 1956. During the War of Independence some Israeli Spitfires operated in the reconnaissance role.

Italy

In 1947 Italy was limited by treaty to an air force consisting of not more than 200 fighters. At the time the Italian Air Force had about 110 Spitfire Mk IXs, and 30 of these aircraft were subsequently supplied to Israel.

Netherlands

One Dutch Spitfire Squadron, No 322, served as part of the RAF in World War II. Late in 1946 the Royal Netherlands Air Force took delivery of 55 ex-RAF Spitfire IXs, and also received a small number of XVIs.

Norway

The two Norwegian Spitfire squadrons that served in WWII were Nos 331 and 332, both of which made a significant contribution to 2nd TAF. In 1947 the Royal Norwegian Air Force purchased 30 Spitfire Mk IXs to equip these two units, further acquisitions bringing the total to 47. Both squadrons rearmed with the Republic F-84G Thunderjet in 1952–53.

Portugal

The Portuguese Air Force was an early overseas Spitfire customer, taking delivery of 15 Mk IAs in August 1943, together with some Hawker Hurricanes and

Below: Portugal took delivery of two batches of Spitfires, comprising 15 Mk IAs and 50 Mk VBs, in 1942 and 1943.

Westland Lysanders. This initial purchase was followed by 50 Spitfire VBs, most of which were also delivered in 1943. The Spitfire Vs remained in first-line service until 1952, when they were replaced by Republic P-47D Thunderbolts.

Sweden

In 1948, Sweden, faced with a growing threat from the Soviet Union, began to upgrade her armed forces, and between then and 1955 bought 50 PR.XIX Spitfires from surplus RAF stocks. Designated S31 in Swedish service, the Spitfires were operated by F11, a reconnaissance unit based at Nyköping. It is ironic that, at one point in World War II, the British Government attempted to bribe Sweden with an offer of 200 Spitfires if the Swedes would stop supplying ball bearings to the Germans.

Syria

Ten Spitfire F22s were delivered to Syria in 1950, drawn from surplus RAF stocks and refurbished by Airwork Ltd. They remained in first-line service until 1953, when they were replaced by Gloster Meteor F.8s.

Thailand

Thirty refurbished Spitfire XIVs were supplied to the Royal Thai Air Force from 1948, replacing a miscellany of elderly types left over from WWII. The Spitfires were replaced by Grumman F8F Bearcats in the mid-1950s.

Above: **Royal Swedish Air Force Spitfire PR.XIXs of F11. Fifty aircraft were purchased from surplus RAF stocks between 1948 and 1955.**

Below: **One of 30 Spitfire XIVs supplied to the Royal Thai Air Force from 1948, replacing a miscellany of elderly Japanese types.**

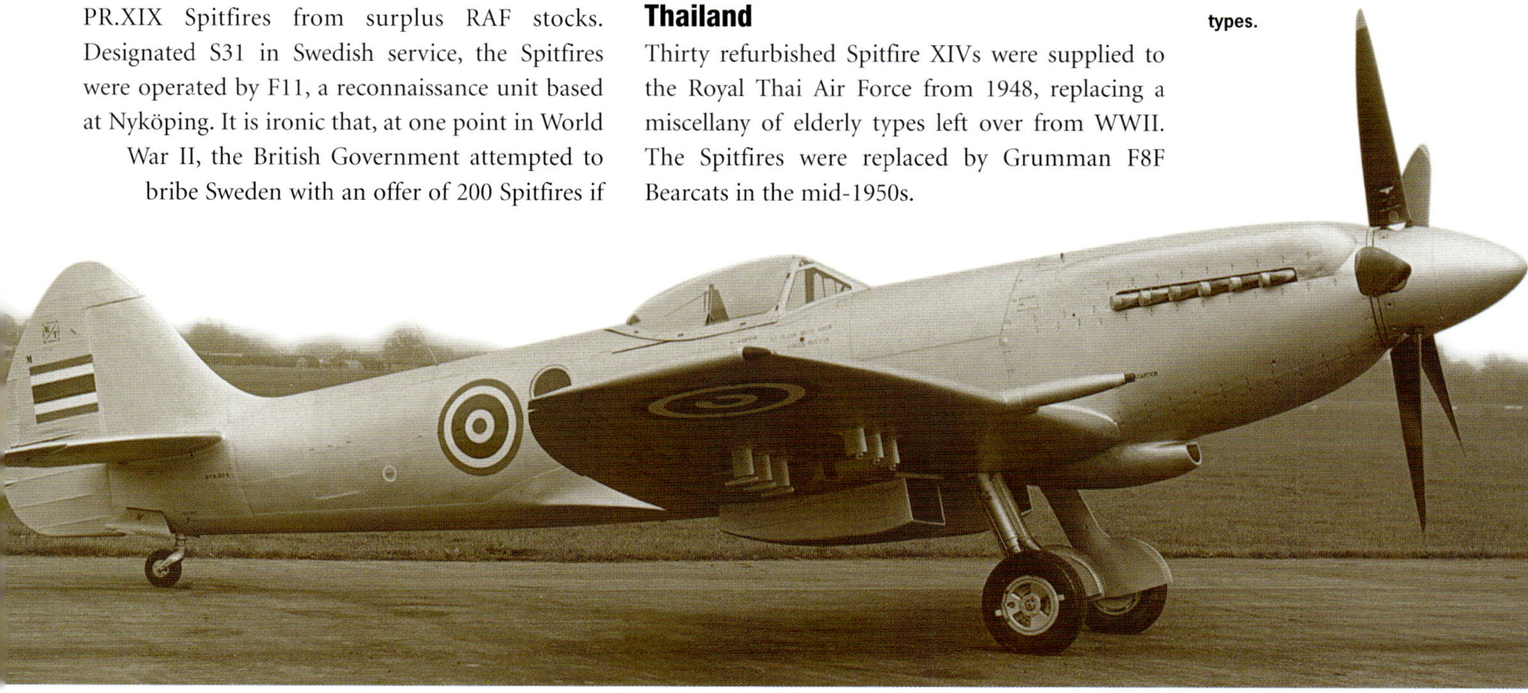

Right: Strange couple: a Turkish Air Force Spitfire VB formates with a Focke-Wulf Fw 190A-5. Turkey received 56 Spitfire VBs and 185 Mk IXs.

Turkey

This country was a major recipient of Spitfires while WWII was still in progress, taking delivery of 56 Mk VBs and 185 Mk IXs from 1943 onwards. The aircraft were sold to Turkey at nominal prices, the British government recognizing the need to keep her in a state of neutrality following the failure of diplomatic efforts to persuade her to join the Allied cause. The Germans supplied the Turkish Air Force with a number of Focke-Wulf Fw 190A-5s, the two types operating alongside one another until they were replaced by P-47D Thunderbolts in the late 1940s.

USSR

The first Spitfire operations from Russian territory took place in September 1942, when two PR.IVs of No 1 PRU deployed to North Russia to provide PR backup for possible air strikes against the *Tirpitz*. On 4 October, the Soviet Ambassador in London presented a request for the urgent delivery of Spitfires to relieve the pressure on the Stalingrad front; this was approved by Winston Churchill and early in 1943 137 Spitfire VBs drawn from Middle East stocks, plus 50 in spares form, were handed over to the Russians at Basrah in Iraq. These aircraft, armed with two cannon and two machine guns, were deployed with units of the 220th and 268th Fighter Divisions in time to take part in the major Soviet counter-attack that led to the encirclement and destruction of the German Sixth Army at Stalingrad.

In addition to the Mk Vs, the Russians also took delivery of 1188 Spitfire IXs before the end of the war, plus five PR Mk IVs and two PR Mk XIs. They fought on every front, but their main area of operations was in the north, where they performed excellent service in the air defence of Leningrad with the 26th Guards Fighter Regiment, and on the Karelian front.

Below: Spitfire VCs of No 352 (Yugoslav) Squadron pictured in Italy, 1944. Its sister squadron, No 351, operated Hurricanes.

Yugoslavia

Two Yugoslav-manned Spitfire squadrons served in the RAF in WWII, Nos 351 and 352, both in the Mediterranean theatre and the Balkans. No 351 operated Hurricanes but No 352 used Spitfire VCs, which continued to be used by Marshal Tito's embryo Yugoslav air arm for some time after the squadron disbanded in June 1945.

***Left:* The Spitfire Mk IX floatplane was the fastest floatplane fighter of WWII, although some contemporary Japanese types were more manoeuvrable.**

SPITFIRE DEVELOPMENTS

Spitfire floatplane (Supermarine Type 335)

In 1940, Spitfire Mk I R6772 was fitted with Blackburn Roc floats in response to a requirement for a fighter floatplane, mainly to operate from Norwegian fjords. A ventral fin was added to increase stability, but trials were generally unsatisfactory and the project was abandoned when the Norwegian campaign ended in defeat for the Allies. But the concept was revived in 1942, when the possibility was examined of establishing clandestine seaplane bases in the Aegean. A Spitfire VB was fitted with a set of floats designed by Supermarine and mounted on cantilever struts attached to the mainplane spars, the aircraft being converted by Folland Aircraft Ltd. The carburettor air intake was extended to avoid spray, a shorter-diameter propeller was fitted, and a ventral fin replaced the tailwheel.

The conversion was a success and the aircraft handled well, but for a marked tendency to yaw when the engine was throttled back (a tendency shared by the Spitfire landplane variants, although not to such an extent). Two Merlin 45-powered conversions, EP751 and EP754, were made by

***Below:* Converted from Spitfire XIV NN660, the prototype Vickers-Supermarine Spiteful was fitted with the Supermarine Type 371 laminar-flow wing.**

Folland, and later on an LF.IXB (Merlin 61 engine) was also converted, but the project was abandoned in 1943 when German forces occupied key Aegean islands in the wake of the Italian surrender. Six float conversion sets were also sent to the Middle East, where three Spitfires were fitted out and used for a time for the air defence of Alexandria. The Mk IX floatplane conversion had a maximum speed of 607km/h (377mph) at 6000m (19,700ft), making it the fastest floatplane in the world. With a 50-gallon auxiliary tank it had a range of 1240km (770 miles) at 362km/h (225mph) and 3050m (10,000ft).

Vickers-Supermarine Spiteful

Directly descended from the Spitfire, but bearing little resemblance to it except in profile, the Vickers-Supermarine Spiteful (Type 371) was designed to Air Ministry specification F1/43 and was in production by the end of World War II. The aircraft had a deeper fuselage than the Spitfire, a larger tailplane and an inward-retracting undercarriage. It also had a high-performance, laminar-flow wing. When F1/43 was issued, very little was known about transonic flight, the area roughly 30 per cent above and 30 per cent below the speed of sound. But experts in aerodynamics were making great efforts to design a wing that would persuade the air to flow more smoothly over a much greater area of the forward wing surface than before, delaying the breakdown of the airflow into the various forms of drag that produce turbulence.

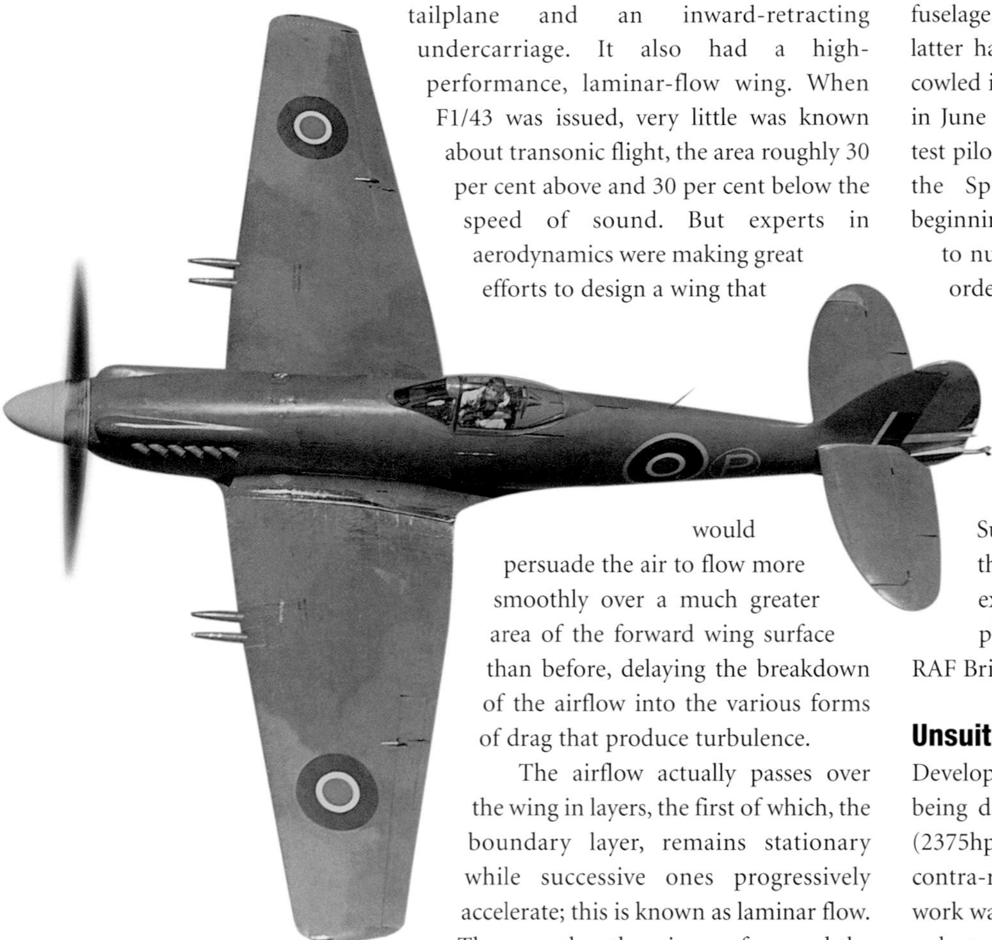

Below: **This photograph of the prototype Supermarine Seafang clearly shows the shape of the laminar-flow wing, totally different from the Spitfire's graceful ellipse.**

The airflow actually passes over the wing in layers, the first of which, the boundary layer, remains stationary while successive ones progressively accelerate; this is known as laminar flow. The smoother the wing surface, and the more efficient its design, the smoother the airflow. As combat aircraft reached speeds in the order of 725km/h (450mph), the airflow over the most curved parts of the aircraft accelerated locally to the speed of sound, causing compression that resulted in heavy drag. The aim of the high-speed, laminar-flow wing was to eliminate much of this, and in December 1942, by which time Supermarine had designed such a wing, three main objectives had been defined. These were to raise as much as possible the critical speed (Mach number) at which the buildup of drag due to compressibility became serious; to obtain a rate of roll faster than that of any existing fighter; and to reduce wing profile drag, so improving performance.

Numerous delays

The first of three Spiteful prototypes, NN660, crashed during the test flight programme. The other two aircraft, NN664 and NN667, differed in that the former had a short air intake under the fuselage, incorporating a tropical filter, whereas the latter had the intake directly aft of the propeller, cowled into the nose. NN664 flew for the first time in June 1944 in the hands of Vickers-Armstrong's test pilot Jeffrey Quill, who had been involved with the Spitfire test programme since its very beginning. Production of the Spiteful was subjected to numerous delays, and only 17 aircraft of 188 ordered were actually built. The first production model, RB515, was completed in March 1945, and the last aircraft was delivered on 17 January 1947. The first Spiteful to be taken on RAF charge was RB516, the sixth aircraft, which was delivered in November 1946. A few were retained by Supermarine for development purposes, and three went to various Ministry and Service experimental establishments; the rest were placed in storage at No 6 Maintenance Unit, RAF Brize Norton.

Unsuitable

Development of the Spiteful continued, the aircraft being designated F14 and powered by a 1772kW (2375hp) Griffon 69 engine fitted with a five-blade contra-rotating propeller. Most of the development work was carried out with NN664, and trials served only to underline the fact that the aircraft was unsuitable for squadron service, particularly in view

Above: **The aerodynamic experiments with the laminar flow wing were put to good use in the design of the Supermarine Attacker, the RN's first jet fighter.**

of its very tricky low-speed handling characteristics. It soon became obvious that the Spiteful did not, as had been expected, achieve a great advance on the later versions of the Spitfire, but the advantages of the new high-speed wing were demonstrated and put to good use in the design of the first generation of jet-propelled aircraft.

A new Griffon engine, the 89 or 90, and the addition of a six-bladed contra-rotating Rotol produced the Spiteful F15, while the sole F16 was powered by a Griffon 101 driving a five-bladed Rotol. This aircraft, RB518, was probably the fastest piston-engined aircraft ever, achieving a level speed of 795km/h (494mph) in 1947. This was only possible by using 25lb of boost pressure, which did the engine no good at all; on subsequent flights the aircraft had to force-land no fewer than seven times because of engine failure. The seventh time, at Chilbolton, its undercarriage legs were pushed up through the wings; it was then dropped from a great height by the salvage crane, bringing an inglorious end to its career. The Spiteful was declared obsolete in 1947, and passed into history.

Vickers-Supermarine Seafang

One of the Spitefuls, RB520, was fitted with an arrester hook to become the prototype of the naval version, the Seafang, produced to Specification N5/45. Before this, orders had already been placed for two new-build prototypes, VB893 and VB895, and 150 production aircraft. As it was, the production version appeared first, VG471 following the fifth Spiteful off the production line. This aircraft went to the Royal Aircraft Establishment on 15 January 1946, as the Seafang F31. As with the Spiteful, the Seafang did not show much improvement over the latest version of the Seafire, the F47. After the relative merits of the two types had been assessed the Admiralty called a halt to Seafang production after ten F31s and F32s (the latter having a Griffon 89 engine driving two three-bladed contra-rotating Rotol propellers, increased fuel capacity, and hydraulically operated folding wings that could be actuated while taxiing) had been delivered. Deck landing trials at Chilbolton and RNAS Ford were carried out by Lieutenant-Commander Mike Lithgow (later to become Supermarine's chief test pilot), and the conclusion was that the Seafang was suitable for carrier operations, with an approach speed of 95 knots, no tendency to float with the throttle closed, and good pilot visibility. By this time, however, the Admiralty had already placed a production order for another Supermarine design, the E10/44; this was to emerge as the Attacker, the Royal Navy's first jet fighter. The story of the Seafang ended with an attempt to sell the type to the Royal Netherlands Navy, which in the event selected the Fairey Firefly instead.

Appendices

SPITFIRE SQUADRONS

Squadron	Code	Spitfire Mks	Dates
1	JX	IXB	Apr 44–May 45
		F.21	May 45–Oct 46
(Converted to Meteor F.3s, October 1946)			
2	OI	XIV	Nov 44–Jan 51
		XI	Sept 45–Jan 46
		XIX	Jan 46–Mar 51
(Began conversion to Meteor FR.9s from December 1950)			
4	UP	XI	Jan 44–Aug 45
(Disbanded at B.118 Celle, 31 August 1945; No 605 Squadron re-numbered 4 Squadron, 1 September 1945)			
5	OQ	LF.16E	Feb 48–Sept 51
(Disbanded at Chivenor, 25 September 1951. Re-formed 1 March 1952 with Vampire FB.5s)			
6	JV	IX	Dec 45–Dec 46
(Converted to Tempest VIs, December 1946)			
11	EX	XIV, XVIII	Jun 45–Feb 48
(Disbanded at Miho, Japan, 23 February 1948. No 107 Squadron renumbered 11 Squadron, 4 October 1948)			
16	UG	XI	Sept 43–Sept 44
		XIX	Mar 45–Mar 46
		XIV	Oct 45–Mar 46
		XVI	Dec 45–Mar 46
(Army Co-operation unit. Converted to Tempest Vs, April 1946)			
19	QV	I	Aug 38–Sept 40
		IIA	Sept 40–Oct 41
		VB/C	Oct 41–Aug 43
		IX	Aug 43–Feb 44
		LF.16E	Mar–Oct 46
(Flew Mustangs, February 1944–March 1946. Converted to Hornets, October 1946)			
20	HN	VIII	Sept–Dec 45
		XIV	Dec 45–May 46
26	XC	VA/B/C	Mar 44–Jan 45
		XI	Oct 45–Apr 46
		XIV	Jun 45–Jan 46
(Converted to Tempest F.2s, June 1946)			
28	BF	IX	Jul–Oct 45
		VIII	Oct–Dec 45
		XIV	Oct 45–Feb 47
		FR.XVIII	Feb 47–Feb 51
(Converted to Vampire FB.5s, February 1951)			
32	GZ	VC	Apr–Nov 43; May 44–Sep 45
		IX	Jun 43–Jul 44; Nov 44–Jun 47
		VIII	Dec 43–Jul 44
		F.XVIII	Jun 47–May 49
(Began conversion to Vampire F.3s, March 1949)			
33	RS/5R	VB/C	Jan–Jun 43; Dec 43–Mar 44
		IXE	Apr–Dec 44
		XVIE	Nov 45–Oct 46
(Converted to Tempest F.2s, October 1946)			
34	8Q	PR.XIX	Aug 46–Jul 47
		LF.XVIE	Feb 49–Mar 51
(Disbanded at Palam, India, 30 July 1947. Re-formed 11 February 1949)			
41	EB	I	Jun 39–Nov 40; Mar–Apr 41
		IIA	Oct 40–Aug 41
		VB	Aug 41–Mar 43
		XII	Feb 43–Sept 44
		XIV	Sept 44–Apr 46
		F.21	Apr 46–Aug 47
(Designated as No 12 Group's instrument flying training unit with Oxfords and Harvards, August 1947–June 1948. Converted to Hornets, June 1948)			
43	FT	VB/C	Feb 43–Jan 44
		VIII	Aug 43–Nov 44
		IX	Aug 43–May 47
(Disbanded at Treviso, Italy, 16 May 1947. Re-formed with Meteor F.4s, 11 February 1949)			
54	KL, DL	I	Mar 39–Feb 41
		IIA	Feb–Aug 41
		IIB	Nov 41–Mar 42
		VA	May–Aug 41
		VB	Jun–Nov 41; Mar–May 42
		VC	Sept 42–May 44
		VIII	Mar 44–Sept 45
(Converted to Tempest IIs, November 1945)			
56	US	IX	Apr–Jun 44
(Converted to Tempest Vs, June 1944)			
60	MU	F.XVIII	Jan 47–Jan 51
		PR.XIX	Mar–Nov 50
(Converted to Vampire FB.5s, December 1950)			
63	UB	VC	May 44–Jan 45
		LF.XVIE	Sept 46–Apr 48
(Converted to Meteor F.3s, April 1948)			
64	SH	I	Apr 40–Feb 41
		IIA/B	Feb–Nov 41
		VB	Nov 41–Jul 42
		VC	Mar 43–Jul 44
		IX	Jul 42–Mar 43; Jul–Nov 44
(Converted to Mustangs, November 1944)			
65	YT	I	Mar 39–Mar 41
		IIA/B	Mar–Oct 41
		VB/C	Oct 41–Aug 43
		IX	Aug 43–Jan 44
		XVIE	May 45–Sept 46
(Operated Mustangs, December 1943–May 1945. Began converting to Hornets, July 1946)			
66	LZ	I	Nov 38–Nov 40
		IIA	Nov 40–Feb 42
		VA/B/C	Feb 42–Nov 43
		IX	Nov 43–Nov 44
		XVI	Nov 44–Apr 45; Sep 46–Mar 47
(Converted to Meteor F.3s, March 1947			
67	RD	VIII	Feb 44–Aug 45
(Disbanded at Akyab, Burma, August 1945. Re-formed 1950 with Vampire FB.5s)			
69	WI	PR.IV	Jun 41–Feb 43
(Disbanded at Wahn on 6 November 1947. Re-formed as a Canberra PR unit, May 1954)			
71	XR	IIA	Aug–Sept 41
		VB	Sept 41–Sept 42
(First 'Eagle' squadron. Transferred to 4th Fighter Group, USAAF, as 334th Fighter Squadron, 29 September 1942. No 71 Squadron re-formed in Oct 1950 as a Vampire FB.5 unit)			
72	RN	I	Apr 39–Apr 41
		IIA/B	Apr–Jul 41
		VB/C	Jul 41–Jan 44
		IX	Jul–Aug 42; Feb 43–Dec 46
(Converted to Vampire F.1s, February 1947)			
73	TP	VC	Jun 43–Oct 44
		VIII	Jul–Nov 44
		IX	Oct 43–Nov 47
		F.22	Nov 47–Oct 48
(Began conversion to Vampire F.3s, August 1948)			

Right: **Tropicalized Mk VB Spitfire AB320 in flight.**

Squadron	Code	Spitfire Mks	Dates
74	4D	I	Feb 39–Sept 40
		IIA	Sept 40–Jan 42
		VB	May–Jul 41; Nov 41–Apr 42
		VB/C	Aug 43–Apr 44
		IX	Oct 43–Apr 44
		IXE	Apr 44–Mar 45
		XVIE	Mar–May 45

(Flew Hurricanes, September 1942–September 1943. Converted to Meteor F.3s, June 1945)

Squadron	Code	Spitfire Mks	Dates
80	W2	VC	Apr 43–Apr 44
		IX	Jul–Nov 43; May–Aug 44

(Converted to Tempest Vs, August 1944)

Squadron	Code	Spitfire Mks	Dates
81	FL	VA	Jan–Apr 42
		VB	Apr–Oct 42
		VC	Nov 42–Nov 43
		IX	May–Jun 42; Jan–Nov 43
		VIII	Nov 43–Jun 45
		FR.XVIII	Aug 47–May 49
		PR.XIX	June 49–Apr 54

(Flew Thunderbolts, June 1945–June 1946, and Mosquitoes 1946. Began conversion to Meteor PR.10s, December 1953)

Squadron	Code	Spitfire Mks	Dates
82	UX	PR.XIX	Oct 1946–Jan 52

(Carried out survey flights over W. Africa with Spitfires and Lancasters. Converted to Canberra PR.3s, November 1953)

Squadron	Code	Spitfire Mks	Dates
87	LK	VB/C	Apr 43–Aug 44
		VIII	Jan–Aug 44
		IX	Jun 43–Dec 46

(Disbanded at Tisano, Italy, 30 December 1946. Re-formed 1952 as a night fighter squadron with Gloster Javelins)

Squadron	Code	Spitfire Mks	Dates
91	DL	IIA	Jan–May 41
		VA/B	Mar 41–Apr 43
		XII	Apr 43–Mar 44
		XIV	Mar–Aug 44
		IXB	Apr 45–Oct 46

(Converted to Meteor F.3s, October 1946)

Squadron	Code	Spitfire Mks	Dates
92	QJ	I	Mar 40–Feb 41
		VB	Feb 41–Feb 42
		VB/C	Aug 42–Sept 43
		IX	Mar–Sept 43
		VIII	Jul 43–Dec 46
		IX	Jun–Dec 46

(Converted to Meteor F.3s, January 1947)

Squadron	Code	Spitfire Mks	Dates
93	HN	VB/C	Jun 42–Aug 43
		IX	Jul 43–Sept 45

(Converted to Mustangs, January 1946)

Squadron	Code	Spitfire Mks	Dates
94	GO	VB/C	Mar 44–Feb 45
		IX	Feb–Aug 44; Feb–Apr 45
		VIII	Feb–Apr 45

(Disbanded at Sedes, Greece, April 1945. Re-formed with Vampire FB.5s, 1950)

Squadron	Code	Spitfire Mks	Dates
111	JU	I	Apr–May 41
		IIA	May–Sept 41
		VB	Aug 41–Oct 42
		VC	Nov 42–Jan 44
		IXC	Jun 43–May 47

(Disbanded at Treviso, Italy, 12 May 1947. Re-formed with Meteor F.8s, 1953)

Squadron	Code	Spitfire Mks	Dates
118	NK	IIA	Mar–Sept 41
		VB	Sept 41–Jul 44
		IX	Jan 44–Jan 45

(Converted to Mustangs, January 1945)

Squadron	Code	Spitfire Mks	Dates
121	AV	IIA	Oct–Nov 41
		VB	Nov 41–Sept 42

(Eagle Squadron. Transferred to USAAF as 335th FS, 4th FG, on 29 September 1942. Converted to P-47s, March 1943)

Squadron	Code	Spitfire Mks	Dates
122	MT	IIA/B	May–Oct 41
		VB/C	Feb–Oct 42; May–Aug 43
		IX	Oct 42–May 43; Aug 43–Feb 44; Aug 45–Feb 46
		F.21	Feb–Apr 46

(Operated Mustangs, February 1944–August 1945. Re-numbered 41 Squadron, 1 April 1946)

Squadron	Code	Spitfire Mks	Dates
123	XE	I	May–Sept 41
		IIA	Sept 41–Jan 42
		VB	Jan–Apr 42
		VC	May–Oct 43

(Operated Hurricanes, November 1943–August 1944. Converted to P-47 Thunderbolts, September 1944)

Squadron	Code	Spitfire Mks	Dates
124	ON	I	May–Oct 41
		IIA	Oct–Nov 41
		VB	Nov 41–Jul 42
		VI	Jul 42–Mar 43
		VII	Mar 43–Jul 44
		IX	Jul 44–Jul 45

(Converted to Meteor F.3s, July 1945. Re-numbered 56 Squadron, 1 April 1946)

Squadron	Code	Spitfire Mks	Dates
126	5J	VC	Mar 42–Apr 44
		IX	Aug–Dec 43; May–Dec 44
		XVIE	Feb–Mar 46

(Also operated Mustangs, December 1944–March 1946. Disbanded at Hethel, Norfolk, on 10 March 1946)

Squadron	Code	Spitfire Mks	Dates
127	9N	VC	Jan–Oct 43
		IX	Mar–Nov 44
		XVI	Nov 44–Apr 45

(Disbanded at B.106 Twente, 30 April 1945)

Squadron	Code	Spitfire Mks	Dates
129	DV	I	Jun–Aug 41
		IIA	Aug 41
		VB/C	Aug 41–Jun 43
		VI	Dec 42–Jan 43
		IX	Jun 43–Apr 44; May 45–Sep 46

(Operated Mustangs April 1944–May 1945. Re-numbered 257 Squadron, September 1946)

Squadron	Code	Spitfire Mks	Dates
130	PJ/AP	II	Jun–Oct 41
		VA/C	Oct 41–Aug 44
		XIV	Aug 44–May 45
		IX	May 45–Oct 46

(Converted to Vampire F.1s, October 1946)

Left: **Spitfire LF IXEs of No 43 Squadron at Zeltweg, Austria in September 1945.**

Right: Refuelling Spitfire TE439, a Mk XVI, prior to an air display at Heathrow on 14 September 1947.

Squadron	Code	Spitfire Mks	Dates
131	NX	I	Jul–Sept 41
		IIA	Sept–Dec 41
		VB/C	Dec 41–Sept 43
		IX	Sept 43–Mar 44
		VII	Mar–Nov 44
		VIII	Feb–Jun 45
(Disbanded at Kuala Lumpur, Malaya, 10 June 1945; number transferred to 134 Squadron)			
132	FF	I	Jul–Nov 41
		IIB	Sept 41–Apr 42
		VB/C	Mar 42–Sep 43; Jan–Mar 44
		IXB	Sept 43–Jan 44; Mar–Jul 44
		IXE	Jul–Dec 44
		VIII	Jan–May 45
		XIV	May 45–Apr 46
(Disbanded at Kai Tak, Hong Kong, 15 April 1946)			
133	MD	IIA	Oct 41–Jan 42
		VA	Jan–Mar 42
		VB	Feb–Sept 42
		IXC	Sept 42
(Eagle squadron. Transferred to USAAF as the 336th FS, 4th FG, 29 September 1942)			
134	GQ	VA	Dec 41–Apr 42
		IIA	Jan–Feb 42
		VB/C	Jun 43–Aug 43
(Also operated Hurricanes, 1943–44. Re-numbered 131 Squadron, 10 June 1945)			
136	HM	VC	Oct 43–Mar 44
		VIII	Jan 44–Feb 45; Apr 45–May 46
		XIV	Feb–May 46
(Re-numbered 152 Squadron, May 1946)			
140	ZW	IV	Sept 41–Jan 44
		XI	Sept 43–Apr 44
(PR unit, formed from 1416 Flight, 17 September 1941. Last Spitfire sortie flown on 27 April 1944; converted to Mosquitoes.)			

Squadron	Code	Spitfire Mks	Dates
145	ZX	IIA/B	Feb 41–Feb 42
		VA/B	Apr 42–Aug 43
		VIII	Aug 43–Aug 45
		IX	Jun 43–Aug 45
(Disbanded at Treviso, Italy, 19 August 1945. Re-formed with Vampire FB.5s, March 1952)			
152	UM	I	Jan 40–Apr 41
		IIA	Apr 41–Feb 42
		VB/C	Feb 42–Nov 43
		IX	Aug–Nov 43
		VIII	Nov 43–Jul 46
		XIV	Jan–Jul 46
(Converted to Tempest F.2s, July 1946)			
153	TB	VIII/IX	Aug–Sept 44
(Primarily operated Beaufighters. Disbanded Reghaia, Algeria, 5 September 1944. Re-formed 7 October with Lancasters)			
154	HT	IIA	Nov 41–Mar 42
		VA/B	Feb 42–Jan 43
		VC	Jan 43–Apr 44
		IX	Jul 43–Sept 44
		VIII	Nov 44–Feb 45
(Converted to Mustangs, February 1945. Disbanded at Calenzana, Italy, 31 March 1945)			
155	DG	VIII	Jan 44–Aug 46
(Disbanded at Thedaw, Burma, 31 August 1946. Re-formed with Whirlwind helicopters, 1954)			
164	FJ	VA	Apr–Sept 42
		VB	Sept 42–Jan 43
		IXE	Jun 45–Aug 46
		XVIE	Jul–Aug 46
(Operated Hurricanes, February 1943–March 1944, and Typhoons, January 1944–June 1945. Re-numbered 63 Squadron, 31 August 1946)			
165	SK	VA/B	Apr 42–Oct 43
		IX	Oct 43–Feb 45; Jun 45–Sep 46
(Operated Mustangs, February–June 1945. Disbanded at Duxford, 1 September 1946)			

Squadron	Code	Spitfire Mks	Dates
183	HF	IX	Jun–Aug 1945
(Converted to Tempest IIs, August 1945. Re-numbered 54 Squadron on 15 November 1945)			
184	BR	VB	Oct–Dec 43
(Converted to Typhoons, December 1943)			
185	GL	VB/C	Feb 42–Sept 44
		VIII	Aug–Sept 44; Mar–Aug 45
		IX	Dec 43–Aug 45
(Disbanded at Campoformido, Italy, 19 August 1945. Re-formed 1951 with Vampire FB.5s)			
186	AP	VB	Feb–Apr 44
(Renumbered 130 Squadron, 5 April 1944)			
208	RG	VC	Dec 43–Jul 44
		VIII	Aug–Oct 44
		IX	Mar 44–Aug 46
		FR.XVIII	Aug 46–Mar 51
(Converted to Meteor FR.9s, March 1951)			
213	AK	VC	Feb–May 44
		IX	Feb–Jun 44
(Converted to Mustangs, May 1944)			
222	ZD	I	Mar 40–Mar 41
		IIA/B	Mar–Aug 41
		VB	Aug 41–May 43
		IX	May 43–Dec 44
(Converted to Tempest Vs, December 1944)			
225	LX	VC	Jan 43–Jan 45
		IX	Jun 44–Jan 47
(Disbanded at Campoformido, Italy, 7 January 1947)			
229	HB/9R	VC	Aug 42–Mar 44
		IX	Jan 43–Dec 44
		XVI	Dec 44–Jan 45
(Re-numbered 603 Squadron, 10 January 1945)			
232	EF	VB	Apr 42–Feb 44
		IX	May 43–Oct 44
(Disbanded at Naples, 31 October 1944. Re-formed as a transport squadron with Wellingtons, 15 November 1944)			
234	AZ/FX	I	Mar–Nov 40
		IIA	Nov 40–Sept 41
		VB/C	Sept 41–Sept 44
		VI	Mar–May 43
		IX	Aug 45–Feb 46
(Operated Mustangs, September 1944–August 1945. Re-numbered 266 Squadron, 1 September 1946)			
237	Uncoded	VC	Dec 43–Mar 44
		IX	Mar 44–Dec 45
(Re-numbered 93 Squadron, 1 January 1946)			
238	KC	VB/C	Jan 43–Apr 44
		IX	Sept 43–Oct 44
		VIII	Jun–Oct 44
(Disbanded at Naples, 31 October 1944. Re-formed as a transport unit, 1 December 1944)			
241	RZ	VB	Feb–Mar 43
		IX	Dec 43–Aug 45
		VIII	Jan 44–Aug 45
(Disbanded at Treviso, Italy, 14 August 1945)			
242	LE	VB/C	Apr 42–Apr 44
		IX	Jun 43–Oct 44
(Disbanded while en route to N. Africa, 4 November 1944. Re-formed as a transport unit, 15 November 1944)			

Squadron	Code	Spitfire Mks	Dates
243	SN	VB	Jun–Sept 42
		VB/C	Jan 43–Mar 44
		IX	Jun 43–Sept 44
(Disbanded at Le Vallon, France, 30 September 1944. Re-formed as a transport unit, 15 December 1944)			
249	GN	VB/C	Feb 42–Sept 44
		IX	Jun–Nov 43; Apr–Jun 45
(Operated Mustangs September 1944–April 1945. Disbanded at Brindisi, Italy, 16 August 1945)			
253	SW	VC	Mar–Nov 44
		VIII	Nov 44–May 47
		XI	Mar–May 47
(Disbanded at Treviso, Italy, 16 May 1947. Re-formed at Waterbeach as a Venom night fighter squadron, 18 April 1955)			
256	JT	VIII/IX	May–Aug 44
(Absorbed Spitfires of the Gibraltar Defence Flight. Disbanded at Nicosia, Cyprus, 12 September 1946. Re-formed with Meteor night fighters at Ahlhorn, November 1952)			
257	FM	I	May–Jun 40
		VB	Apr–May 42
(Used Hurricanes June 1940–September 1942. Spitfire VBs used between relinquishing Hurricanes and converting to Typhoons)			
266	UO	I	Jan 40–Apr 41
		IIA	Sept 40–Sept 41
		VB	Sept 41–May 42
(Began conversion to Typhoons, January 1942)			
268	EG	XIVB	Apr–Sept 45
		XIX	Sept 45
(Re-numbered 16 Squadron, 19 September 1945. No 487 Squadron (Mosquitoes) re-numbered 268 Squadron, same day)			
269	UA	VB	Feb 44–Mar 46
(Air-sea rescue squadron. One Spitfire flight for ASR escort)			
273	MS	VIII	Mar 44–Jan 46
		XIV	Nov 45–Jan 46
(Disbanded at Saigon, 31 January 1946)			
274	JJ	VB/C	Apr 43–Apr 44
		IX	May–Aug 44
(Converted to Tempest Vs, August 1944)			
275	PV	VB	Jan–Apr 43; Apr 44–Feb 45
(Air-sea rescue squadron. One Spitfire flight for ASR escort)			
276	VA	IIA	Apr–May 43
		VB	May 44–Feb 45
(ASR squadron. One Spitfire flight for ASR escort. Disbanded at Dunsfold, 14 November 1945)			
277	BA	IIA	Dec 42–May 44
		VB	May 44–Feb 45
(ASR squadron. One Spitfire flight for ASR escort. Disbanded at Hawkinge, 15 February 1945)			
278	MY	VB	Apr 44–Feb 45
(ASR squadron. One Spitfire flight for ASR escort. Disbanded at Thorney Island 14 October 1945)			
287	KZ	VB	Nov 43–Mar 44
		IX	Nov 44–Aug 45
		XVIE	Jun 45–Jun 46
(Anti-aircraft co-operation squadron. Disbanded at West Malling, 15 June 1946)			
288	RP	IX, XVI	Nov 44–Jun 46
		LF.XVIE	Mar–Jul 53
(AAC squadron. Disbanded on 15 June 1946, but re-formed at Middle Wallop on 16 March 1953. Spitfires replaced by Boulton Baul Balliol T.2s)			
289	YE	XVI	May–Jun 1945
(AAC squadron. Disbanded at Andover, 26 June 1945)			
290	X6	VB	Dec 44–Oct 45
(AAC squadron. Disbanded at B.83 Knokke-le-Zoute, Belgium, 27 October 1945)			
302	WX	VB/C	Oct 41–Sept 43
		IXC/E	Sept 43–Feb 45
		XVI	Feb 45–Dec 46
(Polish 'Poznanski' Squadron. Disbanded at B.111 Ahlhorn, 18 December 1946)			
303	RF	I	Jan–Feb 41
		IIA	Feb–Oct 41
		VB	Oct 41–Jul 44
		IX	Jun–Nov 43; Jul 44–Apr 45
		XVI	Feb–Apr 45
(Polish 'Warsaw-Kosciusco' Squadron. Disbanded at Hethel, Norfolk, 11 December 1946)			
306	UZ	IIB	Jul–Dec 41
		VB	Dec 41–Sep 42; Mar 43–Mar 44
		IX	Sept 42–Mar 43
(Polish 'Torunski' Squadron. Converted to Mustangs, March 1944. Disbanded at Coltishall, 6 January 1947)			
308	ZF	I	Apr–May 41
		IIA/B	May–Sept 41
		VB	Sept 41–Nov 43
		IX	Nov 43–Mar 45
		XVI	Mar 45–Dec 46
(Polish 'Krakowski' Squadron. Disbanded at B.111 Ahlhorn on 18 December 1946)			
310	NN	IIA	Oct–Dec 41
		VB/C	Nov 41–Feb 44; Jul–Aug 44
		VI	Jul–Sept 43
		IX	Jan 44–Feb 46
(Czechoslovak squadron. Disbanded at Prague, 15 February 1946)			
312	DU	IIA	Oct–Dec 41
		VB/C	Dec 41–Feb 44
		IX	Jan 44–Feb 46
(Czechoslovak squadron. Disbanded at Prague, 15 February 1946)			
313	RY	I	May–Aug 41
		IIA	Aug–Nov 41
		VB/C	Oct 41–Feb 44; Jul–Oct 44
		VI	Jun–Jul 43
		VII	Jul–Aug 44
		IX	Feb–Jul 44; Oct 44–Feb 46
(Czechoslovak squadron. Disbanded at Prague, 15 February 1946)			
315	PK	IIA	Jul–Aug 41
		VB/C	Aug 41–Nov 42; Jun 43–Mar 44
		IX	Nov 42–Jun 43
(Polish 'Deblinski' Squadron. Converted to Mustangs, March 1944; disbanded at Coltishall, 14 January 1947)			
316	SZ	VB/C	Oct–Mar 43; Sept 43–Apr 44
		IX	Mar–Sept 43
(Polish 'Warszawski' Squadron. Converted to Mustangs, April 1944; disbanded at Hethel, 11 December 1946)			
317	JH	VB	Oct 41–Sept 43
		IX	Sept 43–May 45
		XVI	May 45–Dec 46
(Polish 'Wilenski' Squadron. Disbanded at B.111 Ahlhorn, 18 December 1946)			
318	LW	VB/C	Feb 44–Mar 45
		IX	Nov 44–Aug 46
(Polish 'Gdanskski' Squadron. Disbanded at Coltishall, 31 August 1946)			
322	VL/3W	VB/C	Jun 43–Mar 44
		XIV	Mar–Aug 44
		IXB	Aug–Nov 44
		XVIE	Nov 44–Oct 45
(Dutch squadron. Disbanded at B.116 Wunstorf, 7 October 1945, but the number later revived for a squadron of the Royal Netherlands AF)			
326	9I	VB/C	Dec 43–Apr 44
		IX	Dec 43–Nov 45
(French GC 2/7 'Nice' Squadron. Released to French command at Grossaschenheim, Germany, November 1945)			
327	7E	VB/C	Dec 43–Apr 44
		VIII	Jul–Sept 44
		IX	Dec 43–Nov 45
(French GC 1/3 'Corse' Squadron. Released to French command at Stuttgart/Sersheim, November 1945)			
328	S8	VB/C	Dec 43–Nov 44
		VIII	Aug 44–Apr 45
		IX	Dec 43–Nov 45
(French GC 1/7 'Provence' Squadron. Released to French command at Grossaschenheim, Germany, November 1945)			

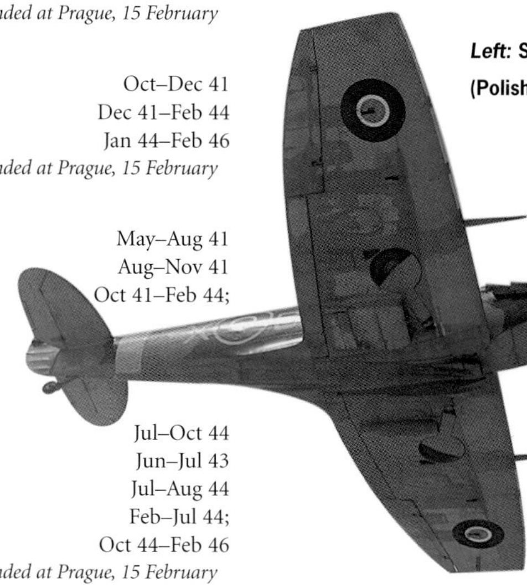

Left: **Spitfire Mk V of 316 (Polish) Squadron.**

Squadron	Code	Spitfire Mks	Dates
329	5A	VB/C	Feb–Mar 44
		IX	Feb 44–Nov 45
		XVI	Feb–Mar 45

(French GC 1/2 'Cigognes' Squadron. Disbanded at Fairwood Common on 17 December 1945)

Squadron	Code	Spitfire Mks	Dates
331	FN	IIA	Nov 41–Apr 42
		VB	Mar–Oct 42
		IX	Nov 42–Sept 45

(Norwegian squadron. Released to Royal Norwegian AF command at Stavanger, 21 November 1945)

Squadron	Code	Spitfire Mks	Dates
332	AH	VA/B	Jan–Nov 42; Apr–Aug 43
		IX	Nov 42–Sept 45

(Norwegian squadron. Released to Royal Norwegian AF command at Stavanger, 21 September 1945)

Squadron	Code	Spitfire Mks	Dates
335	FG	VB/C	Dec 44–Jul 46

(Hellenic squadron. Disbanded at Salonika, 31 July 1946)

Squadron	Code	Spitfire Mks	Dates
336	Uncoded	VB/C	Jan 44–Jul 46

(Hellenic squadron. Disbanded at Salonika, 31 July 1946)

Squadron	Code	Spitfire Mks	Dates
340	GW	IIA	Nov 41–Mar 42
		VB	Mar–Oct 42; Mar 43–Feb 44
		IXB	Oct 42–Mar 43; Jan 44–Feb 45
		XVIE	Feb–Nov 45

(French 'Ile-de-France' Squadron. Released to French AF command at B.152 Fassberg, 25 November 1945)

Squadron	Code	Spitfire Mks	Dates
341	NL	VB	Jan–Mar 43; Oct 43–Feb 44
		IXB	May–Oct 43; Feb 44–Mar 45
		XVI	Mar–Nov 45

(French GC 3/2 'Alsace' Squadron. Released to French command at B.152 Fassberg, 7 November 1945)

Squadron	Code	Spitfire Mks	Dates
345	2Y	VB	Mar–Sept 44
		IX	Sept 44–Apr 45
		XVI	Apr–Nov 45

(French GC 2/2 'Berry' Squadron. Released to French command at B.152 Fassberg, 21 November 1945)

Squadron	Code	Spitfire Mks	Dates
349	GE	VA/B	Jun 43–Feb 44
		VC	Oct 43–Feb 44
		IX	Feb 44–Feb 45; Apr–May 45
		XVI	May 45–Oct 46

(Belgian squadron. Operated Tempest Vs, February–April 1945. Released to Belgian AF command at B.152 Fassberg, 24 October 1946)

Squadron	Code	Spitfire Mks	Dates
350	MN	IIA	Nov 41–Apr 42
		VB	Feb 42–Dec 43; Mar–Jul 44
		VC	Mar–Jul 44
		IX	Dec 43–Mar 44; Jul–Aug 44
		XIV	Aug 44–Oct 46
		XVI	Aug–Oct 46

(First Belgian-manned fighter squadron in RAF. Released to Belgian AF command at B.152 Fassberg, 15 October 1946)

Squadron	Code	Spitfire Mks	Dates
352	Uncoded	VC	Jun 44–Jun 45

(Yugoslav squadron. Disbanded at Prkos, 15 June 1945)

Squadron	Code	Spitfire Mks	Dates
501	SD	I	Apr–Jun 41
		IIA	May–Sept 41
		VB/C	Sept 41–Jul 44
		IX	Nov 43–Jul 44
		LF.XIVE	Nov 46–Jan 49

(Operated Tempest Vs July 1944–April 1945. Converted to Vampire F.1s from November 1948)

Squadron	Code	Spitfire Mks	Dates
502	RAC	F.22	Jun 48–Jan 51

(Auxiliary AF squadron. Converted to Vampire FB.5s, January 1951)

Squadron	Code	Spitfire Mks	Dates
504	RAD	F.22	May 48–Oct 49

(Auxiliary AF squadron. Converted to Meteor F.4s, October 1949)

Squadron	Code	Spitfire Mks	Dates
519	Z9	VI	Aug 43–Jan 45
		VII	Oct 44–Dec 45

(Meteorological squadron. One flight of Spitfires. Disbanded at Leuchars, 31 May 1946)

Squadron	Code	Spitfire Mks	Dates
520	2M	V	Feb–Jun 44

(Meteorological squadron. One flight of Spitfires. Disbanded at Gibraltar, 25 April 1946)

Squadron	Code	Spitfire Mks	Dates
521	5O	V	Aug 42–Mar 43

(Meteorological squadron. One flight of Spitfires. Disbanded at Chivenor, 1 April 1946)

Squadron	Code	Spitfire Mks	Dates
527	WN	VB	Jul 44–Apr 46

(Radar calibration squadron. One flight of Spitfires. Disbanded at Watton, 15 April 1946)

Squadron	Code	Spitfire Mks	Dates
541	E/WY	IV/V	Oct 42–Jun 43
		IX	Nov 42–Jan 43
		XI	Dec 42–Oct 46
		XIX	May 44–Apr 45; Nov 47–Apr 51

(PR squadron. Began conversion to Meteor PR.10s, December 1950)

Squadron	Code	Spitfire Mks	Dates
542	Uncoded	IV	Oct 42–Apr 43
		VII	Nov 42–Apr 43
		X	Jul 44–Apr 45
		XI	Apr 43–Aug 45
		XIX	May 44–Apr 45

(PR squadron. Disbanded at Benson, 27 August 1945. Re-formed with Canberra PR.7s, May 1954)

Squadron	Code	Spitfire Mks	Dates
543	Uncoded	IV/V	Oct 42–Oct 43
		XI	Jun–Oct 43

(PR squadron. Disbanded at Benson, 18 October 1943. Re-formed 1 July 1955 with Vickers Valiant B(PR)1s)

Squadron	Code	Spitfire Mks	Dates
544	Uncoded	IV	Oct 42–Oct 43
		IX	Aug–Oct 43

(PR unit. Disbanded at Benson, 31 October 1945)

Squadron	Code	Spitfire Mks	Dates
548	TS	VIII	Apr 44–Oct 45

(Formed in Australia for air defence duties. Disbanded at Darwin, 9 October 1945)

Squadron	Code	Spitfire Mks	Dates
549	ZF	VIII	Apr 44–Oct 45

(Formed in Australia for air defence duties. Disbanded at Darwin, 9 October 1945)

Squadron	Code	Spitfire Mks	Dates
567	I4	VB	Jun–Sept 45
		XVI	Jul 45–Jun 46

(AAC squadron. Disbanded at West Malling, 16 June 1946)

Squadron	Code	Spitfire Mks	Dates
577	3Y	VB	Jun–Jul 45
		XVI	Jun 45–Jun 46

(AAC squadron. Disbanded at Castle Bromwich, 15 June 1946)

Squadron	Code	Spitfire Mks	Dates
587	M4	XVI	Jul 45–Jun 46

(AAC squadron. Disbanded at Tangmere, 15 June 1946)

***Right:* USAAF Spitfire Mk XIs of 14th Squadron pictured at Mount Farm in April 1944.**

Squadron	Code	Spitfire Mks	Dates
595	7B	VB	Nov 44–Jul 45
		IX	Jul 45
		XII	Dec 44–Jul 45
		XVI	Sept 45–Feb 49
		F.21	Jun 48–Feb 49

(AAC squadron. Re-numbered 5 Squadron, 11 February 1949)

Squadron	Code	Spitfire Mks	Dates
600	RAG	F.XIVE	Jul 46–Jun 48
		F.21	Apr 47–Nov 50
		F.22	Jun 48–Apr 50

(Auxiliary AF squadron. Began conversion to Meteor F.4s, March 1950)

Squadron	Code	Spitfire Mks	Dates
601	UF/RAH	VB	Mar–Apr 42
		VB/C	May 42–Jan 44
		VIII	Jan–Jun 44
		IX	Jun 44–May 45
		LF.16E	Dec 46–Dec 49

(Auxiliary AF squadron. Disbanded at Bellaria, Italy, 7 May 1945. Re-formed 10 May 1946. Converted to Vampire F.3s, November 1949)

Squadron	Code	Spitfire Mks	Dates
602	LO/RAI	I	May 39–Jun 41
		IIA	May–Jul 41
		VB/C	Jul 41–Oct 43
		VI	Sept–Nov 42
		IX	Oct 43–Nov 44
		XVI	Nov 44–May 45
		F.21	Apr 47–Jan 51
		F.22	Jun 48–Jan 51

(Auxiliary AF squadron. Disbanded at Coltishall, 15 July 1945. Re-formed 10 May 1946. Converted to Vampire F.3s, January 1951)

Squadron	Code	Spitfire Mks	Dates
603	XT/RAJ	I	Sept 39–Nov 40
		IIA	Oct 40–May 41
		VA/B	May 41–Apr 42
		VC	Apr–Aug 42
		XVI	Jan–Aug 45; Jun 46–Jun 48
		F.22	Jun 48–Jul 51

(Auxiliary AF squadron. Operated Beaufighters, 1943–44. Disbanded at Turnhouse 15 August 1945. Re-formed 10 May 1946. Converted to Vampire FB.5s, May 1951)

Squadron	Code	Spitfire Mks	Dates
604	RAK	LF.16E	Aug 46–May 50

(Auxiliary AF squadron. Night fighter squadron in WWII. Disbanded at B.51 Lille-Vendeville, 18 April 1945. Re-formed 10 April 1946. Began conversion to Vampire F.3s, November 1949)

Squadron	Code	Spitfire Mks	Dates
607	AF/RAN	VC	Sept 43–Mar 44
		VIII	Mar 44–Jul 45
		XIV	Nov 46–Mar 49
		F.22	Jul 47–Jun 51

(Auxiliary AF squadron. Disbanded at Mingaladon, Burma, 31 July 1945. Re-formed 10 May 1946. Converted to Vampire FB.5s, June 1951)

Squadron	Code	Spitfire Mks	Dates
608	RAO	F.22	Aug 48–Jun 51

(Auxiliary AF squadron. Began converting to Vampire F.3s, December 1949)

Squadron	Code	Spitfire Mks	Dates
609	PR	I	Aug 39–May 41
		IIA	Feb–May 41
		VB/C	May 41–May 42
		LF.16E	Apr 48–Feb 51

(Auxiliary AF squadron. Operated Typhoons, April 1942–September 1943 and Mosquito NF30s, 1947–48. Began conversion to Vampire FB.5s, November 1950)

Left: **A Spitfire Mk VIII at an airshow bearing Southeast Asia Command white recognition stripes and RAF Blue/Sky Blue roundels.**

Squadron	Code	Spitfire Mks	Dates
610	DW/RAQ	I	Sept 39–Feb 41
		IIA/B	Feb–Jul 41
		VB/C	Jul–Aug 41; Nov 41–Mar 44
		XIV	Dec 43–Mar 45; Feb 47–Feb 50
		F.22	Sept 49–Feb 51

(Auxiliary AF squadron. Disbanded at Warmwell, 3 March 1945. Re-formed 10 May 1946. Converted to Meteor F.4s, April 1951)

Squadron	Code	Spitfire Mks	Dates
611	FY/RAR	I	May 39–Mar 41
		IIA/B	Aug 40–Jun 41; Nov 41–Feb 42
		VB/C	Jun–Nov 41; Feb–Jul 42; Jul 43–Jul 44
		IX	Jul 42–Jul 43; Jul 44–Mar 45
		VII	Oct–Dec 44
		XIV	Nov 46–May 48
		F.22	Jun 48–Jun 51

(Auxiliary AF squadron. Operated Mustangs January–August 1945. Disbanded at Peterhead, Scotland, 15 August 1945. Re-formed 10 May 1946. Converted to Meteor F.4s, May 1951)

Squadron	Code	Spitfire Mks	Dates
613	Q3	XIV	Feb 47–Dec 48
		F.22	Jul 48–Mar 51

(Auxiliary AF squadron. Re-numbered 69 Squadron, 7 August 1945. Re-formed as 613 at Ringway, 10 May 1946. Converted to Vampire FB.5s, February 1951)

Squadron	Code	Spitfire Mks	Dates
614	RAU/7A	LF.XVIE	Jun 46–Jul 48
		F.22	Jul 48–Jul 50

(Auxiliary AF squadron. Bomber squadron in WWII. Re-formed 10 May 1946. Converted to Vampire F.3s, July 1950)

Squadron	Code	Spitfire Mks	Dates
615	KW/RAV	VC	Oct 43–Aug 44
		VIII	Jun 44–Jun 45
		XIV	Oct 46–Jan 49
		F.21	Jan 47–Jun 50
		F.22	Jul 48–Sept 50

(Auxiliary AF squadron. Disbanded at Cattack, India, 10 June 1945, and number transferred to 135 Squadron. Re-formed 10 May 1946. Converted to Meteor F.4s, September 1950)

Squadron	Code	Spitfire Mks	Dates
616	YQ/RAW	I	Oct 39–Feb 41
		IIA/B	Feb–Jul 41
		VB	Jul 41–Oct 42
		VI	Apr 42–Dec 43
		VII	Sept 43–Aug 44

(Auxiliary AF squadron. Converted to Meteor F.1s, July 1944. Disbanded at B.158 Lubeck, 29 August 1945. Re-formed 10 May 1946. Received Mosquito NF30s, September 1947, then Meteor F.3s, December 1948. No 616 was the RAF's first jet squadron)

Squadron	Code	Spitfire Mks	Dates
631	6D	XVI	Jun 45–Feb 49

(AAC squadron. Re-numbered 20 Squadron, 7 February 1949)

Squadron	Code	Spitfire Mks	Dates
667	U4	XVI	Jul–Dec 45

(AAC squadron. Disbanded at Gosport, 20 December 1945)

Squadron	Code	Spitfire Mks	Dates
680	Uncoded	IV/V	Feb 43–Jun 44
		VI	Mar–Aug 43
		XI	Aug 43–Jul 46

(PR squadron. Relinquished Spitfires in July 1946 and became entirely equipped with Mosquitoes. Re-numbered 13 Squadron, 1 September 1946)

Squadron	Code	Spitfire Mks	Dates
681	Uncoded	IV	Jan–Sept 43
		XI	Sept 43–Apr 46
		XIX	Jul 45–Aug 46

(PR squadron, formed from No 3 PRU at Dum Dum, India, January 1943. Re-numbered 34 Squadron, 1 August 1946)

Squadron	Code	Spitfire Mks	Dates
682	Uncoded	IV	Feb–Dec 43
		XI	Feb 43–Sept 45
		XIX	Jun 44–Sept 45

(PR squadron, formed from No 4 PRU at Maison Blanche, Algeria, 1 February 1943. Disbanded at San Severo, Italy, 14 September 1945)

Squadron	Code	Spitfire Mks	Dates
683	Uncoded	IV	Feb–Jul 43
		XI	Apr 43–Sept 45
		XIX	Sept 44–Sept 45

(PR squadron, formed from 'B' Flight, 69 Squadron, Luqa, Malta, on 8 February 1943. Disbanded at San Severo, Italy, 21 September 1945. Re-formed as a survey unit with Lancasters, 1950–53)

Squadron	Code	Spitfire Mks	Dates
691	5S	XVI	Aug 45–Feb 49

(AAC squadron. Re-numbered 17 Squadron, 11 February 1949)

Squadron	Code	Spitfire Mks	Dates
695	4M	VB	Sept 44–Jul 45
		XVI	Jul 45–Feb 49

(AAC squadron. Re-numbered 34 Squadron, 11 February 1949)

Squadron	Code	Spitfire Mks	Dates
1435	Uncoded	VB/C	Aug 42–Nov 43
		VC	May–Sept 44
		IX	Mar 43–Apr 45

(Formed from 1435 (Fighter Defence) Flight, Luqa, Malta on 2 August 1942. Disbanded at Gragnano Camp, Italy, 26 April 1945)

COMMONWEALTH SPITFIRE SQUADRONS

Squadron	Code	Spitfire Mks	Dates
400 RCAF	SP	XI	Apr 44–Jul 45

(Formed March 1941. Previously operated Lysanders, Tomahawks and Mustangs. Disbanded July 1945)

Squadron	Code	Spitfire Mks	Dates
401 RCAF	YO	IIA	Feb–Sept 41
		V	Sept 41–May 43
		IX	May 43–Oct 44
		XIV	Oct 44–June 45

(Arrived in UK June 1940; originally designated 1 Squadron RCAF; disbanded July 1945)

Squadron	Code	Spitfire Mks	Dates
402 RCAF	AE	VB	1942–43
		IX	1943–44
		XIV	1944–45

(Formed November 1940; disbanded 2 July 1945. Previously operated Hurricanes))

Squadron	Code	Spitfire Mks	Dates
403 RCAF	KH	V	Aug 41–Dec 42
		IX	Dec 42–Nov 43
		IXE	1944–45
		XVI	1945–45

(Formed 1 March 1941; disbanded 30 June 1945)

Squadron	Code	Spitfire Mks	Dates
411 RCAF	DB	I	Jan–Dec 41
		II	1941–42
		V	1942–43
		IX	1944–46

(Formed 15 June 1941; disbanded 21 March 1946)

Squadron	Code	Spitfire Mks	Dates
412 RCAF	VZ	II	Jul 41–Oct 43
		V	1943–44
		IX	1944–Mar 46

(Formed June 1941; disbanded March 1946)

Squadron	Code	Spitfire Mks	Dates
414 RCAF	RU	IX	Aug 44–Apr 45
		XIV	Apr–Aug 45

(Formed August 1941; disbanded August 1945. Previously used Tomahawks, Lysanders and Mustangs)

Squadron	Code	Spitfire Mks	Dates
416 RCAF	DN	II	Nov 41–Jul 42
		V	Jul–Dec 42
		IX	Dec 42–Oct 44
		XIV	Nov 44–Mar 46

(Formed 18 November 1941; disbanded 19 March 1946)

Squadron	Code	Spitfire Mks	Dates
417 RCAF	AN	II	Nov 41–Jan 43
		VC	Jan–Feb 43
		VIII	Aug 43–Apr 45
		IX	Apr–May 45

(Formed 27 November 1941; disbanded 1 July 1945)

Squadron	Code	Spitfire Mks	Dates
421	AU	V	Apr 42–May 43
		IX	May 43–Dec 44
		LF.XVI	Dec 44–Jul 45

(Formed 9 April 1942; disbanded 23 July 1945)

Squadron	Code	Spitfire Mks	Dates
430 RCAF	G9	XII	Sept 44
		XIV	Sept 44–Aug 45

(Formed 1 January 1943; disbanded 7 August 1945. Armed with Mustangs to September 1944)

Squadron	Code	Spitfire Mks	Dates
441 RCAF	9G	V	Feb–Oct 44
		IX	Oct 44–Aug 45

Squadron	Code	Spitfire Mks	Dates
442 RCAF	Y2	V	Feb–Oct 44
		IX	Oct 44–Aug 45

Squadron	Code	Spitfire Mks	Dates
443 RCAF	2I	V	Feb–Oct 44
		IX	Oct 44–Apr 45
		XVI	Apr 45–Jan 46
		XIV	Jan–Mar 46

(Formed 8 February 1944; disbanded 15 March 1946)

Squadron	Code	Spitfire Mks	Dates
451 RAAF	NI	V	Feb–Dec 43
		IX	Dec 43–Jan 45
		XIV	Jan 45–Feb 46

(Formed in the Middle East, 1941; disbanded February 1946)

Squadron	Code	Spitfire Mks	Dates
452 RAAF	UD	I	Apr–Oct 41
		II	Oct 41–Jan 42
		V	Jan 42–44

(Transferred from UK to Australia, 1942)

Squadron	Code	Spitfire Mks	Dates
453 RAAF	FU	V	Jun 42–Apr 43
		IX	Apr 43–Oct 44
		XVI	Oct 44–May 45

(Formed June 1942; disbanded 31 May 1945)

Squadron	Code	Spitfire Mks	Dates
457 RAAF	BP	II	Jun–Sept 41
		V	Sept 41–Jul 43
		IX	Jul 43–Aug 45

(Formed 16 June 1941; transferred to Australia, June 1942)

Squadron	Code	Spitfire Mks	Dates
485 RNZAF	OU	II	Mar–Nov 41
		V	Nov 41–Jul 43
		IX	Jul 43–Aug 45

(Formed March 1941, disbanded August 1945)

USAAF SPITFIRE SQUADRONS

Squadron	Code	Spitfire Mks	Dates
334th	QP	IXC	Sept 42–Mar 43

(4th Fighter Group. Rearmed with P-47s, March 1943. Formerly No 71 Eagle Squadron RAF)

Squadron	Code	Spitfire Mks	Dates
335th	AV	VB	Sept 42–Mar 43

(4th Fighter Group. Rearmed with P-47s, March 1943. Formerly No 121 Eagle Squadron RAF)

Squadron	Code	Spitfire Mks	Dates
336th	MD	IXC	Sept 42–Mar 43

(4th Fighter Group. Rearmed with P-47s, March 1943. Formerly No 133 Eagle Squadron RAF)

Squadron	Code	Spitfire Mks	Dates
307th	MX	VB/C	Jun 42–Apr 44

(31st Fighter Group. Assigned to Mediterranean theatre, November 1942. Rearmed with P-51s, April 1944)

Squadron	Code	Spitfire Mks	Dates
308th	HL	VB/C	Jun 42–Apr 44

(31st Fighter Group. Assigned to Mediterranean theatre, November 1942. Rearmed with P-51s, April 1944)

Squadron	Code	Spitfire Mks	Dates
309th	WZ	VB/C	Jun 42–Apr 44

(31st Fighter Group. Assigned to Mediterranean theatre, November 1942. Rearmed with P-51s, April 1944)

Squadron	Code	Spitfire Mks	Dates
2nd	QP	VB/C	Jun 42–May 44

(52nd Fighter Group. Assigned to Mediterranean theatre, November 1942. Rearmed with P-51s, May 1944)

Squadron	Code	Spitfire Mks	Dates
4th	WD	VB/C	Jun 42–May 44

(52nd Fighter Group. Assigned to Mediterranean theatre, November 1942. Rearmed with P-51s, May 1944)

Squadron	Code	Spitfire Mks	Dates
5th	VF	VB/C	Jun 42–May 44

(52nd Fighter Group. Assigned to Mediterranean theatre, November 1942. Rearmed with P-51s, May 1944)

Squadron	Code	Spitfire Mks	Dates
12th	ZM	VB	1942–44

(67th Reconnaissance Group)

Squadron	Code	Spitfire Mks	Dates
107th	AX	VB	1942–44

(67th Reconnaissance Group

Squadron	Code	Spitfire Mks	Dates
109th	VX	VB	1942–44

(67th Reconnaissance Group)

Squadron	Code	Spitfire Mks	Dates
153rd	ZS	VB	1942–44

(67th Reconnaissance Group)

Note: The 67th RG deployed to the European theatre in August 1942 and was assigned first to the Eighth and then (in October 1943) to the Ninth AF. In addition to Spitfires, it also used P-38s, P-51s and F-5s)

Right: **Battle of Britain Memorial Flight Spitfire Mk XIX.**

Left: A Seafire battles the mud at a repair and salvage unit in Normandy, July 1944.

OPERATIONAL SEAFIRE SQUADRONS

Squadron	Code	Spitfire Mks	Dates
800		XV/XV11	Oct 46–Apr 49
		FR.47	1949–51
(Previously armed with Hellcats. FR.47s saw action in Malaya and Korea)			
801		IB	Sept 42–May 43
		II	May 43–Feb 44
		III	1944–45
(Operated from HMS Furious during Tirpitz strikes, 1944; HMS Implacable in Pacific. Re-armed with Hawker Sea Fury)			
802		XV	1945
		XV/XVII	1945–May 48
(Previously armed with Martlets. Re-armed with Sea Fury, 1948)			
803		XV	Jun 45–May 46
		XVII	1946
(Previously armed with Fairey Fulmars)			
804		XV	Oct 46–Jan 48
		FR.47	Feb 48–Aug 49
(Previously armed with Hellcats. Re-armed with Sea Fury, 1949)			
805		III	Jul 45
		XV	Jan–May 46
		XVII	Apr 47–Aug 48
(Served with Royal Australian Navy. Operated Sea Furies from HMAS Sydney in Korean War)			
806		XV	1945–46
(Previously armed with Fulmars)			
807		IB	Jun 42–1943
		II/III	1944–45
		XVII	Dec 45–Aug 47
(Took part in Operation Torch, November 1942 (HMS Furious), invasion of Sicily 1943 (HMS Indomitable), Salerno landings 1943 (HMS Battler), invasion of southern France 1944 (HMS Hunter). Re-armed with Sea Fury, 1947; operated from HMS Theseus in Korean War)			
808		IB	Dec 42–43
		III	1943–44
(Re-armed with Hellcats, 1944)			
809		I	Jun 42–43
		II/III	1943–45
(Salerno landings, 1943 (HMS Unicorn); invasion of southern France, 1944 (HMS Stalker); Indian Ocean, 1944–45 (HMS Stalker)			
833		II/III	Jun–Dec 43
(Battle of the Atlantic, HMS Stalker/HMS Activity. Mixed Seafire and Swordfish squadron)			
834		II/III	Apr 43–44
(Battle of the Atlantic, HMS Hunter. Mixed Seafire/Swordfish squadron)			
842		IIC	Jul 43–44
(Battle of the Atlantic, HMS Fencer. Mixed Seafire/Swordfish squadron)			
851		III	Apr–May 44
(Re-armed with Avengers and Wildcats, 1944)			
879		IIC	Mar 43–44
		III	1945
(Mediterranean and Aegean, HMS Attacker, 1944; Indian Ocean, HMS Attacker, 1945)			
880		I	Aug–Dec 42
		II	Jan 43–45
(Operation Torch, November 1942, HMS Argus; invasion of Sicily, July 1943, HMS Indomitable; Salerno landings, September 1943, HMS Stalker; Tirpitz strikes, 1944, HMS Furious; shipping strikes in Norwegian waters, 1944, HMS Implacable; Pacific Fleet, HMS Implacable, 1945)			
883		XVII	Sept 45–Feb 46
(Operated 25 aircraft prior to handing over to Royal Canadian Navy)			
884		II	Nov 42–43
885		I/II	Sept 42–Nov 43
		III	Feb 44–45
886		II	Mar 43–44
		III	1944
(Salerno landings, 1943, HMS Attacker; Battle of the Atlantic, HMS Attacker, 1943–44)			
887		I/II	Dec 42–43
		II	1943–44
		III	1945–Mar 46
(Salerno landings, 1943, HMS Unicorn; Battle of the Atlantic, 1944, HMS Unicorn; Tirpitz strikes, 1944, HMS Indefatigable; shipping strikes in Norwegian waters, 1944, HMS Indefatigable; Indian Ocean and Pacific, 1944–45, HMS Indefatigable)			
889		III	1944
(Indian Ocean, 1944, HMS Atheling)			
894		IIC	Mar 43–44
		III	1944–Mar 46
(Salerno landings, 1943, HMS Illustrious/HMS Unicorn; Tirpitz strikes, 1944, HMS Indefatigable; shipping strikes in Norwegian waters, 1944, HMS Implacable; Indian Ocean and Pacific, 1944–45, HMS Indefatigable)			
895		IIC	Apr 43
897		I	Aug–Sept 42
		II	Apr 43–44
		III	1944
(Salerno landings, 1943, HMS Unicorn)			
899		II	Jan 43
		III	1943–45
(Invasion of Sicily, 1943, HMS Indomitable; Salerno landings, September 1943, HMS Hunter; invasion of southern France, August 1944, HMS Khedive)			
1831		F.XVII	Jun 47–Aug 51
1832		F.XVII	Jul 47–Nov 51
1833		F.XVII/FR.47	Aug 47–Jan 52

Spitfire Variants

The Spitfire prototype

The Spitfire prototype, K5054, adapted to meet the requirements of Air Ministry Specification F.37/34, first flew on 5 March 1936, powered by a Rolls-Royce Merlin 'C' engine. It was first revealed publicly in a flypast at the Royal Air Force pageant, Hendon, on 27 July 1936. By October 1938, K5054 had been brought up to full Mk I standard. It survived several accidents during its test career, but was damaged beyond repair when it overturned in a landing accident at Farnbrough on 4 September 1939. The remains were stored at Farnborough for some time before being broken up, date unrecorded.

The High Speed Spitfire

In 1937, it was decided to use a Spitfire in an attempt to establish a new World Landplane Speed Record. Two Merlin II engines were modified to racing configuration, being tuned to produce 2000hp for a short period with the aid of special fuel (20% straight-run petrol, 60% benzol, 20% methanol and 3.3cc lead per US gallon). A Mk I airframe, K9834, was modified, its wing span being reduced and a revised cockpit canopy fitted, and featuring a four-bladed propeller. First flown on 10 November 1938, resplendent in high gloss blue with a silver trim and registered N17, it reached 656km/h (408mph), but could not surpass the speed of 755.138km/h (469.22mph) attained by Messerschmitt's Me 209 in April 1939. Fitted with a Merlin XII engine, K9834 was allocated to the PRU on 24 November 1940 and served as its communications aircraft throughout the war, being stricken off charge on 21 May 1946.

Spitfire Mk I (Supermarine Type 300)

The first production Spitfire I, K9787, flew in May 1938. The first to enter service was K9789, the third production aircraft, which went to No 19 Squadron at Duxford on 4 August 1938 and went through 240 hours of intensive flying. In all, 1533 Mk Is were built by Supermarine and 50 more by Westland Aircraft. All Mk Is were declared obsolete in February 1945.

Spitfire Mk II (Supermarine Type 329)

The Mk II Spitfire was basically a Mk I built exclusively at the Castle Bromwich factory of Vickers-Armstrongs. Equipment was similar to that of the Mk I, with the addition of a Merlin XII engine developing 1175hp. Production totals were 750 Mk IIAs and 170 Mk IIBs (the A and B suffixes denoted armament variations). Some 50 aircraft, originally designated IICs, were fitted out for air-sea rescue work, equipped with a dinghy and with other survival gear stowed in the parachute flare chutes; these were redesignated Spitfires ASR.II in 1942.

Spitfire Mk III (Supermarine Type 330)

The Spitfire Mk III was intended to be a refined successor to the Mks I and II, with a 1390hp Merlin XX engine, clipped wings, retractable tailwheel and other refinements. Two aircraft were built (N3297 and W3237), but the variant did not enter production, being used for experimental purposes.

Spitfire Mk IV (Supermarine Type 337)

The Mk IV was the first Griffon-engined Spitfire, and was a modified Mk IIB, DP845. This flew for the first time on 27 November 1941, but did not proceed beyond the experimental stage. The aircraft bore no relation to the PR.Mk.IV.

Spitfire PR.Mk IV

The Spitfire PR.IV, 229 of which were converted from MK VA/B airframes, was the main photo-reconnaissance type of the mid-war years. The variant used all the Merlin engine variants applicable to the Mk V, but the Merlin 45 and 46 were the recognized standard. The last PR.IV was withdrawn from service in February 1945.

Spitfire Mk V (Supermarine Type 349)

Converted from Mk I and II airframes, the Mk V, which began to reach the squadrons in March 1941, was to be the major Spitfire production version, with 6479 examples completed. It was produced in six different variants (F.VA/B/C and LF/VA/B/C), developed for high- and low-altitude roles. The majority of Spitfire Vs were armed with two 20mm cannon and four machine guns, affording a greater chance of success against armour plating. The Mk V was powered by a

Rolls-Royce Merlin 45 engine, developing 1415 hp at 5800m (19,000ft) against the 1150hp of the Merlin XII fitted in the Mk II. Nevertheless, the Mk V was essentially a compromise aircraft, rushed into service to meet an urgent Air Staff requirement for a fighter with a performance superior to that of the latest model of Messerschmitt. The debut of the Spitfire V came just in time, for in May 1941 the Luftwaffe fighter units began to receive the Messerschmitt Bf 109F, its service debut having been delayed through technical problems. The Spitfire V, however, failed to provide the overall superiority Fighter Command needed so badly. At high altitude, where many combats took place, it was found to be inferior to the Bf 109F on most counts, and several squadrons equipped with the Mk V suffered heavy losses. It was completely outclassed by the Focke-Wulf Fw 190. The Mk V was declared obsolete for RAF purposes in September 1945, but stocks were retained until March 1948.

Spitfire Mk VI (Supermarine Type 350)

The Spitfire Mk VI was developed specifically to counter enemy high-altitude reconnaissance aircraft, notably the Junkers Ju 86P. It was basically a Mk V airframe with a pressurized cabin, extended wingtips, a Merlin 47 engine and a four-bladed propeller for greater efficiency at height. One hundred examples were produced, one flight being attached to each home defence squadron of RAF Fighter Command. The Mk VI's service ceiling was 12,200m (40,000ft).

Spitfire Mk VII (Supermarine Type 351)

The Mk VII, also with a pressurized cockpit, was powered by a Rolls-Royce Merlin 60 engine, a two-stage, two-speed, inter-cooled powerplant which took development of the Merlin to its ultimate. Like the Mk VI, the VII was a limited production high-altitude interceptor, 140 examples being produced. The aircraft had a service ceiling of 13,420m (44,000ft) and was produced in two variants, the F.VII and HF.VII, the latter with a Merlin 71 engine featuring a Bendix injection carburettor.

Spitfire PR.VII

The Spitfire PR.VII was not a recognized production aircraft, but a service modification of the Mk V; in effect, it was an armed version of the PR.IV, retaining the 'A' type armament of eight Browning 7.7mm (0.303in) machine guns. It had provision for two vertical and one oblique F.24 cameras.

Spitfire Mk VIII (Supermarine Type 359)

The Spitfire Mk VIII was basically an unpressurized version of the Mk VII, intended for low-level air superiority operations. Production reached a total of 1658 aircraft, almost all of which saw service in the Far East and Australia. The major production version was the LF.VIII, with a Merlin 66 engine; the other two variants, the F.VIII and HF.VIII, were respectively fitted with Merlin 61/63 and Merlin 70 engines.

Spitfire Mk IX (Supermarine Type 361)

Early in 1942, the Air Staff envisaged production of both the Spitfire VII and, in much larger numbers, of the Spitfire VIII. The Mk VIII design, however, needed a lot of refinement, including a general strengthening of the fuselage, which meant that production would be delayed for an unacceptably long time, and Air Staff thoughts consequently turned to an interim aircraft: a Mk V Spitfire airframe combined with a Merlin 61 engine. The resulting combination was the Spitfire Mk IX, which for a stop-gap aircraft turned out to be a resounding success. Deliveries to the RAF began in June 1942 and 5665 were built, more than any other mark except the Mk V. The Mk IX was produced in F, LF and HF sub-variants; aircraft with the suffix 'e' (eg LF IXe) featured a universal wing mounting two 20mm cannon outboard and two 12.7mm (0.50in) machine guns inboard.

Spitfire PR.X

The Spitfire PR.X had the shortest operational life of any Spitfire variant, entering service in May 1944 and being discarded in September 1945. Only 16 were built, these being used by No 542 Squadron.

Spitfire PR.XI

The Spitfire PR.XI was a reconnaissance adaptation of the Mk IX; 471 were built, of which 309 were tropicalised for overseas service. Three examples were used by the Royal Navy in the late 1940s, and others were supplied to Greece, the Netherlands, Denmark and Norway.

Spitfire Mk XII (Supermarine Type 366)

The Mk XII, powered by a 1735hp Rolls-Royce Griffon engine, was developed to counter the low-level attacks by German fighter-bombers, mainly the Focke-Wulf Fw 190. It first went into service with No 41 Squadron in February 1943. The squadron shot down its first FW 190 on 27 April, while operating from Hawkinge. The second unit to re-equip with the Mk XII, No 91, destroyed five enemy fighter-bombers in a running battle over the Channel on 25 May 1943. Only 100 MK XII Spitfires were built.

Spitfire PR.XIII

Between December 1942 and May 1943, 18 Spitfire Mk V airframes were fitted with a Rolls-Royce Merlin 32 engine. The type was developed for the low-level tactical reconnaissance role, and remained in service for about two years.

Spitfire Mk XIV (Supermarine Type 379)

Based on a Mk VIII airframe, strengthened to take the extra weight and power of a 2050hp Griffon 65, the Mk XIV was the first Griffon-engined Spitfire variant to go into large-scale production, and the first examples were issued to No 322 (Netherlands) and No 610 Squadrons in March and April 1944. Distinguished from earlier Spitfire marks by its longer nose, cut-down rear fuselage and a clear-view bubble canopy, the Mk XIV was produced in two sub-variants with differing armament fits, as in the Mk.IX. The 527 Mk XIV fighters were complemented by 430 examples of a fighter-reconnaissance version, the FR.XIV, with a fuselage-mounted camera.

Spitfire Mk XVI (Supermarine Type 361)

The Spitfire XVI, which entered service in 1944, was a ground-attack version similar to the Mk IX, but with a Packard-built Merlin 266 engine. It was used in considerable numbers by the RAF at home and abroad in the post-war years, particularly by anti-aircraft co-operation units.

Spitfire F/FR Mk XVIII (Supermarine Type 394)

The Spitfire XVIII was a fighter-reconnaissance variant, just beginning to enter service at the end of WWII, and was the last Griffon-engined development of the original elliptical-wing Spitfire airframe. One hundred were completed as fighters, and a further 200 for the fighter-reconnaissance role. The F/FR XVIII was widely used in the Middle and Far East, and saw action in the early stages of the Malayan Emergency.

Spitfire PR.XIX

The last of the line of photographic reconnaissance Spitfires, and the only PR mark with a Griffon engine, the PR.XIX was basically a late production Mk XIV airframe with a Mk VC bowser wing (a wing adapted for fuel tank stowage) with a universal camera installation based on that of the PR.IV/XI. It was developed early in 1944 to counter German air defences, which were becoming increasingly sophisticated. Production totalled 225 aircraft.

Spitfire Mks 21, 22 and 24

The last variants of the Spitfire, produced until 1947, were the Mks 21, 22 and 24. They bore very little resemblance to the prototype Mk I of a decade earlier. The last of the line, the Mk 24, entered service in November 1946. The Mk 23 was a proposed variant with aerodynamic improvements, which was never built.

Index

Page numbers in *italics* refer to illustrations

Picture Credits

Hugh W. Cowin: 8, 9 (both), 10, 12, 15, 16 (b), 19 (b), 23 (t), 27 (b), 35 (t), 38 (t), 39, 42 (both), 52, 56 (b), 59 (t), 60 (t), 61 (t), 65, 68, 69 (t), 72 (b), 83 (b), 84, 85.

Philip Jarrett: 13, 14, 19 (t), 22, 23 (b), 24 (b), 25, 28, 29 (both), 31, 32, 33 (t), 35 (b), 36 (t), 37, 38 (b), 40, 41, 43, 44 (both), 48, 50-51 (b), 53, 55 (both), 56 (t), 58, 59 (b), 60 (b), 61 (b), 62-63, 66 (t), 67, 69 (b), 70, 71 (t), 74, 75 (both), 76, 77, 78, 79 (both), 80, 81 (both), 82 (both), 83 (t), 86, 87, 88, 89, 90.

TRH: 6, 7, 16 (t) (R. Winslade), 17, 18, 20, 21, 24 (t), 27 (t), 30, 33 (b), 34, 36 (b), 45, 46, 47, 50, 51 (t) (E. Nevill), 54 (both), 57, 64, 66 (b), 71 (b), 72 (t), 73, 91 (R. Winslade), 92 (R. Winslade), 93.

Artworks: Aerospace Publishing